THE ABSENT MARX

THE ABSENT MARX

CLASS ANALYSIS AND
LIBERAL HISTORY IN
TWENTIETH-CENTURY
AMERICA

IAN TYRRELL

CONTRIBUTIONS IN AMERICAN HISTORY, NUMBER 115

GREENWOOD PRESS
NEW YORK • WESTPORT, CONNECTICUT • LONDON

Library of Congress Cataloging-in-Publication Data

Tyrrell, Ian R.
The absent Marx.

(Contributions in American history, ISSN 0084–9219 ;
no. 115)
Bibliography: p.
Includes index.
1. United States—Historiography. 2. Marxian
historiography—United States. I. Title. II. Series.
E175.T86   1985   973'.072'073   85–17709
ISBN 0–313–24876–1 (lib. bdg. : alk. paper)

Library of Congress Catalog Card Number: 85–17709
ISBN: 0–313–24876–1
ISSN: 0084–9219

First published in 1986

Greenwood Press, Inc.
88 Post Road West
Westport, Connecticut 06881

Printed in the United States of America

The paper used in this book complies with the
Permanent Paper Standard issued by the National
Information Standards Organization (Z39.48–1984).

10   9   8   7   6   5   4   3   2   1

To Diane,
For Everything

Contents

Preface

This study had its origins as an essay on the new social history and its limitations. I soon found it necessary to move back in time in order to understand the roots of the difficulties that the discipline was experiencing in the 1970s, but the book that has resulted retains the format of a series of historiographical essays on aspects of the American historical tradition, in which the relations of marxism and liberal interpretations are seen as critical. As a historiographical synthesis, the work maintains no pretense as to finality of judgment or originality of insight. I seek rather to draw attention to sometimes obscure and often diverse work in the marxist tradition, and to bring the insights of that tradition to bear on the much larger and more formidable body of academic literature on American history. Even historiographical works have become fragmented by the specialization of the discipline, and though this study integrates much of that material and explores its connections, an exhaustive coverage is impossible. The reader is, therefore, referred to both the footnotes and the bibliographical essay for further information.

Acknowledgments

Any work of historical synthesis creates its own web of obligations, and this study is no exception. As historiography, especially, becomes more complex, the scale of indebtedness grows. Without the cooperation of a wide range of scholars, who frequently disagreed with the tenor of the project, this book could never have been finished. Charles Grimshaw first awakened my interest in historiography at Queensland University in 1968 when I studied the British empiricists, and Richard Watson revived it at Duke in 1971 when I wrote a paper on William Appleman Williams. The specific interest I have developed in marxist approaches, however, stems from curiosity first raised by reading the works of Eugene Genovese.

In the course of writing this book, several people went beyond the call of duty and read the whole manuscript or large parts of it and saved me from innumerable errors. Bill Rorabaugh's skepticism forced me to rethink many propositions; Jack Blocker gave me the benefit of his knowledge of the quantitative social sciences; Anthony Ashbolt provided many useful suggestions on modern marxism; Pat Buckridge's critique from the vantage point of literary criticism demonstrated the erosion of traditional disciplinary barriers. Among immediate colleagues, I owe most to Dave Rollison, Mark Finnane, Michael Pearson, Andrew Major, Martyn Lyons, and John McQuilton, who set me straight on subjects they know far better than I ever will. In addition, conversations with Ian Bickerton, Max Harcourt, and Beverley Kingston continue to be intellectually fruitful.

Many other scholars around the world provided help which they would never regard as important, but which made the difficult task of writing on American historiography from the antipodes more bearable. They are, especially: Louis Galambos, who supplied me with otherwise inaccessible material; Robert Wiebe, who gave this and another project an impetus through an act of courtesy and generosity to a visiting scholar; Peter Novick, who is working on a related topic, for a stimulating lunchtime discussion in Chicago in September 1981; and Lee Cary, an American friend who as a Fulbright scholar in Australia shared his views of the new labor history and his ongoing research into eighteenth-century slavery.

Martin Ridge and his staff at the Huntington Library made available to me their rich collections in historiography during an enjoyable sojourn there. Among other libraries, I owe most to those at Northwestern University and Duke University, and to Fisher Library at Sydney University, notwithstanding the many fines exacted for late return of books. I am indebted to the staff at the University of New South Wales library for many things, especially their willingness to get so much material on interlibrary loan, no matter how far it had to come.

Without two separate semesters on leave from the University of New South Wales and its School of History, this book would never have proceeded beyond the planning stage.

My editor at Greenwood, Neil Kraner, has worked efficiently with his production team to improve this book. I would also like to thank Greenwood's anonymous reader for a very extensive and helpful critique.

This book is dedicated to Diane Collins, not because she relieved me of my domestic chores, which she didn't, but because of her shrewd observations on the content and because towards the end, when the date of completion seemed to continually recede, she absented herself to ensure that I did finish. Jessica Alice Tyrrell arrived too late to impart wisdom, but soon enough to delay publication.

It should not be necessary to emphasize that this work could not have been written without the rich content of writing by American historians, on whose work I have relied heavily in this survey, and whose contributions are in no way diminished by the critique contained in these pages.

THE ABSENT
MARX

Introduction

American historical writing has never been more sophisticated in a technical sense. Yet never have American historians been so collectively uncertain of the direction that their practice should take. Not since the 1930s has so much attention been devoted to historical explanation, to method, theory, and the purpose of history. Even more unusual is a growing concern over the adequacy of the liberal syntheses so long ascendant in American academic history, and though this questioning mood is not peculiar to Americans or to United States historians, the American case is distinctive in origins and context. One notable difference is the *belated* assertion of a serious marxist presence, another the relationship between the ailing liberal tradition and the promise of a marxist alternative.[1]

The Absent Marx connects these developments in liberal and marxist history, and explores their roots over the course of the twentieth century. Since the marxist influence on liberalism has usually been subterranean, and the overt contact between the two traditions episodic, it did not seem useful to attempt a blow-by-blow account of the relationship in isolation from the main currents of professional activity. Instead, the issue of class analysis is situated in the conceptual terrain of American historiography and its transformation. For all of the recent emphasis on a critical reappraisal, this process is still less advanced than in sociology or economics where the issue of the sociology of the disciplines is now coming onto the agenda. In history we still need studies of the theoretical perspectives, concepts, and methods of the profession.[2]

The present work contributes to this task, but not in the manner of conventional historiography or philosophy of history. Rather, the aim is to show how the concepts and theories employed by American historians have structured the content of the knowledge produced. A secondary goal is to explain how and why the conceptual framework of American historical scholarship has developed in the directions that it has. That involves the study of the relationship between historical concepts and the development of history as a profession. The concepts of American historians have been grounded, I shall argue, not so much in the nature of history as a discipline in the abstract sense, but more specifically in the ways history developed in the United States and was reproduced in an academic setting.

Those who write about the assumptions of others must begin by making their own intentions explicit. This work is not given the imprimatur of an authentic marxist study of American historiography. The project *is* written in sympathy with the claims of marxism, yet conscious of the problematic and provisional character of any marxist formulation. Since I shall be arguing the case that American historians have neglected the insights of marxist analysis to their peril, it is necessary to make clear that I am taking as my point of departure a view of marxism as the cumulative body of social thought derived originally from Marx's concepts. These ideas posit the critical importance of the social relations of production in an analysis of change in complex human societies.[3] That marxists have had a profound impact on many disciplines in many countries is beyond question, but American historiography is not among them. Because of the current interest in marxist history in certain sections of the profession, and because of the more flexible and open character of marxist models in other historiographies, this is an appropriate time to ask whether contemporary marxist theory can enrich American scholarship and delineate the theoretical and empirical weaknesses in the dominant modes of historical understanding. To accomplish this goal, marxist historians must do more than offer critiques of the varieties of liberal historiography that have flourished in the academy. From the diverse conceptual inheritance of their own tradition, marxists need to generate programs of empirical research that can compete with mainstream work.

To effect a claim to the territory of history, marxists must therefore discard one of two strands of analysis present in Marx's own work and that of his followers. That is the predictive theory of social change in which history is fitted into a model of stages. Such an approach can be discerned in the *Communist Manifesto*, and has underpinned much marxist-leninist rhetoric in the twentieth century. No one can blame American historians for repudiating this tendency, but there have always been alternative ways of appropriating the marxist legacy. In Marx's historical works, in Trotsky's analysis of the impact of capitalism on the Russian empire, and in Rudolph Hilferding's reconsideration of Marx's economic theories in *Finance Capital*, to cite just three examples, marxist categories are located in realistic appraisals of the material studied. Though logical analysis and theoretical abstraction are not shunned, the outcome of the inquiry is not determined a priori.[4]

Because American historians have missed the complexity and diversity of marxism, they have generally ignored the potential of an empirical inquiry informed by marxist concepts. They have tended to equate the marxist tradition with the crudities of revolutionary sloganeering and at best have demonstrated an acquaintance with the very intellectually limited forms of marxism that have intermittently appeared in the American environment. Insofar as marxist analysis has been used at all, American historians have assumed that the appropriation of class categories through the work of the progressive historians was about as far as Americans could or would go in the direction of a comprehensive class interpretation. The way in which class analysis was incorporated into American historiography and simultaneously stripped of its intellectual context of political economy still constitutes one of the great neglected themes of American intellectual history, and is consequently one of the central concerns of this study.

In line with the tendency to project a very rigid and limiting knowledge of marxism, Americanists have commonly assumed that marxism was a European phenomenon that did not apply to American history. They have depicted a dichotomy between a Europe beset with a history of class conflict and revolutionary instability and an America in which class lines were not clear, and progress orderly. In the words of Professor Diggins, "an analysis that had its origins in Europe's social structure becomes complicated when applied to America." For a land without feudalism, he writes in an echo of the classic statement by Louis Hartz, "the Marxist babble about 'contradictions' " was an overwhelming irrelevance.[5] Simplifications like these are so persistent that they seem to have rusted onto the content of American historiography. Consequently, certain varieties of radical history in the 1970s as well as the consensus interpretations of the 1950s had affinities with nineteenth- and even eighteenth-century notions of a corrupt and aristocratic Europe against which a virtuous America, a new land and a new people, devoid of tradition, had rebelled successfully. Though hardly new, these conceptions were profoundly reinforced by a twentieth-century experience of the continuity of American institutions in a setting of international turmoil.

In contrast, the understanding of marxism adopted here denies the conventional identification of marxism with the discovery of clear-cut class categories in European history. The whole trend of modern marxism has been away from such a vulgar class determinism. Marxist investigation of hegemonic ideologies, of the cultural dimensions of class, of the complexities of the social formation, of class consciousness, of the political economy of capitalism, and of the material structures of everyday life gives the lie to the hoary caricature. A good deal of marxist theory and empirical research since the Russian revolution, from the work of Georg Lukács, through Antonio Gramsci, to the very different perspective of Louis Althusser, has focused on the failure of the revolution so confidently predicted in the *Communist Manifesto* to follow its expected course.[6] Particular attention has been given to explaining why class divisions in modern societies have been repeatedly complicated by historical circumstances.

As for class in European history, that too has been mangled in American views. These have routinely implied a homogeneous Europe despite vast regional differences in social structure and culture. European historians have not found a simple bipolar model of class conflict linked to a succession of changes in the mode of production particularly helpful in comprehending their own histories. There never was a pure contradiction between labor and capital, nor, for that matter, between the bourgeoisie and feudal structures. But that does not mean class analysis must be abandoned. What historians sympathetic to marxism have been able to do is to take the various elements of the theory and to examine the particular operations of class, class culture, ideology, and so forth in concrete historical settings. Using these approaches, marxist historians during the last thirty years have produced valuable work in Britain, France, Italy, Eastern Europe (especially Poland), and in a number of non-European countries. Not only has some of the best history been marxist, but a marxist influence has also been indirectly felt in the work of the French *Annales* historians, though *Annales* could not in any sense be called a marxist project.[7]

This intellectual production is of immense relevance to American historiography. If Europe's social structure has been as complicated as that of America, it is not necessary that a "Marxist babble" be applied to American history. All that American historians of marxist persuasion could fairly be asked to do is to pursue their subjects with the same rigor and insight that has distinguished the volumes of their European counterparts. That is to say, they must follow the systematic connections that their theories *may* reveal, and explore the complications of class and other material processes in particular historical formations.

Since the 1970s some American historians have been doing just that. They are ignoring the ideological confrontations of the past thirty years, and are busy building a theoretically informed empirical project that focuses on the historically specific social relations of American capitalism. Their work does not attempt to explain every aspect of American history in class terms, but seeks to probe the interrelations of class and nonclass phenomena. Their successes, their failures, and their prospects will be analyzed in the concluding chapters of this study.

Most American historians have been unimpressed and unconvinced by marxism, however. Though there have been notable devotees, and though neither British, nor French, nor German historical writing could be said to be dominated by marxist historians or ideas, it is still true that the impact of marxism on American historiography has been slighter than in any of these cases. Why? Some continue to trot out—in one of its several guises—the argument of exceptionalism. Yet even if the empirical criticisms of the Europe–America dichotomy are discounted, the weakness of marxist historiography still constitutes a significant problem in the sociology of knowledge. The assumption of a correspondence between historical facts and historiography fails to confront the complexities of that relationship. Take the British example. Why did a convincing marxist historiography not develop on the foundations laid by Marx and Engels until recent decades? Since it is hardly tenable to assume that British society prior to the 1950s was not susceptible to a class analysis, there is clearly no direct relationship between historical experience and historiography. If the point is recast in terms of a climate of opinion that has changed in Britain over the past thirty years, then historical explanation is reduced to crude and subjective reflections of the current social and political ethos. Given the undeniable existence of a class structure in both Britain and the United States in the nineteenth century, and the advent of industrial capitalism about which Marx has so much to say, then we can safely dismiss the usual varieties of the exceptionalism theme.

One variation on the exceptionalism theme cannot be so easily discounted. This involves the absence of a powerful working-class political movement to sustain a tradition of radical scholarship. The institutional and cultural supports derived from trade union and working-class experience have been important in both Britain and France to contemporary developments in marxist historiography. Yet, as in the more general case, there is no direct correlation between the fortunes of the working class and the fate of class analysis. Academic marxism in Britain has grown in recent years, but in a period of political retreat on the part of the Labour Party and trade unions.

Another explanation, political and academic McCarthyism, has more validity, and it will be necessary later on to assess the impact of anticommunism after World War II on the state of historical scholarship. This interpretation takes account of power struggles and ideological conflict in shaping historiographical change, but still falls short of making a convincing case. For one thing, marxist history was never strong in the pre-McCarthy era anyway; the decline of interest in and refutation of economic determinism began in the late 1930s, and the decline of marxism was a decline from a molehill rather than a scholarly mountain. Moreover, political and ideological anticommunism had an effect in other western countries, including Britain. The main difference was that whereas American marxists were driven out of most university posts, in Britain those who already had university jobs kept them and laid low, but new marxists were not appointed. A larger degree of political intimidation did occur in the United States, but that alone probably cannot account for the important difference between the vitality of leftist history in the United Kingdom since the 1950s and its weakness in the United States. The question remains with respect to the American case: how was the anticommunist ideology effective at the academic level? Like the other explanations considered above, the reliance on McCarthyism is a reductionist account that does not take sufficient note of historical practice.

The occlusion of a marxist presence must be related to the development of American historical method. Not only was there virtually no marxist history of note published in the period 1940–1965. In those years a powerful strain of American historiography developed, which incorporated certain marxist insights but moved away from any serious consideration of marxist scholarship. Class analysis was not merely denounced by the political witch-hunters. Plausible alternative positions were advanced to occupy space which might otherwise have been appropriated by marxist historians—and ground that was increasingly taken by marxist historians in Great Britain. A scholarly cold war accompanied the more famous political one, but it did not take the blunt forms of anticommunism dominant in the larger political world, though it is easy enough to cite evidence of heavy-handed attacks on totalitarianism from some prominent historians. The refutation of marxism proceeded on a much more subtle basis; genuine disagreement over interpretation occurred, and there was no "party line." Yet pluralism served to mask common methodological and theoretical assumptions which have shaped in complex ways the denial, distortion, and selective use of class analysis in American history.

Studying the conceptual plane of American historiography cannot be advanced by accepting the superficial division of scholarship into scientific, progressive, and consensus periods. While those divisions are valid to some extent for questions of historical interpretation, it is important to see twentieth-century historiography as a piece, in which the meaning of historical debates has been obscured by the failure to examine underlying continuities of theory and method between these different periods and political positions. To understand post–World War II historiography, which some New Leftists saw as conservative and antimarxist, it is necessary to probe the assumptions the writers of the 1950s inherited from their predecessors. It will in fact be necessary to go back to provide a brief outline of American scholarship since professionalization began in the 1880s.

In an incisive review of the limitations of the English historical tradition, Gareth Stedman Jones has provided some clues which will help elucidate these issues in American historiography. He has pointed to the epistemology of empiricism and a positivist program of research as restraining the reform of historical studies in Britain. Fact accumulation, a fixation on events and their succession through time, hostility to theory except that provided by the study of facts through an inductive method, an implicit conception of a simple unilinear causation similar to that adhered to in nineteenth-century physical science, and a belief in progress that provided an overarching moral judgment on the course of history, have all held sway from the Victorian era to the 1950s.[8]

A curious omission in Jones' brilliant essay is the absence of any discussion of the United States. A consideration of American historiography over the same period shows that it would be wrong to make an abstract empiricism divorced from the intellectual setting and the conditions of historical reproduction the critical explanatory force. The empiricist tradition has indeed been present in the United States, but a simple empiricism was in the American case crucially modified in the reform of historical practice which began in the early decades of the twentieth century. These significant differences made American historical interpretation and practice much more innovative and conceptually vital than mainstream British historiography for the first sixty years of the twentieth century. In turn, the innovations in the field of American history made it much less vulnerable to marxist alternatives than its counterpart in Britain, where marxism came by the 1970s to redefine whole areas of historiography.

Beginning in the progressive era, a new liberal tradition gradually developed in the writing of American academic history. This superseded the interpretive program of scientific history, while perpetuating in different and more complex forms some of the key assumptions of that historiography. In particular, the dominant schools of American historiography remained in important ways linked to empiricist conceptions. This did not mean that all American historians continued to regard their interpretations as self-evidently flowing from the facts, though some did. But most American historians would, as we shall see, reproduce empiricism. They tended to select and arrange the materials of the past in accord with perceptions derived from commonsense experience; to treat as facts the most readily observable phenomena; and to adopt an uneasy compromise in which the facts remained inviolable while the interpretations constantly changed. There was also a tendency to locate the historical problem to be solved with reference to existing historiography, and to treat the history of a problem as a given datum to be illuminated through ad hoc borrowing of social science concepts which were, themselves, often profoundly affected by forms of empiricism. These procedures consisted mainly of the use of empirical generalizations based purely on observations, or, in more behaviorist forms, the testing of concepts against the data of the past. Wrenched from their cultural and methodological moorings, such positivist approaches could not confirm or deny the validity of the concepts employed, nor supplant the need for explanatory accounts that were truly historical. The whole range of practices involved the fragmentation of historical reality into sets of factors, and the development of subdisciplinary specializations that truncated historical processes. E. P. Thompson provides a concrete critique of some of these modern forms of empiricism in *The Making of the English Working Class*:

The objection to the reigning academic orthodoxy is not to empirical studies per se, but to the fragmentation of our comprehension of the full historical process. First, the empiricist segregates certain events from this process and examines them in isolation. Since the conditions which gave rise to these events are assumed, they appear not only as explicable in their own terms but as inevitable. . . . But there is a second stage, where the empiricist may put these fragmentary studies back together again, constructing a model of the historical process made up from a multiplicity of interlocking inevitabilities, a piecemeal processional.[9]

The new American tradition of critical history first developed in the early twentieth century was not only empiricist and positivist in its methodological assumptions. It was also liberal because it explained history in terms of an interaction of social and economic forces on the one hand and individuals on the other, championed the concept of progress, became allied with the reform impulse in American history and academic life, and advocated the realization of individual freedoms in a democratic setting. Through the application of social science methods and present-centered political concerns, a problem-oriented discipline emerged to stress the interpretation of facts rather than the accumulation of facts themselves. While this tradition remained rooted in an empiricist conception of historical reality, American liberal historians did reinforce this conception to create a historiography of considerable interpretive power.

If this assessment of the liberal tradition involves a systematic critique of its assumptions, the nascent marxist history must also be read with the same eye to its emphases and omissions. By this measure, radical and marxist scholarship from the New Left onwards has not always passed muster. The British marxist tradition which began in the 1960s to penetrate the United States, primarily through the work of E. P. Thompson, challenged but has not yet supplanted the liberal approaches that have constituted the cumulative heritage of academic history in the United States. British marxism was through the emphasis on a "history from the bottom up" absorbed into existing conceptual systems that are not marxian at all. This is why the study of the current revival of marxist history must paradoxically begin not with marxism but with the liberals.

The critique of liberal historiography in these pages has been influenced by a scattering of methodological appraisals from within the profession of history, and by the assaults on positivism and empiricism emanating from the "western marxist" tradition. One stimulus has been the philosophically inclined strain of modern marxism which sought to recover the Hegelian idealist core from the mechanical orthodoxy of late nineteenth-century marxism of the Second International.[10] Georg Lukács in particular quickened a concern among marxists with the depiction of historical totalities and the interrelations of historical phenomena. From a Hegelian-marxist perspective, the relations between the parts of the whole structure had been crucially neglected in bourgeois social theory and in marxism. Both were dominated very much by positivism, which truncated reality as a set of factors that could ultimately be expressed in statistical terms. Positivism also explained actions in terms of unilinear causal factors that could be identified as acting to produce an effect; this neglected the reciprocal relations in which phenomena were both cause and effect at the same time. Marxist critics influenced by Hegelian readings of Marx also attack empiricism for treating history as the sum of its observable parts, and for its consideration of the facts as entities independent of historical and theoretical mediation.

If Hegelian marxist concerns with totality and the interrelations of phenomena offered cogent means of criticizing aspects of orthodox, positivist social science, these same intellectual currents were less useful in suggesting alternative strategies of research and analysis. A marxist program of research required a division of labor and careful specification of hypotheses, and means for incorporating the substance of non-marxist research, especially in the areas of quantitative methodology. If everything was part of an interrelated totality, then how could causal sequences be established and day to day research be conducted? Under an Hegelian reading, the whole was representative of its internal relations, and could always be expressed as an "essence" in which "the elements of the whole are no more than its phenomenal expression." Dissatisfaction with this essentialism, and with the apparent disregard for empirical formulations inherent in the most extreme Hegelian versions of marxism produced a bewildering series of variations, revisions, and alternatives within the general rubric of western marxism.[11] But an alternative philosophical system to the marxist epistemology of the young Lukács was put most starkly in the work of the French philosopher, Louis Althusser.

The Althusserian project recognizes as inescapable the study of different levels of historical reality, but seeks to relate these levels by treating the parts of the social system as the product of the effects of all of the other parts. Althusser's principle of "structural causality" denies both positivistic notions of unilinear causality on the one hand, and Hegelian essences on the other. Historical epochs are seen in terms of semiautonomous practices related as simultaneous cause and effect to one another in a "structure in dominance." This combination goes to make up the ensemble of relations in a particular "social formation."[12]

Althusser's reinterpretation of marxism appeals to the historian's sense of the complexity of social formations in which there never has been a pure contradiction between labor and capital. Helpful too is the suggestion that the relationship between practice and theory and between ideology and social structure is complicated and not reducible to a simple dependency of "superstructure" on the "base." For historiography, this formulation points towards a more flexible and realistic conception of professional and scientific practice as well.

But such general formulas do not facilitate investigation of the exact circumstances in which historical transformations take place. What does it mean to say, for example, that the political "level" is "relatively autonomous"? When one talks of "structural causality," exactly how is this to be translated into the explanation of actual social practices and their interrelations *over time*? The emphasis on epistemology in Althusser and his disciples stimulates more rigorous criticism of the relations of theories, concepts, and facts in historical analysis. But if such philosophical scrutiny can dissect the limitations of certain forms of empiricism in historical writing, it is true equally that "the abyss of empiricism is only separated by a hair's breadth from the abyss of idealism." Carried away by justifiable attacks on a historical profession too often obsessed with data collection and a concept of time as a unilinear datum, Althusser's followers ran the risk of obscuring the difference between empiricism and empirical research guided by historical theories.[13] Any adequate appraisal of history writing must attend not only to the epistemological status of the concepts used, but also to the actual content of historical analysis and its relation to historical evidence. Without such reference, we are left with a purely internalist critique in which truths are validated according to the systems used to produce them.

It is now increasingly realized that the empiricist-idealist controversy in marxist circles of the 1970s is sterile. If the meaning of evidence is indeed gleaned through theory, the evidence which is produced with its aid is not turned into theory. The accounts of historians are in some sense representations of the real, but they derive power from their claims to illuminate real historical processes, even though these may not be immediately visible or verifiable in a succession of events or facts. Doubtless, a marxist analysis must make the transformation of the material world in its productive and reproductive aspects, the organization and reorganization of classes, and the ways in which men and women become conscious of class the foundations of its concrete investigations, but for the marxist historian concerned with the study of these processes, an abstract or general schematization cannot substitute for analysis of these relations in each historical situation. In this sense, marxist categories can only inform historical analysis, and the value of marxist theory can only be judged heuristically.[14]

I shall view historiography within this framework in a manner superficially akin to Michel Foucault's notion of discourses. In a series of influential works, Foucault treated discourses as systems of thought operating according to their own internal rules, and transforming facts into knowledge.[15] My concern here is not with the individual historian's complex production, but with the relation of the individual production to the whole. These relations will be partly revealed in the conscious intentions of the historian, but this study is not primarily concerned with how the historian meant her or his thought to function. By taking account of underlying methodological and conceptual premises, I hope to elucidate the structures of historical thought.

The discourse of history, to continue for a moment to see the profession in terms similar to Foucault's, has operated through complex disciplinary transformations: through processes of co-optation, accommodation, inoculation, exclusion, and silence, the profession has preserved its own set of priorities and assumptions while continuously modifying its methods to enhance the content of historiography. This mutation of historical practice has (typically) operated not through the exercise of exterior power to prevent acceptance of alternative conceptions of historical reality, but by producing new knowledge which serves its own ends: the extension of its own power and comprehension. This does not mean that historical interpretation has been predetermined by these considerations, only that the questions asked, the kinds of evidence regarded as appropriate, and the direction of research programs have all been conditioned by a set of intellectual ground rules. Nor can these rules be considered—in contrast to much of Foucault's work—in a vacuum, for the institutional setting of historical production and the external political and intellectual environments have in various ways both reinforced and undermined critical assumptions of the discipline. (Though Foucault was apparently moving away from a purely discursive vantage point prior to his death, nowhere did he satisfactorily treat the ways in which the "practical and institutional domains" impinged upon his discourses.)[16] The precise relationship between content, assumptions, and the institutional and political setting of historical practice can only be specified in detailed historical analysis. The transformation of American liberal scholarship, and its relations with marxism, can be viewed on one level as such a case study.

When I speak of American historians, I am referring to historians of the United States who live there or whose work has been influenced by extended periods of residence there, such as attendance in graduate school programs. I have relatively little to say on American foreign policy, the historiography of which is only introduced where developments seem especially pertinent to the central themes of this study. Otherwise I have drawn heavily on those aspects of social, economic, intellectual, and political history with which I am most familiar. I have chosen not to deal with Americans who have written on European history or the third world, partly because that would unduly strain the limits of my comprehension, but also because I believe that those historians were operating in a different historiographical environment. Many of the issues were defined by non-Americans, for example in European history. Moreover, American historians have sometimes been able to look at the histories of other areas with the fresh and skeptical vision of outsiders, and have at times broken out of the narrow confines of a national historiography which limited many of their fellow practitioners at home. I believe, nevertheless, that some of the ideological blind spots and conceptual flaws present in writing on United States history would show up in an examination of work on foreign countries. This subject must, however, be left to others more familiar with the basic literatures of those area studies.

NOTES

1. Among those who treat the crisis as international is Lawrence Stone, "The Revival of Narrative: Reflections on an Old New History," *Past and Present* 85 (1979): 3–24. In addition to the liberal-marxist *relationship*, other distinctive aspects of the American situation are

a. the enormous volume of historical writing and the extent of specialization which American material largesse has facilitated, thus rendering the question of historical synthesis especially difficult.

b. the greater role of social science and quantification which had raised expectations about the consequences of technical breakthroughs.

c. the memory of a coherent liberal synthesis in the interwar period which informs the desire for a synthesis.

These themes have never been adequately treated in comparative perspective, but see Laurence Veysey, "The United States," in Georg G. Iggers and Harold T. Parker, eds., *International Handbook of Historical Studies: Contemporary Research and Theory* (Westport, Conn., 1979), pp. 157–74.

2. Theoretically oriented critiques in other disciplines include Alvin Gouldner, *The Coming Crisis of Western Sociology* (New York, 1970); Marvin Harris, *The Rise of Anthropological Theory: A History of Theories of Culture* (New York, 1968); and Edward Nell, "Economics," in Robin Blackburn, ed., *Ideology in Social Science: Readings in Critical Social Theory* (Glasgow, 1972), pp. 76–95. Developments in the historical sociology of the social sciences can be viewed in the *Journal of the History of the Behavioral Sciences* (1965–   ).

3. I have followed the usage of C. Wright Mills, *The Marxists* (New York, 1962), and refused to capitalize either marxist or liberal. There is no room here to enter the debate over the relevance of marxism to precapitalist economic systems, but see, for example, Marshall Sahlins, *Stone Age Economics* (Chicago, 1972); Barry Hindess and Paul Q. Hirst, *Pre-Capitalist Modes of Production* (London, 1975); Rodney Hilton, ed., *The Transition from Feudalism to Capitalism* (London, 1976 ed.).

4. Karl Marx and Friedrich Engels, "The Class Struggles in France, 1848 to 1850," in *Karl Marx and Friedrich Engels: Selected Works*, 3 vols. (Moscow, 1966), 1:186–299; Rudolph Hilferding, *Finance Capital: A Study of the Latest Phase of Capitalist*

Development, ed. with intro. by Tom Bottomore (London, 1980, orig. pub., 1910); Leon Trotsky, *The History of the Russian Revolution*, 3 vols. (New York, 1932).

5. John Patrick Diggins, "History Through a Wasp: Charles A. Beard and the 1960s Generation," *Reviews in American History* 12 (1984): 340; Louis Hartz, *The Liberal Tradition in America* (New York, 1955).

6. For representative works, see Dick Howard and Karl Klare, eds., *The Unknown Dimension: European Marxism since Lenin* (New York, 1972).

7. See the relevant chapters in Iggers and Parker, eds., *International Handbook of Historical Studies*; Georg G. Iggers, *New Directions in European Historiography* (Middletown, Conn., 1975), pp. 43–79, 123–74; Pierre Vilar, "Marxist History, a History in the Making: Towards a Dialogue with Althusser," *New Left Review* 80 (1973): 67.

8. Gareth Stedman Jones, "History: The Poverty of Empiricism," in Blackburn, ed., *Ideology in Social Science*, pp. 96–115.

9. E. P. Thompson, *The Making of the English Working Class* (New York, Vintage ed., 1966), pp. 204–5.

10. Georg Lukács, *History and Class Consciousness* (London, 1971 ed.). A much more recent study in the Hegelian mold is Bertell Ollman, "Marxism and Political Science: Prolegomenon to an Essay on Marx's Method," in Oliman, *Social Class and Sexual Revolution: Essays on Marx and Reich* (London and Boston, 1979), pp. 99–123. An influential appraisal of idealist elements in western marxism is Perry Anderson, *Considerations on Western Marxism* (London, 1976). More sympathetic is Russell Jacoby, *Dialectic of Defeat: Contours of Western Marxism* (Cambridge, Eng., 1981).

11. Robin Blackburn and Gareth Stedman Jones, "Louis Althusser and the Struggle for Marxism," in Howard and Klare, eds., *The Unknown Dimension*, pp. 370–72. For an outstanding survey of the attempts of western marxists to wrestle with the concept of totality, see Martin Jay, *Marxism and Totality: The Adventures of a Concept from Lukács to Habermas* (Berkeley and Los Angeles, 1984).

12. Louis Althusser, *For Marx*, trans. Ben Brewster (New York, Vintage ed., 1970), pp. 167, 204–7, 209–11, 213–17.

13. Vilar, "Marxist History," p. 67.

14. Gareth Stedman Jones, "History and Theory," *History Workshop* 8 (1979): 198–202; Alan Chalmers, *What Is This Thing Called Science? An Assessment of the Nature and Status of Science and Its Methods* (Brisbane, Qld., 1976), chap. 11; and Gregor McLennan, *Marxism and the Methodologies of History* (London, 1981), pp. 30–38, 87–91.

15. See esp., Michel Foucault, *The Archeology of Knowledge*, trans. Alan Sheridan [Smith] (New York, 1972); Michel Foucault, *Power/Knowledge: Selected Interviews and Other Writings, 1972–1977*, ed. Colin Gordon (New York, 1980); Alan Sheridan, *Michel Foucault: The Will to Truth* (London, 1980); Hubert L. Dreyfus and Paul Rabinow, *Michel Foucault: Beyond Structuralism and Hermeneutics* (Chicago, 1982).

16. Dreyfus and Rabinow, *Beyond Structuralism*, is helpful.

1

New and Old History: Beard, the Progressives, and the Limits to Reform, 1900–1945

This book is concerned primarily with the development of American historiography since World War II. Beginning with Charles Beard and the progressives may therefore seem odd, but even the most determined advocate of modern superiority in scholarship would have to concede the continuing relevance of a man who wrote his most important work more than seventy years ago. Whether Beard is admired or despised, copied or rejected, whether American historians argue the necessity of getting back to, beyond, or around his legacy, there is no denying his reputation.[1] Beard especially concerns a study of marxism and liberal historiography. His own synthesis overshadows the search for a new organizing principle in American history, and of all American historians, Beard is seen as coming closest to the economic and class interpretations which marxists promise as the answer to the current historiographical confusion. For these reasons the next two chapters deal with Beard's place in the context of American historiography in general, and the so-called progressive interpretation in particular. Much of the contemporary debate on this question ignores two important themes that these chapters explore: the theoretical assumptions at the core of the progressive enterprise; and the extent of progressive and, particularly, Beardian influence in the period before 1945.

The debate over Beard since the 1960s has rested implicitly on a reading of the course of American historiography which organizes the subject into a succession of historical schools, beginning with the "scientific historians." These founders of academic history in the 1880s apparently conceived of their discipline as a science. Naive as the belief may now seem, they set out to create a brave new historiography on the basis of the facts, the assembly of which would lead to interpretation, and from there on to a universal history. In the meantime, they believed that historians should steer clear of philosophical questions. On this basis they proceeded to study the evolution of institutions, and produced a dry and narrow historiography focused on political life.

From the 1890s to the 1920s, this scientific historiography was increasingly challenged by a younger group whose view of the past flowed from a sympathy with and involvement in larger movements of reform in American life which are commonly depicted as progressive. The name "the progressive historians" was derived from this intellectual and political milieu which led the new scholars to adopt an activist role in the profession. Influenced by pragmatism, the progressives saw ideas as instruments which could be used to shape future reality; they sought to put history to work for the social good by investigating the social and economic roots of abstract ideas. Whereas the scientific school had concentrated on politics, the progressives stressed economics. The latter enlarged the scope of history to investigate the whole history of a people and its democratic struggles against special interests. The towering figure within this new movement was that of Charles Beard, so much so that Beardian and progressive became, for many commentators, almost synonymous terms. The views of the progressives quickly became dominant themes in American historiography, and held intellectual sway until challenged by the so-called consensus historians of the 1950s, who undermined the idea of a fundamental conflict in American political life.[2]

Variations of this organizing scheme may be found in carefully nuanced form in the writings of a Hofstadter, or rigidified into a set of paradigms by less subtle scholars. As is the case with all such profoundly influential ways of arranging the data, a measure of truth underlies the selection and interpretation. Nonetheless, the achievements of the scientific historians and the shaping of American historical method are thereby distorted if these writers are seen as a mere prelude to the greatness of a progressive school. The lines between the progressives and the scientific historians were not as distinct as the coupling of scholars like Turner and Beard suggests. It makes more sense to conceive of American professional history since the 1880s as a disciplinary discourse in which the contours had been largely laid down by scientific historians prior to 1910. Insofar as they constituted a distinct grouping, the progressives modified continuously the pattern of interpretation and method, but historiography continued to be reproduced in ways that testified to the persistence of the existing structures. This argument does not make the progressive historians unimportant. Their work considered collectively accomplished the gradual *reform* of historical practice which does define the American debate over historiography even today, but unless the progressives are put in the perspective of the theoretical assumptions inherited from the scientific historians, that achievement cannot be understood.

Scientific history actually contained two tendencies. From the beginning of his career at Johns Hopkins in 1876, Herbert Baxter Adams conceived of his subject as the historical equivalent of biology; the "specimens" were his sources, the seminars in which his graduates studied, the "laboratories." The study of the evolution of institutions—the germ theory—would lead to comparison and to universal history. This program soon produced rumblings of discontent. Both future progressives like Turner and more orthodox scholars like Charles McLean Andrews abandoned the germ theory and its evolutionary pretensions, and settled for more modest objectives.[3] They did not, however, forsake all of the canons of Rankean method brought by Adams and others from Germany, for the critical scrutiny of sources survived as the basis of the profession's practice. By the 1890s, the defining metaphor of the discipline had changed from the science of biology to the trade of building. J. Franklin Jameson, one of the most influential of the scientific historians, apparently conceived of the discipline as a matter of pure craftsmanship: "I struggle on making bricks without much idea of how the architects will use them, but believing that the best architect that ever was cannot get along without bricks, and therefore trying to make good ones."[4] Jameson's revelation exposed the positivist assumptions American historians shared with contemporaries in Britain. These articles of faith entailed the observation of the real world as revealed in the documents, the collection of facts, and the development through these inductive procedures of reliable generalizations about the past as actuality. Even though these pioneers of scientific history in America realized that historical accounts would be rendered incomplete by the imperfections in the data, and even though they tended to dismiss the attempts of European positivists like Auguste Comte to advance general laws of human development, they took from the positivist tradition not only a passion for accumulation of data, but also its unilinear conception of causality. Like their British counterparts, the American scientific historians proceeded as if "the facts would fall into place, as if of their own accord, in a chain of events, linked to one another in a mechanical fashion by relations of a simple transitive causality."[5] With the comparative pretensions of Adams discarded, the younger scientific historians wrote within a largely chronological framework, and did not query the idea of history as the study of events and the individuals who shaped them.

This commitment to the actuality of history did not mean their own works were value free. In place of positivistic laws, they put their own belief in evolutionary progress. Progress, interpreted as simultaneously moral and material, they identified with the history of western civilization in general, and with the progress of American civilization in particular. Civilization in turn was equated with the liberal-protestant values believed to be immanent in the historical evidence. These would emerge in a straightforward way from the facts of history. "If the historian took care of the facts," John Higham observed in his summary of these developments in American scholarship, "the values would take care of themselves."[6]

Good reasons exist to qualify this view of the scientific school. J. Franklin Jameson himself wrote a social interpretation of the American Revolution that was praised by supporters of the progressives. In a judicious essay published as early as 1891, Jameson had considered that future historians would have to incorporate economic interpretations into their analyses. In the same work, Jameson also gave notice that the subject matter of history, and historical interpretation, would have to change "with the changing complexion of the present." Neither was Herbert Baxter Adams the mindless advocate of a narrowly political viewpoint that might be inferred from his support for Edward Freeman's dictum that "history is past politics." Raymond Cunningham argues that Adams sought a more comprehensive view of civilization in his teaching and research, and gave "ample consideration" to the social, intellectual, and cultural aspects of history in his lectures. Albert Bushnell Hart, another prominent scientific historian, encouraged the work of Frederick Jackson Turner, and in his presidential address to the American Historical Association went beyond the celebration of mere objective facts to stress the role of an intangible historical insight in fusing the facts into an interpretive whole. Yet another, Herbert Osgood, had conceded before he died that historical interpretation would be bound to change as the problems of the present changed. Osgood told Beard in 1918 that "profound economic questions have now arisen and students of the younger generation, true to their age, will occupy themselves with economic aspects of history."[7]

Reconsiderations of the scientific school have rightly stressed its influence and complexity, but scientific history did not secure the domination of historical *interpretation* that its founders hoped. They remained an obvious target for an intellectual revolt. They *did* write mainly studies of laws, institutions, and national politics. The *American Nation* series, edited by Professor Hart and published between 1904 and 1908, was the principal synthesis of this generation. Hart advocated the inclusion of the social and economic life of "the people" but, Michael Kraus has observed, most volumes in the series "followed conventional lines of political history." The products of the doctoral programs in the period maintained a similar focus and revealed an almost total absence of literary flair as well. The volumes in the *Harvard Historical Studies* and their Columbia and Johns Hopkins equivalents were, with few exceptions, unstintingly dull in conception and execution. Certainly, the image of Ranke and his American disciples in the minds of the later progressive historians was that of a dry-as-dust scientism.[8]

For these reasons the scientific approach came under a series of attacks after the turn of the century from scholars who began to argue that historical method was out of touch with the pressing social problems of the era. Whereas the scientific historians had imported their basic techniques from Germany, the revisionary thrust was fundamentally indigenous and ultimately more influential for the forging of a distinctive American approach to historical interpretation. These scholars included Frederick Jackson Turner, Charles Beard, James Harvey Robinson, Carl Becker, Vernon Parrington, and their many students and followers.

Yet these progressives, as they have been dubbed, displayed no unity of interpretation or professional approach. The prominent cases of Beard and Turner illustrate the diversity. Both advanced varieties of economic interpretation, but Turner emphasized environmental influences while Beard stressed classes and interest groups. Turner had relatively good relations with the larger profession, if his private correspondence with more orthodox, scientific scholars is any guide. In fact, leading conservatives at Chicago and Harvard like Hart went to a good deal of trouble to try to get Turner to come to their institutions. Beard was different. He was much more the outsider after he resigned his academic post in 1917 at Columbia over a matter of academic freedom. Beard attacked what he saw as the petty-mindedness of conventional academic life, and lambasted the historical community for failing to deal with the vital question of the conflict of capital and labor. (No such iconoclastic sentiments issued from the pen of Turner, a moderate Republican and advocate of conservative reform.) Beard was for most of his career seeking to influence by his prodigious capacity as a writer; Turner was famous for writing so little and receiving so much acclaim in return. And the final difference was one of timing; Turner's professional life was more than half over before Beard's *An Economic Interpretation of the Constitution* was ever published.[9]

The institutional and intellectual roots of this diversity will command attention in the following chapter, but first the contribution of the progressives to the reform of American historical knowledge must be analyzed. Only then will explanations of their attitudes and actions be intelligible. Probing the conceptual apparatus of these historians is especially important because it reveals the limits to the innovations the progressives made. Precisely because they strengthened American historiography in the short run, the progressive historians set up barriers to further and more radical reconstruction of the contours of American historiography in the longer term.

Beard looms large in accounts of those who have influenced American historiography, in part because it was Beard who laid down the principal and most highly publicized challenge to the methods and conclusions of the scientific historians. Beard's influence suffered because he did not train any students to perpetuate his methods, and his novel interpretations of aspects of the American past had to be disseminated through the volume of his published writings and his penchant for extravagant and controversial viewpoints. Notwithstanding this impediment, Beard's thirty-seven major books, some two hundred and fourteen book reviews, and two hundred and eighty-five articles would in the long run make him the single most important historian of the period 1900–1950.[10] But volume alone did not distinguish his contribution. Allan Nevins wrote far more, for example. Above all, Beard's conceptual innovations and his arresting interpretations endeared him to younger historians.

Nor can Turner be ignored simply because his output was much smaller than Beard's. Turner commands attention not only because of the fertility of his intelligence, but also because his many students and admirers became significant in the spreading of progressive thought in the interwar years. Vernon L. Parrington, who is typically coupled with Beard as representative of the progressive temper, turned out to be of much less importance in retrospect, but in the 1930s his influence was almost as impressive as Beard's. Though Parrington's major work—*Main Currents in American Thought*—appeared near the end of his life, its colorful prose style and its synoptic interpretation of American letters made the book an inspiration for graduate students. A poll of historians put it at the top of the list of ''most preferred'' books written during the period 1920–1950. Carl Becker is often thought of as an expert in European intellectual history, but his contributions to American history and to discussion of the philosophy of history in America were both voluminous and thought-provoking. Thus he too deserves consideration along with James Harvey Robinson. Though the latter was primarily a Europeanist, his general writings on historical method provided a catalyst for reform.[11]

It was around Robinson's *The New History*, published in 1912, that the movement for a more innovative and flexible historiography rallied. The irony was that neither the theme nor the title was entirely new. The term had been advocated in 1900 by the amateur social historian Edward Eggleston, and there was ample precedent for many of the views of Robinson in the ideas of those dismissed as proponents of a scientific orthodoxy. Nonetheless, the concept stuck to Robinson and his indefatigable intellectual collaborator Charles Beard. Soon students of theirs such as Harry Elmer Barnes and Arthur Schlesinger, Sr., would be described as ''New Historians.''[12] (Though the term is a little narrower and more specific than the more amorphous ''progressive,'' the two can be used interchangeably as they are in this study.)

The Robinson-Beard view departed from the official Rankean notion that the accumulation of facts would lead ultimately and inexorably to universal history. Against the concept of History as a jigsaw puzzle to be completed in cumulative fashion, the New Historians argued that each generation would generate its own distinctive perspectives which would inevitably entail the writing of new versions of the past. They have been credited with vast effects on the practice of American scholarship by taking the subject of American history out of its narrow institutional focus to analyze the social and economic interests which lay behind movements, institutions, and ideas.[13]

The best evidence for this common view of the impact of the New History can be found in Charles Beard's *An Economic Interpretation of the Constitution*, published in 1913. In this work, progressive history produced the first major monograph in the history of the discipline in America. Beard cut through the idea that history was a narrative of surface events to record the underlying realities, as Beard would put it, of economic interests behind the forming of the constitution. His use of collective biography was ahead of its time; it anticipated the work of Sir Lewis Namier and the career-line studies of modern sociology. As Richard Hofstadter correctly says, Beard's book was ''probably the first truly exciting monograph in the history of American historiography.'' It was ''an innovation in form, in American experience a new historical genre.''[14] Compared to English historiography, where the dry traditions of Whig constitutional, administrative, and political history continued to assume a far greater importance in the interwar period, American progressive scholarship was indeed innovative, challenging, and immensely stimulating.

Beard advanced far more than new techniques. He championed the restructuring of historical thinking around an empirical analysis of the impact of economic forces on politics and urged the study of their interrelations. He followed this approach not only in his book on the constitution, but in a series of important additional works, from *Economic Origins of Jeffersonian Democracy* in 1915, through *The Economic Basis of Politics*, to *The Rise of American Civilization*, which appeared in 1927.

Nor was he without followers in this enterprise. Arthur Schlesinger, Sr. and Dixon Ryan Fox were initially attracted to Beard's analysis, and their own dissertations, published as *The Colonial Merchants and the American Revolution* (1918) and *The Decline of Aristocracy in the Politics of New York* (1919), followed the formula of economic groups as the determinants of politics. Later, Howard Beale applied the economic interpretation to the Reconstruction period in *The Critical Year*, and Matthew Josephson became a more journalistic and iconoclastic disciple of the Beardian approach in his exposés of the great, rich, and powerful in *The Robber Barons* (1938) and other works.[15]

The scope of historiography was enlarged to encompass social aspects of history as well. Turner's interest in the west was part of a more catholic enthusiasm for social processes, and under his stimulus, the history of reform, of urbanization, and immigration began to be written in an academic context by Schlesinger and Marcus Hansen. In *A History of American Life*, Schlesinger and Fox edited thirteen volumes whose narratives incorporated subjects as diverse as recreation, religion, politics, art, and economic change. Schlesinger and Mary Beard went so far in the direction of a comprehensive social history as to pioneer the academic study of the role of women in American society, and with her husband, Charles, Mary Beard managed to incorporate material on women's contribution into their synoptic study of the economic, cultural, social, and intellectual life of the people in *The Rise of American Civilization*.[16]

This last volume illustrated another attractive feature of the progressive genre. As no others before or since have done, progressive historians combined the analytical insights of social science with a commitment to an intelligible narrative synthesis. The ultimate aim was to contribute to democratic education and hence to progress. The many works of the Beards, the Schlesinger-Fox series, and the essays of Becker and Turner all illustrate this commitment to making history useful to the democratic purpose. This the Beards' *Rise* achieved to a remarkable degree, while at the same time it served to excite a generation of younger adults in the thirties with the subject of American history. That this work sold 134,000 copies and continues to exert an unacknowledged intellectual influence over many students of American life may seem surprising, until the combination of rich analytical insight, majestic scope, and engaging tone is reconsidered. The attempt to comprehend the total sweep of American historical experience, the frequent comparisons with European history, the setting of individual action and political controversy in the context of larger trends in social and economic change all made the book impressive enough. Completing the triumph is the suggestive theme of civilization that involved the gradual liberation of man from material restraints through the innovations of technology and education. This indeed was a monument to the breadth of vision and social faith that inspired the best of progressive scholarship.[17]

Even the most caustic critic of the progressive temper would have to concede, therefore, the newness of the New History on the level of bold programmatic statements and arresting historical interpretations. Innovation there certainly was in the greater emphasis on the social and economic roots of political behavior; the use of the methods of the social sciences to enliven historical analysis; the attention to contemporary problems to determine the questions historians asked of the evidence; a penchant for treatment of recent times as more relevant to present-day concerns than more distant eras; and a greater focus on American topics as opposed to ancient and European histories.

The pronouncements of the progressives and their innovative approaches can be deceptive, however. Important continuities existed in the ways history was conceived and written. At the levels of historical method and epistemology, the canons of scientific objectivity continued to exercise considerable sway. A certain intellectual and conceptual confusion related to the legacy of scientific history was manifest even in the bible of *The New History*. Robinson's book of that title proclaimed the relativity of historical knowledge, but went on to mix a discussion of philosophical relativism with one which emphasized that improvements in scientific knowledge produced relativism. The kind of relativism that flowed from "our constant increase in knowledge" was very different from the idea that changing philosophical or political viewpoints produced new interpretations. The former was compatible with modern scientific practice while the latter was definitely not. This distinction was blurred in Robinson's account.[18]

Relativism was always part of the progressive program. Men as different as Beard, Robinson, Turner, and Becker all intimated that the changing complexion of the historian and the times produced new questions in historiography, and hence highlighted new facts and relationships. Yet this did not set them apart from the run-of-the-mill scientific historians. With the exception of Becker's 1910 essay on "Detachment and the Writing of History," historians commonly identified with the progressive label did not make clear the tension between the relativism of a present-centered historiography on the one hand, and standards of objective inquiry associated with the scientific historians on the other. Though Ellen Nore reminds us that Charles Beard did not discover relativism in the 1930s, no amount of detail on the lineages of Beard's later position changes the essential point: he was confronting on a philosophical level conflicts in progressive thought which had been neither clearly articulated nor adequately understood by the likes of Beard, Turner, or even Becker.[19] The historians who championed a New History over scientific orthodoxy did not overturn the idea that historical investigation was rooted in a set of facts that were "discrete, atomic and supremely indifferent to the position of the observer." Interpretation in this view established its validity insofar as it flowed from the factual verities. Progressive era historians thus maintained the observer-fact distinction which lay at the heart of nineteenth-century empiricist epistemology, and which underlay British and American historical thinking in that period. To quote again from *The New History*, "our more carefully considered opinions are based ultimately upon observed facts. . . . With our ever increasing knowledge in regard to these facts, our opinions must necessarily change.''[20]

In *An Economic Interpretation*, Beard claimed to be collecting cold, hard facts, described in language that might have gladdened the heart of Fustel de Coulanges.[21] Was that language designed to camouflage Beard's radical purpose in debunking venerable tradition? Perhaps, and yet the commitment to scientific procedures persisted into the 1920s, long after Beard had openly adopted the role of radical gadfly to the historical profession. His assertion that the historical enterprise rested on ''facts, facts, and still more facts, verified and tested,'' still demonstrated the hold of positivism on his thinking a decade after *An Economic Interpretation*.[22] Like others influenced by pragmatism, Beard was trying to penetrate the vapors of idealism which he believed had enveloped the study of American political institutions in the nineteenth century. A critical commitment of Beard's in this enterprise was to fulfill the scientific promise of the scientific historians by applying a dose of social and economic realism often absent from the latter's actual practice. The challenges to this factually and empirically oriented way of looking at the world posed by new developments in European philosophy and historical epistemology—represented, for example, in the early works of Croce—went largely unnoticed. Even after Croce's *Aesthetics* had been translated into English in 1909, there is no evidence that Beard or Carl Becker actually read this work or were aware of its existence before the 1920s. Nor can the superficial resemblances between their own blend of empiricism and pragmatism be equated with the complex idealism of Croce's thought.[23]

The case for a parallel between Croce and the New History is weak, but that should not deter further comparison of the shifts occurring in historical method on both sides of the Atlantic. The progressive reorientation coincided with profound changes in historical thinking in European countries. Georg Iggers' survey of European historiography noted the almost simultaneous questioning of scientific orthodoxy in France, Germany, Italy, and the United States, but perhaps because of the parochial character of American historiographical writing, little has been done to build upon this insight. The survival of a Rankean orthodoxy was, not surprisingly, most marked in Germany, partly due to the structure of the profession there, and partly to the extraordinary circumstances of German national life in the twentieth century. A marxist influence was felt very early and strongly, and had serious intellectual repercussions in the historical sociology of Max Weber. Within marxism itself, promising trends in marxist theory surfaced in the 1920s through the Frankfurt School, but fascism and World War II truncated these developments, as in Italy, and the same experience reinforced in German writing a focus on the nation-state, politics, and diplomacy. For these reasons, the detailed comparisons in this chapter will be made with the French and British cases. In fact, the issue of the ''newness'' of the New History can best be approached by setting the work of Beard beside the equally illustrious contributions of his French contemporary, Marc Bloch.[24]

Though Beard's analysis was received as an interpretive bombshell, its methodological and theoretical advances were considerably less stunning. Beyond the collective biography technique and an interest in economic processes behind political action, Beard broke little new ground. Unlike the French historians who almost at the same time began to question the centrality of political events to the interpretation of historical processes, Beard used socioeconomic data to illuminate the traditional categories of national political history, and the narrative of the realization of democratic and individual liberty which American writers found in that history. Related to this fixation with traditional political and chronological categories was a continuing focus upon the public and political documentary evidence which was derived from scientific historiography. The most innovative progressive work of the period, Beard's *An Economic Interpretation*, could not get beyond what was self-evident in the documents. As Beard stated rather blandly in his discussion of the Connecticut constitutional convention, "no documents, no history."[25]

The first major work of Marc Bloch, *Les Rois Thaumaturges* (1924), translated as *The Royal Touch*, seems on a very superficial level to be a methodologically comparable study to *An Economic Interpretation*, since Bloch, like Beard, probed behind the surface of events and threw light on the sources of elite power. But *The Royal Touch* was fundamentally different in emphasis, for its mode of operation was structural. The book was primarily concerned with the delineation of the mental structures of a past society. Bloch was attempting to uncover the history of a popular myth, the belief in the magical healing powers of medieval kings. The book therefore dealt with elite power as a by-product of its concern with mentalities, and did so in an anthropological way that sought to explore the sources of that power rather than attempt to explain or expose the realities behind political events.[26]

Not simply Beard's method but also the subject matter linked to that method remained strikingly traditional. *An Economic Interpretation* and his *Economic Origins of Jeffersonian Democracy* retained nineteenth-century liberalism's focus on the nation-state, on political events, and on the process of rational decision making among elites. Even in *The Rise of American Civilization*, "the people" do not really appear despite their rhetorical invocation. The reconstruction of their patterns of life and labor he did not begin; they are involved rather as forces which sweep across the stage of American history to enliven a drama in which the central characters are still the great individuals, groups, and parties that articulated contending political forces. This formulation preserves the voluntaristic assumptions of nineteenth-century liberalism while it recognizes that the actions of individuals were powerfully conditioned by material circumstances.

A quieter challenge to orthodoxy came from Frederick Jackson Turner, whose research went further than Beard's in questioning the conventional focus on political events, documentary evidence, and the nation-state. Yet personal and conceptual limitations in Turner's own work combined with changes in the historiographical and intellectual climate after World War II to stifle the best in Turner's contribution. As a result, neither did Turner, any more than Beard, rupture the theoretical and methodological continuity of American historiography's conceptual framework.[27] Turner's pursuit of the illusive theme of sectionalism and his pioneering use of geography in historical studies anticipated in some respects the emphasis on material life found in the work of Fernand Braudel in his consummate product of the *Annales, La Méditerranée*. Turner also resembled *Annales* scholars in his emphasis on a much broader conception of historical sources than most of his American historical contemporaries. He viewed all records, not merely literary evidence and government documents, as critical source materials for the reconstruction of history.

The parallel ends there. While Turner excelled in suggesting new avenues for historical investigation, he was unable to deliver on the promise of his early interpretations, in part because he did not break with the positivist procedures of the scientific historians who trained him. An eclectic in approach, he did strive like Bloch and Braudel for something resembling total history. But he had no disciplined theory which might have helped him to order the totality of relations that he did suggest in his lectures and essays. He was, as Ray Allen Billington says, "a glutton for data" who never did have enough material to make him feel confident that a synthesis of his historical scholarship could be achieved. This stance reflected the profound empiricism of his mind. So too did his belief that modern history was superior to medieval on account of the superior volume and quality of modern historical source materials.[28] As a consequence, Turner's written contribution to American historiography was slight in proportion to his reputation and influence. Including his posthumously published works, he produced two general narrative histories and two books of suggestive but often repetitious essays.[29]

The promise of a materialist interpretation of American history implicit in some of his essays was never realized, and in the absence, his reputation had to rest on the popularity of the "Frontier Thesis." This most famous and influential of Turner's writings combined insights into the importance of geography for historical analysis with a liberal-individualist conception of the American past that celebrated the democratic values of the American polity, and assumed in the process an American national character. The thesis was designed not to challenge those assumptions and the idea of progress associated with them, but to raise the question of how individualistic values could best be preserved in a world increasingly characterized by extremes of wealth, poverty, and class conflict. "However profound the economic changes," Turner wrote in 1922 in anticipation of recent liberal views of marxism, "we shall not give up our American ideals and our hopes for man, which had their origin in our own pioneering experience, in favor of any mechanical solution offered by doctrinaires educated in Old World grievances."[30]

For present purposes it is less important to note that Beard and Turner did not break with the dominant historical tradition than to analyze both the sources and consequences of this crucial episode in the development of American historical scholarship. Its importance is best understood by again comparing the development of American historiography with trends in France, where there occurred "a decisive rejection of the more simplistic assumptions of mid–nineteenth century positivist methodology."[31] Here the comparison concerns not simply obvious differences in techniques, for it cuts to the center of different theoretical constructions of history. Especially important was Henri Berr's *Revue de Synthèse Historique*, established in 1900, which anticipated the rejection of old-fashioned positivism and liberal-individualism within the historical profession. Two of Berr's collaborators in the period before World War I, Marc Bloch and Lucien Febvre, built upon the foundations already apparent in their earliest work to produce in the 1920s mature historical studies reflecting the new orientation, and then established the now-famous *Annales* journal in 1929, devoted to the new historical methods and interpretations.

The method of Marc Bloch, perhaps the most famous historian associated with *Annales*, illustrates the reorientation of historical thought in France. Like Emile Durkheim, the French sociologist in whose intellectual shadow Bloch, Febvre, and Berr developed, Bloch proceeded from the assumption that "the individual could only be understood within the context of a society and that this society manifested itself in concrete forms which could be observed from the outside very much like the phenomena of nature."[32] The progressive historians in America, too, treated individuals and events in relation to social forces, but whereas they viewed society as a backdrop explaining individual events, Bloch and his group made society conceived as a structural entity the basic unit of historical analysis. Since he shifted the emphasis to society, Bloch was not concerned with individual actions but with social facts, especially the depiction of complex relationships within social structures. The approach entailed not merely the study of economic and social backgrounds, as was the case with Beard's *An Economic Interpretation*, but also the reconstruction of the mental landscapes of societies. Thus cultural tradition as well as material circumstances were brought together in an attempt to develop a system of totalistic historical interpretation.

Several related conceptual breakthroughs followed. Especially did his work challenge the ascendancy of political history, the depiction of historical time in terms of the national political narrative of events, and the obsession in much nineteenth-century historical writing with the actions of great individuals. Bloch therefore undermined what Americans know as "the presidential synthesis" in their own history, a revolutionary development which, despite the reform in historical practice initiated by the progressives, had no real parallel in the United States until after World War II. Whereas American historians in the progressive era added socioeconomic aspects to the existing conception of history, French historians began to reconstitute their categories of analysis entirely. Along with this reorientation went Bloch's belief that the traditional periodization of history had to be radically reconstructed. The period of study for any given subject, he argued, must be derived from the concepts under study, not from extraneous considerations derived from superficial events or "facts."[33]

Equally important, Bloch's approach involved a decisive break with the scientific historians' view that the practice of history involved reading the documents and then fashioning an interpretation from the readily observable and accessible evidence. Against Beard's casual concession that "no documents" equaled "no history," Bloch took the emphasis away from literary documents, especially the records of public men and events, to broaden the concept of document immensely. Summing up his viewpoint in the posthumously published *The Historian's Craft*, Bloch noted that "the variety of historical evidence is nearly infinite. Everything that man says or writes, everything that he makes, everything he touches can and ought to teach us about him." This archeological view of history was already being implemented in Bloch's early contributions to the *Revue de Synthèse Historique*, notably his remarkable manifesto, *L'Île de France (Les Pays autour de Paris)*, published in 1913. Not until the 1930s did Beard demonstrate a comparable concern with anthropological evidence, and then only in his programmatic statements on historical knowledge. Underlying Bloch's conception was the conviction that the evidence "will speak only when they are properly questioned." The documents had to be read in spite of themselves—"even against their will"—for what they did not say as much as for what they said.[34] The conception that historical truth was not self-evident in the facts but had to be teased from them by patient reconstruction set Bloch apart from Beard, who in *An Economic Interpretation* depicted the past not as a partial account to be informed by theory, but as a body of historical data to be dredged up with the aid of questions posed by the economic interpretation. These "economic facts" were then presented in the fashion of a "catalogue" from which certain conclusions seemed to flow. Beard merely claimed to be presenting these more or less self-evident conclusions for evaluation by independent students without the theoretical mediation of the historian.[35]

These invidious comparisons should not, however, obscure the positive aspects of the progressive contribution. Though Marc Bloch and Lucien Febvre did excellent service in drawing attention to holistic structures and material forces, their work, in lesser hands, threatened to obscure the relations of individuals, events, ideologies, and classes to structural totalities. The tendency to depict society in organicist, almost biological terms, apparent in some of the more recent inheritors of the mantle of Bloch and Febvre, is as misleading as the liberal-individualism that the founders of *Annales* polemicized against so effectively. Neither did British historiography provide a viable alternative synthesis. No revolutionary break in historical practice occurred there in the comparable period, despite the efforts of R. H. Tawney and the important contribution to the study of political structure by Sir Lewis Namier. Even after World War II, English historians still tended to display an old-fashioned commitment to empiricism, and an attachment to an event-centered, mostly political historiography. Instead of making a history of society its goal, the profession still conceived of social history as history with the politics left out.[36]

United States historians fashioned a blend of these two competing traditions that avoided some of the misconceptions of either. American historians moved away from the event- and fact-centered British empiricist tradition. Much more stress was placed at the level of epistemology and method on the interpretive use to which the facts were put. The arrangements of facts changed according to the application of various social science techniques and particular interests of each generation of historians. At the same time, the autonomy of the facts was preserved from theoretical intervention. This pragmatic liberation of American historiography from a narrow empiricism allowed historians to combine an interest in the individual and the unique with an understanding of the social and economic settings of events. While human actions were never under this formula reduced to purely impersonal and determining structures, the structures themselves could not become the objects of analysis. Events and individuals might be explained in terms of "deeper forces," but knowledge of these forces remained necessarily superficial. This was where the progressives parted with historians like Bloch and Febvre.

The failure to *reconstruct* historical practice had important consequences on several different levels. The most important of these, which shall be dealt with in turn, concerned the conceptualization of historical reality, the subject matter deemed important to historical studies, and the debate over the philosophy of history that occurred through the relativist controversy of the 1930s.

The progressive generation of historians, while they appeared to make history more realistic, could only go so far. To understand these limits, it is important to stress the positivistic residues of traditional historical method in the thinking and practice of the progressives. Their continued emphasis on empirically verifiable realities meant that they focused on what was immediately apparent and either ignored or did not fully understand "non-sensible realities" like mode of production or any patterns of behavior which were not self-evident in the documents.[37] One of the principal consequences of this approach was to make it impossible to throw any light on the concept of class. It is true that class as a concept is associated with the work of Beard as well as Carl Becker's study of the Revolution in New York, Arthur Schlesinger, Sr.'s *Colonial Merchants*, and Dixon Ryan Fox's *The Decline of Aristocracy in the Politics of New York*. In these works, Schlesinger, Fox, Becker, and Beard all tended to take the concept of "class" for granted, and interpreted American history in the light of class rivalries, but class was rarely analyzed and not entirely understood.[38] When Beard spoke of *class* in 1913 he treated the term as interchangeable with *group*, and as he later pointed out, his view did not derive from Marx at all, but from James Madison's depiction of the politics of interests in *The Federalist*. Because Beard interpreted class in terms of what he could see in the documents, the reality he discovered was not the structural relations of classes to the means of production, but the connections of property and other economic interests. Structural relations were not verifiable in the actions of individuals or groups, the events of history, or in the evidence left behind, without patient historical reconstruction in the light of serious theoretical work. Beard was too busy forging a realistic approach to history which would cut through appearances to realize the irony that his own approach involved a surrender to appearances, insofar as he maintained in *Economic Interpretation* and other early works a slavish adherence to the self-evident facts.[39]

If this approach foreclosed any serious attempt to construct a study of social relations at the level of production and reproduction, Beard nevertheless did hold out the promise in the 1920s of a comprehensive reinterpretation of American history focused on the rise of American capitalism. He blasted conventional historians, including Frederick Jackson Turner, for neglect of the "conflict between the capitalist and organized labor." In *The Rise of American Civilization*, the Beards at times come close to an analysis of class and power, but at strategic points their terminology and argument retreat to the formula of interest group politics. The suggestive notion of the second American revolution is variously discussed in terms of "a planter class," or of "men of property" in the south giving way to a "business peerage," which through victory liberated a "large and anomalous class," the ex-slave population. This rhetorical and imprecise use of the class apparatus is reproduced throughout the book. Thus the Beards depict the labor movement and the embattled farmers of the 1870s and 1880s as engaged in "a class enterprise of their own." These are economic interest groups, and nowhere do the Beards attempt to put these phenomena in the context of an explanation of the economic processes they supposedly represent. The "triumph" of the "capitalist class" is located instead in the comparative setting of an eternal spirit of trade and commerce stemming back to the days of Greece and Rome. In a formulation more reminiscent of Henri Pirenne than Marx, we find the rise of "business enterprise" treated as a product of spectacular natural resources interacting with the "spirit" of capitalism. Although the contest between "the capitalists" and "organized labor" remains an important theme, technology and abundance overwhelm incipient class divisions in an analysis as dependent as Turner's on the notion of American exceptionalism.[40]

If Beard stopped short of a class approach, other historians sympathetic to the themes of progressive history felt that he had gone too far. Progressive critics of Beard, however, did not raise the larger issues of class formation in these reservations; they focused instead on the facts of American history and their degree of correspondence with the Beards' description. Arthur Schlesinger, Sr., and Merle Curti conceded, like many of the scientific historians, that Beard had exaggerated the role of economics. At the same time, they preempted the class question by arguing on Beard's ground. Their criticisms implicitly agreed that class analysis consisted in the study of the activities of class representatives in the arena of politics, that class and economic interests were interchangeable, and that class forces could be discussed in terms of factors to be weighed against noneconomic considerations. In short, they did not escape from empiricist and positivist assumptions they shared with Beard and most other American historians.[41]

Nor were there examples in the American marxist literature of the 1930s to encourage the liberal historians of the 1930s to move beyond Beard. The marxists, more than anyone else, wrote in his shadow. That is not to say that marxism and Beardian history were the same thing in the 1930s. The liberals and the marxists attacked one another in the ideological battles of the 1930s, but the left's debt to Beardian categories was prodigious.

This dependence was illustrated in their fuzzy treatment of the economic processes of American capitalism. ''Marxist'' historians like Richard Enmale, Louis Hacker, Herbert Aptheker, and James Allen invoked the terms ''class'' and ''capitalism'' to explain developments such as the Civil War, the Revolution, and Reconstruction, but did nothing to study the structure of the economy in any depth. Like Beard they used economics to inform an overview of American development which focused on events. They did not challenge the essentially political conception of American history and its conventional periodizations, because they acknowledged, indeed embraced, the central importance of the liberal-democratic political struggle in America. Most of these authors were part of the Popular Front of the mid–1930s which inspired the rediscovery of American traditions among communists in the United States. Before that period there was little American history at all written from a marxist perspective. Though earlier works such as Anthony Bimba's *History of the American Working Class* (1927) and Leo Huberman's *We, the People* (1932) gave more space than later texts to the material context of traditional themes, they remained, like the Popular Front studies, superficial narratives designed for general consumption.[42]

Marxist historians of the 1930s thought they were offering a new conceptual dimension which did go beyond the progressive synthesis, but in the writings of Louis Hacker, probably the most sophisticated and certainly the most promising of the marxist historians of that generation, the debt to liberal historical thought is entirely evident. Hacker strenuously attacked Turner's conception of American uniqueness and chastised Carl Becker for a superficial liberal interpretation of the American Revolution, and thus demonstrated his attempt to take marxist scholarship beyond an endorsement of liberal historiography. It was in his criticisms of Becker in 1936 that Hacker came closest to breaking with conventional assumptions. Becker had isolated one class, the articulate middle-class revolutionaries, and sought ''to understand it alone.'' He saw revolution ''not as a force, but as an event,'' claimed Hacker. In contrast, Hacker depicted revolution in terms of relations between classes, and as a dynamic and historical process, rather than something contained in the superficial political and ideological struggle which immediately preceded the revolution. Hacker was particularly critical of what he saw as Becker's tendency to study revolutions from the documents. The focus on the literate minority that penned political arguments eliminated serious consideration of the activity of the inarticulate, and of the profound economic processes which presumably brought about revolutionary situations.[43]

Unfortunately, Hacker did not go so far as to break with the progressives' conception of unilinear economic causation. In both his general historiographical statements, and in his more specialized research work, Hacker remained indebted to this positivistic and empiricist conception. He chastised Becker most strongly because he "never does . . . indicate his willingness to see revolution . . . as a straight line that has its origins in a relatively remote past and continues beyond the actual period of crisis." This crude, unilinear conception of historical time also informs Hacker's more detailed research in the short-lived *Marxist Quarterly* of 1937. In "The American Revolution: Economic Aspects," Hacker offered a chronological account of the "objective economic factors" which he saw as contributing to the coming of the Revolution.[44] Despite Hacker's strictures against Becker's concentration on events rather than processes, Hacker himself presented an analysis (in class terms) of economic facts which were entirely on the surface of American political experience. He did not delve into the relations of classes, the process of class formation, and the connections of classes with the productive system. It may be that Hacker intended to deal with these in the second part of his projected study, "The American Revolution: Social Aspects," but the very fact that Hacker chose to divide his subject into misleading and artificial factors showed how subservient he remained to positivist assumptions that marxist and progressive historians shared. In any case, Hacker's second part did not appear. Instead, the next issue of the *Marxist Quarterly* contained a paper by him on "The American Civil War: Economic Aspects." Here he continued exactly the same analysis that characterized his piece on the Revolution, except that he made much clearer his intellectual debt to the progressive tradition, by explicitly endorsing Charles and Mary Beard's view of the Civil War as "the second American Revolution."[45]

Hacker's belief that the capitalist economic system was on the point of collapse in the 1930s, and that class revolution was imminent, underlay his preference for Beardian class analysis over Turner's emphasis on the influence of geography and regionalism. Hacker dismissed the role of the frontier as a temporary condition which facilitated the swift rise of American industrial capitalism; thereafter, the American experience ceased to be unique, and Turner's frontier thesis could be discounted. Turner had no "understanding of how closely American institutional growth paralleled the European." Truly the future lay not with sections but with classes.[46] Hacker's attempt to find revolutionary class parallels with European experience, explicit in his critiques of both Turner and Becker, would in a few years seem profoundly embarrassing even to Hacker. The United States weathered the Depression and war without revolutionary upheaval, and thus gave renewed emphasis in the post–World War II period to a Turnerian vision of the American past and future. In the process, many American historians, including Hacker, would come to dispense with marxism as a historical analysis.

Among 1930s marxists, Hacker was not the only one who failed to transcend analysis of superficial events of economic and political history, and subservience to simple one-to-one relationships between those events. The failure is also seen in the other historical contributions to *Marxist Quarterly*, which in terms of their theoretical adequacy make Hacker's work seem remarkably good. Philip A.

Slaner's "The Railroad Strikes of 1877" and Harry Frumerman's "The Railroad Strikes of 1885–86" are simply detailed factual accounts presented in a purely narrative form. The traditional division in which philosophy took care of the theory while the historian took care of the facts was dutifully adhered to by the editors.[47]

Of course *Marxist Quarterly* was a renegade publication which survived only three issues because of doctrinal divisions within its editorial councils, yet the same subservience to the conceptual assumptions of the liberal interpretation pervaded other marxist works of the period, even when particular marxist historians claimed to be doing something more. The reviews of liberal historiography in the pages of *New Masses* tried frequently to establish the limitations of such historians as Beard, Becker, Turner, Arthur C. Cole, W. E. Dodd, and W. E. Woodward.[48] But the marxist's supposed distinctiveness represented only an accretion to the liberal theme which added new groups to the progressive story of the struggle for liberal-democratic freedoms. Marxists criticized Beard and others for neglecting the constructive, purposeful role of workers and blacks in the upheavals of revolution and civil war. If it was refreshing to find these groups considered as agents of historical change, their cardboard depiction as militant sources of class mobilization left much to be desired. The racial and ethnic sources of class radicalism and consciousness found treatment only in the work of the black historian W.E.B. Du Bois, but liberals did not pay much attention to his contribution until the 1950s, while marxists were only interested in using his evidence to bolster their superficial incorporation of the role of blacks in the progressive coalition.[49]

The failure of American marxist historians of the 1930s to get beyond Beard was rooted in their political and tactical situation. Most marxist histories written during this period were never intended to be academic studies, and they were written by political journalists, trade union activists, and untenured faculty rather than established scholars. An example was James S. Allen, who wrote the study of Reconstruction in the series Enmale edited. Allen had been an instructor in history at the University of Pennsylvania in the 1920s, but later went into Comintern service, and also edited for a time the first Communist Party newspaper in the south. His book, *Reconstruction: The Battle for Democracy*, was designed to fill a gap in a historical series with Popular Front inspiration. There simply was not the time, given Allen's activist commitments, for him to do the independent historical research to advance a convincing, scholarly, and marxist interpretation, as opposed to a publicist work.[50]

In the absence of sustained historical work of their own, the marxist historians of the 1930s relied for most of their empirical detail, and a good deal of their conceptual apparatus, on the Beardian version of the progressive approach. This reliance was also underpinned by further considerations. One was the search for allies in the Popular Front period of the mid–1930s, which led marxists to champion the same movements for democracy and individual rights that progressive historians had endorsed in their writings. Another was the fact that marxists were a small minority of American historians, and simply had to rely for many aspects of interpretation on the work of those ideologically closest to them. The sheer volume and prestige of progressive scholarship, as well as their use of loose class terminology in many instances, made them obvious candidates for intellectual appropriation.

Thus it is not surprising to find Louis Hacker planning to edit a festschrift for Beard shortly before the outbreak of war; nor to find Richard Enmale in his introduction to Allen's *Reconstruction* praising (with qualifications) the work of Beard and his disciple Howard Beale; nor to find Herbert Morais in 1943 in his *The Struggle for American Freedom* following Beard's view of the constitution. Similarly, Leo Huberman's interesting and useful attempt at popularizing marxist history in *We, the People* relied heavily on Turner, A. M. Schlesinger, Sr., and Charles and Mary Beard. Arthur C. Cole, a liberal, aptly summed up the full measure of this marxist dependence in a review of Allen's book:

After one gets over the strain of identifying well-known forces under the terminology of the modern Marxian, one begins to wonder just what has been contributed that the scorned "liberal" has not included in his picture. The battle for democracy for the Negro is slightly illuminated. . . . But the shifting of classes and of sectional groupings during this dynamic period is largely presented from the fruits of historical scholarship that lack the approved terminology. If there are those who will take their historical medicine only in the form of red-coated pills, one should perhaps encourage those who provide the prescription.[51]

The conceptual poverty and partisan purpose of most American marxist writing of the 1930s encouraged historians of liberal persuasion to ignore the marxist legacy. Like their colleagues in England, they remained largely oblivious of a more diverse and intellectually rich tradition that included Gramsci and Lukács. Language barriers and fascist repression in Germany and Italy were formidable barriers to an assimilation of these ideas anywhere. In the American case, however, the arrival of (mostly Jewish) European intellectuals after Hitler's rise to power might have been expected to dent the ignorance of these new developments. It did not. This remains true even though the critical theorists of the Frankfurt School were so well received in the United States that they were actually able to establish their major base at Columbia University for more than fifteen years after 1933. There they were able to develop important work on mass culture, aesthetic theory, the integration of psychoanalysis with marxism, and other theoretical and empirical concerns. But as Martin Jay's admirable study of this interesting intellectual episode shows, the Frankfurt School had little impact on the American academy as a whole. The publications of the group continued to appear mostly in German, and its members remained for the most part aloof from ordinary academic life. More important, the hostility of critical theorists to positivism did not square well with the dominant intellectual orientation in American social science. The impact of "the European intellectual migration'' was thus selective. ''The ethic of sober objectivity and technological progress'' to be found, for example, in Paul Lazarsfeld's ''brand of quantitative research'' struck ''a respondent chord in American intellectual life.'' In contrast, other, more speculative and theoretically oriented thinkers like Marcuse were not assimilated until the 1960s.[52]

The weakness of the marxist tradition measured in part the appeal of the liberal alternative, but the absence of a sophisticated marxist project threatened in the long run to vitiate the explanatory power of the liberal synthesis itself. Beard had extracted from the challenge of marxism a positivistic program of economic interpretation that did not do justice to the range and complexity of marxist theory. His search for empirical data on the impact of economic forces produced an overly simple view of the political process open to relatively easy refutation. If it could be shown that such issues as the tariff, monetary policy and other economic questions did not ''explain'' the course of national political history, then a good deal of the Beardian synthesis would be thrown into doubt. The tendency of Beard and his followers to subsume a wide variety of issues under the banner of a clash between the people and the special interests, or between polarized groups and classes, could be similarly damaged by detailed research into the complexities of social and economic life. In these ways, the Beardian approach could be overthrown as an imposition of ''interpretation'' on ''the facts.'' In the process, Beard's recognition that political and economic power were interrelated parts of a larger social process could be forgotten. Despite the immense importance of capitalism as an economic system in the United States, and despite evidence of considerable class conflict in the era of industrial growth, the United States did not develop a historical tradition which made the assessment of these phenomena an important part of its intellectual project. The work of Beard and the way in which that work was absorbed into American historiography cannot be ignored in any explanation of that absence.

The failure of the progressives to locate their empirical work in a comprehensive theory of social change also profoundly structured, and limited, their contributions to both social and economic history. Despite their pioneering work in social history, the gulf between social and political history widened as a consequence of the way some progressive social histories were conceived and written. Social history was not treated as the history of society with emphasis upon the changing social structure, but as a descriptive set of institutions and values that contributed to the emerging story of national progress. As in Britain, historians tended to equate social history with nonpolitical subjects, and not until the 1960s did the subdiscipline begin to acquire a method and a prestige to match political historiography. Even the best products of interwar progressive scholarship, such as Merle Curti's socioeconomic interpretation *The Growth of American Thought*, did not entirely escape the accusation that they presented a descriptive catalogue of facts organized around the evolution of democracy. Many of the other social histories of the period were by no means so distinguished. Most volumes in the *History of American Life* series, which incorporated the mono-graphic fruits of the progressive project in social history, produced much inter-esting evidence, but the series as a whole was, Marcus Cunliffe has remarked, "descriptively miscellaneous." The organization of the synthesis in terms of the nation-state and artificially constructed periods obscured relationships between the data and reinforced the impression of eclecticism.[53]

The case of economic history was different. Paradoxical though it may seem, Beard's emphasis on economic interpretation did not stimulate an economic history. This territory remained largely unexamined by the progressives, except in their studies of the relation of politics and business interests. Because pro-gressive historians were chiefly interested in using economic factors to explain political or social history, they left the actual analysis of economic processes to specialist economic historians. From the beginnings of academic history, even before the New History emerged, this specialty was linked with the discipline of economics. As early as 1892, the disciplinary rupture had been created in America with the establishment of the first chair in economic history within the Department of Economics at Harvard. At that time, the division of labor did not matter, since institutional economics had a major interest in historical studies. From the pens of economists like John R. Commons, Frank W. Taussig, Percy Bidwell, and E. R. Johnson came pioneering historical works that culminated in the edifice of the "Contributions to American Economic History" produced between 1904 and 1932 under the auspices of the Department of Economics and Sociology of the Carnegie Institution.

The abdication of the territory of economic history to the specialists seemed appropriate before World War I, when these studies were either planned or appearing, but by the 1920s the division of labor proved to be tactically disad-vantageous to a study of economic and social processes. The economics profes-sion had become steadily more specialized and less historical in orientation, the Carnegie series began to peter out, and what replaced it was of little use to the kind of historical synthesis Beard advocated.[54]

During the interwar period, the developments which did occur in American economic history led away from the totalistic project of a history of society. The influence of Edwin F. Gay and N.S.B. Gras narrowed the focus considerably. "Putting little emphasis upon method," they "stressed the search for facts" which would lead on to "broader conclusions." This positivist commitment to "facts and factors" produced a marked preference for "quantitative data," and, especially in the work of Gras, Gay's most productive student, a penchant for the study of particular industries and individual businesses rather than their connections with larger political, economic, and social processes. Gras even went so far as to declare business history independent of economic history, much to Gay's displeasure. Thus did economic history itself fragment during the inter-war years. In the estimation of Steven Sass, economic history was in 1940 not only fragmented but also "detached from other disciplines because of its values and institutions. In its quest for the inner coherence of particular historical phenomena, it had resisted deductive analysis and had simultaneously lost touch with larger historical contexts.''[55]

The study of political power and class processes languished, and even the investigation of economic interest politics received little attention. The best work by Americans on economic history in this period concerned, by their own admission, European economic history. Not until the late 1930s were there signs of a revival in American economic history. Scholars such as Curtis P. Nettels and George Rogers Taylor had begun the work which ultimately produced several excellent volumes in the Holt, Rinehart, and Winston series on ''The Economic History of the United States.'' Then, from within the subdisciplines of economic and business history, the New Deal experience aroused an interest in the relations of government and business. Particularly through the efforts of Arthur H. Cole and the Committee on Research in Economic History that emerged from these concerns came important initiatives to bring economics and history into fruitful cooperation. But the results of this new research were not published until after World War II, and came too late to inform the progressive syntheses of either Turner or Beard.[56]

A neglect of economic history stymied the progressive project; the relativist controversy of the 1930s unraveled its theoretical assumptions. If one believed, as most progressives apparently did, that history flowed from objective historical facts, *and* in the importance of putting history to work in the interests of reform, then something was bound to give. Carl Becker had already foreshadowed as much in 1910 when he recorded his doubts about the objectivity of historical knowledge, and there were other indications of relativism in the early writings of Beard, James Harvey Robinson, and Turner. The implicit relativism of the pre–World War I period was bound to accelerate, given the momentous impact on the philosophy of science of Einstein's theory of relativity. By the 1920s, the New Physics that emerged on the basis of Einstein's insights had begun to penetrate general academic discourse, including that of the historians. Combined with the dissemination of European idealist philosophies of history, especially the work of Croce, the social thought provoked by the New Physics provided a philosophical basis for the development of the relativist tendencies already present in the New History.[57]

But the way that the new relativist currents were presented by their leading exponents in the 1930s had a lasting impact upon the reception of relativism. Largely because they failed to shed their empiricist and positivistic assumptions entirely, Beard and Becker, the principal exponents, presented muddled philosophies of history that did nothing to free American historical interpretation from its conceptual legacy. The two famous addresses which heralded the crisis of progressive historiography were Becker's 1931 presidential address before the American Historical Association, ''Everyman His Own Historian,'' and Beard's before the same association in 1933, entitled ''Written History as an Act of

Faith.'' Though both addresses conveyed profound doubts about the objectivity of historical knowledge, there were important differences between them.[58]

Becker went further than Beard, asserting a number of times that not only the interpretation but also the facts are given their significance by the historian. ''Left to themselves, the facts do not speak; left to themselves they do not exist, not really, since for all practical purposes there is no fact until someone affirms it.'' Yet Becker was always a little confusing, if not confused, on this point. In private correspondence to his fellow progressive William E. Dodd, Becker sought to explain his famous address by noting that ''the facts may be determined with accuracy; but the 'interpretation' will always be shaped by the prejudices, biasses [sic] needs, of the individual and these in turn will depend on the age in which he lives.'' His aim in writing the address had been to see that ''Mr. Everyman's history'' would be ''so far as possible, in reasonable harmony with what actually happened.''[59] This was very close to Beard's suggestion that historians ought to become aware of their inevitable biases so that they could control them. When they did, they would be less likely to confuse fact and interpretation. If this was Becker's own perception of what he was trying to do in ''Everyman,'' in his public and private utterances he was quite incapable of a consistent exposition of this philosophical position. In a letter written in 1940 to a graduate student, Carl Horwich, Becker sought to distinguish between an event and a fact. The former could be determined with accuracy, but the latter he now took to be fundamentally a conception of the historian who believed it to be true. In this sense the historian did create the facts. The fact was ''merely a symbol which expresses our conviction that something is true.''[60]

Beard's thought also took a confusing turn as he grappled with philosophical implications of the New History. His assertion that historical interpretation was ''an act of faith'' conveyed an extreme relativism which he was soon forced to deny. In ''That Noble Dream,'' he reasserted the importance of scientific method and respect for ''the facts'' which he continued to depict as a given. But how was objective fact to be reconciled with subjective interpretation? Here Beard invoked the frame of reference idea from the sociology of knowledge. Far from conceding an unbridled relativism suggested by the act of faith, Beard's later writings on this subject indicated possible limits to relativism. The frames of reference which historians necessarily used were not infinite in number, and these could be analyzed and tested empirically to put limits on subjectivity.[61]

Had it been possible to detach this intriguing suggestion from the relativist controversy, the study of the sociology of knowledge might well have proven Beard's most fruitful contribution to historiography. Regrettably, this was not to be. Beard's use of the concept merely perpetuated the ambiguities in his theory of knowledge. The frame of reference lessened but did not bridge the gap between fact and interpretation which Beard had conceded. Under his formulation, frames of reference would still have to be assessed against the facts, but how this was to be done remained obscure. Beard could only suggest that the value of the historian's act of faith would become clearer as history unfolded. "The length and correctness" of the historian's "forecasts" would be the measure of the scholar's "influence and immortality," as time provided "the verdict." This suggestion that history could act as judge and juror upon historical interpretation did not explain how or why new historical perspectives would overcome the epistemological problem of the frame of reference. The notion only made sense if one went back to the scientific view of history as a unilinear and given datum to be discovered by the historian.[62]

Beard's own use of the frame of reference was both consistent with this reading and indicative of the concept's explanatory limitations. For Beard, the frames of reference were in essence three: chaos, cyclical patterns, and progress. Since these were far too generalized to provide much help to historians grappling with the New History's proliferation of historical specializations, the act of faith remained just that. Beard made clear from the context that he still favored, despite reservations, movement towards a collectivist democracy in seeking the meaning of history, and to this extent he remained true to the progressive spirit, more so than Becker.[63]

In his own presidential address, Becker made no attempt to bestow meaning on history as a whole. However, instead of using this liberation from the idea of history as a linear progression (and the epistemology of empiricist history) to search for new conceptual foundations of historical truth to replace the pillars of progressive faith, Becker merely proclaimed all interpretations equally valid, provided they squared with the known facts. Yet since he was himself uncertain about the status of historical facts, his position ended in a confusion which excelled that of Beard's. If for Beard the crisis of liberal history produced an act of faith, for Becker in the 1930s it ended in an eclectic and enigmatic relativism that encouraged a mood of despair among historians at the possibility of knowing anything of value about the past at all.

The relativistic temper of Beard and Becker in the 1930s generated considerable controversy within the profession. The direction of the discipline came under attack during the following ten or fifteen years, and unprecedented attention was given at meetings of the leading historical associations and in the scholarly journals to a reassessment of the status of historical knowledge.[64] This discussion was unenlightening because the debate was cast in very misleading terms dictated by the limited range of theoretical positions present in the profession. Essentially the debate raged between the old positivist conception of the objectivity of historical knowledge and the Beardian position of the 1930s which posited a radical distinction between objective facts and changing, subjective interpretations. Beard was unable to provide any rational, objective, and consistent criteria for distinguishing between facts and interpretations, nor for specifying the relations between them. To this extent his position rested on foundations of sand. On the other hand, the positivist argument was both smugly complacent and immensely simplistic in its assumption of a direct and commonsense relation between historical reality and the thought of the historical observer. In this sense

Beard was undoubtedly right in assuming that, after Croce, all history had to be reconstructed through intellectual activity.

Faced with a choice between these two positions, most American historians would follow the *Harvard Guide*, and treat history as a dialogue between "inescapable" interpretation and the "perpetual countercheck of facts" gleaned from the "ideal" of objectivity.[65] The long-term significance of this historiographical compromise that emerged from the controversies of the 1930s would be to shelve consideration of the role of theory in the construction of American historiography, and to sanction the continued preference for an ad hoc approach to the use of historical concepts. In the short run, the considerable confusion over the status of historical knowledge served to reveal the ambiguities which had always been present in progressive historiography. The attempted synthesis of social relevance and objectivity that constituted the New History had been discredited, but the leading spokesmen for progressive historiography in the 1930s could not supply the methodological synthesis which would transcend the drift and confusion they had helped create. The theoretical impasse served the useful function of opening the way in the 1940s and particularly the 1950s for the liberation of younger historians from the *interpretations* though not from the philosophical assumptions of progressive scholarship. With the spokesmen for the older generation uncertain what they believed about history, younger scholars could more easily question the empirical conclusions their mentors had advanced. From these circumstances came the postwar reorientation in historiography.

NOTES

1. See, for example, Thomas Bender, "The New History—Then and Now," *Review in American History* 12 (1984): 612–22; John Patrick Diggins, "History Through a Wasp: Charles A. Beard and the 1960s Generation," ibid., 12 (1984): 336–41.

2. The best available overview is John Higham with Leonard Krieger and Felix Gilbert, *History: The Development of Historical Studies in the United States* (Englewood Cliffs, N.J., 1965). Very influential in shaping current views of the progressive generation and their predecessors is Richard Hofstadter, *The Progressive Historians: Turner, Beard, Parrington* (New York, 1968). In Gene Wise, *American Historical Explanations: A Strategy for Grounded Inquiry* (Minneapolis, rev. ed., 1980), the conventional wisdom is rigidified into a set of paradigms; Charles Crowe, "The Emergence of Progressive History," *Journal of the History of Ideas* 27 (1966): 109–24, lies between these extremes.

3. David D. Van Tassel, "From Learned Society to Professional Organization: The American Historical Association, 1884–1900," *American Historical Review* 89 (1984): 929–56. Still useful is W. Stull Holt, "The Idea of Scientific History in America," in Holt, *Historical Scholarship in the United States and Other Essays* (Seattle, 1967), pp. 15–28.

4. Quoted in Higham, *History*, p. 25; see also George B. Adams, "History and the Philosophy of History," *American Historical Review* 14 (1909): 236.

5. Gareth Stedman Jones, "From Historical Sociology to Theoretical History," *British Journal of Sociology* 27 (1976): 297.

6. Higham, *History*, p. 101; see also Georg G. Iggers, "The Image of Ranke in American and German Historical Thought," *History and Theory* 2 (1962): 18–22.

7. Jameson, *The American Revolution Considered as a Social Movement* (Princeton, N.J., 1926); J. Franklin Jameson, *The History of Historical Writing in America* (New York, 1961 ed.), p. 144; Raymond J. Cunningham, "The German Historical World of Herbert Baxter Adams, 1874–1876," *Journal of American History* 68 (1981): 261–75; Cunningham, "Is History Past Politics? Herbert Baxter Adams as Precursor of the 'New History,' " *History Teacher* 9 (1976): 244–57; A. B. Hart, "Imagination in History," *American Historical Review* 15 (1910): 246–51; Charles Beard, quoting Herbert Osgood, in Beard, "That Noble Dream," *American Historical Review* 41 (1935): 81; see also N. Ray Hiner, "Professions in Process: Changing Relations Between Historians and Educators, 1896–1911," *History of Education Quarterly* 12 (1972): 34–56.

8. Michael Kraus, *The Writing of American History* (Norman, Okla., 1953), pp. 230, 232; Iggers, "Image of Ranke," pp. 23, 25–26.

9. The best sources for these comparisons are Ellen Nore, *Charles A. Beard: An Intellectual Biography* (Carbondale and Edwardsville, Ill., 1983); Ray Allen Billington, *Frederick Jackson Turner: Historian, Scholar, Teacher* (New York, 1973); Charles Beard, "The Frontier in American History," *New Republic* 25 (1921): 350.

10. There are other ways to state the magnitude of Beard's production, but all authorities agree it was immense. See, for example, Howard K. Beale, ed., *Charles A. Beard: An Appraisal* . . . (Lexington, Ky., 1954), pp. 265–84; Forrest McDonald, "Charles A. Beard," in Marcus Cunliffe and Robin Winks, eds., *Pastmasters: Some Essays on American Historians* (New York, 1969), pp. 110, 434; Maurice Blinkhoff, "The Influence of Charles A. Beard Upon American Historiography," *University of Buffalo Studies* 12 (May 1936): 36, 38.

11. Billington, *Turner*, pp. 472–97; John W. Caughey, "Historians' Choice: Results of a Poll on Recently Published American History and Biography," *Mississippi Valley Historical Review* 39 (1952): 289–302; Burleigh T. Wilkins, *Carl Becker: A Biographical Study in American Intellectual History* (Cambridge, Mass., 1961); James Harvey Robinson, *The New History: Essays Illustrating the Modern Historical Outlook* (New York, 1912). I have not discussed Ulrich B. Phillips, whose claim as an innovator and pioneer as a social historian is as great as the claims of these progressives. In fact, a case can be made out for situating Phillips in the general progressive impulse in historical method. See Daniel J. Singal, "Ulrich B. Phillips: The Old South as New," *Journal of American History* 63 (1977): 872–76.

12. Edward Eggleston, "The New History," American Historical Association, *Annual Report for the Year 1900*, 1:35–47; Eggleston, *The Transit of Civilization from England to America in the Seventeenth Century* (New York, 1901).

13. Higham, *History*, pp. 111–15; Crowe, "Emergence of Progressive History," pp. 109–24; Hofstadter, *Progressive Historians*, pp. 211–12.

14. Charles Beard, *An Economic Interpretation of the Constitution of the United States* (New York, new ed., 1935, orig. ed., 1913); Hofstadter, *Progressive Historians*, p. 211.

15. Charles Beard, *Economic Origins of Jeffersonian Democracy* (New York, 1915); Beard, *The Economic Basis of Politics* (New York, 1922); Charles and Mary Beard, *The Rise of American Civilization*, 2 vols. (New York, 1927); Arthur M. Schlesinger, Sr., *The Colonial Merchants and the American Revolution* (New York, 1918); Dixon Ryan Fox, *The Decline of Aristocracy in the Politics of New York* (New York, 1919); Howard

K. Beale, *The Critical Year* (New York, 1930); on Josephson, see David Shi, *Matthew Josephson: Bourgeois Bohemian* (New Haven, 1981).

16. Lois K. Mathews et al., *Essays in American History Dedicated to Frederick Jackson Turner* (New York, 1910); Frederick Jackson Turner, "Social Forces in American History," *American Historical Review* 16 (1911): 217–33; Dixon Ryan Fox and Arthur M. Schlesinger, Sr., eds., *A History of American Life*, 13 vols. (New York, 1928–1943); Beard and Beard, *Rise of American Civilization* 1: 755–61 passim; Arthur M. Schlesinger, Sr., *New Viewpoints in American History* (New York, 1922); Mary Beard, *Woman as Force in History* (New York, 1946).

17. In the absence of sustained critical appraisal, see Nore, *Beard*, pp. 112–26; David W. Marcell, "Charles Beard: Civilization and the Revolt against Empiricism," *American Quarterly* 21 (1969): 65–86.

18. Robinson wrote:

We have learned to recognize that truth is not merely relative, as was clearly enough perceived by an important school of Greek thought, but that this relativity is conditioned by our constant increase in knowledge. . . . Our more carefully considered opinions are based ultimately upon observed facts about man and his environment. With our ever increasing knowledge in regard to these facts, our opinions must necessarily change. To what may be called the innate relativity of things . . . we have added a dynamic relativity which is the result of rapidly advancing scientific knowledge, which necessarily renders all our conclusions provisional.

The New History, p. 130; cf. Higham, *History*, p. 115.

19. Carl Becker, "Detachment and the Writing of History," in Phil L. Snyder, ed., *Detachment and the Writing of History: Essays and Letters of Carl L. Becker* (Ithaca, N.Y., 1958), pp. 3–40; Turner, "Social Forces," pp. 225–26; Ellen Nore, "Charles A. Beard's Act of Faith: Context and Content," *Journal of American History* 66 (1980): 851–65.

20. Gareth Stedman Jones, "History: The Poverty of Empiricism," in Robin Blackburn, ed., *Ideology in Social Science: Readings in Critical Social Theory* (Glasgow, 1972), p. 97; Robinson, *The New History*, p. 130.

21. Denis Numa Fustel de Coulanges was a nineteenth-century French historian with a "zeal for the study of sources." He is reputed to have said: "It is not I who speak, but history which speaks through me." Quoted in Holt, *Historical Scholarship*, p. 23; Harry Elmer Barnes, *A History of Historical Writing* (Norman, Okla., 1938), p. 169. Beard is said to have read Fustel avidly, along with other exponents of the scientific conception of history. Nore, *Beard*, p. 171.

22. Quoted in Marcell, "Charles Beard," pp. 68, 72.

23. Wilkins, *Becker*, pp. 194–96; cf. Nore, *Beard*, p. 156.

24. Georg G. Iggers, *New Directions in European Historiography* (Middletown, Conn.: 1975), p. 27. On Germany and Italy, see the relevant chapters in Georg G. Iggers and Harold T. Parker, eds., *International Handbook of Historical Studies: Contemporary Research and Theory* (Westport, Conn., 1979); H. Stuart Hughes, *Consciousness and Society: The Reorientation of European Social Thought, 1890–1930* (London, Harvester Press ed., 1979).

25. Beard, *Economic Interpretation of the Constitution*, p. 266.

26. Marc Bloch, *The Royal Touch: Sacred Monarchy and Scrofula in England and France*, trans. J. E. Anderson (London, 1973, orig. ed., 1924).

27. Cf. Richard M. Andrews, "Some Implications of the *Annales* School and Its

Methods for a Revision of Historical Writing about the United States," *Review* 1 (1978): 165–80.

28. Billington, *Turner*, p. 481.

29. Frederick Jackson Turner, *The Rise of the West, 1818–1829* (New York, 1906); Turner, *The United States, 1830–1850* (New York, 1935); Turner, *The Frontier in American History* (New York, 1920); and Turner, *The Significance of Sections in American History* (New York, 1932).

30. Turner, *Sections*, p. 339.

31. Jones, "Empiricism," p. 100.

32. Iggers, *New Directions*, pp. 49–50.

33. Marc Bloch, *The Historian's Craft*, trans. Peter Putnam (New York, 1953), pp. 58–59, 63, 183, 194–95; Thomas Cochran, "The 'Presidential Synthesis' in American History," *American Historical Review* 53 (1948): 748–59.

34. Bloch, *Historian's Craft*, pp. 64, 66; Bloch, *The Île-de-France: The Country around Paris*, trans. J. E. Anderson (Ithaca, N.Y., 1971, orig. ed., 1913); see also Peter Burke, "Introduction: The Development of Lucien Febvre," in Burke, ed., *A New Kind of History: From the Writings of Febvre* (London, 1973), pp. ix–xii. Robinson's *New History* came closer to Bloch's usage, but whereas Robinson advocated the broadening of the evidence by borrowing insights from other disciplines, Bloch conducted his own integrated and anthropological interrogation of sources. Robinson, *New History*, p. 92.

35. Beard, *Economic Interpretation of the Constitution*, pp. 275, 280, 324.

36. The limitations of *Annales* will be discussed in Chapter 7. The reproduction of empiricism in English historiography is discussed unwittingly in John P. Kenyon, *History Men* (London, 1982); and effectively in Jones, "Empiricism." Jones carefully notes the exception of R. H. Tawney and his associates in the English *Economic History Review* from the late 1920s to the late 1940s. Pp. 105–7.

37. Jones, "Empiricism," p. 98.

38. Carl Becker, *The History of Political Parties in the Province of New York, 1760–1776* (Madison, Wisc., 1959, orig. ed., 1909).

39. Beard, *Economic Interpretation of the Constitution*, pp. vi, xii, xiii; Hofstadter, *Progressive Historians*, pp. 208, 209, 236.

40. Beard, "Frontier in American History," p. 350; Beard and Beard, *Rise of American Civilization*, pp. 99, 104, 105, 116, 166, 172, 174, 252.

41. Arthur M. Schlesinger, Sr., *In Retrospect: The History of a Historian* (New York, 1963), p. 197; Merle Curti to Frederick Jackson Turner, 13 Aug. 1928, TU Box 39, Frederick Jackson Turner Papers, Huntington Library, San Marino, Calif.

42. "Enmale" was a pseudonym for Herbert Morais, derived from the first two letters of the names Engels, Marx, and Lenin. *New York Times*, 8 Nov. 1941, p. 12; Leo Huberman, *We, the People* (New York, 1932); Anthony Bimba, *The History of the American Working Class* (New York, 1927).

43. Carl Becker, *Everyman His Own Historian: Essays in History and Politics* (New York, 1935); Louis M. Hacker, "Historian of Revolutions," *New Republic* 85 (1936): 260–61.

44. Hacker, "Historian of Revolutions," pp. 260–61; Hacker, "The American Revolution: Economic Aspects," *Marxist Quarterly* 1 (no. 1, 1937): 46–67.

45. Louis Hacker, "The American Civil War: Economic Aspects," *Marxist Quarterly* 1 (no. 2, 1937): 213.

46. Louis Hacker, "Sections—or Classes," *The Nation* 137 (1933): 108–110.

47. Philip A. Slaner, "The Railroad Strikes of 1877," *Marxist Quarterly* 1 (no. 2, 1937): 214–36; Harry Frumerman, "The Railroad Strikes of 1885–86," ibid. (no. 3, 1937): 394–405.

48. See, for example, the review of Arthur C. Cole, *The Irrepressible Conflict, 1850–1865* (New York, 1934), in *New Masses*, 21 Aug. 1934, p. 25; and *New Masses*, 14 July 1936, p. 26 (for Becker), 28 July 1936, p. 26 (for Beard), and 12 Jan. 1937, p. 24 (for W. E. Woodward).

49. Richard Enmale, "Foreword," to Jack Hardy, *The First American Revolution* (New York, 1935), p. 13; Hardy, *First American Revolution*; Enmale, "Interpretations of the American Civil War," *Science and Society* 1 (1937): 127–36; W.E.B. DuBois, *Black Reconstruction in America, 1860–1880* (Cleveland, Ohio, 1969 ed., orig. pub., 1935).

50. Joseph R. Starobin, *American Communism in Crisis, 1943–1957* (Cambridge, Mass., 1972), p. 283; *New York Times*, 8 Nov. 1941, p. 12; James S. Allen, *Reconstruction: The Battle for Democracy (1865–1876)* (New York, 1937).

51. Herbert M. Morais, *The Struggle for American Freedom: The First Two Hundred Years* (New York, 1943), p. 249; Beale, *Beard*, p. vi; Huberman, *We, the People*, p. vii; Allen, *Reconstruction*, pp. 10–11; Arthur C. Cole, rev. of Allen in *American Historical Review* 44 (1938): 163; see also Paul Buhle, "Marxism in the United States, 1900–1940," Ph.D. diss., University of Wisconsin, 1975, pp. 289–300.

52. Martin Jay, *The Dialectical Imagination: A History of the Frankfurt School and the Institute for Social Research, 1923–1950* (London, 1973), p. 297; Bernard Bailyn and Donald Fleming, eds., *The Intellectual Migration: Europe and America, 1930–1960* (Cambridge, Mass., 1969); Martin Jay, rev. of Bailyn and Fleming in *Commentary* 49 (1970): 78–85.

53. Marcus Cunliffe, "Arthur M. Schlesinger, Sr.," in Cunliffe and Winks, eds., *Pastmasters*, p. 353; Merle Curti, *The Growth of American Thought* (New York, 1943). Though published in 1943, the latter work was underway in the late 1930s.

54. The Carnegie project and other early works in economic history are listed and discussed in N.S.B. Gras, "The Rise and Development of Economic History," *Economic History Review* 1 (1927): 25–29; and Herbert Heaton, "Recent Developments in Economic History," *American Historical Review* 47 (1942): 27–29. See esp., John R. Commons et al., *History of Labor in the United States*, 2 vols. (Washington, D.C., 1918); Emory R. Johnson et al., *History of Domestic and Foreign Commerce of the United States* (Washington, D.C., 1915); Percy W. Bidwell and John I. Falconer, *History of Agriculture in the Northern United States, 1620–1860* (Washington, D.C., 1925); Lewis C. Gray, *History of Agriculture in the Southern United States to 1860*, 2 vols. (Washington, D.C., 1932); Frank W. Taussig, *The Tariff History of the United States* (New York, 8th ed., 1931).

55. Gras, "Rise and Development of Economic History," p. 26; Arthur H. Cole, A. L. Dunham, N.S.B. Gras, comps., *Facts and Factors in Economic History: Articles by Former Students of Edwin Francis Gay* (New York, 1967 repr., orig. pub., 1932), p. 5; Steven A. Sass, "Entrepreneurial Historians and History: An Essay in Organized Intellect," Ph.D. diss., Johns Hopkins University, 1977, p. 51.

56. Oscar and Mary F. Handlin, *Commonwealth: A Study of the Role of Government in the American Economy: Massachusetts, 1774–1861* (Cambridge, Mass., rev. ed., 1969), pp. viii–x, for the operations and fruits of the Committee on Research in Economic History; Carter Goodrich, *Government Promotion of American Canals and Railroads,*

1800–1860 (New York, 1960); Curtis P. Nettels, *The Money Supply of the American Colonies before 1720* (New York, 1934); of the Holt, Rinehart, and Winston series, George R. Taylor, *The Transportation Revolution, 1815–1860* (New York, 1951), stands out for its durability.

57. Cushing Strout, *The Pragmatic Revolt in American History: Carl Becker and Charles Beard* (New Haven, 1958), p. 33; Turner, "Social Forces," pp. 226, 231; Nore, "Charles A. Beard's Act of Faith," pp. 851–65.

58. Carl Becker, "Everyman His Own Historian," *American Historical Review* 37 (1932): 221–36; Charles Beard, "Written History as an Act of Faith," ibid., 39 (1934): 21–24.

59. Becker, "Everyman," pp. 232–33; Michael Kammen, ed., *"What Is the Good of History?" Selected Letters of Carl L. Becker, 1900–1945* (Ithaca, N.Y., 1973), pp. 156–57.

60. Kammen, ed., *Letters of Carl Becker*, p. 272.

61. Beard, "That Noble Dream," pp. 74–87; Beard, "Written History," pp. 226–29; Beard and Vagts, "Currents of Thought in Historiography," *American Historical Review* 42 (1937): 481.

62. Beard, "Written History," p. 226. His position was similar to that offered later by E. H. Carr, *What Is History?* (Harmondsworth, Middx., 1962). For a critique, see Jones, "Empiricism," p. 114.

63. Beard, "Written History," pp. 226–29.

64. See esp., Social Science Research Council, Bulletin 54, *Theory and Practice in Historical Study: A Report of the Committee on Historiography* (New York, 1946); Higham, *History*, pp. 128–31.

65. The "compromise" is best expressed in Oscar Handlin et al., *Harvard Guide to American History* (Cambridge, Mass., rev. ed., 1954), p. 20.

2

Reproducing Knowledge: Historical Practice and Progressive History

Historiographers are usually content to chart changes in the patterns of historical interpretation, or to measure those differing accounts against the reality of past events. Explaining these patterns has lagged far behind. Presumably the fear of determinism lies behind the failure to treat the sociological and political context of historical thought. Or perhaps the very complexity of studying one's own profession from the inside renders the exercise off-limits. Whatever the reason, historians have produced excellent works on the institutional, social, and intellectual roots of other disciplines, but they have seldom done the same for history. No legitimate reason beyond convention can be given for this neglect. Certainly, we cannot provide definite causal links between particular historical interpretations and the social backgrounds, experiences, and institutional connections of historians. What can be done is to consider the social and intellectual context that impinged upon the thought and practice of historians, and both promoted and resisted changes in historiographical assumptions. Not what was discovered when the evidence was assessed, but the kinds of historical inquiry and the criteria of explanation adopted were intimately connected to everyday historical practice.[1]

The present inquiry may be illuminated in several ways by a sociological focus. Investigating the conditions of historical production may explain the failure of the progressives to reconstruct historical practice as extensively as the historians of *Annales* did in France, and yet at the same time show why the American innovation went further than its British equivalent in the period from the turn of the century to 1945. The institutional and intellectual impediments to historiographical change also throw light upon the continuing debate about the contemporary relevance of progressive history. For that debate assumes that sometime in the past, usually the period between the second and fourth decades of the twentieth century, a coherent progressive historiography dominated historical scholarship. This is a caricature of the true situation, but only the study of the sociology of the profession in that period can put the progressives in a more realistic perspective.

The persistence of innovation, of historiographical reform that breaks with a narrow empiricism, is one of the features of the American historical profession most likely to impress an observer from elsewhere in the Anglo-Saxon world. If the achievements of mainstream British scholarship are compared with the legacy of the progressives at midcentury, then the success of Americans in creating a vital historiographical tradition in touch with major social and political debates seems assured. This comparison is quite easily understood. The American scholars betrayed at every turn a desire to produce a useful history that shed light on contemporary issues. No doubt this revealed the less secure place of intellectual life in American culture, but what underlay that demand for relevance was the social position of the intellectuals and the nature of the university system.

In the period 1890–1920, it was children of respectable farmers, small-town merchants, and professionals, often from the midwest, who came into prominence in the historical profession. Their interpretations often challenged those of various scientific historians, but the progressives were also part of a larger shift in recruitment patterns in the historical profession that included the scientific historians, broadening the discipline's social base beyond an eastern and amateur bias. What occurred in the progressive era was therefore partly a regional shift in the composition of the historical elite, and partly the growing power of professionals over gentleman amateurs. Beard, Turner, Becker, Parrington, and Robinson were all midwesterners who conformed to the pattern. The new academic elite was solidly middle-class, and the process of professionalization may have made it more so over time, as a recent case study of academic recruitment in a midwestern university suggests. Nonetheless, professionalization did involve the principle of meritocracy, and by the creation of a national market in higher education, it facilitated the challenge of the products of the midwest against eastern dominance.[2]

The different patterns of recruitment of the academic elites may help explain the continuing adherence to political and constitutional history in the British case, and its modification in the United States. In Britain the purpose of the profession was still to educate the aristocracy and the upper middle classes for politics, the cloth, and civil or colonial service. The view of history as past politics could not merely survive but prosper as the rationale of this system, in ways that it could not in the United States, where the profession was drawn from more diverse social origins, and where the purpose of education was to provide a broad democratizing and Americanizing influence. These forces conditioned the reshaping of American historical interpretation.

Turner provides suggestive evidence of the impact that the social background of the historian can have on historical innovation. In a passage that is strikingly evocative of his regional inspiration, Turner reminisced about his early frontier childhood, and its implications for his historical interpretation:

I have polled down the Wisconsin in a dug-out with Indian guides . . . through virgin forests of balsam firs, seeing deer in the river, . . . hearing the squaws in their village on the high bank talk their low treble to the bass of our Indian polesman,—feeling that I belonged to it all. . . . The frontier in that sense, you see, was real to me, and when I studied history I did not keep my personal experiences in a watertight compartment away from my studies.[3]

Turner's evocative testimony notwithstanding, the theme of social background can easily be pushed too far. A meritocracy also operated in France, and the social backgrounds of the founders of *Annales* were similar. Like Turner, Febvre and Bloch both had strong regional roots, and both were middle-class in origins. Yet France and the United States soon diverged in the paths that their historiographical orientation would take. The political, social, and cultural context in which these similar backgrounds were experienced seems more pertinent than the abstract sociological comparison of occupation, income, or ethnic and regional origin.

Among the many different social conditions impinging on intellectual syntheses, the one which has received most attention in European historiography is the confrontation of the intellectuals with marxism. The importance of marxism on the continent of Europe, where the new intellectual currents in historiography and social science ran strongest, prompts consideration of the role of that absent intellectual and political force in the American case. Few of Marx's mature works were accessible to the general reader in the United States, especially those unfamiliar with European languages. Neither his *Contribution to the Critique of Political Economy* nor any of the later volumes of *Capital* had been translated into English at the turn of the century. The major American interpreters of Marx's historical views in the United States had to fill the footnotes of their books with quotations and citations from the German and French editions of Marx's work.[4] The fragmentary fourth volume of *Capital* (*Theories of Surplus Value*) was not even published in German until 1909, while the important *Economic and Philosophical Manuscripts* and the *Grundrisse*, Marx's notebooks on political economy, remained unknown until 1931 and 1939 respectively. When added to the massive size and conceptual difficulty of the more learned of Marx's works, it is no surprise that American historians turned to the synthesizers and superficial interpreters in forming their conclusions on marxism.

The foremost synthesizer was Edwin R. A. Seligman, whose *Economic Interpretation of History*, published in 1902, became the major American conduit for consideration of Marx's views by American historians. Beard, for one, cited Seligman approvingly and Seligman's version of Marx made an unmistakable impression on Beard's views.[5] Through Beard's interpretations of American history, the flaws in Seligman have profoundly influenced subsequent American scholarship in history. Though claiming sympathy with the thrust of Marx's work, it was a benign and emasculated economic interpretation of Marx that

Seligman advanced. Seligman was a cautious reformer of the progressive type, but in his comments on "the economic interpretation of history," he seemed to lean over backwards to assimilate marxism to the values of American industrial capitalism of the late nineteenth century. Perhaps mindful that advocacy of socialist views had caused more than one American academic in the 1890s to come to grief at the hands of business-oriented trustees of private universities, Seligman reassured nervous American readers that the economic interpretation of history could be detached from the class question and from socialist politics. His view of Marx's theories the Rockefellers and Carnegies might well have found congenial. Seligman's version of the economic interpretation merely called "attention, among other things, to the influence which private capital has exerted on progress." Discounting Marx's theories of surplus value and profits, and choosing instead to concentrate on the beneficial effects of capitalism, Seligman announced that "the principle of private property" was "a logical and salutary result of human development." Seligman did not follow Marx in enunciating an anti-individualist methodology and interpretation based on social *relations*. In fact, Seligman remained wedded to the conceptual framework of liberal individualism; he claimed that it was possible to be the "staunchest individualist" yet believe in an economic interpretation; he suggested that "the individual or corporate entrepreneur" and "private property and private initiative" were "the very secrets of the whole modern movement" of industrial progress.[6]

The result of Seligman's work was not to encourage Americans to read Marx, but to assure them that they did not need to. Beyond that misleading assurance, Seligman's principal contribution was to convince the emerging generation of talented progressive historians that the economic factor ought to be taken into account. Divorcing Marx's historical insights from his economic theory and socialist politics, Seligman proclaimed that "the economic factor has been of the utmost importance in history."[7] His work did not encourage historians to reconstitute their categories of thought, but rather to use the economic analysis to help explain political events, and to add an economic component to a pluralistic social philosophy. This is precisely what happened in the case of Beard's study of the founding fathers.

Yet it remains an essentially superficial explanation to credit Seligman for the failure of American scholars to reconstruct historical practice. The most famous progressive era scholars—Beard and Turner—probably had better command of European languages than their counterparts today, and Beard certainly reviewed works both in French and German. Turner did not read Italian, but he was nevertheless familiar through translation with the theoretically sophisticated writings of the Italian socialist Labriola. Beard was definitely aware that socialist history entailed "a disintegration of the intellectual synthesis upon which the defence of the present order rests" through reopening "the whole question of historical interpretation and construction." Beard made this clear in a review of Jean Jaurès' *Histoire Socialiste de la Révolution française* as early as 1906. But Beard did not go so far as to agree with Jaurès' "avowed [socialist] purpose" nor did he understand the reconstruction of the historical landscape to require a challenge to the scientific notions of history then ascendant in the profession. In fact, his chief criticism of Jaurès was the absence of adequate documentation rather than a discussion of the theoretical foundations of the French socialist's enterprise. "There is no way of telling," Beard concluded, "how thoroughly evidence has been sifted or of verifying statements."[8]

It is also easy to exaggerate the availability of marxist works in countries where historical thought underwent profound changes. Volume I of *Capital* had been translated into French, for example, in the early 1870s, but then nothing more for over twenty years. A recent survey of the impact of marxism in France concludes that "during the lifetime of Marx and Engels, their considerable theoretical achievements did not make much of an impact and were certainly not followed up or discussed in intellectual circles." The foundations of a marxist historiography in France were "laid in the middle 1930s and just after World War Two," as they were in England.[9] One must conclude that the progressives interpreted Marx through Seligman not because of ignorance of marxism, but because of opposition to its philosophical premises and political implications.

This assessment is confirmed by the greater volume of evidence available on the liberals' attitude to marxism in the 1930s. With American intellectuals turning to marxism in significant numbers for the first time, and with the emergence of a popular base of support for the Communist Party, American liberals like Barnes, Becker, and Beard felt compelled to articulate their views on marxism lest their own efforts be confused with the marxist currents. All rejected marxism as essentially utopian and speculative, at odds with the spirit of pragmatic inquiry and optimistic reform which animated the original progressive impulse in scholarship.[10]

Perhaps the absence of significant marxist political parties rather than the impact of marxist theory as such limited the challenge to existing intellectual syntheses in the United States. But on the subject of marxist political activity per se, it is relevant that marxism was also of little importance in the British case in the late nineteenth century, yet the reorientation of historical thought went further in the United States than in the United Kingdom. The impact of marxist thought and practice cannot alone explain that important difference, and it is probably not sufficient to account for the limitations upon the reform of historical practice in the United States either. Much more important were the differing structures of the university systems in the various countries concerned and their capacities for absorbing intellectual and social change. More important, too, was the degree and character of social upheaval which intellectuals had to confront in those countries. Marxist political action was part of that social context, but only part.

A better understanding of the divergent paths of historical method in France and the United States leads inexorably to the political and social upheaval of the Third Republic period, and the related unrest in French education. The contribution of the French sociologist Emile Durkheim as an influence on *Annales* and as a model of intellectual imperialism was extremely important in this milieu. Marc Bloch's first mature work, *The Royal Touch*, is inconceivable without the Durkheimian rejection of individualism and the development of a study of collective representations or mentalities.[11] Durkheim's new and very influential synthesis took shape amid intellectual and social crises that profoundly affected members of the French intelligentsia, threatening their own ambitions within the education system and challenging conventional interpretations of individualistic morality.[12] The political repression of the Commune, the rise of marxist parties and labor movements, the social and political turmoil surrounding the Dreyfus affair, and the bitter anticlericalism of the entire Third Republic period had no parallel in either Britain or the United States. Faced with an attack on the institutions of the Third Republic by the anti-Dreyfusards, a new defense of republican values emerged. Politics no longer seemed to promise a rational adjudication of individual interests but rather involved the conflict of often irreconcilable social forces. This realization led social theorists away from a preoccupation with the preservation and extension of individual autonomy to a search for a holistic social philosophy that gave rise to Durkheim's sociology. The rebellion against nineteenth-century liberalism which Durkheim led in turn had profound implications for other areas of French scholarship, including history, where Bloch and Febvre were influenced by the reorientation of French thought which Durkheim's anti-individualist sociology entailed. Within the historical profession itself, therefore, a similar tactic was employed. Faced with bureaucratic structures and vested interests, Bloch and Febvre came to repudiate the traditional centers of scholarship, and eventually to found their own journals and develop their own methods. *Annales* was the end result.[13]

In the United States, only World War I had a comparable effect on liberal values, though the impact of war was by no means as devastating for the political and intellectual fortunes of liberalism as in some European cases. The aftermath had disillusioned some Wilsonian liberals, including Carl Becker, and the repudiation of both progress and liberalism was temporarily fashionable in the younger intellectual set that included the future progressive historian Matthew Josephson.[14] This cultural and aesthetic radicalism paralleled developments in Europe. Yet in the historical profession, most scholars, including most progressives, had been pro-war, and the impact of the war did not undermine their liberal convictions of democratic freedom, the role of the individual, and the possibility of progress through rational action and the application of technology. Carol Gruber's impressive study of historians in the Committee on Public Information is relevant to the theme of war and the resilience of American liberalism. As enthusiastically as the scientific historians they allegedly opposed, progressives like Turner and Guy Stanton Ford rushed into Creel Committee work fashioning anti-German, pro-war, and later anti-Bolshevik propaganda to demonstrate their usefulness to the state and its liberal ideology. These historians depicted the war as a clash between democratic and pluralistic values on the one hand, and authoritarian European traditions on the other. This experience was bound to reinforce the liberal belief in the superiority of American institutions. Even those who like Becker and Beard became quickly disillusioned with the war's conduct and outcome concluded that American democracy suffered when entangled in European politics and militarism. Thus Becker remained, "in spite of the lessons he took from the Great War, a liberal democrat who wished man well and granted him the right to experiment radically with his institutions."[15]

One suspects that the reasons for the attachment of historians to the liberal state, and their continued preference for reform of it rather than alternatives to it, lie as much in the domestic as in the international sphere, and specifically in the academic situation of this particular segment of the American intelligentsia prior to World War I. The liberal historians who subsequently influenced American historical interpretations, and advanced the most important methodological innovations, had already formed their attitudes in the optimistic era of American material growth between the 1890s and 1919. When Vernon L. Parrington drew attention to the prewar experience in explaining the survival of liberal values, he was talking about himself as well as others. In his thinly veiled piece of intellectual autobiography, "A Chapter in American Liberalism," he admitted to a certain postwar disillusionment with progressive reform, but maintained his Jeffersonian "trust in the individual" and conceded that the older generation of American liberals never doubted "the finality or the sufficiency of the democratic principle."[16]

The same confident spirit underpinned the faith of younger historians like John D. Hicks (born 1890), Roy Nichols (born 1896), Merle Curti (born 1897), and Arthur Schlesinger, Sr. (born 1888). Schlesinger was already twenty-nine when America entered the war, and his early experience confirmed the promise of American liberal values. "My youthful environment . . . provided an image of America as a pluralistic society as well as a land of opportunity, and nothing in later life has dimmed the vision." Hicks was born into the world of "small-town America" and grew to maturity in a period of "peace and prosperity." Nichols was "politically . . . a child of the Progressive era and dedicated to reform."[17] In the prewar United States, political repression and social upheaval could be discerned, but the latter seemed manageable within the democratic process, while the former hardly matched the French (or German, or Russian, or Italian) in extent. Nor did it affect the liberal intellectuals in the same way, because no incident of repression rocked the integrity of the American state structure the way the Dreyfus affair affected the French.

It is this tenacity of a faith in the possibility of reform which stands out as a common characteristic. Whether they advocated radical adjustments of social arrangements like Beard, or more modest tinkering of the kind favored by Turner, the belief in pragmatic change and democratic procedures prospered and survived. Their understanding of marxism was conditioned in important respects by this political solidity of the democratic state, and by the optimistic cast of liberal values. Those most enamored of the potential benefits of an economic interpretation favored Seligman because his view of a marxism divested of class conflict and exploitation matched their desires for orderly progress and the amelioration of the conditions created by the emergence of industrial society.

Since Charles Beard was the principal exponent of an economic interpretation, it is important to realize that he shared the reformist disposition, despite his iconoclastic criticisms of accepted shibboleths. Though more radical in politics and social philosophy than most of his fellow progressive historians, like them he strongly endorsed progress and the rational amelioration of the social order. Beard's interest in reform went back to his Quaker-Methodist roots which instilled a concern with social justice already well in evidence during his interlude as a student at Oxford. There he joined with Walter Vrooman and other social reformers to open Ruskin Hall, "the first laboring man's college at Oxford," in 1899. Faced with the social squalor of the English industrial revolution, Beard favored at first the cooperative movement and was immensely attracted to John Ruskin's moral and aesthetic condemnation of the evils of industrial capitalism. Harnessing his own considerable outrage, he worked with labor leaders and trade unionists to reform the industrial system in the interests of all. "Let us hope," he wrote, "that the new century will witness the triumph of the Co-operative ideal, and that humanity will have freed itself from the injustice, ignorance, and folly which to-day allow the few to live upon the toil of the many."[18]

After his return to the United States in 1902 and his appointment as a lecturer at Columbia University's Department of History in 1904, Beard continued to espouse social reform through interclass cooperation. In the context of evolving progressive era politics, however, this meant in effect a shift from the promotion of working-class self-help to a growing concern for the application of professional expertise to social problems. Beard's participation in the work of the National Municipal League for more efficient and responsive local government was characteristic of that era's impulse to control laissez-faire capitalism through efficient administration. That way "the freedom of the individual" could be preserved in a society increasingly riven by great disparities of wealth and power.[19]

This freedom he did not define in terms of inviolable property rights along the lines of classical liberalism, but rather more broadly if more vaguely as the realization of individual potential in its social setting. His position was similar to the left wing of the New Liberalism in England. Like L. T. Hobhouse and J. A. Hobson, he recognized the need for state intervention to promote public welfare and condemned imperialism abroad, yet had no clear theory of society that would account for the evils he identified, and promote their elimination. Like them, too, he believed social injustice could be removed through a form of social engineering without a radical rejection of liberal individualism, and he explained imperialism not as a product of capitalism's inexorable drives but rather as a result of evil individuals, groups, and classes.[20] The task was to restore the Jeffersonian promise of democracy and individual freedom through the extension of rational planning and social welfare. On the constitutional plane, this involved bringing government "under the control of the people" by easing the process of constitutional amendment. This faith in the capacity of democracy to reconcile individual freedoms with collective responsibilities remained intact even after the onset of the Great Depression, despite differences of opinion with the Roosevelt administration. During the New Deal period, Beard argued for centralized planning but he opposed nationalization and was vague as to how his own alternative of a technological utopia was to be realized.[21]

Turner illustrates from a more moderate perspective the same connection between an optimistic liberalism and a disinterest in apocalyptic theories of social change. Turner was a liberal Republican who celebrated the values of American democracy but feared the impact that the development of trusts might have on individual freedom. Like Theodore Roosevelt (*and* Robert M. La Follette), he favored regulation of the trusts to preserve the economies of scale they had produced, but also to allow the fruits of American capitalism to be shared more equally by workers and consumers. If the cautious Turner was not given to the enthusiasm for visionary change that sometimes overtook Beard, he believed as Beard did in the value of history to a democratic state. History could, Turner argued, "hold the lamp for conservative reform." Along with the other social sciences, the discipline could help produce the experts that could mediate between the contending interests of the "capitalistic classes" and "the proletariate" in modern America.[22]

Associated with this faith in liberal democracy was a resistance to theories of historical change which might have promoted a reconstruction of historical interpretation and practice. As much as for Beard and for Carl Becker, marxism was for Turner a "mechanical solution" of "doctrinaires" which compared unfavorably with the "ideals" of American democracy. For Turner, America's "pioneering experience" taught not class warfare but the reality of "sectional and class compromises."[23] There might have been incentive to depart from this pragmatic temper had personal experience unsettled inherited convictions. Yet Beard, Turner, Becker, Robinson, and others like them did not come from immigrant or blue-collar backgrounds. All were comfortably placed in a financial sense. Even if they had had working-class affiliations, there is no guarantee that they would have been drawn to marxist analysis, since we know from a host of studies that American workers were rarely attracted to socialist doctrines of the marxist kind at this time. Little pressure therefore existed for these writers to probe the implications of marxist thought for the survival of liberal values and progressive interpretations of history.[24]

Thus far I have been seeking to explain why the progressives sought to modify rather than to reconstruct historical practice and interpretation in a radical way. For all that, Beard, Turner, Becker, Robinson, and their followers did attempt to broaden the scope of historical method in ways that must not be forgotten. These efforts achieved only partial success, and the political and social milieu within which these historians operated cannot supply an adequate explanation for the limits to their initiatives. In these cases, a failure of will or of conceptualization did not occur. An answer must be sought instead in the institutional and intellectual impediments to historiographical change. This does not mean that the historian's practice determined historical interpretation. Rather, the framework of the discipline and the university system set limits to conceptual innovation and helped shape the theoretical and methodological contours of historiography. Exploration of these matters may also provide an underlying explanation for the reluctance of the progressives to discard systematically the positivist and empiricist assumptions of their scientific colleagues and teachers.

The concept of professionalism is crucially important here. Though history is one of the learned disciplines which has its own specific procedures, one cannot discuss the structure and content of this knowledge in a vacuum. Thomas Haskell has noted that "knowledge . . . does not grow or subdivide of its own inner nature." It emerges in the context of "potent institutional realities" that involve the "certification" of some kinds of knowledge, the "conferring" of "authority on some people and some ideas while withholding authority from [others]." Haskell concedes that no simple dichotomy existed between "amateur" and "professional" historians or other academics. (After all, the professionals were happy to lend prestige to their enterprise by co-opting prominent amateur historians like Theodore Roosevelt for the A.H.A. presidency.) What did occur, however, was a gradual displacement of the amateur "to a lower level of authoritativeness." Amateur history continued to be written, but it simply became increasingly irrelevant to what professional historians were doing and thinking.[25]

Studying professionalization in the academic world involves the intersection of power and knowledge.[26] For the reproduction of existing forms of knowledge, the power structure of the discipline is particularly important. Scientific historians continued to exercise influence because they had already attained a fairly entrenched position by 1910 through their publication, their teaching, and their attainment of high honorific positions in the professional associations. They had established a linkage between professionalism and the scientific method as then understood. This meant that the knowledge they produced and defended became institutionalized and closely identified with history as a concept. To attack their achievements meant assaulting more than the specific interpretations they offered.

If there was a break of real consequence in the continuity of historical scholarship, the scientific historians can lay as impressive a claim as the progressives, because of their role in the professionalization of their discipline. This process rested on several underlying assumptions, including the assertion of a privileged status for professional historians trained in the techniques of criticism available only to formal apprentices socialized within a guild of scholars; the development of specialization within the discipline; the mastery of small, complementary areas as part of the cooperative accumulation of knowledge of the whole subject; the notion of scholarly productivity, not sales or literary value, as the criteria of professional assessment; the elimination of idiosyncratic bias; the establishment of societies for professional interaction and intellectual sustenance; and the creation of scholarly paraphernalia in the form of an array of journals, documents, historical series, degrees, prizes, and honorific positions.[27]

In these respects, the scientific historians were innovators par excellence. They founded the graduate programs at the great universities and chartered the American Historical Association in 1884 as the central professional focus. They established the monograph as the vehicle for the presentation of original research in the primary sources. They gathered, criticized, and edited vast and invaluable collections of documentary material, and generally strove to establish the framework of facts upon which later American scholarship would be largely based. They were probably more alive to developments in European historiography in the 1870s and 1880s than later generations of American historians would be of their own eras. They were, too, concerned with the teaching of history and participated actively in campaigns to promote concepts of good citizenship through the study of the past in the high schools. At the graduate level, they trained a large number of doctoral candidates. Whereas there were only twenty trained professional historians in 1884, by 1894 there were already nearly one hundred. Herbert Baxter Adams of Johns Hopkins was especially successful in wielding patronage because he was virtually present at the creation of the doctoral system, and established colonies of scientific historians in most of the major universities. The influence of scientific history was considerable in part because the Johns Hopkins seminar produced such a large proportion of the Ph.D.s in North America. In fact, Johns Hopkins conferred one-third of the total number of Ph.D.s up to 1900, and with five other major private universities, accounted for 80 percent of the total output.[28]

The mere volume of orthodox scholars produced in the Rankean tradition prior to 1910 was impressive. By the time Beard and Robinson announced their departures from conventional practices in the second decade of the twentieth century, more than four hundred and fifty doctorates had been granted. From the inquiry of Marcus Jernegan into graduate productivity in 1927, we know that most of these spent their days living off the intellectual capital of their graduate experience.[29] For those who did try to introduce new subjects and methods, the relatively slow attrition rate among these older scholars constituted a serious institutional impediment. Arthur Schlesinger, Sr., reported in 1929 that "the dissenters" of the New History had "by no means won the field" over the exponents of facts, dates, and political events. As late as 1938, Harry Elmer Barnes lamented that the "younger men" who promoted the New History often had to teach in history departments controlled by older scholars with views "much more venerable and antique." Because of a tendency for orthodoxy to reproduce itself through patronage and influence, "perhaps a majority of men who have shaped and are shaping the new history are not now teaching in university departments of history."[30] Like Barnes himself, some found themselves teaching by choice or necessity in other disciplines. Others, like Beard, left orthodox academia, complaining of its small ideas and conventionality. Still others in the depression decade of the 1930s, especially, were unable to get jobs at all.

Major syntheses from orthodox scholars, such as that produced by Charles McLean Andrews, continued to appear in the 1930s, and scholars ready to defend the standard of "objective truth" against relativism and marxist partiality were not in short supply. When Beard announced his "act of faith" in 1933, Theodore Clark Smith was quickly into the lists to defend professional objectivity, and to attack those "doctrinaire" supporters of the view that "American history, like all history, can and must be explained in economic terms." Though scientific orthodoxy as remembered in the 1930s underwent serious questioning in that decade, scholars like Smith, Andrew C. McLaughlin, and others kept alive notions of the self-evident facticity of history until the Beardian influence began to subside. As much as Beard's relativism, these views contributed to the postwar compromise on historical method.[31]

The apprenticeship system of historical training was one important mechanism for the transmission of this orthodox historiography. John D. Hicks has provided us with a testimony of the system as it operated in the period of his graduate education at the University of Wisconsin during World War I.

In those less frantic years, when university professors were not so harried by numbers, a kind of academic apprentice system prevailed; each graduate student learned his trade by close association with a few more experienced practitioners, and in particular, a major professor, with whose name and fame he was branded for life.[32]

The language of apprenticeship involved the concept of a guild of historians possessing an esoteric knowledge of professionals. The master craftsman like Charles McLean Andrews initiated the apprentice into the secrets of the trade. The craft concept demonstrated the widely held view that historical knowledge was accumulated through experience of the particulars of historical periods. Historical understanding was in the craft concept the antithesis of philosophical knowledge, which was speculative and deductive. Emphasis in the training of the apprentice was therefore placed upon technique rather than upon the theory that could be taught a priori or copied from a book. Technique meant in particular the critical appraisal of evidence, but historians generally believed that critical skills were best learned by "doing" history under the supervision of one who possessed the profound knowledge of particulars.[33]

The most important single element within the apprenticeship system making for historiographical continuity was the operation of patronage networks. Hicks, for example, owed his first job to his mentor, Frederick Paxson, and Hicks' own experience is reproduced in his characterization of other scholars in terms of their relationship to a powerful patron or mentor. Oscar Handlin also offers a description of the system as he encountered it, largely unaltered, in the 1930s: "A few score professors who knew one another personally decided which among their students deserved prizes, fellowships, and positions in the highly varied array of American institutions of higher learning."[34] There is an element of romantic nostalgia in this recollection but a collegial concentration of influence was possible. When Handlin first studied at Harvard in the mid–1930s, ten prestigious schools, seven of them private and all in the northeast and midwest, were producing over half the total number of Ph.D.s. (Forty-six other departments accounted for the rest.) From nine of the ten schools came all of the twenty-five American-trained presidents of the American Historical Association between 1920 and 1951 bar two, including eleven of the twelve Americanists with Ph.D.s from American universities. The six major schools which had produced 80 percent of all history doctorates in 1900 still accounted for a third in 1936–1940, and again in 1946–1950. With the number of jobs almost always small, the question of who received the best of them strengthened the hands of senior practitioners in the elite institutions still further, despite the opening up of a "varied array" of universities.[35]

But patronage could be wielded by a variety of groups, and was. The papers of Frederick Jackson Turner are an archeological site for evidence that progressives as much as more conservative scholars could participate in the thousand scholarly exchanges and courtesies that constituted ordinary historical activity. Conversely, scientific historians found long before the 1930s that they had no monopoly of authority. J. Franklin Jameson had been unable to exert the control over the "standard of workmanship" in the profession which he had hoped to effect through the editorship of the *American Historical Review*. The Mississippi Valley Historical Association provided as early as 1907 a focus of revolt against the centralizing pretensions of the A.H.A., and by the 1920s the many regional and state historical journals and societies made *American* history less susceptible to centralized and hierarchical networks of influence than other specialties, or the discipline of history as a whole in France.[36] Centrifugal tendencies were furthered by the growth in the interwar years of graduate programs at state universities like California, North Carolina, Texas, Illinois, and Ohio State. This development was especially important for American history because the newer programs, particularly those in the south and west, stressed American history more than did those of Harvard, Yale, or Pennsylvania.[37]

The lines of patronage which stemmed from these fragmenting tendencies were quite naturally pluralistic. A survey of graduate placement done by William B. Hesseltine and Louis Kaplan found strong regional patterns of preferment in 1939. About 10 percent of all graduates from 1926 to 1935 were still teaching in the universities which had awarded them doctoral degrees, and 46 percent in the region in which they had studied. Each departmental chairman attempted, apparently with some success, "to control the part of the market nearest him and where he [could] exert his greatest influence."[38]

Pluralistic patterns along regional lines did not, however, change the fact that existing scholarly practices were being reproduced. It is even possible that the newer and less prestigious departments were more likely to encourage a reproduction of scientific orthodoxy if they remained isolated from larger and more cosmopolitan historiographical currents. Hesseltine and Kaplan pointed to this danger when they attacked "inbreeding" and "provincialism" revealed in the placement statistics. The growth of local history journals and societies which undermined Jameson's role as a professional watchdog to the craft similarly did not mean innovation in method. While the regional movement could produce a work of intuitive skill like Walter Prescott Webb's *The Great Plains* (1931), which married personal insight with a study of geographic forces, in lesser hands the possibility of regional studies on the *Annales* model of a total history degenerated into state and local histories, which could and often did allow for the survival of fact gathering and a parochial empiricism.[39]

If patronage was an important element in professional socialization, the reproduction of historical knowledge entailed far more. A critical reason for the failure of the New History to transform the profession was, according to Schlesinger, the fact that "graduate instruction continued to be organized along the lines laid down a generation ago" by the scientific historians. Students studying for preliminary examinations had to ingest a political history, in which facts, names, and dates, underlined by a conception of time as a unilinear datum, assumed critical importance. Barnes complained that things were much the same a decade later when he argued that there "has been little change in the external forms of historical instruction in the last generation." Still another ten years on, when Roy F. Nichols became Dean of Arts at the University of Pennsylvania, the doctoral program in history there was "operating about as it had when [Nichols] was a graduate student thirty years before. The degree candidates certainly amassed a great deal of fact" but "in so many instances there was an absence of literary style or depth of understanding, of capacity for interpretive analysis. Often there seemed more learning than understanding, more drudgery than inspiration."[40]

Originally, the patterns of historical instruction and the content of courses testified not only to the Rankean influence, but also to the process of academic specialization. The graduate programs had been established to create for the new professionalized discipline of history its own distinctive subject matter and approach. The movement of other social sciences at the turn of the century away from historical analysis reinforced this defensive posturing as historians reasserted the value of their discipline. Because historians were especially concerned to establish their own credentials, they were unwilling to admit reliance on the theories of society being developed by newer and more aggressive social sciences. And what did history have that made it distinctive but its emphasis upon particulars, the sequence of events, and the theme of national progress?[41]

These conceptions of historical training proved, however, to be notoriously difficult to shift once established. Surveys done in the 1950s, particularly the Perkins-Snell study, prepared for the American Historical Association, still made the same claims as the partisans of the New History had done in the 1920s and 1930s. The degree programs were, by and large, overspecialized, protracted, and tailored to produce a descriptive and conventional conception of history.[42]

How the structures of learning actually operated would require a separate book. What can be indicated here is how the student entering graduate school in history was expected to undertake extensive coursework designed to give the apprentice a firm grounding in a number of fields of history. The aim of acquainting the student with a broad historical knowledge was laudable, but in effect the coursework had to substitute for deficiencies in the undergraduate programs brought about by the immense variations in standards applying to liberal arts colleges. Coursework often took up two-thirds of the period of full-time study, and together with the onerous oral and written exams, usually taken at the beginning of the third year, left the student able to do little serious research before he or she was forced out into the job market. Nor did the coursework truly compensate by giving students a breadth of approach or an interdisciplinary framework. As Marcus W. Jernegan argued in his survey of graduate productivity in 1927, the oral and written examinations often focused on "more minute memory-knowledge . . . than should be exacted."[43]

Course requirements for the doctorate were diversified at many universities in the interwar period, and there were wide differences from one school to another. Yet the changes occurred incrementally and in the direction of a greater topical, geographical, and especially chronological specialization. Knowledge of the philosophy and theory of history and related social sciences, which might have integrated historical studies, languished as a minor part of the curricula. Though the relativist controversy rekindled interest in these questions, Perkins and Snell could still justly lament the inadequate attention to philosophical and historiographical training in the 1950s.[44] Neither did the academic structures encourage the genuinely interdisciplinary exchange which in France was facilitated through the programs of the elite Ecole Normale Supérieure. Thus, for example, the future leaders of the historical profession like Bloch and Febvre who passed through this centralized institution were required to study geography and history together, and in fact Bloch graduated in both subjects. The result was a systematic attempt to integrate the different fields of study into a totalistic approach. In the United States, those like Turner and Walter Prescott Webb, who both took a similar interest in geography and interdisciplinary studies, did so in an uncoordinated, idiosyncratic, and necessarily eclectic way. The minor fields that historians were required to study for the doctorate were intended to connect history with that larger world of learning, but as the fields became more specialized after the turn of the century, the taking of one or two courses in outside subjects became inadequate to the task. By the 1930s, an increasing dissatisfaction with the formalism of the existing programs of study was felt, as the inception of American civilization courses at Yale, Harvard, and other universities testified. Ironically, however, the American studies movement which emerged from their initiatives as a major interdisciplinary focus after World War II would itself succumb to the perils of academic specialization through the institutional atrophy of its reformist impulse.[45]

Another way in which the existing arrangements proved resilient was the choice of research topics within the graduate seminar. These were structured quite naturally by the interests of the seminar director, and seminar work in turn conditioned the choice of the doctoral dissertation. In this way the older generation of scholars could influence to some extent the content of the most important piece of work most historians would ever do. Roy Nichols "did not blink" when his supervisor, W. A. Dunning, steered him into a study of the antebellum Democratic Party, even though Nichols was a "rock-ribbed Republican." Frederick Paxson "brushed aside" John D. Hicks' desire to do a study of the Populists, and insisted that he write his thesis on "state-making" in the West. Though Hicks found the topic to be a "morass" of an assignment, he persisted to the point of publication. This he "later came to regret," and after obtaining his degree he "did not pursue the subject further." Howard K. Beale's *The Critical Year* has been commonly attributed to Beard's influence, but Beale himself noted that he owed the conception and topic to the conservative narrative historian Edward Channing. Other supervisors were less directive, like Charles McLean Andrews, who "preferred that the subject of the dissertation be chosen by the students themselves." Yet no one could deny that Andrews exerted a profound influence over the scope of studies through his seminar, his style, and his supervision. Thus the studies in the *Yale Historical Series* he edited for about twenty years were "mainly institutional, and the scope of concern" was "almost entirely political and administrative." Similarly, the festschrift for an orthodox scientific scholar like Dunning as much as for Turner demonstrated the influence in subject matter and treatment that teachers had on the questions taken up by the succeeding generations.[46]

The seminar structure and the patronage networks on which historical training was founded did not prevent innovation. That depended on the individual interests and capacities of the student. Beard and Turner quickly went their own ways in relation to their scientific teachers John W. Burgess and H. B. Adams on the level of interpretation, but the institutional context of learning made it much more difficult for progressives or any one else to transcend the empiricist and positivist assumptions which underlay the scientific contribution to American historiography. Such conceptual advances as did occur tended to be gradually absorbed by the larger profession, and the continuity with existing practice was not disrupted. Outstanding individuals could not transform the discipline while orthodox methods and interpretations were being reproduced in textbooks, course structures, and in the routine career patterns of lesser scholars. This last point must be emphasized. Since the doctorate was, according to Perkins and Snell, "fairly often the only substantial work of research scholarship in which the [average] history Ph.D. engages in a lifetime," the influence of the doctoral training was profound indeed for everyday historical practice.[47]

Confronted by this institutional and intellectual grid of power and knowledge, partisans of the New History could either work within the existing framework or opt out and develop a radical critique of the operation of scholarship and disciplinary reproduction. The New Historians tried elements of both approaches. Attempts were made to influence school and university curricula. N. Ray Hiner has shown how this process produced some alteration in the scope of historical studies, but the pace of change in the methods of historical instruction was glacial, largely because of the institutional circumstances. Those who first mounted campaigns for reform before World War I encountered a newly entrenched establishment. It was necessary for progressives to make compromises if they wished to influence the structures the profession controlled. James Harvey Robinson followed such a procedure while a member of the Committee of Five of the American Historical Association, set up in 1907 to recommend a high school curriculum for history. Robinson was successful in getting "an increase in the time allotted to the study of modern history" and gained, according to Hiner, a "more liberal statement of the role of history in the schools." But the group of reformers that Robinson represented, which soon included Charles Beard, Carl Becker, and others, "was not powerful enough to gain control of the profession" before World War I.[48]

After World War I, the second approach was tried when both Beard and Robinson left academic employment dissatisfied with the conservatism of Columbia. From that time onwards, they operated more and more as critics outside the system but were unable to exert an influence commensurate with their eloquence. Detached from the academic environment, Beard's work took on an increasingly eclectic air, and he never returned to complete the detailed research needed to substantiate his earlier program for the economic interpretation. The powerful and majestic synthesis of *The Rise of American Civilization* did not fill the gap, though it did inspire the next generation of scholars.[49]

The opportunity to influence future scholars through the power of his prose and his personal example remained. Beard was certainly not an inaccessible figure, but great teaching gifts were lost after 1917, if the testimony of those who knew him can be believed. The absence of a coterie of dedicated students dependent on his patronage weakened and changed the pattern of absorption of his ideas. His influence was felt, but was assimilated in ways which made his interpretations more reliant on the climate of opinion than on the patterns of professional productivity. It would be a mistake to think that charisma and intellectual vitality could entirely overcome this lost opportunity. The case of Arthur Schlesinger's relationship with Beard is a useful and instructive example. *The Colonial Merchants and the American Revolution* is usually depicted as a product of Beard's influence even though Schlesinger was nominally a student of the conservative, Herbert Osgood. But it would be wrong to conclude that this work of Schlesinger's was wholly Beardian in conception and assumptions. The way in which Beard was absorbed demonstrated other academic influences as well. *The Colonial Merchants* combined, reminisced Schlesinger, "the research methods [of Osgood] with the insights of Beard." Although Beard was a major influence, Schlesinger conceded the "complexity of forces, governmental and religious," which must be assessed to arrive at a definitive account of the Revolution. In a sense, this was simply a prudent attempt to distance himself from the charge that he really was a Beardian. Beard himself had advised Schlesinger not to thank him in the preface of the book. But this concession of history as a multicausal system of explanation is consistent with Schlesinger's later career, and with his assessment that Beard had overstated the economic factor in history.[50]

If the system of graduate training in history and the processes of professional advancement help explain the tenacity of older conceptions of history, the structure of the university system also encouraged the assimilation of the New History *in modified form*. The university structure of the late nineteenth and early twentieth centuries combined toleration of moderate reform in a professional framework of sober objectivity with repression of some opinions that university trustees deemed too radical. Value-oriented social criticism had characterized a good deal of American social science in the second half of the nineteenth century, but professionalization and the workings of the university system made radical political and moral commitment more difficult to sustain within the academy after the 1890s. Social science increasingly took on the air of objectivity and abandoned the notion that ultimate causes could be assigned to social problems. Instead, an interlocking set of variables was analyzed in empirical research, and the old notion of moral condemnation of social evils became obsolete. The emerging professional associations were careful to confine their defense of dissent to limited areas of professional competence.[51] Though celebrated cases of academic freedom did arise, the results in the 1890s warned historians of the costs of unconventional viewpoints. The attacks on Richard Ely at Wisconsin in 1894 over his alleged support for socialist doctrines could not be lost on a generation which produced Frederick Jackson Turner. Indeed, Turner was one of Ely's students and defenders. Beard, too, was very much aware of the issue of academic freedom long before he resigned from Columbia in 1917. In 1910 he noted in a review that "it is notorious that several of the worst violations of academic liberty have been" not in private colleges but "in state institutions managed by politicians." He may have been thinking of the case of Vernon Parrington at the University of Oklahoma, who fell foul of a despicable piece of sectarian intolerance in 1907.[52]

The attacks on dissent worried progressive historians, but the issue must be seen in larger perspective. Provided historians remained within the bounds of professional controversy, their novel contributions to academic life were encouraged. The university system required such encouragement because the emergence and expansion of higher education created competition between a number of universities; the effort to build new faculties meant that talented people were welcomed despite or even because of their divergence from the scholarly norm.

If the New Historians could not immediately conquer Harvard or Hopkins, they could go elsewhere to Columbia or Wisconsin and be professionally satisfied. This is why Turner achieved such early prominence. Several departments courted him, irrespective of his reformer status, and Harvard eventually lured him from his beloved midwest in 1910, to spend the rest of his teaching career alongside conservative historians like Edward Channing. Unlike the centralized

French university system which encouraged a head-on clash between the adherents of *Annales* and their Rankean opponents, in the university system of the United States new viewpoints were absorbed as alternatives within a pluralistic system, and the edge was taken off the impulse to effect a revolutionary break in historical practice.[53]

In this way, the academic system reinforced the reformism which the progressive generation of historians brought to their work from wider intellectual and cultural experience. John R. Commons, whose contribution to labor history was as substantial as his efforts for an institutional economics, never lost his faith in an American capacity for pragmatic reform, despite persecution in the 1890s for "socialist" opinions. Dismissed from Syracuse University in 1899, he merely concluded that political interference from private trustees and administrators could be effectively overcome through the establishment of a strong system of public universities. At Wisconsin after 1904, Commons attempted with some success to put his pragmatic and incremental reforms into operation. Commons' experience was not unusual. Individual cases of political repression, in the absence of some theory to explain the workings of the structures of education, did not shake the conviction that a pluralistic academy was in the process of being constructed.[54]

World War I shattered this kind of complacency among some progressives, as the foundation in 1919 of the New School for Social Research in New York attests. Robinson and Beard joined in the movement to "establish an institution of learning at which the social sciences may be as emancipated from lay interference as the natural sciences." At its inception, the New School held the promise of an imposing intellectual program which could have competed with and ultimately displaced conventional learning. But though some progressives, notably the political critic, Herbert Croly, envisaged an American version of the French écoles, such ambitions for a citadel of higher learning were bound to be disappointed, and not only because of divisions within the advocates of reform. The New School functioned as part of New York culture; it did not and could not have a special status as the focal point of a centralized, national system of education.[55]

The New School's establishment actually confirmed the existence of a pluralism in American higher education which made radical change difficult to effect then, and much later in the 1960s. The selective incorporation of progressive concepts at times obscured the boundaries between "schools." All American historiography tended toward an eclectic framework of interpretation which incorporated both the positivist and empiricist legacy of the scientific approach, and the concern for a broader and more methodologically sophisticated historiography associated with the advocates of the New History.

The ad hoc absorption of progressive concepts applied especially to the profession's assessment of Charles Beard. His ideas did achieve a preeminent place in the thinking of American historians for a time, but the process of assimilation was uneven and protracted. The ways in which Beardian concepts of class and economic interpretation were absorbed are particularly important for an understanding of American liberal historiography in the post–World War II period. This assimilative process is captured in an early comment by Merle Curti, a historian influenced by both Beard and Turner. Curti told Turner in 1928: "It is this very catholicity, this synthetic quality, which makes your methodology superior, it seems to me, to that which selects and emphasizes any single factor." Curti suggested that Beard, "recognizing the great importance of industrial capitalism in our own day, has possibly let his interpretation of our earlier history be colored by a kind of an ex-post-facto industrial bias."[56] Even in the work of scholars sympathetic to progressive historiography, no simple triumph of an economic interpretation of history or class analysis occurred. Rather, historians selectively incorporated such hypotheses within a multicausal analysis of factors.

Curti's letter might have been differently phrased had he been assessing the relationship between Turner and Beard ten years later. The 1930s did provide the conditions for an apotheosis of Beardian influence in certain quarters. The Depression helped make class and economic analyses convincing in a way they had not been for large numbers of American historians before then. The research of Maurice Blinkhoff on Beard's influence showed that the economic interpretation of the constitution had overcome early resistance and had been adopted in most college-level texts and in an impressive number of other works. A series of monographs on the constitution written in this decade backed up Beard's analysis, even where empirical evidence was presented that appeared to later observers to contradict Beard's hypothesis.[57]

Blinkhoff's study is useful to those who may wish to demonstrate the pervasive influence of Beard, but another of Blinkhoff's findings casts doubt on the conventional wisdom. According to Blinkhoff, American historiography evidenced an "almost complete absence of economic interpretation of United States history as a whole." Though Beard certainly shaped the historiography of particular topics and brought the question of economics to the fore, the existing frameworks of a narrative political history of the American nation remained in Blinkhoff's estimation the organizing conception.[58]

Within this context, the more important and more lasting aspect of the progressive legacy was not Beard's economic interpretation but the larger and more diverse methodological contribution. That involved the integration of an empirical study of the American past with all of the techniques and insights that could be gleaned from the social sciences. In the late 1930s, this opened the possibility of a new and more vigorous synthesis of social history, built upon the best that both the progressives and the scientific historians could offer. The promise was illustrated in the unprecedented content of the annual meetings of the American Historical Association held in 1939 and 1940. Particularly noticeable was the emphasis upon a social history "from the bottom up," as Gerald Capers put it in his own paper. For the very first time at the A.H.A., a panel on women's history was held, and a lively session on blacks under Reconstruction also demonstrated the concern for recovering the history of inarticulate groups. Proposals were advanced for the collaboration of the folklorist and the historian, for the use of oral history, and for the exploitation of a wider range of sources that included photography, cinema, and local history archives. Historians familiar with the radical pronouncements of the 1960s may experience a feeling of *déjà vu* on reading again these old programs, but these earlier efforts to study the common folk somehow managed to avoid the rhetorical excesses of the New Left equivalent.[59]

The innovative programs in part stemmed from the strategic placement of the progressive Merle Curti on the organizing committees; nevertheless, a new maturity in American scholarship was manifest. The programmatic statements of the New History seemed about to be transformed into a project for a sociologically sophisticated history of American society. Some of the papers presented at the 1939 convention and published as *The Cultural Approach to History* illustrated the promise. Caroline Ware's introduction to that volume drew together the methodological strands, and pointed to the trend of interpretation. She based her advocacy of the concept of culture as a unifying feature of historiography on the claim that "every society has a structure of institutions, of values, of ideologies." "No part," she continued, "is to be understood without reference to its place in the whole." The New History had offered a kaleidoscope of "diverse approaches," and "multiplied materials and ideas"—but without "a basis for selection, organization, and interpretation." The explosion of historical knowledge had engendered doubts that historians could grasp the actuality of history, and so produced a debilitating relativism represented in the work of Beard and Becker. Ware believed that the concept of culture could provide the organizing principle to overcome this crisis of confidence.[60]

This is not to say that the old theoretical and conceptual difficulties of progressive history had been overcome. The grab for a totalistic analysis of culture would prove to be too vague and diffuse to reintegrate a fragmenting historiography. The reliance on modern anthropological theory in *The Cultural Approach* presupposed that particular and fashionable branches of social sciences could, in the tradition of the progressives, supply a reliable and durable conceptual framework. Nevertheless, the A.H.A. programs demonstrated a new and more catholic approach to historical evidence, a greater willingness to examine explicitly the use of sociological concepts, and a broadening of the content of historiography.

World War II interrupted this promising set of developments, and when peace returned, political, intellectual, and academic controversies had dramatically changed. Soon the repudiation of deterministic and economic explanations would become so fashionable that the continuity between the work of the postwar historians and the new departures in historical method illustrated in *The Cultural Approach* would be thoroughly obscured. The historians who refashioned historical interpretation in the 1950s had first come to study history in the decade of Depression. Given Beard's prominence in those years and his role as the mentor of the intellectual left, it was tempting for historians trying to come to terms with their predecessors to focus unduly on the aspect of economic interpretation in Beard's most controversial and influential works. Yet to target the economic interpretation would be to obscure the long-term contribution that the progressives made to American historical method. Rather than transcend that contribution, the postwar historians would ironically reproduce its conceptual strengths and limitations.

NOTES

1. Examples of the conventional genre are Robert Skotheim, *American Intellectual Histories and Historians* (Princeton, N.J., 1966); Michael Kraus, *The Writing of American History* (Norman, Okla., 1953); Harvey Wish, *The American Historian: A Social-Intellectual History of the Writing of the American Past* (New York, 1960). An exception is William R. Keylor, *Academy and Community: The Foundation of the French Historical Profession* (Cambridge, Mass., 1975), and this deals with the discipline in another country.

2. Alan Creutz, "Social Access to the Professions: Late Nineteenth Century Academics at the University of Michigan as a Case Study," *Journal of Social History* 15 (1981): 73–87, argues that as the academy's professoriate became more professionalized, it became more restricted to the middle class. Yet this does not change the fact that within the ranks of the doctors, lawyers, and clergymen's sons that Creutz identifies, the process of selection became more meritocratic. No adequate study of this process exists for the historical profession, but see John Higham, with Leonard Krieger and Felix Gilbert, *History: The Development of Historical Studies in the United States* (Englewood Cliffs, N.J., 1965), pp. 62–65. More generally, see Alexandra Oleson and John Voss, eds., *The Organization of Knowledge in Modern America, 1860–1920* (Baltimore, 1979).

3. Turner to Carl Becker, 18 Dec. 1925, TU Box 34, Frederick Jackson Turner Papers, Huntington Library, San Marino, Calif.

4. On the European encounter with Marx, see H. Stuart Hughes, *Consciousness and Society: The Reorientation of European Social Thought, 1890–1930* (London, Harvester Press ed., 1979). For the key American contemporary view, Edwin R. A. Seligman, *The Economic Interpretation of History* (New York, 1902), esp. p. 48.

5. Richard Hofstadter, *The Progressive Historians: Turner, Beard, Parrington* (New York, 1968), p. 109.

6. Seligman, *Economic Interpretation of History*, pp. 106–9.

7. Ibid., p. 159.

8. Beard, rev. of Jaurès, in *Political Science Quarterly* 21 (1906): 111, 120.

9. Pradeep Bandyopadhyay, "The Many Faces of French Marxism," *Science and Society* 36 (1972): 132.

10. Carl Becker, *Everyman His Own Historian: Essays on History and Politics* (New York, 1935), pp. 113–31; David W. Marcell, "Charles Beard: Civilization and the Revolt against Empiricism," *American Quarterly* 21 (1969): 79; Harry Elmer Barnes, *A History of Historical Writing* (Norman, Okla., 1938), pp. 395–96.

11. Steven Lukes, *Emile Durkheim: His Life and Work: A Historical and Critical Study* (Harmondsworth, Middx., 1975), p. 403; Terry N. Clark, *Prophets and Patrons: The French Universities and the Emergence of the Social Sciences* (Cambridge, Mass., 1973), pp. 166, 172, 173, 177; Marc Bloch, *The Royal Touch: Sacred Monarchy and Scrofula in England and France*, trans. J. E. Anderson (London, 1973); Georg Iggers,

New Directions in European Historiography (Middletown, Conn., 1975), pp. 54–55; Keyler, *Academy and Community*, chaps. 9–10, is very pertinent to the French comparisons in this chapter.

12. Clark, *Prophets and Patrons*, pp. 173, 190; Gareth Stedman Jones, "History: The Poverty of Empiricism," in Robin Blackburn, ed., *Ideology in Social Science: Readings in Critical Social Theory* (Glasgow, 1972), pp. 100–104; Lukes, *Durkheim*, pp. 332–50.

13. Iggers, *New Directions*, pp. 49–50, 56–57; Lukes, *Durkheim*, pp. 338–44.

14. David Shi, *Matthew Josephson: Bourgeois Bohemian* (New Haven, 1981), pp. 152–53; Henry F. May, "The Rebellion of the Intellectuals," *American Quarterly* 8 (1956): 114–26; Phil L. Snyder, "Carl L. Becker and the Great War: A Crisis for a Humane Intelligence," *Western Political Quarterly* 9 (1956): 1–10.

15. Carol S. Gruber, *Mars and Minerva: World War One and the Uses of the Higher Learning in America* (Baton Rouge, 1975), pp. 8, 121–22, 124, 144–45, 151–57, 159, 241, 255–57; Ellen Nore, *Charles A. Beard: An Intellectual Biography* (Carbondale and Edwardsville, Ill., 1983), p. 86; Snyder, "Becker," p. 9.

16. Vernon L. Parrington, "A Chapter in American Liberalism," in Parrington, *The Beginnings of Critical Realism in America, 1860–1920* (New York, 1930), pp. 400–413; Granville Hicks, "The Critical Principles of Vernon L. Parrington," *Science and Society* 3 (1939): 466.

17. Arthur M. Schlesinger, Sr., *In Retrospect: The History of a Historian* (New York, 1963), p. 195; John D. Hicks, *My Life with History: An Autobiography* (Lincoln, Neb., 1968), pp. 354–55; Roy F. Nichols, *A Historian's Progress* (New York, 1968), p. 277; Warren Sussman, "Merle Curti," in *International Encyclopedia of the Social Sciences*, vol. 18, Biographical Supplement (New York, 1979), p. 133.

18. Beard, quoted in Cushing Strout, *The Pragmatic Revolt in American History: Carl Becker and Charles Beard* (New Haven, 1958), p. 89; Harlan B. Phillips, "Charles Beard, Walter Vrooman, and the Founding of Ruskin Hall," *South Atlantic Quarterly* 50 (1951): 186–91; Charles Beard, "Ruskin and the Babble of Tongues," *New Republic* 87 (1936): 370–72; John Braeman, "Charles A. Beard: The English Experience," *Journal of American Studies* 15 (1981): 165–90, esp. pp. 177, 185–86.

19. John Braeman, "Charles A. Beard: Historian and Progressive," in Marvin C. Swanson, ed., *Charles A. Beard: An Observance of the Centennial of His Birth* (Greencastle, Ind., 1976), p. 59; Hofstadter, *Progressive Historians*, p. 181.

20. Jones, "Empiricism," pp. 103–4; Stefan Collini, *Liberalism and Sociology: L. T. Hobhouse and Political Argument in England, 1880–1914* (Cambridge, Eng., 1979); Bernard C. Borning, *The Political and Social Thought of Charles A. Beard* (Seattle, 1962), pp. 183–84, 193; Michael Freeden, *The New Liberalism: An Ideology of Social Reform* (Oxford, 1978).

21. Quoted in Braeman, "Beard: Historian and Progressive," pp. 55, 59.

22. Frederick Jackson Turner, *The Frontier in American History* (New York, 1920), pp. 285, 324.

23. Frederick Jackson Turner, *The Significance of Sections in American History* (New York, 1932), p. 339.

24. For an introduction to this vast subject, see the essays in John M. Laslett and Seymour Martin Lipset, eds., *Failure of a Dream? Essays in the History of American Socialism* (Garden City, N.Y., 1970).

25. Thomas L. Haskell, "Are Professors Professional? The Organization of Knowledge in Modern America, 1860–1920," *Journal of Social History* 14 (1981): 488–90.

26. I have been influenced in what follows by Michel Foucault, *Power/Knowledge: Selected Interviews and Other Writings, 1972–1977*, ed. Colin Gordon (New York, 1980).

27. W. Stull Holt, *Historical Scholarship in the United States and Other Essays* (Seattle, 1967), pp. 3–63.

28. William B. Hesseltine and Louis Kaplan, "Doctors of Philosophy in History: A Statistical Study," *American Historical Review* 47 (1942): 766; Warren F. Kuehl, *Dissertations in History, 1873–1960* (Lexington, Ky., 1965), pp. xii–xiii.

29. Kuehl, *Dissertations in History*, pp. xii–xiii; Marcus W. Jernegan, "Productivity of Doctors of Philosophy in History," *American Historical Review* 33 (1927): 1–22.

30. Arthur M. Schlesinger, Sr., "History," in Wilson Gee, ed., *Research in the Social Sciences* (New York, 1929), p. 217; Barnes, *History of Historical Writing*, p. 368.

31. Theodore Clark Smith, "The Writing of American History in America from 1884 to 1934," *American Historical Review* 40 (1935): 445, 447. On Andrews' contribution, see A. S. Eisenstadt, *Charles McLean Andrews: A Study in American Historical Writing* (New York, 1956).

32. Hicks, *My Life with History*, p. 83.

33. Eisenstadt, *Andrews*, pp. 144–59. It is not implied that only historians trained in the United States conceived of history primarily as a craft, though it is possibly significant that Marc Bloch's *Apologie pour L'histoire ou Métier d'Historien* was translated into English under the narrower title of *The Historian's Craft*, trans. Peter Putnam (New York, 1953).

34. Hicks, *My Life with History*, e.g., pp. 147–48, 157; Oscar Handlin, *Truth in History* (Cambridge, Mass., 1979), p. 60.

35. Kuehl, *Dissertations in History*, pp. xii–xiii; Frank Freidel, "American Historians: A Bicentennial Appraisal," *Journal of American History* 63 (1976): 6–11; Hesseltine and Kaplan, "Doctors of Philosophy," pp. 782–83; Emil Pocock, "Presidents of the American Historical Association: A Statistical Analysis," *American Historical Review* 89 (1984): 1020, 1022–23. The Americanists among this group of A.H.A. presidents have been checked against the relevant editions of *Who Was Who in America* and the *Dictionary of American Biography*.

36. Morey D. Rothberg, " 'To Set a Standard of Workmanship and Compel Men to Conform to It': John Franklin Jameson as Editor of the *American Historical Review*," *American Historical Review* 89 (1984): 957–75; James L. Sellers, "Before We Were Members—the MVHA," *Mississippi Valley Historical Review* 40 (1953): 3–24; Clark, *Prophets and Patrons*, pp. 84–87; on the Turner Papers, see, for example, Turner to Prof. L. C. Marshall, 17 Feb. 1925, TU Box 34.

37. Kuehl, *Dissertations in History*, pp. xii–xiii; Hesseltine and Kaplan, "Doctors of Philosophy," pp. 756–57.

38. Hesseltine and Kaplan, "Doctors of Philosophy," p. 784.

39. Ibid.; Gregory M. Tobin, *The Making of a History: Walter Prescott Webb and "The Great Plains"* (Austin, Tex., 1976); Necah Stewart Furman, *Walter Prescott Webb: His Life and Impact* (Albuquerque, N.Mex., 1976).

40. Schlesinger, "History," p. 223; Barnes, *History of Historical Writing*, p. 367; Nichols, *Historian's Progress*, pp. 241–42.

41. Higham, *History*, pp. 100, 107.

42. Dexter Perkins and John Snell, *The Education of Historians in the United States* (New York, 1962), pp. 151, 157, 171, 186–87.

43. Jernegan, "Productivity," p. 15.

44. Perkins and Snell, *Education of Historians*, p. 171; Hesseltine and Kaplan, "Doctors of Philosophy," p. 769.

45. Richard H. Shryock, "Nature and Objectives of the American Civilization Program," in report of the sixty-third annual meeting of the American Historical Association," in *American Historical Review* 54 (1949): 739; Sussman, "Merle Curti," p. 135; Handlin, *Truth in History*, pp. 79–80; Gene Wise, "An American Studies Calendar," *American Quarterly* 31 (Bibliographical issue, 1979): 414–15. For the *Annales* parallel, see Tobin, *Webb*, pp. 111–12; cf. Peter Burke, ed., *A New Kind of History: From the Writings of Febvre* (London, 1973), pp. ix–xi.

46. Walter Prescott Webb, "The Historical Seminar: Its Outer Shell and Its Inner Spirit," *Mississippi Valley Historical Review* 42 (1955): 3–23; Nichols, *Historian's Progress*, p. 33; Hicks, *My Life with History*, pp. 87–88; Howard K. Beale, *The Critical Year: A Study of Andrew Johnson and Reconstruction* (New York, rev. ed., 1958), p. viii; Eisenstadt, *Andrews*, pp. 152–53; W. L. Fleming et al., *Studies in History and Politics Inscribed to W. A. Dunning* (New York, 1914); Lois K. Mathews et al., *Essays in American History Dedicated to Frederick Jackson Turner* (New York, 1910).

47. Perkins and Snell, *Education of Historians*, p. 152.

48. N. Ray Hiner, "Professions in Process: Changing Relations between Historians and Educators, 1896–1911," *History of Education Quarterly* 12 (1972): 48–52.

49. Nore, *Beard*, p. 127.

50. Schlesinger, *In Retrospect*, pp. 53, 197.

51. Mary O. Furner, *Advocacy and Objectivity: A Crisis in the Professionalization of American Social Science, 1865–1905* (Louisville, Ky., 1975); Thomas L. Haskell, *The Emergence of Professional Social Science: The American Social Science Association and the Nineteenth-Century Crisis of Authority* (Urbana, Ill., 1977); Dorothy Ross, "Socialism and American Liberalism: Academic Social Thought in the 1880's," *Perspectives in American History* 11 (1977–1978): 62–63; Edward A. Purcell, Jr., *The Crisis of Democratic Theory: Scientific Naturalism and the Problem of Value* (Lexington, Ky., 1973).

52. Beard, rev. of J. A. Hobson in *Political Science Quarterly* 25 (1910): 530; Ray Allen Billington, *Frederick Jackson Turner: Historian, Scholar, Teacher* (New York, 1973), pp. 147–48, 293–94; Hofstadter, *Progressive Historians*, pp. 285–86.

53. Laurence Veysey, *The Emergence of the American University* (Chicago, 1965), pp. 317–32; Clark, *Prophets and Patrons*, pp. 86–89; Billington, *Turner*, pp. 154–56, 297–300, 385–86; George Weisz, *The Emergence of Modern Universities in France, 1863–1914* (Princeton, N.J., 1983), pp. 270–71, 290–91, 292; Oleson and Voss, eds., *Organization of Knowledge*, p. 298.

54. John R. Commons, *Myself: The Autobiography of John R. Commons* (New York, 1934), pp. 58, 95; George D. Blackwood, "Frederick Jackson Turner and John Rogers Commons: Complementary Thinkers," *Mississippi Valley Historical Review* 41 (1954): 479; Joseph Dorfman, *The Economic Mind in American Civilization*, 3 vols. (New York, 1949), 3: 288, 291.

55. Nore, *Beard*, p. 87; Veysey, *Emergence of the American University*, p. 87; Alvin Johnson, *Pioneer's Progress* (New York, 1962), p. 275.

56. Curti to Turner, 13 Aug. 1928, TU Box 39, Turner Papers.

57. Maurice Blinkhoff, "The Influence of Charles A. Beard Upon American Historiography," *University of Buffalo Studies* 12 (May 1936): 31, 36, 38.

58. Ibid., pp. 31, 75; Hofstadter, *Progressive Historians*, pp. 218–20, 477.

59. Reports of the fifty-fourth and fifty-fifth annual meetings of the American Historical Association in *American Historical Review* 45 (1940): 509, 510, 516; and ibid., 46 (1941): 525, 531, 544–48.

60. Caroline Ware, ed., *The Cultural Approach to History* (New York, 1940), pp. 10, 13–14.

3

The Postwar Reorientation:
Political and Ideological Contexts

The drift away from Beard and the tidy labels of subsequent historiographers notwithstanding, there was no such unified movement as consensus history in the post–World War II period. In certain senses, the writing of history in the period was extraordinarily diverse. Some historians like Louis Hartz dwelt upon the history of political ideas and thought, while others like Daniel Boorstin wrote of a pragmatic American past in which doing had taken precedence over thinking. Some, like Samuel Eliot Morison, proclaimed "sane" conservative values, yet others, like Henry Steele Commager and Howard Beale, continued to champion liberal ideals. Many historians of the 1950s were politically and intellectually hostile to communism, but important differences separated the anticommunism of a "vital center" liberal like Arthur Schlesinger, Jr., and the increasingly conservative stance of others like Boorstin. Some historians called loudly, as Conyers Read did, for a scholarly war against totalitarian communism, but many more condemned marxism only indirectly through their attacks on the dangers of relativism. There were writers in the fifties like Richard Hofstadter who made delicious use of irony on almost every page while others—Boorstin again comes to mind—did not. Some of the most prominent historians, like C. Vann Woodward and Schlesinger, were not consensus historians at all. Change over time was also evident. The immediate postwar period, ending roughly around 1950, was very much a transitional phase in which the Beardian influence was still important. Though the 1950s was the high point of anti-Beardian, conservative, and consensus varieties of thought, by the end of the decade the counterattack of John Higham against the "cult of consensus" anticipated the reaction of the New Left in the 1960s.[1]

What still stands out amid this diversity and complexity in American historical interpretation is firstly the repudiation of economic determinism of the Beardian variety, and then secondly the growing importance of social science to the creation of an alternative, if more politically conservative, liberal synthesis.

Because these two trends have exerted such a lasting impact upon contemporary American historiography, they shall be systematically analyzed in the next two chapters.

It is important to realize that the historians who shaped the study of American history in the first two decades after 1945 perpetuated the liberal tradition. This does not mean they were all liberals in the sense of supporting Adlai Stevenson, though many were. Much of the scholarship of the fifties and early sixties was increasingly conservative in its political and ideological implications. There was a growing distrust of mass political action and criticism of the role of and need for ideology in many histories, including those of such writers as Stanley Elkins, David Donald, and Richard Hofstadter. The need for strong institutions to restrain popular "excess" also figured prominently, as did the focus on the importance of astute and pragmatic rather than idealistic or revolutionary leadership and thought.[2]

For all that, most historians did not abandon the boundaries of liberal history. The most important scholars of the 1950s all wrote within the methodological and epistemological shadows of the progressives, as the next chapter will demonstrate. In political and philosophical terms, too, they remained men and women who were deeply attached to the liberal state. For all the talk about the new conservatism in America, it is worth remembering that the leading historians of the period still believed in the special virtues of an American-style democracy, and the role of the individual within that system. Those writers like Hofstadter, Donald, Handlin, and Elkins who were critical of aspects of the reform tradition in the American past nevertheless tended to support in their historical analysis pragmatic reform, and often aligned themselves with the New Deal tradition of positive liberalism and the use of government to improve the welfare of individuals. Their representative publications still shared, moreover, a conception of American history ordered in terms of critical public events associated with the evolution of democracy, and the strengthening of the nation-state. Indeed, the wartime and postwar problems intensified this focus so that even the interest in social history now tended to be forced back into this mold. A series of essays edited by Daniel Aaron in 1952—*America in Crisis*—containing contributions from prominent historians like Richard Hofstadter, pursued precisely these themes translated into the uncertain postwar era.[3]

As in any complex intellectual tradition, some prominent authors only partially conform to these generalizations or provide exceptions to them. Yet even writers who proclaimed conservative values drew heavily on the accumulated tradition of American liberalism. While Samuel Eliot Morison called for a conservative history to balance the dominant liberal tradition, he confessed that his "own approach" was the "Jefferson–Jackson–F. D. Roosevelt line." He still believed that this line "is the one that the mainstream of United States 'actuality' has followed, just as British 'actuality' is best explained by historians who write in the Whig-Liberal-Labour tradition."[4] Daniel Boorstin's discovery of the nonideological character of the American people had politically conservative implications, but Boorstin drew on ideas of America's unique experience and its superior material and philosophical resources that informed the writings of progressive historians. He never doubted that American history was the Whiggish story of the unfolding of the democratic experience of individual freedom forged and maintained by a practical people. What distinguished him from both Beard and Hofstadter was his *uncritical* endorsement of America's practical achievements, and it was this celebratory attitude above all else which gravely limited the acceptance of his work within the academy.[5]

The new generation of historians played down or in many cases entirely abandoned the Beardian notion that American history was characterized by conflict between economic groups or classes. The United States was a middle-class society, and unlike European societies, it displayed little or no disagreement over its basic political ideology. This emphasis upon common political beliefs accounts for the tendency to label these writers as consensus historians. Yet it would certainly be a mistake to assume that most of them presented views of American history devoid of conflict and change. In place of the economic conflict of Beardian history, they tended to substitute conflict over cultural, social status, or intellectual questions. Where they did depict economic controversy, it was presented as much more pluralistic or complex in character than the simple dualism of the progressive historians.

The range of issues challenged in this reorientation stretched across the topography of American history from the colonial era to the New Deal. The Revolution was reinterpreted as a pragmatic revolt against British dominance, not an internal social conflict. Simultaneously, Beard's view of the constitution was exposed to sustained empirical critiques by Forrest McDonald and Robert E. Brown. Scholars of the antebellum years found rising, expectant capitalists, not democratic populists, when they examined Jacksonian democracy, while the significance of the Civil War as a bourgeois economic revolution came under attack from several historians who tried to show the divisions within northern capitalism over Civil War and Reconstruction policies. When the postprogressive historians turned to that great failure of consensus, the origins of the Civil War, they interpreted it in very politically conservative terms as a breakdown of institutional restraints, or the product of irrational abolitionist agitators suffering status anxiety. The same approach adopted in analyses of the abolitionists was meted out to the participants in another great movement for social and political change in nineteenth-century America: the populists appeared no longer as embattled farmers pitted against robber barons, but as psychologically disturbed or prejudiced protesters against an urban industrial order that threatened their status. The robber barons of Beardian history themselves reemerged in the work of Allan Nevins as farsighted industrial statesmen who created the material foundation for international leadership against communism. Not all of these interpretations won easy or complete acceptance within the profession but the trend of scholarship in the 1950s was clear enough.[6]

The relationship of the historians who produced these new postwar interpretations and syntheses to marxism is complex. On one level the rejection of Beardian interpretation involved a common rejection of marxism as a more extreme form of Beardian error. But the major efforts of the postprogressives were directed against their historiographical mentors, and their relations to marxism were tangential to that scholarly debate. Hence references to marxism are rather rare and cryptic, and undoubtedly do not reveal the complex dimensions of that relationship. These historians were, so far as it is possible to make out from their published writings, less concerned with rejecting marxism as a social theory than they were with repudiating the manifestations of American marxism that they had encountered in the late 1930s, or the marxism manifest in the contemporary Soviet state. The latter, in particular, was a difficult cross to bear for marxism's reputation in the United States after 1945.

Daniel Boorstin was one historian who tended to conflate marxism and the experience of communism as a "political dogma." He failed in his references to Marx to give attention to the latter's important theoretical and empirical contributions to the study of society, and instead concentrated on criticisms of the "terrifying" twentieth-century experience of revolution inspired by "a blueprint for remaking society." Boorstin felt that all such attempts to revolutionize social relationships through the overthrow of existing institutions and "by abolishing economic classes," such as Marx had proposed, were bound to fail. Boorstin favored a more pessimistic view that "the prior limitations of human nature" had "made exploitation and institutions inevitable." America's "genius" consisted in the absence of such theoretical delusions of perfectibility. The interpretation Boorstin offered of the American past was closely bound up with his understanding and rejection of marxism. Boorstin's explicit anticommunism led him in the 1950s to seek a unique, nonideological American history grounded in the realities of American experience.[7]

If Boorstin felt marxist theories could not fit the facts of America's unique history, so too in different ways did Louis Hartz. *The Liberal Tradition in America* was, read on one level, an extended commentary on the irrelevance of European marxism to American development. Hartz explicitly rejected marxism, therefore, as "a single factor theory" whose claims were essentially "religious." This is not to say that Hartz was uninfluenced by marxism, however. One of the strengths of Hartz's book was its incorporation of certain marxist insights within a nonmarxist framework. Hartz believed that "Marxist categories" of analysis could, when creatively applied to the American scene, prove illuminating. It was out of an understanding of the dialectic between feudalism, liberal capitalism, and socialism that the notion of a "liberal society" sprang. The United States differed from Europe in that it had no feudal past. Lacking a feudal regime struggling against bourgeois reform, it failed also to develop a strong socialist movement struggling for radical change. Yet insofar as this analysis drew on Marx, it was the marxism of the Popular Front and revolutionary sloganeering. Hartz talked in such broad terms as feudalism, capitalism, and socialism, and treated these as undifferentiated abstractions without discussing their specific economic or cultural content. Interested only in the realm of political ideas, Hartz produced a book based in part on a caricature of marxism derived from his understanding of Stalinist marxism, as experienced in the United States in the 1930s and 1940s. If Hartz knew more of the variety and complexity of the marxist tradition, he did not display it in his text and footnotes. In fact, the only direct reference to European marxist writings was *The Communist Manifesto*, cited from a one-volume handbook of marxism published in the United States in the 1930s. In contrast, American marxist writings of the 1930s are directly engaged in Hartz's text in a way which suggests a more complex acquaintance.[8]

Richard Hofstadter, like Boorstin and Hartz, was intimately acquainted with the Popular Front marxism of the 1930s, and he too tended to dismiss the complexities of marxist method and philosophy on the basis of this brief encounter. His reference in later works to marxism were tantalizingly slight, but he did focus on the weak and vulgar determinism which passed for marxism in the Depression decade in America. He drew heavily on Seligman's view, which he described as "sensible" in its assessment of marxism and the importance of the "economic factor" in history, but concluded against any endorsement of a single factor theory of history.[9]

Just as the views of the past developed by Boorstin and Hartz were influenced by their understanding and rejection of marxism, so too was this true of Richard Hofstadter. Neither Boorstin's synthesis nor Hartz's was to prove, however, as useful or as influential as Hofstadter's narrower concept of symbolic politics. Hartz's liberal society notion seemed too abstract, too confined to the realm of articulate political ideas, too independent of changing historical contexts. Boorstin's view seemed too disparaging of ideas to be taken very seriously. Hofstadter, in contrast, focused on popular ideology and thus provided the crucial link between intellectual history on the one hand and political and economic history on the other. Hofstadter's theory apparently had its origins in his dissatisfaction with the base/superstructure formulation of orthodox marxism. The notion that the economic base determined the political and ideological superstructure "in the last instance" begged the question of what constituted the last analysis. Hofstadter, like many others, saw the possibility of an infinite regression of causes which ultimately explained nothing.[10]

Instead, Hofstadter proposed a new pluralistic liberal compromise that would incorporate economic causation in a larger and more diverse theory of historical explanation. As always the most thoughtful of the postwar historians, Hofstadter did not attempt in theory to deny "the reality, or even the primacy, of the problems of money and power." He claimed only that too much attention had been devoted to such matters at the expense of defining "their reality by turning attention to the human context in which they arise and in which they have to be settled." He professed only to agree that to this concern with structure and economic reality there should be "supplemented . . . another which amplifies our sense of political life and does justice to the variety of political activity." Hofstadter adopted the term *symbolic politics* to describe the territory where popular ideology, politics, and culture intersected. To underpin his focus on symbolic perceptions, he drew on the textual analyses of modern literary criticism, Karl Mannheim's conception of ideology as mediating between reality and perception, and American anthropology's increasingly influential depiction of culture as a unifying and pervasive force.[11]

Hofstadter's attempt to provide a pluralistic alternative to economistic theories of material causation was innovative and challenging, but not without its own ambiguities and facile reasoning. His formulation left important problems unresolved. It tended to suggest a dichotomy between the empirical reality of economic interests and the symbolic ways in which those interests are perceived. By doing so, Hofstadter's formulation perpetuated the progressive historians' naturalistic presentation of that dichotomy. Then, having distinguished analytically between material reality and symbolic perceptions, Hofstadter said that noneconomic influences must be taken into account, and that more attention should be paid to the symbolic aspects of human life. Such a vague formulation skirts rather than settles the question raised by his methodology: exactly how important are economic and structural influences, and how important are the symbolic, cultural issues that Hofstadter gives prominence? Hofstadter implied at times in some of his more general statements of principle that the latter were not so important as the former, but his own detailed historical writing suggests the opposite conclusion. His treatment of prohibition, for example, as symbolic politics and thus "a historical detour" from "the great economic interests" and from "the main trend of class politics" is a pertinent example. Hofstadter did not supplement an economic interpretation of prohibition with his own symbolic one. He used the example of prohibition to propose an alternative to political economy, and to reinforce the general thrust of his interpretation in *The Age of Reform*. This was to depict the political conflicts of the progressive era as battles of status groups, not economic "interests."[12]

The problem of primary causation over which Hofstadter is so deliberately evasive would evaporate if we ceased to view the intellectual, cultural, and economic domains of human action in positivistic terms as causes or factors to be ranked hierarchically to explain human actions. At times Hofstadter comes close to abandoning this positivistic formulation; in the preface to *The Paranoid Style in American Politics and Other Essays*, Hofstadter hints that there is a sense in which the symbolic representations actually "define the reality" and not merely the representations of economic and other "material" interests of politics. Yet if we read Hofstadter in this way, he only resolves the problem of a positivistic formulation of human action by a sleight of hand that *reduces* economic phenomena to their symbolic representations.[13]

If the major historians of the 1950s shared, despite differences of emphasis, a common intellectual orientation that rejected both Beardian economic interpretation and marxism as a cruder form of Beardianism, the sources of this repudiation of economic class interpretation remain much more deeply controversial. The most obvious explanation would seem to lie in the virulent and pervasive anticommunist purge which took place in the late 1940s and early 1950s, yet this explanation has recently been challenged by a number of intellectual historians. The flight from Marx and Beard has in various ways been located by Robert Skotheim, John P. Diggins, and Gene Wise in an antitotalitarian reaction which called into question in the late 1930s naive assumptions about liberal progress, particularly faith in reason, in human nature, in the use of government to change mankind, in progress itself. The experience of fascism and Stalinism in Europe combined to make American intellectuals more wary of utopian ideologies, less inclined to endorse movements of social protest associated with them. One result of this intellectual reorientation was an equation of marxism with German Nazism, and their simultaneous rejection by liberals. Another consequence was a reaffirmation of American democratic values while at the same time questioning those American historical interpretations of a left-liberal variety which had emphasized the economic conflict between the people and big business.[14]

There are, however, severe problems with an interpretation which locates the rejection of Beardian history in the antitotalitarianism of the late 1930s. The alleged discovery of totalitarianism among the progressive historians did not entail abandonment of their progressive interpretation of American history until the early 1950s. Merle Curti's *Growth of American Thought*, as Robert Skotheim himself admits, was "a historical Bible for reformers" *as well as* "a book for free men in an era of totalitarianism." It is true that Carl Becker, under the impact of events in Europe in the late 1930s, began to take a more genial view of American history that emphasized the democratic consensus rather than economic conflict and social injustice. He began to reaffirm the "generalities that still glitter" in American democracy, and he stressed that the flexible American system was infinitely preferable to Nazism or Stalinism. This intellectual mood of democratic affirmation did not lead, however, to a cold war anticommunism. Unlike some later liberals such as Arthur Schlesinger, Jr., who turned their faith in American democracy into an anticommunist holy war, Becker warned shortly before his death in 1945 against trying to impose an American solution on Eastern Europe at the expense of world peace, since the Russians clearly had the largest stake there.[15]

Nor was the change in the liberal historians to an anticommunist perspective immediately apparent in the early work of Schlesinger. The threat of totalitarianism was plain enough, if only implicit in the Foreword to his *Age of Jackson* in 1945, but Schlesinger did not repudiate there his indebtedness to the progressive interpretation. Instead, the progressive interpretation of Jacksonian Democracy was utilized as evidence of democracy's flexibility and capacity for orderly change, thus rendering violent social and political upheaval such as had occurred in Europe in the 1930s and 1940s unnecessary in America.[16]

Gene Wise, in his *American Historical Explanations: A Strategy for Grounded Inquiry*, attempts to resolve the problems in the antitotalitarian view by invoking

Thomas Kuhn's concept of an intellectual paradigm of scholarship. The paradigm—for Wise—is a set of assumptions or "intervening filters" governing intellectual inquiry in a particular discipline. There was one set of assumptions filtering reality under the progressive paradigm, and another under the counterprogressive paradigm of the 1950s. The first centered around concepts of progress and faith in human nature, while irony, complexity, and symbolic meaning defined the counterprogressive paradigm. Under the impact of economic and foreign crises, the first set of assumptions had been, Wise argues, irretrievably undermined in the late 1930s. The anomalous evidence contradicting the old view had become overwhelming, even though occasional reaffirmations of the liberal progressive faith would still occur. Yet Wise dwells unduly on the initial breakup of the alleged progressive paradigm, and is unable to tell us how or why the new counterprogressive view emerged as the dominant force in the 1950s. He focuses too mechanically on identifying the shift in the intellectual orientation of the profession, while largely ignoring the surrounding social and political context in which the shift took place. Part of the problem lies in Wise's adoption of the concept of paradigm; it is not at all clear that progressives and counterprogressives each constituted a definable intellectual paradigm in the manner of the physical sciences. It is for this reason that Wise is unable to tell us precisely when or why the presentation of new and potentially anomalous evidence can no longer be contained within the paradigm. Whatever the merits of this attempt to apply Kuhn's controversial theories of science to the more amorphous methodologies and concepts that have characterized historical scholarship, Wise is at pains to deny the political and social context in so profound a way that it is essential to confront his analysis of the postwar political situation and its impact on scholarship.[17]

If Wise has not satisfactorily explained the divergent tendencies in postprogressive scholarship, and located far too rigidly a crucial turning point in the late 1930s, he has also underrated the importance of political anticommunism in the late 1940s and early 1950s. The two go together; in order to show the significance of totalitarianism, it was necessary to gloss over changes in politics and ideology after 1945 that were profoundly important for American historiography.

He plays down the role of political McCarthyism in the 1950s, denying that the postprogressives minimized conflict or were uncritical of American social and political institutions. Wise buttresses his point of view with reference to a study by Paul Lazarsfeld and Wagner Thielens, Jr., on the academic community and McCarthyism. This study, Wise tells us, shows that

McCarthyism may have cowed high school teachers, or professors at the more vulnerable state colleges and fundamentalist religious institutions. But scholars at Harvard and Minnesota and Yale and Berkeley and Michigan are not likely to be that vulnerable to outside pressures. Their home institutions can serve as a buffer for them, so also their national professions. This may not insulate them from all outside influences. But it does give them distance and leverage, so they can usually respond to such influences in their own way, and often in their own time.[18]

Wise ignored the obvious point that peer group pressure may be the greatest in maintaining uniformity, and that the very illusion of detachment may lead to bias in favor of pluralist as opposed to class analysis. He also ignores the fact that private, elite institutions were not immune to the subtle but effective presentation of marxism as crude, and does not consider the possibility that group pressure indirectly inhibited the development of marxist scholarship.

It seems necessary therefore, despite Wise's assurances, to look again at the postwar ideological and political transformation of the United States which goes under the general name of the cold war against communism. Here the evidence of influence is profound though indirect. Even Lazarsfeld and Thielens' own survey analysis, on which Wise relies, demonstrates the very real atmosphere of coercion and political conformity that helped to set back marxist studies for a generation. Of those social scientists interviewed in the survey, 63 percent perceived increased political pressures against radical ideas and commitments at their institutions, and they expressed concern at this trend. Leftists and liberals testified that they felt uncomfortable discussing current political attitudes. They also felt it necessary to balance any leftish opinions with more conservative ones, and they noted that they were sometimes reported by students to university administrators, politicians, and others for leaning toward the left. Lazarsfeld and Thielens conclude: "Broadly speaking . . . American social scientists felt in the spring of 1955 that the intellectual and political freedom of the teaching community had been noticeably curtailed, or at least disturbingly threatened."[19]

True, the coercion was most often felt at the state schools, rather than private universities and colleges, but on the other hand, pressure increased or rather was perceived to have increased "as we move up the quality rating of institutions." While "quality" institutions had administrations that were more likely than others to defend their faculty from outside attacks, the authors made the very valid point that "the difficult years" of McCarthyite hysteria "put the superior college under especially heavy strain," showing that "the problem goes considerably beyond the realm of the rights of individual teachers. It was the very quality of social science teaching and of inquiry as a whole which was put into jeopardy."[20]

More recently, David Caute's *The Great Fear: The Anti-Communist Purge under Truman and Eisenhower* has demonstrated how extensive the anticommunist influence was. He notes that the attack extended beyond teachers and small state colleges to such "great universities" as the Massachusetts Institute of Technology and Harvard. Those who refused to take the state-imposed anticommunist oath in the University of California system in 1950 were fired, and as a result, the university lost "men of great distinction." After reviewing the wide range of available evidence concerning this and similar episodes in the struggle for thought control, Caute concludes sensibly that "it is surely no coincidence'' that ''the whole concept of ideology'' was at this time declared obsolete, and left-wing opinion equated with fascist irrationality.[21]

Nor should it be assumed that the anticommunist hysteria was merely a product of McCarthy. Academic repression of communists had actually occurred as early as 1941, when the Rapp-Coudert hearings in New York City had removed some fifty teachers from the school and university system for their communist associations. Among those victimized were Philip Foner, Irving Mark, and Herbert Morais, all young scholars of United States history. After World War II, the purge resumed on a national scale, with professional journals generally excluding the academic work of these and other scholars while universities denied them jobs. Herbert Aptheker, a Columbia Ph.D. of 1943 who studied under John Krout, did not receive an academic appointment until 1969–1970, when he taught for one semester at Bryn Mawr. Though Aptheker's work was often strident in tone, he did pioneer many aspects of the study of black history and slavery. Yet approximately fifty universities in the two decades after World War II thought him unworthy of even a temporary appointment. As late as 1976, a controversy raged around his attempt to teach a one-semester course on W.E.B. DuBois at Yale in the Davenport College seminar series. Members of Yale's history department opposed the proposal and delayed its implementation, though Aptheker subsequently taught the course under the auspices of the political science department. The quality of Aptheker's scholarship is not at issue here. After all, among other temporary appointments at Yale was Howard Cosell, who taught a course on ''Big Time Sport and Contemporary America.'' What must be noted, rather, was the unwillingness of Yale's history department to give Aptheker's views even a temporary airing.[22]

Some of the historians affected by the purges may not have been candidates for professional prominence in any case, but some clearly were. Sir Moses Finley (Moses Finkelstein), who was a victim of the Rapp-Coudert inquisition in the early 1940s, and again under the Senate Internal Security Subcommittee in 1952, was one whose subsequent career as a historian (in Britain) has been most distinguished. Dismissed from Rutgers in 1952, he took part-time jobs until he left the country in 1955. Philip Foner had been called a ''non-indoctrinating Communist'' at the time of the Rapp-Coudert hearings, and a number of prominent historians had objected to his dismissal from New York's City College. His *Business and Slavery* had been favorably reviewed in leading historical journals. Nevertheless, Foner had considerable difficulty in returning to academic life after World War II, and not until 1967 did he receive a (minor) university post. Another historian affected was Sigmund Diamond, who has subsequently worked as a sociologist at Columbia. He was denied a minor administrative and teaching post at Harvard in the mid–1950s for prior Communist Party associations. Still others were not marxists. John W. Caughey of UCLA was one of three historians dismissed from the University of California system for refusal to take the noncommunist oath mandated by the Board of Regents. Caughey did not suffer long term damage to his career, if his later presidency of the Organization of American Historians is any guide. But he did, like many other victims of the hysteria, incur a protracted legal battle to regain his job, a battle which lasted three years.

Such episodes are not merely important in themselves. These cases had a more insidious effect, since they represent only the visible portion of the structure of intimidation. At California, for example, a total of twenty-six academics in a variety of disciplines received dismissals, but nearly double that number of outsiders, including leading scholars, refused to take appointments in the state system. The impact of such pressure on historiography can only be surmised. Certainly the influence of anticommunist hysteria cannot be precisely quantified, or measured against the yardstick of the few celebrated cases of historians who were directly coerced. There was in addition the indirect intimidation and the impact of a climate of fear on the unknown number of possible, future historians of marxist persuasion.[23]

When all is said and done, the significance of these purges in inhibiting marxist scholarship must not be exaggerated. Far more important was the production of new knowledge which bypassed and supplanted the Beardian formulations and contemporary caricatures of marxism. Nonetheless, the purges constituted a process of exclusion which complemented the intellectual transformation of scholarship. Exclusion and transformation interacted in such a way that it is difficult to separate coercion from the productive processes of professional change. The hysteria foreclosed the possibility that Popular Front marxism would mutate in significant theoretical and intellectual directions after World War II, as it did in Britain. The purges also foreclosed the possibility that talented younger people would consider marxism in the 1950s. One consequence was that when the intellectual challenge to liberalism came in the 1960s, the radicals reflected in their rejection of Old Left orthodoxy and their search for a usable radical past the atrophy of a stymied marxist tradition as much as did the attitudes and historiographical approaches of the liberals they opposed.[24]

While some leftist scholars were actively discouraged from pursuing academic careers in history and related disciplines, governments, businesses, foundations, and universities sponsored after World War II a range of studies that developed more positive interpretations of American capitalism than had characterized the antibusiness studies of the Josephson genre in the 1930s. The multivolume history of the oil industry, partly supported by Standard Oil itself, provides a well-known example of this postwar trend. The implications of the oft-cited example of the postwar reinterpretation of Standard Oil are frequently misunderstood, however. The oil industry was one of a number of business groups aware that noncooperation or interference with the independent scholarly assessment of their concerns would be counterproductive. Much more important was the kind of positive knowledge that could be produced to show the complexity of business life. Such complexity inevitably contended with the simplistic polarities of business and people associated with the progressive indictment. For every historian hastening to reinterpret business in the light of postwar politics, there were many more like Thomas Cochran and Alfred D. Chandler, who were "much more interested in understanding American material success" than in "glorifying it." Nevertheless, the mere promotion of a new object of study had a pervasive impact. Foundation largesse and the proliferation of institutional networks for the study of business history did not determine the interpretations that emerged. Rather, such developments fostered attention on business history as a specialization, and this shifted the boundaries of historical discourse. Specialization was carried to an extreme in the genre of company histories that was one very important product of the new study of business. As William Miller noted in 1962, the spate of company histories which emerged in the 1940s and 1950s "indeed snuggle so closely to the 'administrative art' inside the company under study that its competitors, its customers, and indeed its relation to the country itself are characteristically slighted."[25]

Ideological conformity was promoted in much more subtle ways, however. Complementing overt repression and efforts to promote a more favorable view of business were developments which emphasized the diversity of American responses to the threat of communism. Ironically, the principled stand of certain liberals against McCarthyism reinforced an underlying consensus. Howard K. Beale and Henry Steele Commager were two historians who spoke out courageously against the political witch-hunters; but it is difficult to escape the conclusion that in denouncing McCarthy, they believed that they were upholding pluralistic American values against Russian thought control. Howard K. Beale's attack on Conyers Read's call in 1949 for historians to enlist, in effect, in the postwar ideological struggle against Soviet communism is an instructive example. Beale retorted that to suppress dissent or produce histories that served a partisan, cold war cause would be no different from "what on a large scale . . . the USSR has done to the destruction of all freedom."[26] The result of this laudable defense of dissent, in the context of cold war politics, however, was to take the focus away from repression to emphasize the democratic, pluralistic heritage of the United States, and to reinforce American images of Soviet totalitarianism. After all, McCarthy was eventually called to order and "good sense" did prevail. It was easy for Americans to forget the real results of the intimidation that occurred, and to become very self-congratulatory about the way McCarthyism was conquered. It was also easy to equate anticommunism with McCarthyism, and to forget that the phenomenon went much deeper, had begun much earlier, and lasted much longer than McCarthy's short period of notoriety. Only recently, through the fine research of Robert Griffith and others, have these points become clear. Only as a result of this work has the study of this crucial episode in American intellectual and political history begun to command the attention that it so urgently deserves.[27]

The responses of Communist Party historians actually underlined the pluralist reading of American institutions. To defend themselves against the witch-hunters, they were forced, as Herbert Aptheker was, to resort to concepts of democratic fair play and to applaud those liberals like Commager who dissented from

McCarthyism. Commager did not equate the intellectual theories of marxism with conspiratorial activity. But he did argue that membership in the Communist Party was "presumptive evidence of a lack of critical acumen," and conceded that communists were "not desirable as teachers in colleges and universities." (Under such a formula, someone like Eric Hobsbawm would not be fit for university service.) When Aptheker applauded Commager's defense of civil liberties, he was forced to ignore the contradictory tendencies in Commager's position. In the interests of building alliances, Aptheker had to overlook the fact that Commager's position also served to reinforce negative conceptions of communism and positive conceptions of American tolerance.[28]

The cold war did, then, in all these concerted and indirect ways have a serious effect on the intellectual climate. The end result was that marxism was virtually excluded from the intellectual life of the nation in the 1950s, leaving a bland ideological consensus. The consequences were far-reaching and quite subtle in their operation.

The absence of marxism as a serious intellectual force can perhaps be illustrated on one level by personal anecdote. When I told an Australian class that included one American student that Americans had not included marxism in the educational dialogue, the American told me that his experience in the 1960s at a prestigious private university in the East contradicted my argument. After all, while he was studying economics, his department had given the marxists a chance; in fact they had gone to the trouble of importing a Swedish economist to give the marxist point of view. The American student could not see the irony of the incident: it was necessary to import a marxist with a foreign accent, thus emphasizing the exotic character of marxism; moreover, one paltry marxist was pitted to give "the marxist view" against a department of many neoclassical economists. The prejudicial assumption that marxism was a monolithic system of interpretation while American economic theory was pluralistic and tolerantly diverse was thus emphasized in the very attempt to show impartiality.

Stripped of a dialogue with various strands of marxist theory, the postwar search for a new historical synthesis took place in a narrow conceptual framework. The debate among American historians of that period, between the progressives and their opponents, centered around the role of economic factors and whether they explained, in an empirical sense, American development—that is, whether they fitted the facts of American history. A case in point was the debate in 1954 between Allan Nevins and Matthew Josephson over the role of economic entrepreneurs in the industrial revolution. Nevins spoke of industrial statesmen and Josephson of robber barons, but Josephson, the defender of the Beardian tradition, did not argue for a comprehensive marxist view but instead asserted merely that the economic motive was important, and invoked the arguments and name of Edwin Seligman to justify his views. For his part, Nevins argued for a Whig interpretation of American economic history which was entirely compatible with the economic interpretation set out in Seligman's study. Each author claimed that his interpretation fitted the facts better than the other. Neither went beyond a simplistic argument over economic causation. Neither questioned the epistemology which polarized facts and interpretations and insisted that the latter flowed inexorably from the former. Nevins called his view a "fair presentation of the facts," in place of the "tendentious writing" of the progressives, while Josephson could only reply by appealing to "the corpus of ascertainable facts." Despite all this invocation of factual verities, the argument nevertheless involved much swapping of moral judgments—whether the late nineteenth-century entrepreneurs were immoral or whether they were farsighted agents of national progress. True to the progressive tradition, this mixture of facts and irrelevant moral judgments continued to plague serious analysis of the economic past of the nation within the historical profession.[29]

The impact of political repression on the intellectual composition of marxist history itself was as severe as the consequences for the quality of debate between progressives and revisionists. Since the 1950s, marxist history in both Britain and France has clearly been superior in quality to its American counterparts, as well as more abundant in quantity. But the gap between the marxist historiographies of these countries, in terms of quality, is a recent product. In the 1930s, positivism and economic determinism plagued the marxist tradition in all three countries. After the war, there was in Britain and France a core of communist and other leftist historians already in the universities and colleges who could despite some discrimination build upon existing work, and particularly in the post-Stalin years, begin to rethink orthodoxy.[30] In contrast, the focus across the Atlantic was much more upon defending the beleaguered political interests of the party against intimidation. Joseph Starobin's analytic memoir of the American Communist Party's turbulent decade of decay recalls the development of "an inner circle of self-justification" that "militated against any re-examination within the Party's ranks." A similar pattern occurred among historians identified with the party. Foner, Aptheker, Morais, and others like them could and did continue to write history, mostly as independent scholars, but neither the intellectual climate nor the political positions of these people encouraged rethinking of orthodox marxist positions. As David Montgomery, himself a member of the party in the 1950s, has testified, the dynamics of political repression reinforced "the siege mentality" of the dwindling marxist fraternity. Forced to subordinate theoretical work to the most elementary forms of partisan self-defense, it is hardly surprising that intellectual atrophy set in among those committed to the party.[31]

Neither McCarthyism nor the new emphasis upon a positive interpretation of capitalism was a purely American phenomenon. It was probably as great a liability to be a marxist in the academic employment market in Australia in those years, and as Eric Hobsbawm has observed, in Britain the marxist group remained for a number of years a derided minority. Capitalism's ideologues among historians crossed national boundaries too. The most famous of all the pro-capitalist tracts was F. A. Hayek's *Capitalism and the Historians*, published in 1954, which drew together celebratory papers authored by British, American, and continental European scholars. What differed was the historical context. The relative weakness of socialist parties and the widespread identification of marxism as foreign, subversive, and Soviet certainly ensured the marginality of marxist analysis in American life, but the structure of political institutions exerted a more immediate and more devastating effect. The nature of the anticommunist attack was more open and more virulent than in other comparable democracies, as befitted a society in which democratic participation and public disclosure were parts of the official creed. This is why the impact of anticommunist hysteria on marxist writing was more lethal than in Britain.[32]

The impact on liberalism was more complicated. One aim of the anticommunist crusade was to identify radicals and left liberals as fellow travelers. I have already noted that certain liberal historians were among those affected by the loyalty purges in the universities. Yet other liberals, like those who formed the Americans for Democratic Action, were among the leaders in a movement to dissociate liberalism from the communist stigma. This was the position of Arthur Schlesinger, Jr., in *The Vital Center*. Though usually identified with the "liberal intelligentsia," the great majority of American historians did not conform to either of these extremes, and the impact of anti-communism was indirect. The hysteria of the late 1940s and early 1950s did not destroy their careers, directly suppress their political convictions, or seriously limit the scope of their historical research. But the domestic and international offensive against communism was part of a historical conjuncture which perpetuated and strengthened liberal social thought and historical methodology. Contributing was the experience of the New Deal and the war which seemed to give the lie to marxist predictions. If the Great Depression had not brought a workers' revolution in the United States, then what would? American democracy's record did look good under the challenge of depression, war, and international revolution. The resiliency of democracy in the United States impressed the liberal historians who found in that recent experience confirmation for the idea of American uniqueness which was always contained in American liberal thought. Jack Pole, an astute English observer who studied in the United States in the early 1950s, was especially impressed by the pervasive commitment among American historians to the New Deal tradition, and by the impact of "the sense of justified ideological nationhood of the war years" in producing the climate for consensus in the 1950s.[33]

Yet if the work of Hofstadter, Boorstin, Hartz, David Potter, and others is closely examined, we find that the consensus views usually identified with them had not fully developed in the 1940s. Hofstadter's Foreword to *The American Political Tradition* is commonly thought to be the herald of the new approach, but Arthur M. Schlesinger, Jr., has observed that this appeared to be something of an afterthought in the 1948 edition, and was not clearly argued throughout the book. Boorstin had not yet discovered the nonideological character of the American people, and Louis Hartz's important statement of consensus theory, *The Liberal Tradition in America*, was still several years away from completion. The so-called consensus interpretation was not fully fashioned until the 1950s, and it is in this setting that political anticommunism could be said to have influenced the views of the leading postwar liberals.[34]

As Richard Hofstadter noted in several acutely autobiographical passages in *The Paranoid Style*, the liberals who had been critics of the social order in the depths of the Depression gradually became the entrenched defenders of the status quo which was, in fact, the liberal state of the New Deal and its pragmatic reform tradition. They became, as a consequence, more conservative in their political outlook while defending the achievements of reform against attacks from both the left and the right. The McCarthyism of the early 1950s merely demonstrated to these liberal social critics and historians the strength and value of the political consensus that was a product of New Deal liberalism. Mc-Carthyism revealed the left as insignificant while the right appeared hysterical and irrational in its attacks on domestic communism. To those who theorized upon the "new right," it could not possibly be a movement exercising real power and enforcing ideological consensus. Its flailing at inconsequential foes and its rapid demise and disgrace after 1954 were evidence that a fundamental consensus already existed. That consensus excluded the irrational anxieties of the radical right as much as it excluded the totalitarian left.[35]

From their observations of ideological conformity and economic prosperity in the 1950s, the liberals completed the new synthesis of American history. Their depiction of the exceptional economic abundance of America as the underlying condition of political consensus in such important works as David Potter's *People of Plenty* rested transparently on the American economy's transformation since the Depression. Their analysis of the United States as politically consensual rested both on the relative political conformity of the post-McCarthy years, and on the contrast between the American experience of the 1930s and 1940s and the European conflagration. If a vital marxist tradition had existed, then the liberals might have had to reconsider their judgments of liberal democracy and what they called "mass culture." Instead, they were faced only by the surviving relics of 1930s marxism. There was no reason for the liberals to question the identification of communism as the greatest external threat to world peace. By and large they accepted the cold war rhetoric as ample analysis of both the political situation and the theoretical adequacy of communism and marxism's historical claims.[36]

It was under the influence of these political, economic, and ideological changes that the postwar historians came to reject Beardian and class analysis, but it can be easily demonstrated that the new synthesis remained profoundly indebted to the methodological legacy of the progressive historians. The postwar consensus historians were the inheritors of the old progressive historiography in a new political climate and new historical perspective. An analysis of the nature of the postwar historiographical transformations which produced these continuities is absolutely essential to understanding the weaknesses of marxist history and the eventual degeneration of the liberal historical tradition.

NOTES

1. John Higham, "The Cult of the 'American Consensus': Homogenizing Our History," *Commentary* 27 (1959): 93–100; Higham, "Beyond Consensus: The Historian as Moral Critic," *American Historical Review* 67 (1962): 609–25; Richard Reinitz, "Niebuhrian Irony and Historical Interpretation: The Relationship between Consensus and New Left History," in Robert H. Canary and Henry Kozich, eds., *The Writing of History: Literary Form and Historical Understanding* (Madison, Wis., 1978), pp. 93–128, esp. pp. 115, 126–27; Samuel Eliot Morison, "Faith of a Historian," *American Historical Review* (1951): 261–75; Conyers Read, "The Social Responsibilities of the Historian," *American Historical Review* 55 (1950): 281–84; Arthur M. Schlesinger, Jr., *The Vital Center* (Boston, rev. ed., 1962).

2. Richard Gillam, "Richard Hofstadter, C. Wright Mills, and the Critical Ideal," *American Scholar* 47 (1978): 79; Arthur Mann, "The Progressive Tradition," in John Higham, ed., *The Reconstruction of American History* (New York, 1962), pp. 157–79; David Donald, "An Excess of Democracy," in Donald, *Lincoln Reconsidered: Essays on the Civil War Era* (New York, 1956), pp. 209–35; Stanley Elkins, *Slavery: A Problem in American Institutional and Intellectual Life* (Chicago, 1959); Richard Hofstadter, *The Age of Reform: From Bryan to F.D.R.* (New York, 1955).

3. Daniel Aaron, ed., *America in Crisis: Fourteen Crucial Episodes in American History* (New York, 1952), esp. pp. x–xi. Richard M. Andrews, "Some Implications of the *Annales* School and Its Methods for a Revision of Historical Writing about the United States," *Review* 1 (1978): 167–68 is illuminating on this point.

4. Morison, "Faith of a Historian," pp. 272–73.

5. Daniel Boorstin, *The Americans: The Colonial Experience* (New York, 1958); Boorstin, *The Americans: The National Experience* (New York, 1965); and Boorstin, *The Americans: The Democratic Experience* (New York, 1973).

6. Edmund Morgan, *The Birth of the Republic, 1763–89* (Chicago, 1956); Forrest McDonald, *We the People: The Economic Origins of the Constitution* (Chicago, 1958); Robert E. Brown, *Charles Beard and the Constitution: A Critical Analysis of "An Economic Interpretation of the Constitution"* (Princeton, N.J., 1956); Brown, *Middle-Class Democracy and the American Revolution in Massachusetts, 1691–1780* (Ithaca, N.Y., 1955); Richard Hofstadter, *The American Political Tradition and the Men Who Made It* (New York, 1948), pp. 56–57; Marvin Meyers, *The Jacksonian Persuasion: Politics and Belief* (New York, Vintage ed., 1960); Irwin Unger, *The Greenback Era: A Social and Political History of American Finance, 1865–1879* (Princeton, N.J., 1964); Stanley Coben, "Northeastern Businessmen and Radical Reconstruction," *Mississippi Valley Historical Review* 44 (1959): 67–90; Kenneth M. Stampp, *The Era of Reconstruction, 1865–77* (New York, 1965); Elkins, *Slavery*; Donald, *Lincoln Reconsidered*; Hofstadter, *Age of Reform*; Allan Nevins, *Study in Power: John D. Rockefeller: Industrialist and Philanthropist*, 2 vols. (New York, 1953).

7. Daniel Boorstin, *The Genius of American Politics* (Chicago, 1953), pp. 3, 4, 7; Boorstin, *The Lost World of Thomas Jefferson* (Boston, 1960), p. 177.

8. Louis Hartz, *The Liberal Tradition in America* (New York, 1955), pp. 21, 248–55, 277–83, 317 n. 1; E. Burns, ed., *A Handbook of Marxism* (New York, 1935).

9. Richard Hofstadter, *The Progressive Historians: Turner, Beard, Parrington* (New

York, 1968), pp. 197–200, 452; Arthur M. Schlesinger, Jr., "Richard Hofstadter," in Marcus Cunliffe and Robin Winks, eds., *Pastmasters: Some Essays on American Historians* (New York, 1969), p. 279; Hofstadter, "Beard and the Constitution: The History of an Idea," in A. S. Eisenstadt, ed., *The Craft of American History: Selected Essays*, 2 vols. (New York, 1966), 2:156; Gillam, "Hofstadter," pp. 71–72; Daniel J. Singal, "Beyond Consensus: Richard Hofstadter and American Historiography," *American Historical Review* 89 (1984): 980.

10. Hofstadter, *Progressive Historians*, pp. 199–200, 312–13.

11. Richard Hofstadter, "Introduction" to Hofstadter, *The Paranoid Style in American Politics and Other Essays* (New York, 1965), p. x; Stanley Elkins and Eric McKitrick, "Richard Hofstadter, A Progress," in Elkins and McKitrick, eds., *The Hofstadter Aegis: A Memorial* (New York, 1973), p. 309.

12. Morton White has picked this key evasion. See his *Pragmatism and the American Mind: Essays and Reviews in Philosophy and Intellectual History* (New York, 1973), p. 208; Hofstadter, *Age of Reform*, p. 289.

13. Hofstadter, *Paranoid Style*, p. x.

14. John P. Diggins, *The American Left in the Twentieth Century* (New York, 1973), pp. 145–48; Gene Wise, *American Historical Explanations: A Strategy for Grounded Inquiry* (Minneapolis, 2d ed., 1980), pp. 214–15, 229–33, 273–76, 282–84; Robert A. Skotheim, *Totalitarianism and American Social Thought* (New York, 1971), chaps. 2–3.

15. Robert A. Skotheim, *American Intellectual Histories and Historians* (Princeton, N.J., 1966), pp. 148–49, 156; Merle Curti, *The Growth of American Thought* (New York, 1943); Carl Becker to Mrs. Max Kesterson, 16 Feb. 1945, in Michael Kammen, ed., *"What is the Good of History?" Selected Letters of Carl L. Becker, 1900–1945* (Ithaca, N.Y., 1973), p. 342; Carl Becker, *New Liberties for Old* (New Haven, 1941), p. 145.

16. Arthur M. Schlesinger, Jr., *The Age of Jackson* (Boston, 1945), pp. ix–x.

17. Wise, *American Historical Explanations*, pp. ix–x; Thomas S. Kuhn, *The Structure of Scientific Revolutions* (Chicago, 1962).

18. Wise, *American Historical Explanations*, p. 347.

19. Paul F. Lazarsfeld and Wagner Thielens, Jr., *The Academic Mind: Social Scientists in a Time of Crisis* (New York, 1958), pp. 35, 37, 198, 207–10, 212–13.

20. Ibid., pp. 164, 165, 167, 177–78. It should be noted that of this national sample, 28 percent were historians. Ibid., p. 4; see also Merle Curti, *Probing the Past: Paths to the Present* (Gloucester, Mass., 1962); pp. 30–31.

21. David Caute, *The Great Fear: The Anti-Communist Purge under Truman and Eisenhower* (New York, 1978), pp. 410–14, 430; David P. Gardner, *The California Oath Controversy* (Berkeley and Los Angeles, 1967), pp. 250–51.

22. Lawrence H. Chamberlain, *Loyalty and Legislative Action: A Survey of Activity by the New York State Legislature, 1919–1949* (Ithaca, N.Y., 1951), pp. 68–186; Robert W. Iversen, *The Communists and the Schools* (New York, 1959), pp. 208–23; *American Institute for Marxist Studies Newsletter*, May–June 1970, p. 3, Sept. 1976, p. 1; *New York Times*, 13 Oct. 1976, p. 48; "Yale University and Dr. Aptheker. A Report of the American Historical Association-Organization of American Historians Committee on the Defense of the Rights of Historians Under the First Amendment. December 1977," *Organization of American Historians Newsletter* 5 (Jan. 1978), suppl., and 6 (July 1978), suppl., for the report and responses to it among historians.

23. Caute, *Great Fear*, pp. 414–15, 425, 551, 553–54; Gardner, *California Oath Controversy*, pp. 350–51, 353; Iversen, *Communists and the Schools*, pp. 211–12; *New York Times*, 8 Nov. 1941, p. 21; *Directory of American Scholars* (New York, 1969 ed.), for biographical data.

24. See Chapter 5.

25. William Miller, "The Realm of Wealth," in John Higham, ed., *The Reconstruction of American History* (New York, 1962), p. 154; Nevins, *Rockefeller*; Herbert Aptheker, *Laureates of Imperialism* (New York, 1954), pp. 19–35.

26. Howard K. Beale, "The Professional Historian: His Theory and His Practice," *Pacific Historical Review* 22 (1953): 254; Read, "Social Responsibilities," pp. 281–84.

27. See, for example, Robert Griffith and Athan Theoharis, eds., *The Specter: Original Essays on the Cold War and the Origins of McCarthyism* (New York, 1974).

28. Aptheker, *Laureates of Imperialism*, p. 77; Henry Steele Commager, *Freedom and Order: A Commentary on the American Political Scene* (New York, 1966), pp. 82, 83.

29. Allan Nevins and Matthew Josephson, "Should American History Be Rewritten?" in Eisenstadt, ed., *Craft of American History*, 1: 185, 189, 192.

30. The rudimentary and populist character of much 1930s marxism can be discerned in the examples of Raphael Samuel, "British Marxist Historians, 1880–1980: Part One," *New Left Review* 120 (1980): 37–41; and Pradeep Bandyopadyay, "The Many Faces of French Marxism," *Science and Society* 36 (1972): 133–36.

31. Joseph R. Starobin, *American Communism in Crisis, 1943–1957* (Cambridge, Mass., 1972), p. 197; "Once Upon a Shop Floor: An Interview with David Montgomery," *Radical History Review* 23 (1980): 42–43.

32. F. A. Hayek, ed., *Capitalism and the Historians* (London, 1954), p. v; Edward A. Shils, *The Torment of Secrecy: The Background and Consequences of American Security Programs* (London, 1956).

33. J. R. Pole, *Paths to the American Past* (New York, 1979), p. xv.

34. Schlesinger, "Richard Hofstadter," p. 286.

35. Hofstadter, *Paranoid Style*, pp. 42–43.

36. David Potter, *People of Plenty: Economic Abundance and the American Character* (Chicago, 1954); Daniel Bell, *The End of Ideology: On the Exhaustion of Political Ideas in the Fifties* (New York, rev. ed., 1962).

4

Social Science and the Renewal of Liberal History, 1945–1965

Conventional accounts of American historiography depict the late 1930s and 1940s as a crucial dividing point which saw the demise of the progressive synthesis and its replacement by a consensus school or counterprogressive approach. On the level of interpretation and political temper, this generalization has some validity, though even there the lines were less clearly drawn than is often supposed.

The consensus–progressive dichotomy is less helpful in understanding the development of historical method and the continuity of historical practice. While the new counterprogressive historians tended to take a more detached view of reform movements, and depicted themselves as intellectuals interested in the past for its own sake, their actual practice was compatible with the progressive impulse to use history to illuminate (and hence implicitly to solve) current political and social problems. Richard Hofstadter's assessment of populism as an irrational mass movement with sociopsychological roots similar to McCarthyism fell into this mold. Indeed, the choice of apt subjects in the light of current political or intellectual concerns is a theme running through most of Hofstadter's mature work, from the *Paranoid Style* essay of the early 1950s to his documentary survey on violence in America, compiled after the momentous civil disobedience of the 1960s.[1] Also in the tradition of activism was the work of Daniel Boorstin, especially his attempts to resurrect the lost world of Thomas Jefferson and establish an authentic American conservative tradition in *The Genius of American Politics*. Boorstin, it is true, attacked the progressive historiographical urge to "cull apt phrases for current needs" from the past, and argued instead for "observing in all their tantalizing complexity" the ideas and events of history. He admitted, however, that his own purpose in reconstructing that "complexity" was to strengthen "the philosophical foundations of a moral society." Read in connection with his famous testimony before the House Un-American Activities Committee in 1947, Boorstin's scholarly activism and "present-mindedness'' were obvious to all. There he explained that his ''opposition'' to communism had taken the form of ''an attempt to discover and explain to students, in my teaching and in my writing, the unique virtues of American democracy.''[2] Louis Hartz, too, disclosed his own present-mindedness at the end of his *Liberal Tradition in America*. He sought in that work to inform Americans that their liberalism did not equip them to handle the international crisis of the 1940s and early 1950s. A nation which had had no revolutionary discontents or ideological conflicts could not, in Hartz's view, easily sympathize with the need for genuine change in the rest of the world. Only by coming to an understanding of the limited range of experience offered by the liberal political tradition could the nation provide rational and progressive leadership against ''the threat of Russian communism.'' This present-minded purpose underlay his attack on those progressive era historians and reformers who had advanced simple Beardian and/or marxian explanations of the American past.[3] In such works, the counterprogressives displayed activist concerns as clear and precise as Beard's attempts to demystify the American constitution in the muckraking era of reform before World War I.

In addition to retaining the activism of progressive scholarship, the consensus historians of the 1950s adopted a very similar attitude to that of progressives on the status of facts and interpretations. The leading historians in the post–World War II period spoke in naturalistic terms of an underlying historical reality against which they measured both theory and popular misconceptions of the American past. (They differed from progressives, of course, in their belief that a class conflict approach was fanciful.) Louis Hartz's 1948 volume on *Economic Policy and Democratic Thought: Pennsylvania, 1776–1860* is a case in point. Hartz tested the ideology of laissez-faire against the evidence and found the former a myth. Then, in the 1950s, Hartz became especially concerned with the gap between an American reality and European social theory, though he shifted over time from a critique of the poverty of American ideological experience to a more positive assessment of its pragmatic democractic qualities.[4] Daniel Boorstin was another who reflected continuities with progressive styles of thought. In the 1950s Boorstin became well-known for his celebration of empirical (American) behavior over abstract (European) ideas, and thereby adopted categories of analysis of intellectual history familiar to Charles Beard. The same dualistic framework lingered also in influential early exemplars of the American studies genre. In *Virgin Land: The American West as Symbol and Myth*, published in 1950, Henry Nash Smith analyzed the agrarian tradition which arose out of the American encounter with the wilderness. Against man's illusions of what the frontier might be, Smith repeatedly drew attention to the empirical realities of the West. The interplay of consciousness and material reality in this analysis was undervalued, as Smith has since conceded.[5]

The counterprogressive dichotomy of underlying empirical reality and superficial appearances was but one legacy of Beardian thought. Another revolved around the difficulties historians faced in transcending the crisis of relativism

bequeathed to them by progressive scholarship. The postwar historians incorporated rather than resolved the epistemological confusion raised in the 1930s.
As Oscar Handlin put it, they had "learned to live with relativism."[6] A key
episode in bringing about a reaction against excessive relativism was the presidential address of Conyers Read before the American Historical Association in
1949. Read had been a disciple of Beard, and his call for American historians
to serve American interests in the cold war was a manifestation of the relativism
of the 1930s under different political circumstances. But Read's address was so
extreme a presentation of the implications of relativism and so overtly political
that it was profoundly embarrassing to many American historians. If the comments of influential senior figures within the profession are any guide, Read's
address "was not enthusiastically received" by historians. In this respect, the
attempts of various New Left historians to paint a gloomy picture of an historical
profession in the early 1950s dominated by outright cold war partisans are
incorrect. Nonetheless, the counterattack on relativism illustrates the development of more subtle pressures that worked to limit and effectively to exclude a
serious marxist historiography from the profession.[7]

One approach was taken by historians who argued that the claims of historical
investigators could and ought to be measured against the simple tests of historical
"truth." Chester McArthur Destler, for example, argued against the relativists
that there was much in the way of factual information on which historians could
rely. History was not a morass of shifting interpretations but a solid and growing
fund of empirical detail. Destler's article, in particular, showed the continuing
appeal of old-fashioned scientific notions of history that persisted despite the
Beardian offensive. Andrew C. McLaughlin, A. O. Lovejoy, and Theodore
Clark Smith had advanced similar objections to Beard in the 1930s. The reassertion of the possibility of an objective or, at least, an impartial history based
upon an accumulation of evidence was directed against any intellectual system
that strayed from the path of empiricism, but one important consequence was
to condemn marxism.[8]

Equally subversive of relativism but much more intellectually promising was
the position of the Historiography Committee of the Social Science Research
Council. The authors of its important Bulletin 64 were Thomas Cochran, Hugh
G. J. Aitken, Shepard B. Clough, Bert J. Loewenberg, Jeanette P. Nichols, and
Samuel H. Brockuner. These writers tried to escape from the dilemmas of
relativism by arguing that the best way out of bias was to make hypotheses more
explicit, and by the use of concepts drawn from the social sciences. If few
historians were prepared to accept a wholesale importation of social science into
history, a remarkably large number made some selective use of the concepts
which the Bulletin 64 authors publicized.[9]

Social science did not immediately triumph over historical relativism or old-
fashioned history of the scientific type. Rather, social science was gradually
assimilated to the relativist position in such a way as to combine elements of
both. Then, as the claims of social science grew stronger by example, and those

of relativism weaker as time put its distance between the postwar historians and the controversies of the 1930s, relativism faded from its significant place in the synthesis, leaving a rejuvenated liberal history strongly informed by social science methods.

To summarize the outcome of the complex process of postwar accommodation: historians could not know all the facts. Some indeed were irrecoverable, but a partial account of the past could be given with accuracy. Bias was inevitable, but it could be controlled by making one's hypotheses explicit. The new liberal historians did not use the relativist crisis to concede the theoretical basis of historical knowledge, and to make the construction of historical concepts the foundation of empirical inquiry in the discipline; they chose to accept the relativity of history, and sought to compensate for the loss of objectivity by ad hoc borrowing from the social sciences. If all historical knowledge was problematic, the employment of social science methods and concepts might both illuminate historical problems and provide a firmer empirical foundation for the discipline.

A key figure in this process of accommodation was Richard Hofstadter. It is amply rewarding to focus for a moment on Hofstadter who, helped by his numerous publications and his keen historical insight, became the most accomplished historian of his generation and a worthy successor in this and in other respects to Charles Beard. "To those of us who encountered *The Age of Reform* in graduate school," recalled Robert Wiebe, himself a distinguished liberal historian, "he [Hofstadter] more than any other writer, framed the problems, explored the techniques, and established the model of literate inquiry that would condition our study of the American past." This was true not only in the matter of historical interpretation, but perhaps more importantly in the area of methodology.[10]

In one of his more obscure but very important publications, "History and the Social Sciences," Hofstadter put down on paper his thoughts on the relationship as of 1956. Starting out from an appreciation of the value of the social sciences, and advocating "conceptual borrowings" from them, he married this approach with the relativist emphasis of the later progressive historians. His insight was strikingly similar to a suggestion made by Beard and Alfred Vagts in 1937. It was impossible, they concluded, to comprehend the actuality of history conceived as the sum total of things that had happened in the past, but historians could through the use of the methods of the social sciences expand "the range of [history's] interests . . . to the fullness of its subject matter—history as actuality." A history which broached all areas of human experience came closer to the spirit of history as actuality than the old-fashioned political variety, even though the newer version was unable to promise definitive accounts of the past. Though Beard and Vagts had proposed this solution, it awaited historians like Hofstadter to take up the suggestion and implement a compromise between relativism and social science that illustrated the continuing conceptual legacy of the progressive tradition. According to Hofstadter, social science could not provide exactitude for historians, encumbered as they were by the need "to reconstruct partially hypothetical accounts from fragmentary evidence.'' Social science did not provide a means to certitude, but served rather to liberate the discipline from a narrow concentration on the problem of historical ''facts,'' and to add complexity and ''speculative richness'' to the analysis.[11]

While Hofstadter's account has been read, for example by Elkins and McKitrick, as a diffident essay on the limitations as well as the uses of social science for historians, the meaning of these thoughtful reservations will remain unclear without reference to the historical context of progressive relativism and its place in the profession in the 1950s. It is a significant indication of the impact of Beardian relativism that Hofstadter's concessions to the relativist currents rested upon a continuing adherence to an empiricist conception of knowledge. Hofstadter agreed that history became most objective in the narrow monographic form when ''historians exhaustively explore an extremely narrow segment of reality'' (that is, when the facts were most complete). The social sciences, he argued, were capable of more though never complete objectivity precisely because of their sounder empirical foundations. They possessed ''such masses of material focussed upon a given subject'' compared to the ''fragmentary [historical] evidence'' derived not, as in the case of much sociology, from ''direct access to their subjects,'' but from ''surviving documents.''[12]

Hofstadter did not abandon a conception of autonomous facts as the basis of historical truth: he merely despaired, as some exponents of the progressive tradition in its declining phase had, at the possibility of knowing them all. Building implicitly on the insight of Beard and Vagts, he saw a way out of the paralyzing relativism of the 1930s. Empirically grounded social science theory could be applied to produce a problem-oriented discipline that would be richer in heuristic power though always lacking definitive answers. Despite Hofstadter's reservations about the role of the social sciences in historical inquiry, it was Hofstadter's attention to the possibilities of using social science theories to enrich historical analysis which has marked his methodological legacy. Moreover, Hofstadter's reservations about the value of social science did reflect their proximity in time to the relativist controversies. When he came to write again on the subject of social science and its application to history, in 1968, Hofstadter's emphasis on social science's limitations for historical analysis had completely evaporated.[13]

While the alliance between social science and history was a practical compromise, not a carefully articulated philosophical position, it did provide a new lease on life for the methodological synthesis of progressive history. That had rested above all on the application of social science methods to historical facts in order to throw light on contemporary problems. Prominent post–World War II historians perpetuated this legacy by increased reliance on the same strategy, and thereby imparted enhanced explanatory power and intellectual influence to a continuing historical tradition: one that was problem-oriented, analytical, relativist in its concern with making history speak to the current social, political, and moral questions of the day yet firmly grounded in the empirical realities of the past. This was progressive, liberal history in a different political setting.

Changes in interpretation aside, Beard's methods had their most extensive and fruitful application through the so-called counterprogressives. The key link is again found in the new generation's most able spokesman, Richard Hofstadter. His work in particular represented not a challenge to the progressive tradition as has been conventionally thought, but rather a fulfillment of its methodological drives and a perpetuation of its epistemological assumptions. In his very perceptive early appraisal of Beard's legacy, published in 1950, Hofstadter praised his invention of the "career-line analysis" in *An Economic Interpretation*. Far from attempting to demolish Beard's methods, Hofstadter actually noted how little they had been exploited by American historians in the intervening forty years. He realized quite well that the pre–World War II period had not seen the triumph of Beardian methodology, "which American historians have hardly used at all," only of Beardian interpretation.[14]

Hofstadter's sympathetic early treatment of Beard, and his advocacy of career-line analysis, has to be read against the presentation, just five years later, of his *Age of Reform*. This classic and critical account of the progressive mind embodies precisely the type of analysis—a profile of the socioeconomic backgrounds and motivations of reform movement leadership—that Hofstadter had admired in Beard's early work. The difference lay at the most superficial level, where Hofstadter substituted the then-current vogue for psychological and status explanations of motivation for Beard's exposure of the reality of economic interest. Even here, Hofstadter gave ground to Beard. Hofstadter conceded the rationality of economic interests, and posed against these the irrational anxieties of the status revolution. Thus rationality and interest were conceived too narrowly, as the continuing legacy of Beard revealed. Nor did Hofstadter challenge the orientation of the historiographical debate in terms of the conventional issues of national political history, or the tendency to explain political behavior in terms of deeper and supposedly more realistic motivating drives.[15]

Hofstadter's *Age of Reform* was merely the most famous and influential of a series of studies that popularized the use of career-line analysis, and made it perhaps the most widely known and used social science technique among historians in the 1950s and 1960s. Other authors were adopting the collective biography approach at about the same time, and some even preceded Hofstadter. George Mowry had published an article on the social backgrounds of the California progressives in 1949, and Alfred Chandler profiled Progressive Party leaders across the nation in a 1954 publication. Neither of these inspired Hofstadter's study, but Hofstadter willingly drew upon their empirical research and gave it wider currency in the course of a general interpretation of the progressive mind.[16]

Ironically, the critics as much as the enthusiasts ensured the influence of his methods. When Robert Skotheim and Richard Sherman took David Donald and Hofstadter to task for loose applications of the collective biography technique, the attacks did not discourage its use. By setting up concrete historiographical controversies, and by providing practical lessons in the construction of a research design, these critiques actually encouraged more historians to perpetuate the approaches Hofstadter had employed, though in a more rigorous fashion and with different interpretive results. Particularly important was the comparison of the groups of individuals studied with control groups, and with the characteristics of the larger population. Armed with this emendation of the Hofstadter approach, the social analysis of group behavior in politics became steadily more precise.[17]

Through the debate that Hofstadter's thesis set off, the themes of progressive history did not die an ignominious death at the hands of the counterprogressives. The underlying methodological and theoretical structures which the progressives had championed were modified and strengthened to produce a new historiography influenced by social science concepts and techniques.

So far, the continuity between the work of the progressive historians on a methodological plane and that of the so-called counterprogressives of the 1950s has been examined through a critical case of a historian commonly conceived as the nemesis of the progressive interpretation. That continuity was also evident in the work of historians who more openly defended the progressives. Merle Curti was an excellent example of the other strand of progressive influence in the 1950s. His prestige was at its peak in this period. He served as a President of the American Historical Association and of the Mississippi Valley Historical Association. He had trained a list of historians that was both long and prestigious. The importance of men like Curti (and Arthur Schlesinger, Sr.) has been undervalued because it has been thought that their progressive paradigm was under strain in the 1950s, their interpretations "embattled." Yet Curti not only topped a 1952 poll of historians evaluating the major works written between 1936 and 1950; he also produced in 1959 *The Making of an American Community*. This book constituted more than an empirical testing of the frontier thesis; it exemplified the potential of the methodological residue of progressive historiography: an empirical inquiry guided by social science concepts employed to illuminate an analytical problem in the history of American democracy. Given the growth of social science history in the 1960s, the emergence of quantitative empirical testings of the central myths of American history, and the penchant for case studies of communities as a means of probing the historical social structure, it is not accurate to describe Curti as a man whose time or paradigm had passed in the late 1950s. Like Hofstadter's *Age of Reform*, Curti's *Making of an American Community* illustrated what could be done to transcend the "major historical controversies" over relativism and progressive historiography by applying social science techniques to limited and carefully focused community studies. Curti intended the book to fulfill this function, and to an impressive extent he had succeeded.[18]

This is not to suggest that an unconditional surrender occurred in the longstanding battle between the social science–influenced New History and more traditional conceptions of historical scholarship. Something more eclectic was going on. John Higham has argued that the post–World War II years marked a declaration of independence by historians against old feelings of inferiority toward social science. The 1950s saw, Higham believed, a resurgence of humanistic scholarship. There are echoes of this interpretation in other views, and in the general scholarly prescriptive literature of the postwar period. Generalizations and the discovery of historical laws were out; the importance of the particular and the individual event was in. Timothy Donovan has even gone so far as to suggest that the period witnessed a return to "the individual as [the historian's] central object of concern." In a numerical sense, there is no denying that many historians carried on their daily work without much reference to social science theories. Factual evidence remained the chief criterion of scholarly excellence in the discipline to an extent which would be considered irrelevant in, for example, economics. As late as 1963, A. S. Eisenstadt could claim that the "great majority" of American historians were "not impressed" by the methods or the achievements of social science.[19]

If there is a paradox here, it is easily solved. Higham has the answer in his argument that the relationship between history and social science became more eclectic. Since historians no longer felt obliged to make Manichean choices between acceptance or rejection of social science, the chance for concepts derived from other disciplines to exert influence actually increased at the very time Higham was proclaiming that a humanistic revival had occurred. As for Donovan's argument, one must distinguish between the pronouncements of historians on method and actual historical practice. The protests against social science in the 1950s and after were by and large protests against the current of change. Carl Bridenbaugh's 1963 diatribe against the "bitch-goddess" of quantification in "The Great Mutation" should not be taken as evidence of an important anti-social science trend. (Bridenbaugh himself was a social historian with a lineage going back to Arthur Schlesinger, Sr.) What Bridenbaugh's rhetoric did signify was the movement of American historiography towards a more comprehensive accommodation with social science and with quantification, at the expense of the more impressionistic and intuitive practice of many of the earlier social historians. As Bridenbaugh implicitly recognized, American liberal history was already undergoing another mutation, potentially as important as the reform of historical practice in the progressive era.[20]

It is also important to appreciate the way in which social science concepts have helped define the theoretical and methodological framework of liberal history in the past three decades. The influence of social science in this way far exceeded its numerical importance in the scholarship of the 1950s. Social science concepts figured in a great number of the best and most influential of the historical works of the 1950s. There are obvious examples in the writings of Thomas Cochran, David Potter, Stanley Elkins, David Donald, Lee Benson, Bernard Bailyn, and Oscar Handlin. Beyond these most prominent cases, the penetration of social science can be seen in the publication of such anthologies as Edward Saveth's *American History and the Social Sciences* (1963) which gathered together some of the previous decade's most innovative scholarship. There was too the influence of social science in the American studies movement which burgeoned in the 1950s. American studies rested implicitly on the introduction of the methods of psychology and cultural anthropology to comprehend the patterns of myth and symbol in American experience.[21]

The assessment of a trend against social science in the 1950s rests on the mistaken assumption that the New History had triumphed in the interwar period. We have already seen in an earlier chapter how Beard, Robinson, Schlesinger, and Barnes tried along with others to reshape American historiography, with only partial success. The 1950s represented a change in the fortunes of the historical innovators insofar as there was a move away from declarations of support for the newer ways of history to actual practice of a history influenced by social science.

This shift had roots in the increasing prestige of social science in the American academy, and reflected larger changes in the political economy of higher education and research in the United States after World War II. Sociology, anthropology, and political science gained new importance in the American university structure after 1945 and this new influence rested in turn upon the heightened valuation of scientific research in the larger society. Saveth, one of the leading social scientific historians of the postwar period, noted that history's "public prestige has been diminished" to the extent that it resisted "being categorized as a science." The social scientists had "captured the public imagination" and carried out the essential tasks that a "practical society" demanded, such as "predicting election returns" and "selling deodorants." Saveth was well aware that the newly prestigious disciplines such as anthropology and psychology offered new concepts and techniques which seemed promising for historical analysis. Voter opinion studies, survey methods, quantitative techniques, the concept of culture, and reference group theory were only a few of the developments in the social sciences which conveyed the very real possibility of conceptual advance in history. He might also have noted that immense amounts of money were spent in the postwar period by governments and business to fund research in social science designed to contribute to the solution of practical problems in social policy. The depression, war, and post–World War II international tensions spawned big government in the United States, which in turn generated increasing state intervention in the shaping of university research.[22]

The impact was felt mainly in the scientific, military, and medical fields, with the social sciences being dragged in by the coattails. Twice as many social scientists as humanists who applied for research grants from all sources in the period 1945–1950 received some support (31 percent compared to 16 percent) while scientists did even better at 44 percent. The estimated average support for researchers working in the humanities was $800 per capita, compared to $2,000 in the social sciences, and $4,100 in the natural sciences. Much of the difference in funding came from greater governmental support for the natural and social sciences. As early as 1945–1950, with the vast institutional juggernaut of cold war agencies hardly assembled, military and governmental sources already provided more than 50 percent of all expenditures in the natural sciences to individual faculty members polled in a Social Science Research Council survey, but less than one-seventh of social science money, and no humanities money at all.[23] The percentage of research and development monies provided by government continued to rise; from just over half in 1953, it had reached two-thirds by 1963. By 1965, the federal government was spending enormous amounts of money on military and space research, and far more on defense and related industries than on education and social research, let alone humanities.[24]

These trends in funding provoked some consternation over the future of the discipline. Howard K. Beale, the president of the Pacific Coast Branch of the American Historical Association, noted in 1953 that governmental support for science was growing, to the detriment of the humanities. ''If history is to preserve its place in the world, it will have to compete with the other social studies in discovering solutions for current problems.'' For Beale, this meant a renewed commitment to the kind of critical history that Beard had pioneered, while others like Saveth more explicitly championed the cause of social science concepts in American historiography.[25]

Those who advocated the incorporation of social science concepts into a rejuvenated, humanistic discipline gradually and quietly triumphed over those who sought a return to the older version of scientific history and against those who championed narrative, facts, free will, and the role of the individual against the heresy of positivism that had produced orthodox marxism. This point is brought into sharp relief if we examine the position of social science in English historiography in the same period. There the disciples of sociological method had hardly penetrated the very traditionally structured universities, let alone seriously influenced English historical scholarship. There was little attempt at even the cross-fertilization with the social sciences which American historians preached and to some extent practiced.

The discipline's empiricist tendencies were reinforced in Britain by political developments in philosophy and the history of ideas. Karl Popper's attacks on marxist metaphysics and Isaiah Berlin's assaults on deterministic formulas did not serve to promote a more sophisticated understanding of research strategies. Rather, in the polemical context of the cold war era these works strengthened the tendency of British historians to view history as a sequence of unique events and to focus even more heavily than before on the facts. In the United States, these same currents of historiography were manifest, but in a more muted fashion and in a wholly different intellectual context in which they took on new meanings. The battle lines were not so clearly drawn in the American case. Some who expressed in articulate terms reservations about the role of social science theory, like David Potter, Hofstadter, and Oscar Handlin, were among the most vigorous in popularizing social science concepts.[26]

Because American historians were much more open to innovation in methods, the discipline there could easily generate new and more formidable defenses for its liberal empiricist assumptions. In Britain, the vitality of empiricism actually weakened the capacity of English liberal historiography to defend itself against a resurgent marxist history in the post-Stalinist era. With a theoretical vacuum ensured by the attack from the academic right, the ground was left open for innovative marxist historians centered around the journal *Past and Present*, founded in 1952, to propose serious theoretically informed alternatives. In this way marxism had come by the 1970s to influence whole areas of British historiography.

That this did not happen in the United States must in part be attributed to the prestige and intellectually imposing edifice of postwar liberal history. The historians who defended the liberal tradition through the selective application of empirical social science techniques and issues thereby succeeded in counterbalancing philosophical idealists like Lloyd Sorenson who railed against positivism, and made them voices in the academic wilderness. They also made a liberal like Arthur Schlesinger, Jr., who echoed the call of Isaiah Berlin for a reassertion of the role of individual free will and moral responsibility, increasingly antique in a methodological sense, despite his popularity with Pulitzer Prize committees. While the defenders of traditional narrative political history were fighting these ideologically inspired battles, the most impressive and influential liberal historians were creating a corpus of scholarship which recognized the importance of the individual, but encompassed that sacred liberal concept in its social setting.[27]

If social science helped to guard the liberal tradition against the influence of reactionary forms of empiricism, it also served to preempt the chance that more radical methodologies might take root. The social science approach shared one important characteristic with those who fetishized facts and emphasized the individual and the unique in history. This was the conviction that marxism represented a utopian and delusive social theory based on economic determinism, and that it must be combated at all costs. Social Science Research Council Bulletin 64 claimed to have demolished "the Marxist interpretation of change" because of "its limited purview of operative forces" while Chester M. Destler similarly denounced "Marxist economic-revolutionary thought" which resulted not from "the inexorable processes of mature capitalism" but from "fifth-column conspiratorial tactics." But where Destler could only offer denunciatory platitudes, the social science historians were able to promote concepts which retained an ideological content upon closer examination, but nonetheless could serve as manageable frames of reference for the accumulation of vast quantities of data by assiduous researchers. This empirical material, fortified with the innovative appearance of social science method and theory, would then have to be confronted by a generation of historians, analyzed, and theoretically scrutinized before alternative and potentially more radical conceptions could be advanced.[28]

The concepts put forward by the authors of Bulletin 64 are especially important to an understanding of this process. Those historians modified rather than abandoned basic liberal tenets and helped to inoculate liberal history against a possible class analysis. The new concepts such as status anxiety, stratification, social mobility, reference groups, and role theory placed individuals in a social context wherein they were shaped. Moreover, individuals were typically viewed under the social science approaches in group terms, consonant with the pluralism that was a fundamental article of the modern liberal worldview. Rather than depict society as marxists tended to do in terms of polarized and irreconcilable forces, liberal social science history since the 1950s has depicted a complex, pluralistic society in which there were a great many overlapping patterns of social action.

The analysis was not only pluralistic; it was also ultimately compatible, despite the emphasis on social factors, with the individualist conception of social reality held by American liberals. Social mobility theory, for example, involved the comparison of individual patterns of material acquisition. Society was depicted for purposes of analysis in terms of competing individuals. The individual results were then combined to show social trends and to measure the extent of individual freedom. As might be expected, these historians rarely spoke of class. They preferred to use the more descriptive categories of social status or stratification, by which "the members of a society rank each other in terms of prestige, and other types of social rewards." When class was used at all, it was *social* class or *economic* class which historians discussed. Class itself as a phenomenon was broken down into artificially constructed parts, and in fact meant merely "aggregates of individuals," not a set of relationships tied to the world of work as Marx had argued. Such concepts as role, social mobility, and status anxiety could be used to reinforce the existing worldview so as to provide it with more apparent rigor and a mystique of scientific objectivity. Thus Thomas Cochran reassured readers that "role theory" was "useful" for the historians who saw society "as a background for the actions of individuals."[29]

The ways in which these concepts could provide defenses against class analysis are subtle and profound, for the influence went much further than those enamored of the Social Science Research Council bulletins. Oscar Handlin was a prominent historian who did not agree with the extreme statements of relativism, nor with the more enthusiastic champions of social science history, and he went so far in one book written during this period to stress the role of chance in history. Nevertheless, through his wide reading in the social sciences, his teaching contributions, and many of his publications, he became an influential publicizer of sociologically informed history. While these talents are best known through his evocation of immigrant life in *The Uprooted*, published in 1951, the themes went back to his more scholarly works of the 1940s. Absorbing the concern of the New History with depicting the life of the people, Handlin skillfully synthesized close empirical research with concepts drawn from urban community studies and cultural anthropology to chart the adaptation of immigrants to the American environment, and later to explain the role of government in the American economy in the antebellum years.[30] In the process, he bypassed class dimensions of these phenomena that other historians have noticed. In *Boston's Immigrants* (1941), Handlin offered an analysis of the Irish in which a collective identity and experience in the urban environment took precedence over class divisions within Irish-American society. Because Handlin focused on the functional adaptation of the group he studied, he drew attention away from the important tradition of Irish labor radicalism which the recent research of Eric Foner demonstrates.[31] In his other important early book, *Commonwealth*, written in 1947 with Mary Flugg Handlin, the avoidance of class explanations was also latent in the analysis. Here, the Handlins discussed the role of government in a period of rapid social and economic change from the Revolution to the Civil War. Like *Boston's Immigrants*, the central theme of this study was the breakdown of traditional social controls that results in "social disorganization." From this threat to the functional stability of society came the institutional response leading to the reintegration of Massachusetts society around "humanitarian" governmental regulation of the economy. For all its strengths, the Handlins' book embodied the questionable assumption of social cohesion before the Revolution, and failed to look beyond the promotion of entrepreneurial change to the activities of workingmen who might have opposed the processes described. Central to these weaknesses was the functionalist description of a society's normal condition as one of cohesion and stability. When people protest, or conflict arises, that is described by the Handlins as "disorganization." One wonders whether it might not be better to ask whether it was some form, muted, masked, or fragmented perhaps, of class conflict. But whatever historians think about that controversial point, the Handlins have covered a complex question with the deceptively neutral concepts of functionalist sociology. For the themes of organization and disorganization preempt the question: "Who is organizing and who is being organized?"[32]

The sociological conception of the organization and disorganization of a whole society has penetrated other fields than immigrant history. Its assumptions provided historians with ways of controlling large quantities of data and understanding the systematic character of social relations. Using this framework either explicitly or implicitly, they could interpret larger-scale historical change without succumbing to marxian formulations. One of Handlin's students, David Rothman, has taken over the order-disorder-reform formulation to fashion a very influential interpretation of antebellum reform movements in *The Discovery of the Asylum*, which won a Beveridge Prize for the best book written in the field of American history in 1971. The same functionalist viewpoint also pervades the growing literature on social control as it pertains to the study of reform movements, popular culture, and social protest, though its sociological sources have not been mediated exclusively through the influence of a particular historian like Handlin.[33]

Perhaps the most useful social science methods for the preservation of liberal history against marxism, however, were those that involved quantitative techniques. Here the benefits of conceptual innovation could be combined most successfully with massive data collection. Thus empiricism could be reconciled with theory, and the development of computer technology could be harnessed to justify increasing governmental, foundation, and university support.

The quantitative social science history movement had its effective beginnings in the work of Lee Benson in the 1950s, and in particular in Benson's development of the ethnocultural interpretation of American voting. Benson proposed and in part carried out a plan to make American history more conceptually rigorous. For him history involved the testing of concepts against the record of the past. In *The Concept of Jacksonian Democracy*, the method chosen was statistical analysis of voting returns and the correlation of this data with a number of variables. The aim was to test the economic interpretation of Jacksonian democracy as a battle between the people and the special interests, as advanced by such historians as Charles Beard and the early Arthur Schlesinger, Jr. Benson drew heavily on the work of American behaviorist social scientists, especially Paul Lazarsfeld's "voting and opinion formation studies" and Robert K. Merton's role and reference group theories. Using these analytical tools, Benson came to the conclusion that religious and cultural variables were more important than economic class in determining voting patterns.[34]

Benson's failure to honor the standards of statistical precision he raised so high has proven to be the major source of criticism of his views in recent years. David Hackett Fischer notes that Benson employed "the fallacy of statistical impressionism." His statistical information was greatly reduced in value because of a failure to ensure the representativeness of his samples.[35] To focus on the representativeness of his data or his crude statistical techniques is legitimate, but it does not go far enough. That would be to pick holes in his inquiry without asking whether the assumptions underlying it were worthwhile in the first place. Benson's major failing is in fact a product of the intellectual legacy of the progressive historians, and illustrates the failure of their successors to transcend their methodology and conceptions. Though Benson set out to disprove the economic determinism of Beard and his followers, he did not challenge the idea of looking at politics in terms of economic or other factors to explain political reality. He spoke disparagingly of the terminology of "factors" or "forces," but substituted a set of "variables" which were "determinants" of "behavior." In actuality, Benson substituted a new range of causal factors, particularly ethnicity, religion, and cultural attitudes. This effectively created a new cultural determinism in place of Beard's economic schema. Benson's positivistic formulation assumed that society could be divided up into such discrete factors, and that some combination of them could be invoked to explain reality. Though Benson's "variables" were clearly abstractions from reality, he did not seem to appreciate that the relationship between and the interpenetration of the aspects of reality chosen for study ought to have been central. Instead, politics is analyzed in terms of group behavior that is actually the sum of individual, measurable phenomena like voting choices.[36]

Benson's work also suffered from a crude conception of class which reflected, as in his factor analysis, misleading constructions of reality derived from positivistic social science. His view of class he took from conceptions current in American sociology in the 1950s. Nowhere in his book did he define class, but his characterization of the phenomenon as "economic class" and his discussion of class "variables" in voting in terms of wealth and (very vaguely) occupation left no doubt of his position. Benson fully accepted the 1950s social stratifica-tionist view of class which located individuals within the social structure in terms of wealth, income, social status, or occupation.[37] These were categories more or less arbitrarily imposed upon (contemporary) American society by social scientists, who took little or no account of the relations of power between classes. Moreover, they neglected the elements of community and culture which con-tribute to the creation and maintenance of class structures. They thereby assumed that the most significant things that could be said about class could be reduced to quantifiable propositions. Yet as E. P. Thompson has argued, class is not a thing but a relationship rooted in historical transformations centered around productive processes. To abstract class from this context, as the social stratifi-cationist view adopted by Benson did and must do, is to miss the phenomenon of class entirely, and to ensure that the investigator will not find class to be of much historical significance.[38]

Despite these weaknesses, Benson had created a powerful impression of the-oretical rigor and statistical precision. More important, he had advanced his own concept of Jacksonian democracy to replace the economic class interpretation. His ethnocultural approach, backed by quantitative evidence, appealed to a profession still easily lulled into a sense of security by empirical detail. Many students took up this fresh and exciting approach, and refined Benson's insights into an imposing series of books and articles detailing the ethnic and cultural variables determining voting behavior. By the early 1970s, after the publication of important books on nineteenth-century electoral politics by Richard Jensen, Paul Kleppner, Ronald P. Formisano, and Michael Holt, the new approach had become very influential within the profession generally.[39]

The most difficult question for radical and marxist historians has been what to do with this vast amount of empirical material and its interpretive and meth-odological thrust. One early response, felt mainly in the rhetoric of the New Left, was to turn against quantification entirely, because it allegedly reduced the materials of history to the positivistic formula of bourgeois social science.[40] But there never was anything so simple as two paradigms, one a social science approach espousing and the other a radical approach rejecting quantification. Even in the 1960s a few thinkers influenced by marxism tried to incorporate quantification into radical analyses of American history. Stephan Thernstrom's *Poverty and Progress* and his criticisms of ahistorical social science showed how quantification could be geared toward radical criticism of American liberal ide-ology. Unfortunately, Thernstrom's later work, and that of those who emulated his study of social mobility, tended toward a narrower and more technical ap-proach that blocked off into a specialized field the promise of his early research. For these and other reasons, the incorporation of quantification in radical and marxist analysis did not make obvious progress until much later.[41]

Whether they were hostile, indifferent, or enthusiastic in their response, New Left historians accomplished little in the way of serious assessment of the new quantitative social science history of the 1960s. Staughton Lynd was one of the few radicals of the period to discuss the quantitative part of Benson's work, but he merely conceded Benson's statistical competence in order to make more general historiographical objections. The only sustained leftist criticism of Benson at the time of the *Concept*'s publication came from Michael Lebowitz.[42] It is probably no accident that Lebowitz's background was more in the fields of economics and statistics than in history as traditionally conceived, and his subsequent career as an economist is also consistent with this interpretation.

Most of the significant methodological discussion occurred within the quantitative fraternity, and some of the most telling criticism of the ethnocultural approach came from this source.[43] In the main, radical historians of the 1960s looked back at the consensus history of the 1950s. Thus preoccupied, they failed to come to grips with the complexity, the data, the methods, and the interpretations of the new quantitative historians. Radical historians were busy demolishing a structure which was already mutating into something more complex and impervious to purely political criticisms of "bias" and "interpretation."

Though the infusion of social science methods strengthened liberal history against attack in the 1960s, reliance on social science also entailed longer term dangers for the discipline. The historical profession was thereby made the recipient of theory rather than the formulator of its own theories. This was not, however, the intention of the apostles of social science, as David Potter's *People of Plenty* illustrates. For Potter as for Hofstadter, the new emphasis on social science did not mean a return to simpleminded positivism or a blind subordination to the social sciences. It meant selective borrowing to enrich historical explanation, and the new liberal and ethnocultural historians firmly believed that history could reciprocate by influencing the social sciences. Thus the intention was not subservience but mutual interaction.[44]

Yet the practical effect was to make the discipline more reliant on social science. In *People of Plenty*, Potter sought principally to investigate the advances made by social scientists in the areas of culture and personality, so as to throw light on the historical dimensions of the problem of a national character. As a second aim, he proclaimed the "potential value to the behavioral sciences . . . of a more active awareness of historical forces." To this end he advocated the concept of abundance to illustrate how the study of national character by social scientists could be advanced by better attention to historical specifics. While Potter thus offered to return to the social sciences as much as he borrowed, he did not fulfill these high expectations. The historian's contribution to the reciprocal enterprise turned out to be a reworking of the old theme of the frontier thesis, hardly a theoretical or methodological advance upon liberal historiography's established concerns. Potter argued that it was not merely the frontier that explained the "distinctiveness in the American character," but rather the larger "factor of abundance" of which the frontier was a special and only temporary part. Technology acted upon environment to produce the "plenty" that underwrote America's unique democratic forms. Democracy, in turn, provided the setting for the technological innovation. The distribution of plenty was not an issue, except at the level of national political ideology through the absence of class politics. Nor was the existence of that abundance clearly established. The evidence was drawn largely from post–World War II economic data, and the presence of large-scale unemployment and labor-capital conflict in American history over long periods was not woven into the consensual synthesis. Poverty was treated as the exception to the rule, an argument which more recent social historians would severely qualify. In all, *People of Plenty* involved a restatement in different terms of certain critical myths about the American nation: in particular its unique constellation of resources, and the consensual character of its civilization.[45] Potter's work was hailed within the history profession as the masterpiece of thoughtfulness, compression, and lucidity that it undoubtedly was, but it is significant that the book had little impact on the social sciences which became more and more antihistorical in the 1950s. The actual though unintended result of Potter's work was therefore not to provide cross-fertilization between disciplines but to furnish impressive social science concepts which appeared to bolster one of the central themes of the liberal historical tradition.

This borrowing process exposed the profession to fads, to concepts scarcely advanced within the discipline before they were declared outmoded in the social sciences. The historians advised to shop around for concepts ran the risk of acquiring outdated models. Conceptual borrowing meant wrenching theories out of context and obscuring their ideological content and political functions in the original disciplines which formulated them. The use of modernization theories as a central explanatory device or organizing principle is a justly famous example of this process. Even radical historians employed the polarities of modernity and tradition without realizing, at least at first, the conservative origins of modernization theory, not to mention its ahistorical and mechanical schema for assessing change. They then found themselves quickly overcome by the protests of sociologists who justly exposed the intellectual limitations and ideological implications of the whole modernization framework.[46]

When not buying shoddy goods, historians have usually shopped for familiar products. Thus the innovative character of conceptual borrowing has often been more illusory than real. The most recent example is to be found in the fashionable field of anthropology. Here the borrowing has, unfortunately, been overwhelmingly from the subdiscipline of cultural anthropology. Even some anthropologists have been struck by the one-sided use of Clifford Geertz, Mary Douglas, and other cultural anthropologists, while those who have presented more materialist theories of culture, such as Marshall Sahlins, have been neglected. Says anthropologist John W. Adams: "Historians have borrowed only what was most like history as currently practiced."[47]

Those historians who drew on social science in the 1950s tended to ignore or play down the systematic theoretical context within which particular concepts were located, in favor of specific insights that could be gleaned from the empirical work of social scientists. These historians could be found more often citing the work of Robert Merton than that of his more abstract mentor, Talcott Parsons. Perhaps this predilection stemmed from the historian's professional eye for particulars, or from the belief that Merton's structural-functionalism was less politically conservative in its implications for the liberal historians, though the state of sociological thought also justified the choice. As Thomas Cochran noted in the course of a reference to Merton, sociologists had not "worked out any generally accepted model of the structure and interaction of society."[48] In the absence, historians could only provide "general descriptions of some of the concepts used in the various areas of interest." Avoiding grand theory was aided, too, by the fact that the real strength of American sociology, at least until the rise of Parsons, had been in such areas as community studies and the empirical investigation of behavior. The emergence of survey research in the 1940s as a major field built upon this tradition and provided American historians with yet another model which did not challenge but rather endorsed their antitheoretical instincts.[49]

The whole concept of borrowing as developed by the Social Science Research Council historians of the 1950s and other liberal historians like Potter and Hofstadter was misconceived. Borrowing ironically perpetuated the antitheoretical nature of historical study. Under this approach, theory was applied to history from the outside; it did not arise from historians' attempts to fashion their own theory that was sensitive to the complex, dynamic character of historical change. Yet despite the difficulties involved in selecting appropriate theory from the social sciences, the idea of ad hoc borrowing persists to this day as the most common solution to the poverty of historical analysis.

In the final analysis, the liberal historian's response to the rise of social science theory was to incorporate theoretically derived concepts into an empiricist framework and methodology. Despite the advent of social science language and manifestos, conceptions of history and historical inquiry remained remarkably conventional. Even the most advanced prophets of a social science history did not question the national, political conception of history derived from liberal historiography, and they tended to view the past according to the fact-interpretation dichotomy. The past was a record of events to be dredged up, against which the concepts of social science would be empirically tested. Using this most publicized formula, Lee Benson sought to "test" the "concept" of "Jacksonian Democracy" against the historical record; there was little appreciation of the extent to which the concepts involved in social science could actually produce certain kinds of evidence (for example, statistical series, estimates, and oral evidence), while obscuring some relationships which could not be easily tested via statistical data, or observed in the facts. Nor was there recognition that the ideological and political status of concepts ought to be scrutinized, not simply their logical status or their correspondence with the hard data. Ubiquitous advocates of social science like Samuel Hays spoke in impressive terms of the "constant interaction between conceptualization and evidence," and denounced the distortion involved in the historian's "empiricist" use of evidence. But the concepts used in this way constituted nothing more than a miscellany of empirical generalizations of interest to contemporary American social science. Testing these ad hoc observations against historical data did not supply the theories that explained the observed phenomena, nor explain why particular generalizations deserved attention.[50]

Because the liberal historians did no more than utilize specific empirical data and concepts of American social science, the history which resulted from their efforts tended to be synthesized in ways that had important continuities with prior historiography. Postwar historians overturned, in true Beardian fashion, the myths associated with traditional issues, as Benson did with Jacksonian Democracy, as Hofstadter did in his critique of populism, and David Donald accomplished through his essays on Lincoln and the Civil War era. Sometimes the best liberal historians went so far as to shift the terms of debate by asking, as Stanley Elkins did for slavery, fresh questions of old problems, but Elkins' comparative approach was an exception to the perpetuation of a national and political conception of American history.[51]

A related difficulty was an inability in many cases to get beyond the more superficial aspects of social history. Social protest and reform, as manifest in political life, was well covered. Donald raised important questions about the motivation of antislavery agitators, Hofstadter and Mowry probed the social roots of progressive politics, influential figures in the American studies movement explored the symbolic aspects of political rhetoric in the Jacksonian era, Gusfield related the prohibition movement to status politics, and so on. These were studies of individual or group action which used the 1950s preoccupation with status, mobility, myth, and symbol to elaborate upon a political arena taken as given, but the organization of society which underpinned the sociological concepts historians imported never became the central object of historical investigation. The burden of these works, for all their efforts to bring social science and history into fruitful cooperation was to convey to American historiography an ephemeral character precisely because so much attention was devoted to social reform questions that lay at the center of the liberal concern with democratic and political progress. This impression of drift and superficiality could only have been countered with a serious and sustained attempt to construct a history of American social relations, a project that had hardly begun by 1960, and then only for limited periods and places. When Rowland Berthoff's *An Unsettled People* appeared in 1971, analysis of the social structure as it changed over time was still grossly inadequate for a historical synthesis.[52]

The quantifiers of the 1960s and 1970s did not do much better in reshaping the conceptualization of American history. Superficially more rigorous and zealously committed to social science theory and the use of computer technology, they nevertheless tended to take the political system as the central focus of their analysis, though they stressed the need for a broader examination of the social processes that underlay political life. "The time [was] ripe," claimed Samuel Hays, "for a new consideration of political life as the major context of historical inquiry.'' Hays held out the aim of studying ''the entire range of the clash of goals in society,'' but in practice the research he cited in support of his program of ''social analysis'' focused on the explication of formal democratic politics.[53]

Much of the research devoted to quantification in the 1960s and even in the 1970s revolved around the traditional democratic political issues of voting and, to a lesser extent, legislative behavior. Thus in 1961 the University of Michigan established an Inter-University Consortium for Political Research (I.C.P.R.) which has since that time gathered immense quantities of data focused on electoral history. They have collected data on computer tapes covering all American elections for president, governor, and United States senator and representative since 1824. Demographic data has more recently been added, but principally because it was ''needed to interpret election returns.''[54]

While appearing to do something new, the voting studies have actually reinforced the preoccupation of American historians with the political process in general and democratic electoral politics in particular. The ethnocultural historians did look at the social roots of political behavior, but they did so in much the same way as Beard had done. They tried to expose the real issues that constituted the engine of the formal democratic process rather than question the efficacy of the voting process itself to an understanding of American life. They may complain that it is unfair to criticize them for what they did not do rather than what they did, but the selection of a historical subject is in itself an important policy decision which can and in this case did help determine much larger areas of discourse within the profession.

The emphasis on voting flowed in part from the preoccupation of the research establishments and theorists from which computer-oriented historians took their funding and methodology. The Inter-University Consortium drew upon the behaviorist political science theory and political survey research methodology employed by the Survey Research Center of the University of Michigan which originally sponsored and funded the I.C.P.R. program. Voting was also emphasized for the simpler reason that it provided a large body of data that could easily be quantified. Political power, in contrast, could not be quantified, and its study was therefore largely neglected by the rising generation of numerate historians. In reality, however, electoral history is only a small part of political history. It is a justly famous but rarely pursued truism that the poor have had unequal access to the electoral process in America. Voting restrictions, the difficulties of the registration process, the complexity of electoral politics, and the unequal distribution of wealth and influence generally have helped to make the major American parties effective instruments for the preservation of the existing social order, for example from the 1870s to the 1930s. As James Green has pointed out, nonvoting was a widely practiced political act in late nineteenth-century America. In a political party system in which both major political parties were controlled effectively by the wealthy and powerful, nonvoting may have been a realistic response by the workers to their class situation.[55]

The point is not to damn quantification. More recently, historians such as J.

Morgan Kousser have shown that quantification far more sophisticated than that developed by ethnocultural historians can be employed to analyze race and class-based inequalities that have dominated the electoral process over long periods of American history. Kousser showed, through the use of ecological regression techniques, the effectiveness of laws in the late nineteenth-century South which were designed to exclude blacks *and* poor whites from politics. His methodology, however, is useful for measuring the social, economic, and racial basis of non-participation in other electoral contexts as well.[56] Quantification has been and must therefore remain an essential tool of analysis, but American historians have tended more than any other national grouping in the discipline of history to confuse technical competence with theoretical adequacy. Sometimes, as in the case of *Time on the Cross*, the obsession with technique has had tragic consequences when the methodological tools at the disposal of eager historians have vastly exceeded the precision, reliability, or quantity of data available.[57] One can only agree with the sensible comments of Stedman Jones on British history:

To have nineteenth-century voting patterns systematized and codified is without question a major service—but of a technical rather than a theoretical kind. . . . Given the complexities of class relations and the still as yet largely unexplored ideological shifts, it can by no means be assumed that the political behaviour of different social groups can be adequately deduced from their voting patterns merely because this is the most obvious and easiest evidence to handle.[58]

As the example of voting returns indicates, another consequence of the accommodation between social science and history after the 1950s was to reinforce the obsession with data collection which had always been an occupational hazard in the profession. Relativism had challenged the point of mindless data collection, but given the explicit use of social science concepts, it was now possible to justify rampant empiricism in terms of its use in the advancement of some concept. Backed by government grants such as those provided by the National Institute of Mental Health to the Philadelphia Social History Project and by the National Science Foundation to the Inter-University Consortium for Political Research, the sheer accumulation of data assumed renewed importance. The foundations naturally wanted results in return for their money. Computer-based research of increasingly entrepreneurial scale could provide those results and at the same time justify the infusion of further large sums of money required to build the academic empires themselves.

The Philadelphia Social History Project (PSHP) directed by Theodore Hershberg is a case in illustration of a kind of academic Parkinson's law in which the funding of research and the accumulation of data appear in a symbiotic relationship of ever increasing proportions. After eight years of lavish funding (by historical standards) from the National Institute of Mental Health, the PSHP had gathered on tape "a machine-readable data base without precedent. . . . Data are currently available on a block-by-block basis describing the 2.5 million persons who lived in the city in the years 1850, 1860, 1870, and 1880 and hundreds of thousands of individual persons and families as well as the city's housing, businesses, manufacturing firms, and transportation facilities. . . . ''[59] If the data thus gathered is impressive testimony to the value of organization, funding, and cooperative scholarly endeavor, the project has been less successful in conceptualizing research programs or producing works of historical synthesis that illustrate the value of the quantitative data. When the results of this unprecedented collective effort appeared in 1981 under the title *Philadelphia: Work, Space, Family, and Group Experience in the Nineteenth Century*, the response from within the profession was somewhat less than adulatory. There was no denying the value of the data base, nor the worth of several of the individual papers. Yet the project did not result, as Olivier Zunz pointed out, in "an integrated history of the city," nor "a convincing overall reinterpretation of urban and rural processes."[60]

Hershberg's defenders would probably reply that the absence of a grand synthesis is hardly a flaw. Hershberg himself has consistently applauded "the absence of an all-embracing theoretical framework," and asserted that PSHP workers preferred the heuristic potential of "middle range" theory. Such rhetoric notwithstanding, the PSHP project does indeed embody deeply embedded theoretical assumptions which inform the project's practice. The self-conscious absence of theory is itself a kind of theoretical framework, but more salient is the use of a frame of reference drawn from functionalist sociology. Almost with the same breath that Hershberg renounces grand theory, he proclaims that the "engine" of historical change is the process of "industrialization" and that his purpose is to chart the adaptation and differentiation of the social system under its impact. Not class relations, but that more impersonal and ostensibly neutral concept of industrialization, informs Hershberg's contribution.[61]

The 1960s move into quantification may seem here to be unfairly connected with the 1950s liberal historians discussed earlier in the chapter. After all, what does a humanist like Hofstadter have in common with a quantifier like Hershberg? Yet the more recent obsession with quantification is in part an elaboration of the themes and methods set down by the major liberal historians of the 1950s. In a revealing comment in the introduction to *Philadelphia*, Hershberg explicitly recognizes his inspiration in the conceptual framework of David Potter, "that remarkable man under whom I studied in graduate school" who "was responsible for introducing me to the social sciences and encouraging my search for a more systematic and interdisciplinary history."[62] In a further indication of important continuities between the liberal historians of the 1950s and the quantifiers, Lee Benson explicitly recognized that one purpose of his famous work, the *Concept of Jacksonian Democracy*, was "to consolidate and extend the complementary theses presented by Richard Hofstadter in *The American Political Tradition* (1948) and Louis Hartz in *The Liberal Tradition in America* (1955)." The work of that growing legion of historians who have focused on the quantification of individual social mobility is, as James Henretta has perceived, yet another "unexamined legacy of 'consensus' historiography.'' While the quantifiers, notably Samuel P. Hays, implicitly renounced part of Hofstadter's legacy—his excessive focus on ideology at the expense of behavior—Hays and others have extended Hofstadter's concern for the application of social science concepts to the empirical study of the past, and his support for the use of quantification as a component of that social science methodology.[63]

Nor did the formative figures in the postwar liberal tradition who did so much to import social science concepts into historical study repudiate the new developments in quantification. In an important comment published in *Sociology and History: Methods*, in 1968, Hofstadter praised the movement toward a more social scientific history. He identified it as the fulfillment of the "new historical genre" of "analytical history" which he had first hailed and heralded in his 1950 essay on Beard and exploited in *The Age of Reform*. Hofstadter clearly (and correctly) identified his own work with the mainstream of new social science–oriented history of the 1960s.[64]

Finishing this chapter with reference to the recent monumental work of Theodore Hershberg on Philadelphia is appropriate since certain positivist and empiricist assumptions are here reproduced in the context of an immensely complex and yet methodologically and theoretically flawed project. This same work also provides ample evidence for the continuing force of an activism and instrumentalism which first entered the liberal historical tradition in the reform of historical practice undertaken by the progressives. The sheer volume of statistical data collected and analyzed, and research papers published is awe-inspiring for historians used to individual historical enterprises. Since this data bank will continue to be available to scholars of differing persuasions, there is the prospect that its value will extend beyond the usual limits of individual projects. Moreover, the work of the Hershberg team has been so relatively good that the limitations of its methodology and its assumptions must be treated especially seriously. Hershberg's economic structural analysis of mobility in Philadelphia is superior to other mobility studies in its emphasis on what Hershberg calls "material factors" in limiting or creating individual opportunity.[65] Yet the very strength of Hershberg's analysis, his attention to actions rather than intentions, entails its own weakness. A false sense of precision and historical actuality flows from the project, because the gathering of data is governed by assumptions derived from a social science tradition which equates the study of material life with the measurement of individual behavior. Hershberg lauds his superior analysis of social mobility, but does not ask whether one ought to abstract the study of individual mobility from its collective and cultural settings in the first place. The only place for the latter in Hershberg's strategy is found in the division of social action into "material" and "attitudinal factors." Thus the workers of Philadelphia have their lives truncated into two sets of factors in the positivist mold, and the accumulation of data within this framework assumes, in practice, an over-riding importance. While Hershberg has presented a different interpretation, more radical in its implications than the interpretations of other students of social mobility, he has not questioned the theoretical assumptions of the liberal historical tradition in its social science mutation.[66]

These are not the only links with the liberal tradition. Equally important is the liberal-democratic activist orientation in Hershberg's work. He has announced as the major finding of his research so far that while the nineteenth-century city did provide for the social mobility of white immigrants, the contemporary economic structure does not provide a comparable "opportunity structure," and that modern American blacks cannot be expected to get ahead simply through self-help. Hershberg has also given notice that the policy concerns revealed in his treatment of social mobility among twentieth-century blacks reflect the increasing orientation of the PSHP toward a new goal: "the purposeful study of history to shed light on issues of contemporary social policy." This they seek to achieve through the fusion of history with the social sciences in interdisciplinary research. The goal is reflected in the move of the PSHP from its original auspices under the Department of History at the University of Pennsylvania to the School of Public and Urban Policy.[67] Clearly, the Beardian tradition of presentism, social science methods, factor analysis, and reformism is not dead, but, by way of the 1950s counterprogressives, is alive and well in Philadelphia.

The liberal history of the postwar period, of which Hershberg's work stands as the latest and one of the finest examples, has had much to commend it. One cannot help but admire the ingenuity in pressing into service a kaleidoscope of social scientific theories, the flexibility and adaptability to new intellectual currents, the increasingly sophisticated command of technical details, the engaging concern to make history relevant to present concerns, and the understanding of history as a problem-oriented discipline. The failings of liberal history were inextricably tied to these strengths, however; in many cases what were strengths if looked at from one angle became weaknesses looked at from another. These weaknesses revolved around the uncritical fascination with technique and method over theoretical adequacy, the insatiable appetite for empirical data, the failure to challenge the political conception of an American historical synthesis, the general disinterest in dissolving the geographic boundaries that restrict historical analysis, and the fragmentation of historical reality into artificially constituted causative factors.

For all this, there is no denying that the liberals built in the post–World War II period a powerful and partially effective historical tradition for comprehending the American past. The generation of Hofstadter, Potter, Handlin, Donald, Benson, Hartz, Cochran, and others perpetuated and in many ways brought to fruition the reform of historical practice begun by Beard and Turner. But they did not transcend the methodological and epistemological framework bequeathed to them by the progressives. This failure has reflected their profound attachment to the American liberal democratic state and its values. Just as the progressives had attempted to reform rather than revolutionize the American nation–state, and had developed a historical practice based on that attachment to democratic institutions, so too did the postwar historians seek to defend the reformed state against more revolutionary or reactionary theories. The New Deal and the subsequent world crisis had demonstrated the capacity of the American state for pragmatic reform, as Hofstadter pointed out.[68] The United States had escaped the disasters of social revolution and military upheaval which befell Europe. This experience impelled the defense of the democratic nation–state and its values against both right and left. One could not have expected from such liberal intellectuals any fundamental reconceptualization of the nature of historical reality, no profound reassessment of the liberal tradition in historical analysis.

Not only did they fail to transcend the progressive legacy in these ways. They abandoned the search for a synthesis that revolved around the changing economy and the life of the people in favor of a greater methodological and topical specialization that the New History itself encouraged. And they trusted to the concepts of culture and status to provide a new coherence. In the short run this choice allowed for greater complexity of analysis and enhanced technical competence, but the issue of how the parts related to the larger social structure and how the structure moved through time could not be avoided, and would inevitably be raised again. To these the liberal historians who supplanted Beard would have no answer.

NOTES

1. Richard Hofstadter, *The Paranoid Style in American Politics and Other Essays* (New York, rev. ed., 1965); Hofstadter and Michael Wallace, eds., *American Violence: A Documentary History* (New York, 1970).

2. Daniel Boorstin, *The Genius of American Politics* (Chicago, 1953); Boorstin, *The Lost World of Thomas Jefferson* (Boston, 1948), pp. ix–xi. U.S. Congress, House of Representatives, Committee on Un-American Activities, Communist Methods of Infiltration (Education), Part 1, 83rd Cong., 1st sess., 1953, pp. 51–52, 59–60.

3. Louis Hartz, *The Liberal Tradition in America* (New York, 1955).

4. Louis Hartz, *Economic Policy and Democratic Thought: Pennsylvania, 1776–1860* (Cambridge, Mass., 1948), pp. xi, 287, 289.

5. John Higham, "The Cult of the 'American Consensus': Homogenizing Our History," *Commentary* 27 (1959): 93–100; Henry Nash Smith, *Virgin Land: The American West as Symbol and Myth* (Cambridge, Mass., 1970 ed.), pp. viii, x.

6. Oscar Handlin, quoted in Richard D. Challener and Maurice Lee, Jr., "History and the Social Sciences: The Problem of Communication" (Notes on a conference held by the Social Science Research Council), *American Historical Review* 61 (1956): 331.

7. J. H. Hexter, *On Historians: Reappraisals of Some of the Makers of Modern History* (London, 1979), p. 16 n. 5; R. K. Webb, cited by Jesse Lemisch, *On Active Service in War and Peace: Politics and Ideology in the American Historical Profession* (Toronto, 1975), p. 4; Oscar Handlin, *Truth in History* (Cambridge, Mass., 1979), p. 411.

8. Chester McArthur Destler, "Some Observations on Contemporary Historical Theory," *American Historical Review* 55 (1950): 525; John Higham, with Leonard Krieger and Felix Gilbert, *History: The Development of Historical Studies in the United States* (Englewood Cliffs, N.J., 1965), p. 128.

9. Social Science Research Council Bulletin 64, *The Social Sciences in Historical*

Study: A Report of the Committee on Historiography (New York, 1954), pp. 6–7, 85, 86–88, 141–42; Challener and Lee, "History and the Social Sciences," pp. 333–34, 337–38.

10. Robert Wiebe, "Views But No Vista," *The Progressive* 33 (February 1969): 47.

11. Richard Hofstadter, "History and the Social Sciences," in Fritz Stern, ed., *The Varieties of History: From Voltaire to the Present* (New York, 1956), pp. 350–70, esp. p. 364; Charles Beard and Alfred Vagts, "Currents of Thought in Historiography," *American Historical Review* 42 (1937): 482.

12. Hofstadter, "History and the Social Sciences," pp. 368–69; Stanley Elkins and Eric McKitrick, "Richard Hofstadter, A Progress," in Elkins and McKitrick, eds., *The Hofstadter Aegis: A Memorial* (New York, 1973), p. 361.

13. Richard Hofstadter, "History and Sociology in the United States," in Seymour Martin Lipset and Richard Hofstadter, eds., *Sociology and History: Methods* (New York, 1968), p. 18.

14. Richard Hofstadter, "Beard and the Constitution: The History of an Idea," in A. S. Eisenstadt, ed., *The Craft of American History: Selected Essays*, 2 vols. (New York, 1966), 1: 157–59.

15. Richard Hofstadter, *The Age of Reform: From Bryan to F.D.R.* (New York, 1955).

16. George E. Mowry, "The California Progressive and His Rationale: A Study in Middle Class Politics," *Mississippi Valley Historical Review* 36 (1949): 239–50; Alfred D. Chandler, Jr., "The Origins of Progressive Leadership," in Elting Morison, ed., *The Letters of Theodore Roosevelt*, vol. 8 (Cambridge, Mass., 1954), pp. 1462–65; Hofstadter, *Age of Reform*, pp. 144–45; Hofstadter, "Beard and the Constitution," p. 158 n. 27. Studies in a similar vein to Hofstadter's include Stanley Elkins and Eric McKitrick, "The Founding Fathers: Young Men of the Revolution," *Political Science Quarterly* 76 (1961): 202–6; Elkins, *Slavery: A Problem in American Institutional and Intellectual Life* (Chicago, 1959), part 3; Otis L. Graham, Jr., *An Encore for Reform: The Old Progressives in the New Deal* (New York, 1967); David Donald, "Toward a Reconsideration of Abolitionists," in Donald, *Lincoln Reconsidered: Essays on the Civil War Era* (New York, 1956), pp. 19–36. Donald influenced Ari A. Hoogenboom, *Outlawing the Spoils: A History of the Civil Service Reform Movement, 1865–1883* (Bloomington, Ind., 1962), pp. viii–xi, 190–97. See also Jack P. Greene, "Foundations of Political Power in the Virginia House of Burgesses, 1720–1776," *William and Mary Quarterly*, 3rd ser., 16 (1959): 485–506.

17. Richard B. Sherman, "The Status Revolution and Massachusetts Progressive Leadership," *Political Science Quarterly* 78 (1963): 59–65; Robert Skotheim, "A Note on Historical Method," *Journal of Southern History* 25 (1959): 356–65. One of many studies that has absorbed the lessons of these critiques is Leonard L. Richards, *"Gentlemen of Property and Standing": Anti-Abolition Mobs in Jacksonian America* (New York, 1970).

18. Merle Curti, *The Making of an American Community: A Case Study of Democracy in a Frontier Community* (Stanford, Calif., 1959), p. 1; John W. Caughey, "Historians' Choice: Results of a Poll on Recently Published American History and Biography," *Mississippi Valley Historical Review* 39 (1952): 289–302; Warren Sussman, "Merle Curti," in *International Encyclopedia of the Social Sciences*, vol. 18, Biographical Suppl. (New York, 1979), pp. 133–35.

19. Timothy A. Donovan, *Historical Thought in America: Postwar Patterns* (Norman, Okla., 1973), pp. 5, 47, 73–74; Higham, *History*, pp. 132–57; A. S. Eisenstadt, "American History and Social Science," in Eisenstadt, ed., *Craft of American History*, 2: 116.

20. Carl Bridenbaugh, "The Great Mutation," *American Historical Review* 68 (1963): 315–31.

21. Edward N. Saveth, ed., *American History and the Social Sciences* (New York, 1963).

22. Edward N. Saveth, "A Science of American History," in Eisenstadt, ed., *Craft of American History*, vol. 1, p. 133.

23. Social Science Research Council, *Items* 4 (1950): 13–17; Howard K. Beale, "The Professional Historian: His Theory and His Practice," *Pacific Historical Review* 22 (1953): 227; Loren Baritz, *The Servants of Power: A History of the Use of Social Science in American Industry* (Westport, Conn., 1974 repr., orig. ed. 1960), pp. 166–67.

24. Irving Horowitz, *Professing Sociology: Studies in the Life Cycle of Social Science* (Chicago, 1968), pp. 267, 269, 271; Martin Shaw, *Marxism and Social Science: The Social Roots of Knowledge* (London, 1975), p. 34.

25. Saveth, ed., *American History and the Social Sciences*, p. 22; Beale, "Professional Historian," p. 227.

26. Hofstadter, "History and the Social Sciences"; Challener and Lee, "History and the Social Sciences," pp. 332–33; W. Stull Holt, "History and the Social Sciences Reconsidered," in Holt, *Historical Scholarship in the United States and Other Essays* (Seattle, 1967), pp. 73–83; David Potter, *People of Plenty: Economic Abundance and the American Character* (Chicago, 1954); Isaiah Berlin, *Historical Inevitability* (London, 1954); Karl Popper, *The Poverty of Historicism*, 2d ed. (London, 1960); Popper, *The Open Society and Its Enemies*, 5th ed. (Princeton, N.J., 1966); Gareth Stedman Jones, "History: The Poverty of Empiricism," in Robin Blackburn, ed., *Ideology in Social Science: Essays in Critical Social Theory* (Glasgow, 1972), pp. 96–115; John P. Kenyon, *History Men* (London, 1982).

27. Lloyd Sorensen, "Historical Currents in America," *American Quarterly* 7 (1955): 234–46; Arthur M. Schlesinger, Jr., "The Historian and History," in Eisenstadt, ed., *Craft of American History*, vol. 1, pp. 108–9; Schlesinger, "The Limits of Social Science," in Saveth, ed., *American History and the Social Sciences*, pp. 535–36.

28. SSRC Bulletin 64, pp. 109, 147 n. 27; Destler, "Some Observations on Contemporary Historical Theory," p. 517.

29. SSRC Bulletin 64, pp. vii, 48, 49.

30. Maldwyn A. Jones, "Oscar Handlin," in Marcus Cunliffe and Robin Winks, eds., *Pastmasters: Some Essays on American Historians* (New York, 1969), p. 245; Oscar Handlin, *Chance or Destiny: Turning Points in American History* (Boston, 1955), p. 210; Handlin, *The Uprooted: The Epic Story of the Great Migrations That Made the American People* (Boston, 1951); David J. Rothman, "*The Uprooted*: Thirty Years Later," *Reviews in American History* 10 (1982): 311–19.

31. Oscar Handlin, *Boston's Immigrants, 1790–1865: A Study in Acculturation* (Cambridge, Mass., 1941); Eric Foner, "Class, Ethnicity, and Radicalism in the Gilded Age: The Land League and Irish-America," *Marxist Perspectives* 2 (Summer 1978): 6–55; Robert Sean Wilentz, "Industrializing America and the Irish: Towards the New Departure," *Labor History* 20 (1979): 581–85.

32. Oscar and Mary F. Handlin, *Commonwealth: A Study of the Role of Government in the American Economy: Massachusetts, 1774–1861* (Cambridge, Mass., rev. ed., 1969), pp. 189–244. Jones, "Handlin," has an excellent critique which has influenced my argument; see pp. 251–52.

33. Gareth Stedman Jones, "Class Expression Versus Social Control," *History Work-*

shop 4 (1977): 163–70; David J. Rothman, *The Discovery of the Asylum: Social Order and Disorder in the New Republic* (Boston, 1971); Michael Katz, *The Irony of Early School Reform: Educational Innovation in Mid–Nineteenth-Century Massachusetts* (Cambridge, Mass., 1968); William Muraskin, "The Social-Control Theory in American History: A Critique," *Journal of Social History* 9 (1976): 559–69.

34. Lee Benson, *The Concept of Jacksonian Democracy: New York as a Test Case* (Princeton, N.J., 1961), pp. 264, 281–87, 329–31.

35. David Hackett Fischer, *Historians' Fallacies: Toward a Logic of Historical Thought* (New York, 1970), p. 113; Alan Bogue, Jerome Clubb, and William H. Flanigan, "The New Political History," *American Behavioral Scientist* 21 (1977): 205.

36. Though Benson talked disparagingly of "factors" in *Concept*, p. 337, the methodological foundations of this work published in 1957 (in Mirra Komarovsky, ed., *Common Frontiers of the Social Sciences* [Glencoe, Ill., 1957]) had developed similar arguments about the characteristics of voter behavior using the "factor" terminology. See Benson, "Research Problems in American Political Historiography," in Benson, *Toward the Scientific Study of History: Selected Essays of Lee Benson* (Philadelphia, 1972), p. 69.

37. Marx is not mentioned in Benson's book. Instead, there is a discussion of "economic status" and this term is used interchangeably with "economic class," "lower class," and "social class," in a critique of Beard and Turner's "economic determinism." "Economic status" equals, according to Benson, the average value of dwellings per family in the localities studied. See *Concept*, pp. 141, 142, 149, 156, 165. In a much more recent publication, "Group Cohesion and Social and Ideological Conflict: A Critique of Some Marxian and Tocquevillian Theories," *American Behavioral Scientist* 16 (1973): 745, Benson distinguishes between "economic class" ("the nominal members of a demographic group") and "social class" ("the conscious members of a communal group"). This remains a purely descriptive approach based on stratificationist principles. See E. F. Jackson and R. F. Curtis, "Conceptualization and Measurement in the Study of Social Stratification," in H. M. Blalock and A. B. Blalock, eds., *Methodology in Social Research* (New York, 1968), pp. 112–41, for a classic analysis of the techniques of stratificationist sociology and their limitations.

38. E. P. Thompson, *The Making of the English Working Class* (New York, Vintage ed., 1966), pp. 10–11.

39. Ronald P. Formisano, *The Birth of Mass Political Parties: Michigan, 1827–1860* (Princeton, N.J., 1971); Michael Holt, *Forging a Majority: The Formation of the Republican Party in Pittsburgh, 1848–1860* (New Haven, 1969); Paul Kleppner, *The Cross of Culture: A Social Analysis of Midwestern Politics, 1850–1900* (New York, 1969); Richard Jensen, *The Winning of the Midwest: Social and Political Conflict, 1888–1896* (Chicago, 1971). A more recent addition, with a reply to the critics of ethnocultural history, is Paul Kleppner, *The Third Electoral System, 1853–1892: Parties, Voters, and Political Cultures* (Chapel Hill, 1979).

40. On the rejection of quantification in a section of the New Left, see the wise remarks of Erik Olin Wright, *Class, Crisis and the State* (London, 1979), p. 10; see also Irwin Unger, "The 'New Left' and American History: Some Recent Trends in United States Historiography," *American Historical Review* 72 (1967): 1262; James Green, "Behavioralism and Class Analysis: A Review Essay on Methodology and Ideology," *Labor History* 13 (1972): 89–106.

41. Stephan Thernstrom, *Poverty and Progress: Social Mobility in a Nineteenth-Century City* (Cambridge, Mass., 1964); Robert F. Berkhofer, Jr., "The Two New Histories:

Competing Paradigms for Interpreting the American Past,'' *Organization of American Historians Newsletter* 2 (May 1983): 9–12; James Henretta, ''The Study of Social Mobility: Ideological Assumptions and Conceptual Bias,'' *Labor History* 18 (1977): 165–78; Bruce Laurie, *Working People of Philadelphia, 1800–1850* (Philadelphia, 1980), pp. ix, xi–xii.

42. Staughton Lynd, ''Scientific History,'' *Commentary* 33 (1962): 366–68; Michael Lebowitz, ''The Significance of Claptrap in American History,'' *Studies on the Left* 3 (Winter 1963): 79–94; Lebowitz, ''The Jacksonians: Paradox Lost,'' in Barton Bernstein, ed., *Towards a New Past: Dissenting Essays in American History* (New York, 1968), pp. 65–89.

43. J. Morgan Kousser, ''The 'New Political History': A Methodological Critique,'' *Reviews in American History* 4 (1976): 1–14; Bogue, Clubb, and Flanigan, ''New Political History,'' p. 205; Walter Dean Burnham, ''Quantitative History: Beyond the Correlation Coefficient: A Review Essay,'' *Historical Methods Newsletter* 4 (1971): 62–66.

44. Potter, *People of Plenty*, pp. x, 77.

45. Ibid., pp. x, xvi, xix, xx, 141.

46. The most systematic attempt to apply modernization theory to American history is in Richard D. Brown, *Modernization: The Transformation of American Life, 1600–1865* (New York, 1976), which is in turn convincingly dissected by James Henretta, '' 'Modernization': Toward a False Synthesis,'' *Reviews in American History* 5 (1977): 445–52. Among the many applications are Regina Morantz. ''Making Women Modern: Middle Class Women and Health Reform in 19th Century America,'' *Journal of Social History* 10 (1977): 490–507; Robert Wiebe, *The Search for Order, 1877–1920* (New York, 1967); Daniel Walker Howe, *The Political Culture of the American Whigs* (Chicago, 1979). The impact of modernization theory on leftist historians can be seen, for example, in Eric Foner, ''The Causes of the American Civil War: Recent Interpretations and New Directions,'' *Civil War History* 20 (1974): 197–214; cf. his reconsiderations in Foner, *Politics and Ideology in the Age of the Civil War* (New York, 1980), p. 7. For a critique of the use of modernization in the new labor history, see Daniel T. Rodgers, ''Tradition, Modernity, and the American Industrial Worker,'' *Journal of Interdisciplinary History* 7 (1977): 655–81. Standard critiques from within sociology are Dean C. Tipps, ''Modernization Theory and the Comparative Study of Societies: A Critical Perspective,'' *Comparative Studies in Society and History* 15 (1973): 199–227; and Joseph Gusfield, ''Tradition and Modernity: Misplaced Polarities in the Study of Change,'' *American Journal of Sociology* 72 (1967): 351–62. Yet modernization theory can still command a ''muted cheer'' from prominent social historians. See Peter N. Stearns, ''Modernization and Social History: Some Suggestions and a Muted Cheer,'' *Journal of Social History* 14 (1980): 189–90.

47. John W. Adams, ''Consensus, Community and Exoticism,'' *Journal of Interdisciplinary History* 12 (1981): 253.

48. SSRC Bulletin 64, pp. 42–43. For examples, see Stephan Thernstrom, ''Quantitative Methods in History,'' in Lipset and Hofstadter, eds., *Sociology and History*, p. 69; Eric McKitrick, ''The Study of Corruption,'' ibid., pp. 358–70; Robert F. Berkhofer, Jr., *A Behavioral Approach to Historical Analysis* (New York, 1969), pp. 195–97; Benson, *Concept*, pp. 264, 281–87.

49. Edward A. Purcell, Jr., *The Crisis of Democratic Theory: Scientific Naturalism and the Problem of Value* (Lexington, Ky., 1973), p. 27; Baritz, *Servants of Power*, pp. 167–68; Saveth, ''A Science of American History,'' p. 133.

50. For a conventional view, see Robert R. Palmer, "Generalizations about Revolution: A Case Study," in Louis Gottschalk, ed., *Generalization in the Writing of History* (Chicago, 1963), pp. 66, 74–75. Benson, *Concept*, p. 331, presents the more rigorous social science position; Samuel Hays, "New Possibilities for American Political History: The Social Analysis of Political Life," in Lipset and Hofstadter, eds., *Sociology and History*, p. 203.

51. Benson, *Concept*; Donald, *Lincoln Reconsidered*; Elkins, *Slavery*; Hofstadter, *Age of Reform*.

52. Joseph Gusfield, *Symbolic Crusade: Status Politics and the American Temperance Movement* (Urbana, Ill., 1963); Rowland T. Berthoff, *An Unsettled People: Social Order and Disorder in American History* (New York, 1971); Donald, "Toward a Reconsideration of Abolitionists," pp. 19–36; Hofstadter, *Age of Reform*, chap. 3; Mowry, "California Progressive," pp. 239–50; Marvin Meyers, *The Jacksonian Persuasion: Politics and Belief* (New York, Vintage ed., 1960).

53. Hays, "New Possibilities," p. 182.

54. Ibid., p. 213.

55. Ibid., p. 212; Green, "Behavioralism and Class Analysis," pp. 104–5.

56. J. Morgan Kousser, *The Shaping of Southern Politics: Suffrage Restriction and the Establishment of the One-Party South* (New Haven, 1974). How this data and methodology relate to class is treated in Michael Katz, "Social Class in North American Urban History," *Journal of Interdisciplinary History* 11 (1981): 579–605.

57. Thomas L. Haskell, "The True and Tragical History of *Time on the Cross*," *New York Review of Books*, 2 Oct. 1975, pp. 33–39.

58. Gareth Stedman Jones, "From Historical Sociology to Theoretical History," *British Journal of Sociology* 27 (1976): 303.

59. Theodore Hershberg, "The Philadelphia Social History Project: An Introduction," *Historical Methods Newsletter* 9 (1976): 43. Another case is the work of Carl F. Kaestle and Maris A. Vinovskis, *Education and Social Change in Nineteenth-Century Massachusetts* (Cambridge, Eng., 1980). For a critique of the latter work, with implications for much social-scientific history, see Michael Katz, "Hardcore Educational Historiography," *Reviews in American History* 8 (1980): 504–10.

60. For persistent reservations about the project's conceptual value, see the assessments in *Journal of Urban History* 8 (1982): 449–84, quote at p. 464. Theodore Hershberg, ed., *Philadelphia: Work, Space, Family, and Group Experience in the Nineteenth Century: Essays Toward an Interdisciplinary History of the City* (New York, 1981). Criticisms aside, the book did reprint individual contributions of great value. See Bruce Laurie, Theodore Hershberg, and George Alter, "Immigrants and Industry: The Philadelphia Experience, 1850–1880," *Journal of Social History* 9 (1975): 219–48; and Frank Furstenberg, Jr., Theodore Hershberg, and John Modell, "The Origins of the Female-Headed Black Family: The Impact of the Urban Experience," *Journal of Interdisciplinary History* 6 (1975): 211–33.

61. Hershberg, "Philadelphia Social History Project," p. 44.

62. Hershberg, *Philadelphia*, p. xvi.

63. Benson, *Concept*, p. 272; Henretta, "The Study of Social Mobility," p. 165; "A Conversation with Stephan Thernstrom," in Bruce Stave, ed., *The Making of Urban History: Historiography through Oral History* (Beverly Hills, Calif., 1977), p. 239; Hays, "New Possibilities," p. 206.

64. Richard Hofstadter, "History and Sociology in the United States," in Lipset and Hofstadter, eds., *Sociology and History*, p. 18.

65. Hershberg, *Philadelphia*, pp. 13–20.

66. Ibid., pp. ix, xiii.

67. Ibid., pp. 457–58, 462.

68. Hofstadter, *Paranoid Style*, pp. 42–43, 225–26; Hofstadter, *Age of Reform*, pp. 324–28.

5

A Mirror to Orthodoxy: Aspects of the New Left

The decade of the 1960s produced the first and most ineffectual challenge to the liberal synthesis. Earnest young radicals issued clarion calls to reform the profession, and angrily denounced the consensus interpretation. For a time, this New Left movement seemed refreshing in its reassertion of moral questions, its rediscovery of conflict, its rehabilitation of Charles Beard, and its emphasis upon the history of common people and minority groups. The New Left approach has also brought some lasting advances to the profession, notably in the consideration of nonelite history—from the bottom up, as it has been put—and in the economic analysis of foreign policy in the work of William Appleman Williams and his students.

In retrospect, however, and these caveats aside, the New Left must be pronounced an intellectual failure. A New Left reinterpretation of American history has not materialized. Fifteen years after publication, the manifesto of New Left academic history, *Towards a New Past*, seems curiously insignificant in relation to subsequent developments in American historiography. With few exceptions, the achievements of its contributors have hardly rocked, let alone transformed, the historical establishment. Why the gap between promise and performance has been so vast is complex. One or two of the contributors to *Towards a New Past* ran afoul of the establishment they attacked because their partisanship was more explicit than the political interventions of the liberal historians of the 1950s.[1] There was, too, the failure of some of the New Left historians to do the hard work necessary to supplant existing historiography. In several cases discussed in this chapter, political activism in various ways took precedence over scholarship. But there was also a theoretical failure which conditioned gratuitous intellectual and political difficulties. It was the failure of the New Left historians to transcend the conceptual and methodological legacy of liberal historiography that condemned their laudable crusade to ignominious defeat. Despite their radical credentials and brash claims, the central figures among New Left American historians remained empiricists, and more important, they remained trapped within a liberal problematic bequeathed to them from the tradition going back to Beard and Becker.

Though the radical historians who tried to take consensus history apart failed to make much impact on the profession, there was a much broader though more diffuse intellectual reorientation derived from the radical experience of the 1960s which has profoundly altered the substance of American historical research. This change involved the emergence of the "new social history," a history aimed at the study of social structures and processes, and especially at the role of racial, sexual, cultural, and class forces in the making of that history. Assessing the impact of the New Left therefore involves the study of both phases of this intellectual reorientation.

New Left history was of course a product in part of the social ferment of the 1960s associated with civil rights and anti-Vietnam protests. The unedifying spectacle of America's imperialist adventure in Asia was especially critical in radicalizing many young Americans in this decade. It is not surprising, therefore, that strident attacks on liberal historiography and especially on consensus history should develop. Some of this work began to appear in Students for a Democratic Society (SDS) pamphlets, some in radical and socialist periodicals, such as *Studies on the Left*, and some of it was published in the mainstream professional journals and scholarly presses. An important early institutional focus, both for New Left historians and for *Studies on the Left*, was the University of Wisconsin, where William Appleman Williams and Fred Harvey Harrington had, among others, been instrumental in developing alternative analyses of American society with potentially radical implications. Their work on the economics of American imperialism, especially that of Williams, is so important that it receives extensive treatment in this chapter. I have reserved for a later chapter considerations of contemporaneous work done in *Studies on the Left* and other forums by such authors as Gabriel Kolko, James Weinstein, and Eugene Genovese, all of whom wrote within an identifiably marxist context. In this chapter, I deal only with the aspects of the New Left (c. 1960–1970) that were not closely identified with marxism.[2]

What is most striking about early radical history in retrospect is not its daring innovation, but its conformity with traditional topics and methods. New Left historians concentrated their vitriol on the consensus school and its interpretations, not its methods. This meant locking horns with the liberals on their own ground of established historical debates derived mostly from the liberal problematic and national political issues. More important, it meant accepting the conceptualization and periodization imposed by the liberals themselves. The New Left, having chosen such unfavorable ground on which to fight, tried to criticize the specific interpretations and evidence of the liberals. Thus Norman Pollack took issue with Hofstadter and Handlin in their views of Populism without questioning that category of analysis in any serious way. Similarly, Lynd and Jesse Lemisch criticized consensus views of the Revolution and brought conflict back into interpretations of that upheaval, but the focus remained national and political. They seemed to think that if social and economic divisions could be put back into the interpretive picture, the historiography of the period could be radically transformed. They spent much time trying to resurrect a radical tradition, and showing the contribution of radicals to the unfolding of the freedom of the American people and the creation of democratic institutions. Thus Lemisch attempted to interpret popular radicalism as contributing to the Revolution and democratizing its aims. Lower-class seamen, in Lemisch's study of impressment, are added to "the causes" of the Revolution, and their riots interpreted within the language of Lockean political ideology.[3]

Another defining characteristic of the New Left was its renunciation of marxist orthodoxy. This they equated as the liberal historians did with the economic marxism of the Old Left. Howard Zinn demonstrated how little attraction New Left writers and activists found in the Old Left. He noted that "the traditional marxian idea of revolution because of a breakdown in the capitalist mechanism and its replacement by an organized, class-conscious proletariat" was "hardly tenable today." Socialist revolutions had "been possible mostly because war had weakened or destroyed a state and created a power vacuum." The workers in a highly developed industrial society like the United States seemed quiescent, while students and blacks, not Marx's proletariat, "were the forces for revolutionary change." To make matters worse, the Old Left was saddled with the embarrassments of "socialism" at work in the "East" in the form of Stalinist and post-Stalinist political repression and Russian territorial aggression. Given these understandable perceptions of postwar marxism, the New Left felt free to cut loose both from past orthodoxy and from the reliance on theory itself. Much more persuasive than Marx for the New Left was C. Wright Mills, whose study of *The Power Elite* not only exploded the pretensions of liberal pluralism, but also undermined simplistic marxist notions of class conflict as well.[4]

Against the mechanical and vulgar determinism of the Old Left, New Left writers like Zinn and Staughton Lynd put emphasis upon the creative application of marxist principles of activism. They took as their cue the famous aphorism that "the philosophers have interpreted the world in various ways, the point however is to change it." By "it" they meant to change marxism as well as the world. For Lynd, marxism became an existential philosophy, marxist theory "a backdrop to the stage on which historical protagonists play their self-determined parts." For Zinn, too, it was necessary to "act out" marxism rather than take "all the exact propositions about the world that Marx and Engels lived in." As Zinn recognized, this approach entailed not only existentialism, but an "admixture of pragmatism [and] empiricism into Marxist theory." Though Zinn and Lynd invoked rhetorically the marxist concept of praxis, the actual operation of their existential marxism meant an abdication of theoretical tools of analysis for the tactical imperatives of everyday experience.[5]

Hostility to the economism of the Old Left rubbed off in the historical issues that New Leftists treated. They tended to deemphasize the economic class struggle associated with vulgar marxism, in favor of stressing conflicts of other kinds. They did not deny the reality of economic forces, especially in the determination of American foreign policy, and there was some rehabilitation among them of the reputation of Charles Beard. But cultural and racial questions impressed them more than economics.

The shift from economic to cultural questions and from theory to activism was of course a product not only of revulsion against the Old Left, but also of the practical experience and programmatic objectives of the larger New Left political movement. Most of the leading New Left historians were in some way connected to the civil rights and anti-Vietnam agitation, and their careers were sometimes transformed by that experience. For Staughton Lynd, the shift to new cultural and racial questions took place in the context of his teaching in Atlanta and his association with the southern civil rights movement in the early 1960s. Similarly, Howard Zinn's major activist works, *SNCC: The New Abolitionists* and *The Southern Mystique*, drew on his experience as chairman of the department of history at Spelman College, Atlanta. Zinn, like Lynd, began with a scholarly monograph, *LaGuardia in Congress*, but his work was transformed by the civil rights experience and his part in it.[6]

The response meted out in the discipline to dissenting history was as diverse as the interpretive stances of the practicing historian. Generally speaking, there was no blanket denunciation of the New Left. New Left historians were allowed to speak at the major professional conferences, and some of their work did appear in the leading journals. Scholarly assessments of the New Left were not uniformly hostile either. Critics tended to suggest that the work of the radicals was uneven, ranging from careful empirical study to wildly partisan exaggeration. The larger profession thus drew lines to distinguish ''good'' from ''bad'' New Left history, and those lines were mostly drawn on the questions of evidence and impartiality. Those who breached these guidelines were condemned, refuted, or ignored, but the insights of New Left writers that appeared to be based on the facts were selectively incorporated into the existing synthesis. This process of preserving the existing historical practice through absorption and mutation occurred most obviously in textbooks, where publishers rushed to incorporate new sections on the Vietnam war, black protest, and other topics familiar to New Left rhetoric, but the process was also seen in the comments of leading practitioners. Contributors to John Garraty's *Conversations with Historians*, an ''oral history'' of historiography by such people as Arthur Schlesinger, Jr., Hofstadter, Ernest May, and C. Vann Woodward, repeatedly welcomed the addition of new viewpoints to the diverse American historical tradition. At the same time, they warned against biased New Left work.[7]

The activism of the New Left became not only its defining characteristic but also the target of criticism from the mainstream of the profession. The stridently partisan tone in some New Left writing and its tendency to play down the value or possibility of unbiased history opened the young radical historians to the wrath of liberal critics. David Donald's acidic appraisal of *Towards a New Past* in the

American Historical Review found fault with the New Left's belligerently revisionist "cannibalizing" of their "predecessors." Rather than engaging in strident critiques of other historians, they ought to be getting on "with the writing
of their own books." Phrased in another forum to encompass all such historical
revisionism, Donald reaffirmed the importance of scholars' getting "on with the
historian's main task, that of rediscovering the past."[8] Jerold S. Auerbach offered
a similarly misleading point of view drawn from his empiricist epistemology
when he wrote: "The historian who is a partisan for or against the present
deprives himself of the insights that only come after he permits the present to
frame his questions and insists that the past alone provide his answers—on *its*
terms, not his." This commonplace and almost anthropomorphic view of the
past as an entity that could provide an objective and independent retort to the
present's questions surfaced again and again, most notably in a critique by Irwin
Unger. "If history has any pragmatic value," Unger concluded after a long
survey of New Left partisanship, "surely it must be history that is allowed to
speak for itself. Let the New Left ask its own questions of the past, but let the
past then say its piece."[9]

The adoption by certain New Left historians of a deliberately partisan tone
and their denial of historical objectivity played into the hands of the historical
establishment. It was easy for liberal historians not only to dismiss the general
programmatic assertions of New Left writers, but also to cast doubt on their
more specific interpretations as irretrievably biased. In some cases, as with Jesse
Lemisch and Staughton Lynd, the accusations of bias were used to justify professional discrimination as well as intellectual denunciation.[10]

Up to this point I have analyzed the New Left in terms of its general unities,
but further understanding of its weaknesses will not come until we break the
general category of New Left writers into more specific subgroupings. This is
essential because there was much diversity within the New Left, which is best
treated as a loose coalition of individuals clustered around two intellectual positions. First there were those who adopted an activist approach to life and history.
These included historians like Martin Duberman, Lynd, and Zinn. Zinn, for
example, asked historians to decide "from a particular ethical base what is the
action-need of the moment, and to concentrate on that aspect of the truth complex
which fulfills that need." Then there were those like Jesse Lemisch, William
Appleman Williams, and Norman Pollack, who professed the need for a more
objective history and sought to change interpretations of the past by the traditional
historical methods of presentation of evidence and professional debate. While
Lemisch often seemed in his attacks on the historical establishment to be as
partisan as Lynd was, Lemisch was actually attacking the partisanship of the
liberals and arguing for a more complete, more objective history that would
encompass radical perspectives. The differences between the two broad groupings
were, of course, matters of emphasis. Lynd and Zinn, for example, both believed
at least to some degree that they were advancing historical truth through the
interjection of present-mindedness into the historical debate, while historians

critical of "movement" or "relevant" history like Lemisch conceded that any attempt to redress the balance in favor of conflict interpretation rather than consensus must add to the total picture of the past, whatever its initial motivation.[11]

Though each professed different aims and methods, the two approaches both foundered, in different ways, upon their confrontation with the legacy of empiricism and positivism in the historical discipline. The "movement" historians found that their attempts to create a relevant history conflicted with historical objectivity, and the result was not a reorientation of historical thought but disillusionment with history because it did not easily succumb to the radical assaults. The second group tried, in effect, to beat the liberals at their own game, and they too failed in varying degrees. The result was either absorption of the new evidence into the existing liberal synthesis or the rejection of the new interpretations as empirically inadequate.

Martin Duberman illustrates some of the dilemmas that a search for a usable past raised in the practice of historians sympathetic to the new radical currents. His intellectual odyssey amply demonstrates the debilitating effects of a subservience within the New Left to empiricism. Duberman came to the study of the past in the late 1950s with the "initial expectation" that it "*could* help us 'problem solve,' could help us to understand not only how we got where we are, but also where we want to go and how to get there." Although he never totally dismissed the value of history, Duberman came by 1969 to espouse a profound disillusionment with the discipline because it could not in his opinion serve those important activist ends. Duberman's growing dissatisfaction with history stemmed from an empiricist conception of truth that was entirely compatible with the liberal historical tradition. Contextual differences and the "limited evidence" of the past left historical study "of marginal utility for those"— like Duberman—concerned with "acting in the present." There was simply not enough evidence to build up a reliable picture of past motivations or actions. Despite years of study of the abolitionist poet James Russell Lowell, Duberman still felt unable to explain the man's deepest motives, and therefore felt unable to generalize about historical processes governing the activities of radical social movements in the past. Those interested in finding the sources of social movements would, Duberman argued, be better off reading contemporary sociological studies, which "provide that very abundance of detail and analysis so absent in historical efforts."[12]

Duberman's confidence that social science could provide certainty in the area of human understanding where history had failed was quite misplaced. His confusion rested on the delusion that because students of present behavior had more evidence they could get closer to "the truth" about that behavior. The methods and ideological assumptions underlying social research were not subjected by Duberman to critical scrutiny, and the logical conclusion of his position was abandonment of history entirely. Though Duberman did not cease to profess history in the sense of teaching it, he did move increasingly toward valuing creative writing as a means of self-expression and critical social insight. It is probably a fair judgment to conclude that he has not fulfilled his early promise of becoming one of the nation's most productive as well as insightful historians.[13]

The effects of this debilitating empiricism on the radical offensive are even better illustrated in the recent career of Staughton Lynd than they are in the case of Duberman. Lynd was like Duberman and Zinn a man with "an activist orientation to life." History seemed to Lynd to offer service in that quest for "a better world which mattered very much to me." In the search for that activist past which could help contemporary radical needs, Lynd first tested the economic interpretation of Charles Beard, then studied slavery and race relations and their connection to the making of the constitution, and finally turned to a study of the origins of American radicalism that emphasized the links between eighteenth- and nineteenth-century radical movements, and the political and intellectual concerns of the 1960s. By the early 1970s, Lynd had become increasingly dissatisfied with the limitations placed upon his activist mentality by the need for historical objectivity.

I found myself more and more frustrated by the fact that a historian is not supposed to attach values to his or her conclusions, a historian is not supposed to say at the end of the book, "Now this means we should all go out and do so and so." And I felt as a person with an activist orientation to life, that I had trapped myself into a discipline which was inherently schizophrenic for a person like myself. If you try to infuse your objective work with your values, to comment on it, then of course you are "presentist." If, on the other hand, you bend over backwards not to do that, you run a danger of losing track of who you are, of disassociating yourself from your own values. I wasn't happy with that dilemma. . . . [14]

Lynd's dilemma arose because he saw a tension between historical truth and present perspectives which mirrored the larger tension between mind and action that debilitated New Left thought generally. Like Howard Zinn, Lynd first tried to think his way out of the dilemma by asserting that there were many truths, and that provided the historian grabbed hold of one of them, then he or she had satisfied the demands for historical objectivity. Truth, Lynd argued (adopting an old philosophical analogy), "is an elephant with many sides, and if a scholar grasps that leg which is closest to him he nevertheless lays hold of something that is really there."[15] A detailed analysis of this view and its implications is instructive for an understanding of the failure of New Left scholarship, since Lynd's analogy—and his epistemology—was widely accepted in the New Left. Phrased somewhat differently in another of his papers as "like a mountain" which "can be viewed from many different standpoints, all equally 'objective,' " Lynd's view of historical truth won the support of Alfred F. Young in his *Dissent: Explorations in the History of American Radicalism*. Despite apparent differences, it was also the view of Jesse Lemisch. Though Lemisch was a ferocious and sensible critic of mindless relevance in radical scholarship, he nevertheless conceded that present-mindedness "is not all bad," and offered as support none other than Lynd's elephant analogy.[16]

This was a very weak and unsatisfactory answer to the problem of historical objectivity and knowledge raised by the activism of the New Left. Every truth became under this formula equal to all others; nothing was said about the relationship between different truths; it was as if, to extend Lynd's ungainly analogy, the tusks of the elephant were as indispensable as its heart. The implication of this view was that if each historian grasped that part of the elephant which most interested him or her, then what would result was a comprehensive picture of the whole elephant. Nothing could be further from the truth. It was necessary to assess logically and empirically the contribution of both old and new views, and to show how the different aspects of a particular historical object could be related to one another to elucidate its structures and processes. This the New Left consistently failed to do. Given this failure to transcend the idea of historiography as the sum of individual views, it is small wonder that the New Left historians remained open to the charge of partisanship which their liberal colleagues duly issued.

Equally significant was the larger question of empiricism on which the New Left's attitude to historical truth was founded. The content and effects of that empiricism upon the New Left are amply illustrated in Lynd's recent career. By the early 1970s, Lynd chafed at the need to adhere to the profession's standards of objectivity, but he did not question the validity of the historian's conventional notion of the past. History's truth was still something "out there" and open to the historical observer independent of theoretical mediation. Lynd sought to reconcile the dilemma of activism versus objectivity not by a reappraisal of empiricist notions of truth, but by moving into a new type of history—oral history—as "a way to break through the methodological impasse of being an observer." He decided to interview union organizers from the 1930s to make available for the New Left their experiences of life and labor so that intellectual and practical bridges could be built between working-class people and the New Left. This way he could be faithfully presenting the evidence of historical actors while serving a useful activist aim.[17]

Yet Lynd's oral history did not resolve the dilemmas stemming from his subservience to empiricist assumptions. In fact, the oral history phase of Lynd's career illustrated in poignant fashion the paralyzing and intellectually debilitating effects of failing to challenge the dominant epistemology. This point can be made clearer by looking at Lynd's view of history from the bottom up, how he proposed to further that history through oral evidence, and how his attempt degenerated into a celebration of pure experience.

Though Lynd was, like Lemisch, concerned with the history of the inarticulate, common people, he differed from Lemisch in his skepticism about the possibility of recovering that history from purely written records. His "own quarrel" with Lemisch's efforts to set the record straight was "not with its contention that history has been distorted but with its hope that the truth can be restored."[18] "From the standpoint of knowledge," he argued, "I question how much about the bottom really can be derived from the fragmentary documentary sources that we're perforce driven to use." From the point of view of the New Left historian trying to redress the balance in historical scholarship by focusing on the inarticulate, it seemed preferable to work on the recent past, where the techniques of oral history could be employed as they never could in the history of earlier periods. For Lynd, studying the recent past was more fruitful since more of the evidence was available; radical history was to be judged in terms of the quantity of its evidence. The efforts of historians to reconstruct, patiently from "assiduous digging" and "innovative use of evidence," the history of medieval and early modern times had limited yields since after all that work, he argued, "how much do you really know about those people?"[19] Whereas Duberman's question conceded in practice the superiority of social science methodology and contemporary research, Lynd opted for the oral history technique and the raw experience of living historical actors.

Taken to its logical conclusion, Lynd's view left no place for the historian at all; the historian was simply someone whose ego came between the data and the reader. And Lynd did take his radical philosophy far in that direction. Still concerned to produce a history with relevance to present needs, yet reluctant to editorialize, he decided to opt for the role of "a catalyst, an organizer" who prepared the stage on which the historical protagonists could speak without scholarly intervention.

Naturally Lynd was taken to task by perceptive critics within the profession. David Brody, for example, noted simply that the material Lynd assembled with Alice Lynd in *Rank and File: Personal Histories by Working-Class Organizers* did not speak for itself. The book was not an oral history of the rank and file at all but rather of radical organizers. Lynd did not seem to understand or care at that time that the meaning of the data was unclear. From the traditional standpoint of the historian, Lynd had not checked each and every episode against other sources for veracity and significance.[20] Lynd might have overcome these objections, had he realized or made clear that the oral evidence could not be employed to open a window onto the actuality of the past. Since the evidence was culturally and historically constructed, it ought to have been assessed in that light for possible meanings. Instead, Lynd capitulated by default to the empiricist conception, and received just criticism for his failure to act out the role of the historian as gatekeeper between fact and fantasy. Lynd could perhaps have appropriated to his own purpose the constructed meanings of the oral evidence through the aid of theory, but theory was something in short supply among the radicals of the New Left. By 1977, Lynd had come full circle to concede explicitly the legitimacy of traditional historical practice. Convinced that the critical responsibilities of the historian to remain objective were incompatible with his own sense of social injustice and activist temperament, Lynd had ceased to work as a historian, and moved into a field that he found more intellectually congenial: labor law. Thus foundered upon an inadequate conception of historical inquiry one of the most promising historians of the 1960s.[21]

Lynd's career (and to some extent also that of Duberman and Zinn) is particularly instructive when placed alongside the career of E. P. Thompson, another committed radical active in the 1960s. The gap between mind and action was not so strongly evident in the English case. There committed scholars like Thompson, Hobsbawm, and Hill could mix historical work and political commitment without any sense that these aims might be conflicting. It is true that Thompson eventually left his teaching post at Warwick University but he did not leave off writing history of a high academic standard. He resigned instead because of disillusionment with increasing pressure to turn Warwick into a more practical, business-oriented university, and because the pressures of university teaching interfered with his ambitious writing projects. The question of activism versus intellectual commitment to history simply did not arise as a problem at that time.[22]

The career of Jesse Lemisch brings us to a set of cases illustrating different aspects of the dilemmas stemming from the empiricist epistemology of the radical historians. This was the attempt by various New Left historians not consciously to champion partisan causes, but rather to use traditional standards of evidence to challenge liberal interpretations. While the perils of this approach were apparent in many of Lemisch's specifically historical works, an appraisal of his historiographical essay entitled "Present-mindedness revisited," originally delivered at the American Historical Association convention in December 1969, is especially instructive. There Lemisch recognized that the liberal history of the 1950s was in some sense both partisan and conservative in its implications. He insisted further on a conspiratorial view of the historical profession, in which radical opinions were consciously but surreptitiously suppressed while liberal alternatives shot through with political import were bandied about the length and breadth of the profession.[23]

Lemisch did not choose to demonstrate these points by laying bare the methodological and epistemological roots of liberal history. His contentions rested rather, as did much of his more specific historical work, on faith in historical facts. He emphasized the importance of "evidence," not "relevance," in sectarian battles within the New Left.[24] He wrote eloquently and perceptively on the ideology that passed for objective history among certain liberals, but naively believed that the balance of historical interpretation could be redressed by presenting the evidence of what had really happened in the past. His historiographical critique of the liberal interpretation erred chiefly in its presentation of *examples* of discrimination against the left, or *examples* of allegedly biased interpretation. He did not present any systematic exposition of the profession's biases or show how they were produced. His error was further revealed in his confession that although he had not done the detailed research in historical interpretations which he had originally hoped to complete, his work showed the *tendency* within the profession. He had no theory of the operation of the profession beyond the evidence of individual examples. His method was simply to pile one case upon another, without discriminating between liberal and conservative bias. The result was a simplistic account of the exercise of established power; the complex processes whereby new viewpoints were incorporated into the existing historiography were not studied.

As a consequence, fruitful lines of inquiry suggested by Lemisch's essay could be easily dismissed in the profession as a whole. R. K. Webb, the editor of the *American Historical Review*, was able to refuse publication by citing counterexamples. Webb simply declared Lemisch's evidence unrepresentative, leaving Lemisch with the impossible task of trying to prove that his cases were indeed typical, and that Webb's assertion that they were atypical and extreme was false.[25] As for Lemisch's specific claim of overt political bias against radicals, this could easily be deflected by pointing to examples of liberal tolerance of deviant left-wing opinion. Thus Irwin Unger could question the bias against the left by pointing to the fact that Walter LaFeber, an important New Left writer, had won the Albert J. Beveridge Award in 1962 for his *The New Empire*. "That it should win this prestigious award casts some doubt," Unger remarked, "either on the hostility of the establishment toward the New Left or on their academic influence."[26] So long as the issue rested on examples, rather than the elucidation of the structure of the profession, and so long as it rested on the question of overt bias rather than on the appraisal of the profession's assumptions, writers like Unger could escape with such misleading half-truths.

Norman Pollack, author of a controversial reinterpretation of populism, displayed equally unwittingly the perils of a failure to transcend the fact-theory dichotomy. Pollack claimed that his interpretation in *The Populist Response to Industrial America* grew "directly out of the evidence itself. It was reached inductively, and not deductively."[27] Pollack criticized such liberal historians as Richard Hofstadter and Oscar Handlin for political and ideological bias. In his "Fear of Man: Populism, Authoritarianism, and the Historian," Pollack noted the "preoccupation with present-day values" of the so-called consensus historians "and the attempt to read [those values] back into the past."[28] This claim that the consensus historians had disregarded the evidence while Pollack's account flowed from the facts left Pollack very vulnerable to the charge that he too had composed an account which was not factually accurate, and which did nothing but impose the present on the past. This was precisely the charge that Irwin Unger made in his critique of Pollack's interpretation. Pollack's attack on Hofstadter thus ended in inconclusive assertions and counterassertions of factual accuracy, while Pollack himself could be easily dismissed as an ungracious and irresponsible critic.[29]

The New Left foreign policy of the so-called Williams School, centered around William Appleman Williams and Fred Harvey Harrington, similarly failed to transcend the limits of liberal history, though its practitioners did come to specific interpretive conclusions which were to have a considerable effect on the discipline. The role of Walter LaFeber's *The New Empire* in recasting the debate over late nineteenth-century foreign policy in terms of the economic imperatives of a productive crisis in the capitalist economy is generally acknowledged. Not only did the book win professional awards and wide praise. A session of the

1971 Organization of American Historians convention devoted to the book's impact showed that two-thirds of the diplomatic historians surveyed acknowledged that "they had been greatly to moderately affected by LaFeber's volume."[30]

More important still than the work of LaFeber was that of Williams himself. Carl Degler, in his presidential address before the Organization of American Historians in 1980, went so far as to claim that "the influence" of William Appleman Williams had "largely transformed" the "history of foreign relations" in the United States. The element of truth behind this acknowledgment of his influence can be made clear not only by noting his own works, such as *Tragedy of American Diplomacy* and *Roots of the Modern American Empire*, but also by listing a few of the works of his many protégés. These have included Thomas McCormick, *China Market: America's Quest for Informal Empire, 1893–1901* (Chicago, 1967); Carl Parrini, *Heir to Empire, United States Economic Diplomacy, 1916–1923* (Pittsburgh, 1969); and Lloyd C. Gardner, *Economic Aspects of New Deal Diplomacy* (Madison, Wisc., 1964).[31]

These historians have had considerable influence on the profession because they have been prepared to do the hard empirical research necessary to establish new interpretations, but they have also succeeded because their work has been mutually reinforcing. Almost all have had connections with the Wisconsin graduate program, and they have generally complemented each other's work while consciously building upon the indefatigable labors of their mentor, Williams. They bear as a consequence the marks of a school of interpretation in a way that has not been common in American historical scholarship since the time of Turner. It is largely a result of the existence of this quasi-collective enterprise that Williams' impact has been greater than that of any other historian "of socialist persuasion" in the United States.[32]

Yet for all the influence that Williams has exerted, it could not be said that he and his admirers have transformed the profession, as Charles Maier's essay on recent work in diplomatic history makes clear. The shape of scholarship in international and diplomatic history remains very pluralistic, and the Williams approach is only one of a number of competing *interpretations*. As Robert Beisner's survey of diplomatic historians in 1971 indicated, many had been influenced by the work of LaFeber, but "few had changed the chronological structures of their courses as a result."[33] Neither has the Williams School succeeded in restructuring the method of diplomatic history. "Rankean exegesis," Charles Maier notes, "still forms the basis of the craft" of international and diplomatic history in the United States.[34]

In part the failures of the Williams School stemmed from the obvious fact that American historical scholarship was too broad, diverse, and amorphous to be easily susceptible to radical assault. For every interpretation there has always been and always will be another view, so long, at least, as liberal pluralism lasts. Those who in the 1960s ran the most prestigious departments, the professional journals, and the major historical associations tended to reflect the mainstream liberal position as reinterpreted in the 1950s. With some exceptions, they favored analyses which played down the significance of economic interests, stressed a plurality of factors, and emphasized that the United States was not so wicked, greedy, or irresponsible as some New Left historians seemed to be claiming.[35]

The traditions and practice of diplomatic historiography also limited the potential impact of the Williams approach. He and his students wrote in the context of an established historiography in which traditional methods were probably more entrenched than in any other field of American history. The main issues of diplomatic and foreign policy history were quite naturally drawn from the national history of the American republic and its geographic expansion and political involvement in the international community. As left-liberals or radicals, passionately concerned with the direction of American policy in the postwar world, Williams and his disciples wished to contribute to that debate over the course of American expansion, and as a consequence, the issues that they tended to become involved in were usually old ones: the origins of the American territorial empire in 1898, the failures of Wilsonian diplomacy, and the coming of World War II. The study of the origins of the cold war was of course a much more novel topic, but it was so mainly because it referred to events in the very recent American past that connected in direct ways with the conduct of present-day American foreign policies. Like Beard who had tried to find the economic causes of political events, the Williams School tried to find the economic causes of diplomatic events and foreign policy decision making. They tended to neglect analysis of the economics of foreign relations except insofar as this was connected to political decision making. To be sure, economic and political issues in twentieth-century foreign policy have been interlocking and must be treated together as Williams and his followers have insisted, but the focus of their inquiry has been very much upon critical periods of national policy-making rather than upon analysis of the dynamics of the economic structures themselves, which remained either subordinate or unexamined. In their most innovative work, such as Williams' important contribution to the hackneyed topic of isolationism versus internationalism, the New Left historians did put the old issues and chronological frameworks in new and more realistic perspectives. But when the dust settled, the profession was still left, under the Williams formula, with a historiography which emphasized the power and free destiny of American purpose, while neglecting the "comparative dimension" which might have given an understanding of the limits to and forces shaping conceptions of America's power in the post–World War II period.[36]

As these comments imply, Williams' view of American foreign policy remained very much within the voluntaristic traditions of the progressives. His approach showed insufficient attention to the dynamics of an international system qua system. Yet it is precisely this analysis of systemic forces which has distinguished some of the best recent work on international politics and history. The concept of an international system has been broadened by writers like Charles Maier to include interlocking domestic and international pressures of the social, cultural, and economic as well as political kind. It is likely that future writers on American foreign policy will be attracted to such approaches rather than continue to stress domestic drives for manipulation and expansion. That preference and its insights may well reflect the growing interdependence of the international capitalist order in the post–World War II period. But whatever the intellectual origins of concepts of international systems, they can be used to study more than contemporary politics. They could illuminate earlier periods of American international involvement as well. Despite considerable achievements, the Williams School has had little to offer to this enterprise. Their research led away from a multinational approach to a consideration of specifically American and, particularly, domestic impulses, and to the question of American choices in diplomacy.[37]

Further problems have stemmed from the economic interpretations of these historians. Critics have repeatedly claimed that Williams' work seemed on one level to represent a sophisticated perpetuation of Beard's own approach to foreign policy in the 1930s. There is no doubt that Williams was an admirer of Beard but he was an admirer who sought to transcend the progressive interpretation from which his work was originally derived. Williams tried to reconstruct the progressive argument that economic factors had been the most important influence on politics by showing how politics and economics shared a common ground of economic ideas shaping foreign policy. The question whether economics "caused" politics or vice versa simply did not arise. This approach represented an advance on the more simplistic varieties of progressive thought that stressed real and underlying motives in history that were based on economic interests. As Carl Degler has noted, Williams thereby expanded the limits of the progressive synthesis, though it could also be said that this expansion built upon the ambiguities in the progressive project that were not entirely overcome by Williams.[38]

Two separate difficulties arose. The emphasis on economic ideas tended in practice to produce intellectual histories of foreign policy in which the material context of economic process was neglected in favor of an analysis of *Weltanschauung*. The overarching idealism of this approach was manifest not only in his seminal *Tragedy*, but also in *Contours of American History*, and in his representations of Marx's own theory of history in *The Great Evasion*. As Eugene Genovese notes, the tendency to slide from interests to ideas leaves the neo-Beardians (of whom Williams is the preeminent representative) without a coherent account of the economic processes that policymakers purport to represent.

These neo-Beardians . . . usually end where Beard did. . . . For all their pages devoted to economics, what often emerges is an account of how members of the ruling class perceive their economic interests. What does not emerge is a coherent critique of the economic process itself and of the objective validity of those perceptions. . . . [It] makes a great deal of difference whether people in command of policy are perceiving their interests on the basis of an analysis that corresponds to objective reality or whether they have been misled into a series of strategic estimates that do not conform to objective reality.

This question Williams' analysis was unable to answer.[39]

On the other side, Williams' emphasis on economic ideas gave rise to defensive strategies from more conventional diplomatic historians. Since Williams did not directly challenge the positivist formula which treated ideas and interests as factors exerting independent influences on politics, the way was clear for other historians to retort that Williams had overestimated the role of economic ideas in shaping policy, and that his work really was a form of economic determinism which still neglected the political and other supposedly noneconomic factors in policy-making. Thus Daniel M. Smith indicted the New Left school in diplomatic history as "on the whole seriously marred by monolithic economic interpretations, to the neglect of other motivating forces in history." Similarly, Lloyd Ambrosius argued that Williams' insights in *Roots of the Modern American Empire* were "severely restricted" by "rigidly adhering to an economic interpretation."[40] At the same time, Williams' works prompted another and not incompatible response: to accept economic ideas and interests as one of a number of considerations to be taken into account in any overview. Thereby it has been possible to absorb the findings of the Williams School into the body of liberal historical interpretation as part of a larger, pluralistic pattern of causal explanation, leaving the conceptual framework and intellectual structure of liberal history essentially untouched.

An equally important failure was the inability to transcend a liberal historical view of what constituted evidence or documentation. Williams stated in *Tragedy of American Diplomacy* that he was not "content with rhetoric and other appearances" and wanted "instead to establish by research and analysis a fuller, more accurate picture of reality."[41] This concern, both for accuracy and reality, could, unless given further explanation of a methodological and epistemological character, lead defenders of traditional historical practice to conclude that Williams was basing his new interpretations on nothing more than a thorough reading and presentation of the facts. In none of his methodological discussions, nor in his most influential works, did he make clear the extent to which he was attempting to break with traditional historical method. He came closest in a 1962 essay, "Fire in the Ashes of Scientific History," an unnecessarily tangential and enigmatic discussion of these issues of historical method. However, his rather old-fashioned, or so it seemed, commitment to scientific history in an era of historical relativism, and his concern that men could "get closer to the truth" with the help of a "set of intellectual ground rules" that they agreed upon, could mean that historians were entitled to expect adherence to empiricist canons of truth. A review of Richard Hofstadter's *Age of Reform*, published in *The Nation* in 1956, added substance to this confusion. There Williams was especially concerned to tax the Pulitzer Prize–winning author with a failure to undertake "extended research in the primary evidence." Elsewhere in the same review he stressed that "it is not possible to write valid History by using social-science concepts . . . as substitutes for facts."[42]

To some extent, Williams' position on method and theory could be inferred from his detailed treatment of foreign policy. In *Tragedy*, politics and economics are shown as interacting forces in an approach which implicitly breaks from the more simplistic formulas of positivism. Moreover, it was possible for the careful reader to ascertain that Williams regarded the overall context of a social system as of prime significance in his account. What remained unspecified at the time, and unclear in his analysis, was the way Williams selected and presented data in accordance with these antipositivist principles.[43]

Williams' failure to clarify his attitudes toward the problem of historical facts exposed his work to the damaging criticism that he had done violence to the historical record. Robert Maddox was able to make great play of the extent to which Williams and other New Left diplomatic historians had "engaged in unscholarly manipulation of the evidence." Lloyd Ambrosius, in a review in *Civil War History*, also pointed to the fact that Williams had "misrepresented some of the most important documentation," and emphasized his "inaccurate use of evidence." Oscar Handlin gloated that the "revisionist historians" of American foreign policy claimed "a right to impose on it [the evidence] what meaning they wished to accord with their total world-view."[44]

Unfortunately, Williams did not attempt to answer these objections until after his major work had been long published and subjected to embarrassing criticism. Even when he did reply, in the pages of the *New York Times Book Review*, his response left much to be desired. Limply defending the technique of stringing together quotations to give what the speaker or writer really meant, Williams called the method "seriatum quotation." The profession was not likely to be impressed with this claim, not only because it was issued *ex post facto*, but also because it violated the sacrosanct canons of traditional historical method. Other writers sympathetic to revisionist arguments considered the charges and concluded that the alleged distortions involved "questions of interpretation." They thereby played into the hands of empiricist critics by conceding the commonplace view of the existence of a body of facts open to historical investigation without theoretical and critical mediation, and thus quite separable from interpretation. Facts appeared in this analysis as objective entities, but interpretation was, by implication, merely a matter of opinion.[45]

There was a defense to be made against the critics which would expose the defects of the empiricists' own methodology and their persistent misunderstanding of the revisionist case. Yet that defense did not emerge until Williams appeared at the American Historical Association convention in 1973. On that occasion, Williams stressed that "the primary issue between me as a revisionist and my serious critics involves our different theories of knowledge." He professed to be following the antiempiricist views of Spinoza, Marx, and Lukács in "positing one organic world in which seemingly separate parts are in reality always internally related to each other; a universe in which an ostensibly positivistic fact is in truth a set of relationships with all other facts and therefore with the whole.''[46] At last Williams had made clear his philosophical assumptions, though his defense would still not satisfy empiricists (and many others) because he remained unable to demonstrate convincingly how one got from the individual facts to the sets of relationships. Williams merely intimated that a leap of historical imagination occurred which enabled him to transform the seemingly isolated elements of the whole into an understanding of the historical *Weltanschauung*. The latter idea, drawn from the work of William Dilthey, provided the concept which enabled Williams to relate individual factors in an intelligible synthesis.[47] Just as his historical interpretation ended in idealism, so too through his invocation of Dilthey and Spinoza did Williams reveal the idealist cast of his philosophical assumptions. At least, however, Williams had declared his philosophical independence from the empiricist assumptions which underlay the attacks of his critics. It is a pity for the reputation of his work and the edification of the profession that he did not do so earlier.

The failure to present these issues clearly, and the failure to expose their opponents to systematic theoretical scrutiny in the formative period of New Left writing, marked a major strategic blunder. The Williams School historians did not challenge the Rankean procedures and empiricist assumptions which underlay the critiques of the New Left. At times, Williams and his associates made statements that involved actual concessions to the conventional methods, and for this reason their work lost some of its potentially revolutionary impact on the profession. When they were not rejected, as other New Left historians often were, as biased, partisan, or methodologically unscrupulous, they encouraged through their approach to evidence the idea that their findings were simply empirical results which did not challenge the structure of historical method or the way of conceiving American history as a whole, but merely presented new and interesting interpretations of American foreign policy.[48]

On the whole, the record of the New Left historians of the 1960s was not a very impressive one. Some attempted to revitalize the profession with their activism, while others challenged the interpretations of the profession with new ones based on reexamination of the historical record. Either way they failed. The first approach generated tension between a concern for a usable past and the canons of objectivity supposedly adhered to within the profession. Having failed to transform either the society or the profession, the moral activists tended to defect from history entirely or to become disillusioned with the historical enterprise because it was not amenable to their activism. If they did fight on the level of empirical, objective history, they saw their evidence met with counter-examples, or their particular findings were incorporated into existing syntheses.

The New Left failed so dismally to transcend the limits of liberal history for several important reasons. When the radicalism of the 1960s erupted unexpectedly, leadership of the New Left naturally fell upon those more advanced graduate students and young professors who were articulate, beginning to publish, and eager to participate in a radical movement arising from the ashes of a defeated left. While Lynd, Lemisch, and Zinn were able historians, they had begun their basic historical training prior to the shattering of the political and ideological consensus. They had already received rather traditional graduate school educations in the best history departments the nation could offer. Schooled in the empiricist and positivistic assumptions of the liberal historians, their dissertations and early publications tended to be fairly conventional in subject matter and method.

Neither did New Left historians have the opportunity to draw on a vital oppositional historical tradition. McCarthyite repression had combined with the persuasive and well-funded power of the liberal consensus to put an end to that in the 1950s. The popular working-class tradition which informed the contemporaneous English work of Hobsbawm, George Rudé, and E. P. Thompson was not available to the American radicals. Gradually radicals would import the English issues and concepts, but the very fact that importation of a foreign tradition was required to create an oppositional history revealed the conceptual poverty of American radical history.[49]

New Left history's failure to transcend liberalism's legacy had, of course, more general roots in the theoretical weakness of the political protest movements of the 1960s from which radical history took inspiration. A romantic radicalism and a widespread hostility to theory was, I have already argued, a product of the New Left's revolt against the seemingly stale and tawdry ideologies of the Stalinist left and against those liberal theories which did not explain the persistence of inequality or the resurgence of ideological conflict in American society.

The New Left historians railed against liberalism, but their relationship with liberal values remained too ambiguous to enable them to mount an effective critique. While they attacked the workings of the liberal "creed," particularly in contemporary America, they sought to resuscitate a radical democratic tradition that sprang from the eighteenth-century liberal values of the declaration of independence. This meant that their critique of American society could only be framed in terms of moral outrage. Bereft of a historical analysis of where the liberal state was actually heading, they focused instead on the ephemera of student and radical protest in contemporary American society. That emphasis upon the facts of resistance and prejudice at the expense of theoretically informed perspective left them unable to comprehend the subsequent decline of activism. Nor was their moral and rhetorical analysis able to illuminate the systemic economic stagnation into which international capitalism slid after 1973.[50]

These critics of the establishment had to engage a historiographical tradition which was institutionally entrenched, which constituted the very ground of discourse of professional activity, and which had produced a huge body of rich historical material backed up by the growing prestige of social science theory. The New Left did not work out ways of incorporating this inheritance into theoretical systems of their own making which could move beyond the liberal syntheses. Instead, they took issues with specific interpretations of the liberals, and far too often created a mirror image of the existing historiography.[51]

NOTES

1. Barton Bernstein, ed., *Towards a New Past: Dissenting Essays in American History* (New York, 1968); Jesse Lemisch, *On Active Service in War and Peace: Politics and Ideology in the American Historical Profession* (Toronto, 1975), pp. 43–46.

2. See James Weinstein and David Eakins, eds., *For a New America: Essays in History and Politics from "Studies on the Left," 1959–1967* (New York, 1970), pp. 3–33.

3. Jesse Lemisch, "The American Revolution Seen from the Bottom Up," in Bernstein, ed., *Towards a New Past*, pp. 3–45; Staughton Lynd, "Beyond Beard," ibid., pp. 46–64; see also Lemisch, "The Radicalism of the Inarticulate: Merchant Seamen in the Politics of Revolutionary America," in Alfred F. Young, ed., *Dissent: Explorations in the History of American Radicalism* (DeKalb, Ill., 1968), pp. 38, 47, 51, 54, 57–58; Norman Pollack, *The Populist Response to Industrial America: Midwestern Populist Thought* (Cambridge, Mass., 1962), pp. 8–9, 10–11, 143 passim.

4. Howard Zinn, "Marxism and the New Left," in Young, ed., *Dissent*, pp. 369, 370, 358, 359; C. Wright Mills, *The Power Elite* (New York, 1956); Howard Zinn, *Postwar America: 1945–1971* (Indianapolis, 1973), pp. 110–12.

5. Ibid., p. 362; Staughton Lynd, "Historical Past and Existential Present," in Theodore Roszak, ed., *The Dissenting Academy* (New York, 1968), p. 109.

6. Young, ed., *Dissent*, pp. 2, 356.

7. John A. Garraty, *Interpreting American History: Conversations with Historians*, 2 vols. (New York, 1970).

8. David Donald, *Charles Sumner and the Rights of Man* (New York, 1970), p. xii; Donald, rev. of Bernstein, ed., *Towards a New Past*, *American Historical Review* 74 (1968): 533.

9. Jerold S. Auerbach, "New Deal, Old Deal, or Raw Deal: Some Thoughts on New Left Historiography," *Journal of Southern History* 35 (1969): 18–30, quote at p. 28; Irwin Unger, "The 'New Left' and American History: Some Recent Trends in United States Historiography," *American Historical Review* 72 (1967): 1237–63, quote at p. 1263.

10. Lemisch, *On Active Service*, pp. 43–45, 118–20.

11. Howard Zinn, "Abolitionists, Freedom-Riders, and the Tactics of Agitation," in Martin Duberman, ed., *The Antislavery Vanguard: New Essays on the Abolitionists* (Princeton, N.J., 1965), pp. 430–31; Lemisch, *On Active Service*, pp. 10, 148.

12. Martin Duberman, *The Uncompleted Past* (New York, 1969), pp. 22, 353, 355, 356.

13. Ibid., p. 22.

14. "An Interview with Staughton Lynd," *Radical History Review* 4 (Spring-Summer 1977): 60–75, quote at p. 60; Lynd, "Historical Past and Existential Present," pp. 96–97; Lynd, *Class Conflict, Slavery, and the United States Constitution* (Indianapolis, 1968); Lynd, *Intellectual Origins of American Radicalism* (New York, 1968).

15. Lynd, "Beyond Beard," p. 49.

16. Young, ed., *Dissent*, pp. v–vi; Lemisch, *On Active Service*, p. 92.

17. "Interview with Lynd," p. 62.

18. Lynd, "Historical Past and Existential Present," p. 105.

19. "Interview with Lynd," pp. 63–64.

20. Alice and Staughton Lynd, eds., *Rank and File: Personal Histories by Working-*

Class Organizers (Boston, 1973); David Brody, "Radical Labor History and Rank-and-File Militancy," *Labor History* 16 (1975): 117–26.

21. "Interview with Lynd," pp. 65, 67, 68, 75.

22. E. P. Thompson, ed., *Warwick University Ltd.: Industry, Management and the Universities* (Harmondsworth, Middx., 1970), chap. 1; "An Interview with E. P. Thompson," *Radical History Review* 3 (Fall 1976): 14–15.

23. Jesse Lemisch, "Present-mindedness Revisited," published by the obscure New Hogstown Press as *On Active Service in War and Peace*, in 1975.

24. Ibid., p. 10.

25. Ibid., p. 4.

26. Unger, "New Left," p. 1247.

27. Pollack, *Populist Response*, p. 11.

28. Pollack, "Fear of Man: Populism, Authoritarianism, and the Historian," *Agricultural History* 39 (1965): 59–67, esp. p. 61.

29. Unger, "Critique of Norman Pollack's 'Fear of Man,' " ibid., p. 75.

30. Robert Beisner, quoted in Daniel M. Smith, "Rise to Great World Power, 1865–1918," in William Cartwright and Richard L. Watson, Jr., eds., *The Reinterpretation of American History and Culture* (Washington, D.C., 1973), p. 446; William A. Williams, *The Tragedy of American Diplomacy* (Cleveland, Ohio, 1959); Walter LaFeber, *The New Empire: An Interpretation of American Expansion, 1860–1898* (New York, 1963).

31. Carl Degler, "Remaking American History," *Journal of American History* 67 (1980): 12.

32. "An Interview with William Appleman Williams," *Radical History Review* 22 (1979–1980): 65–92.

33. Smith, "Rise to World Power," p. 446.

34. Charles S. Maier, "Marking Time: The Historiography of International Relations," in Michael Kammen, ed., *The Past Before Us: Contemporary Historical Writing in the United States* (Ithaca, N.Y., 1980), p. 357.

35. For a restatement of such views, see Richard M. Abrams, "United States Intervention Abroad: The First Quarter Century," *American Historical Review* 79 (1974): 72–102.

36. Lloyd Ambrosius, "Turner's Frontier Thesis and the Modern American Empire: A Review Essay," *Civil War History* 17 (1971): 332–39; Maier, "Historiography of International Relations," pp. 366–67, 383–87; Williams, "The Legend of Isolationism in the 1920s," *Science and Society* 18 (1954): 1–20.

37. See, for example, Charles Maier, *Recasting Bourgeois Europe: Stabilization in France, Germany, and Italy in the Decade after World War I* (Princeton, N.J., 1975); Fred Block, *The Origins of International Economic Disorder: A Study of United States International Monetary Policy from World War II to the Present* (Berkeley and Los Angeles, 1977); Akira Iriye, "Culture and Power: International Relations as Cultural Relations," *Diplomatic History* 3 (1979): 115–28.

38. Degler, "Remaking American History," p. 12; William A. Williams, "Fire in the Ashes of Scientific History," *William and Mary Quarterly*, 3d ser., 19 (1962): 278; Williams, "A Note on Charles Austin Beard's Search for a General Theory of Causation," *American Historical Review* 62 (1956): 59–80.

39. Eugene Genovese, "Charles Beard's Economic Interpretation of History," in Marvin C. Swanson, ed., *Charles A. Beard: An Observance of the Centennial of His*

Birth (Greencastle, Ind., 1976), p. 37; William A. Williams, *The Contours of American History* (Cleveland, 1961); Williams, *The Great Evasion: An Essay on the Contemporary Relevance of Karl Marx* . . . (Chicago, 1964); Williams, *Tragedy*; Genovese, "William Appleman Williams on Marx and America," *Studies on the Left* 6 (Jan.–Feb. 1966): 75.

40. Smith, "Rise to World Power," p. 445; Ambrosius, "Turner's Frontier Thesis," p. 336.

41. Williams, *Tragedy*, p. 308.

42. Williams, "Fire in the Ashes," pp. 274–87; Williams, *History as a Way of Learning: Articles, Excerpts, and Essays* (New York, 1973), pp. 162, 164.

43. Williams, *Tragedy*, pp. 30, 72n., and passim.

44. Robert J. Maddox, *The New Left and the Origins of the Cold War* (Princeton, N.J., 1973); Oscar Handlin, *Truth in History* (Cambridge, Mass., 1979), p. 156; Ambrosius, "Turner's Frontier Thesis," p. 337.

45. Francis Loewenheim, "The New Left and the Origins of the Cold War," *New York Times Book Review*, 17 June 1973, p. 5; Ronald Steel, "The Good Old Days," *New York Review of Books*, 14 June 1973, p. 34; Ronald Radosh, "Re-Revising Revisionism," *Radical History Review* 2 (no. 2, 1974–1975): 22–23.

46. William A. Williams, "Confessions of an Intransigent Revisionist," *Socialist Revolution* 3 (Sept.–Oct. 1973): 93–98.

47. Ibid., p. 95.

48. As recently as 1983, John Braeman was able to survey New Left foreign policy writings without a hint that Williams had broken with the positivism of Beard's economic interest analysis. Braeman, "The New Left and American Foreign Policy during the Age of Normalcy: A Re-Examination," *Business History Review* 57 (1983): 73–104.

49. See Chapter 6.

50. See, especially, Zinn, *Postwar America*, p. xiii.

51. This point is noted by James Weinstein in "Can a Historian Be a Socialist Revolutionary?" *Socialist Revolution* 1 (May–June 1970): 99.

6

The New Social History of a Radical Kind

The failure to shed liberal assumptions and methods should not obscure the very considerable long-term impact that the New Left has had on the subject matter of American history. One of the most important consequences of the radical scholarship of the 1960s has, according to Peter Stearns, been a reconsideration of the role of "ordinary people" and "the framework of their daily lives," particularly the oppressed and "minority" groups. As Stearns has noted, the concept of "history from the bottom up" devised by Jesse Lemisch has become a "litmus test" for the success of social inquiry. Associated with this trend, the 1970s witnessed such a boom in the study of social history that it had by the end of the decade become the most vital of the discipline's subfields.[1]

The proliferation of social history cannot of course be correlated closely with the academic or political influence of radical history. "History from the bottom up," as originally envisaged, had radical political implications, but there is no evidence that these views have been systematically accepted by the new social historians. Indeed, much of the new social history seems devoid of any political content. The stirring calls of Lemisch have been appropriated by others whose interests have been primarily academic; they have produced more detailed, more detached, and more technically sophisticated studies of a whole range of social history topics. The most important developments have occurred in women's, black, and labor history, though the study of the family, sexuality, popular culture, and other nascent fields has also boomed. Much of this work goes under diverse and rather confusing labels such as "the new labor history" or "the new urban history," but the trends of these fields have been so interrelated and so strikingly similar that it is surely appropriate to consider them together.

Although not all of this scholarship has been radical by any measure, the work of some historians of oppressed groups and minorities such as women, slaves, and working-class people has had important radical implications. It is on this phase of social history that this chapter concentrates. Historians using the wider variety of sources and techniques of the new social history have been able to challenge effectively the condescending notion of the 1950s liberals that oppressed and minority groups lacked their own cultural traditions. The new view has offered important evidence of resistance to liberal and capitalist values, and has undermined superficial assumptions of an American consensus. Yet if this radical version of the new social history has been impressive in producing evidence of oppositional subcultures, its focus on culture has also raised problems for those historians seeking to supplant the liberal tradition and to incorporate the insights of the new social history into a marxist synthesis. These problems partly stem from the character of the marxist revival, but they have been complicated by the interests and origins of the new social history itself.[2]

The promise of the new social history was tied up in some measure with the infusion of new social groups into the historical profession. The discipline which one scholar has stated was until the 1950s "the preserve of a privileged segment of American society" now opened up gradually to "people with working-class and immigrant backgrounds." If this brought a new interest in the social history of workers and immigrants, social background alone could not transform the profession while existing scholarly practice remained intact. Like the New Left, the new social historians multiplied through their interests and demands the specializations of the discipline, and reproduced orthodox theoretical and methodological concerns precisely because they worked and trained within the boundaries of a larger and vital historiography informed by the liberal synthesis.[3]

Economic history conceived broadly to encompass political economy might have supplied the integrating design, but social historians followed the trend of the discipline to move away from economics in the 1950s and 1960s. The increasing complexity of economic theory, the narrowing of the scope of economic analysis to questions of growth, and the impact of quantification made the territory of economic history more forbidding. This material would have been difficult enough to encompass in the best of circumstances, without the additional burden of historical topics introduced by the radicals of the 1960s and the new social history. In addition to these professional impediments, ideological and political pressures came into play. Those historians who were trying to establish the important contribution of oppressed minorities to the making of American history tended to shy away from the study of vast economic structures because those structures called into question the intellectual validity and the substantive findings of much of the new social history. The latter moved instead toward a history of minority subcultures. As an unintended result, the ground has been laid for the incorporation of the history of minorities and oppressed groups, stripped of radical political content, into the liberal mainstream under the guise of cultural pluralism.[4]

The best way to appreciate the strengths—as well as the weaknesses—of the new social history of a radical kind is to begin by examining in detail the work of its most influential spokesman. Herbert Gutman was probably the most innovative and thoughtful of the recent breed of social historians committed to the study of "inarticulate" groups, or "history from the bottom up." Gutman began his career as a historian working on labor radicalism: especially that centered around strike activity. His early research on labor unrest in the 1873–1874 period, for his doctoral dissertation, led him to revise the portrait of society in the Gilded Age as one increasingly dominated by the large-scale entrepreneurs and companies, and to assert that workers did not accept these developments passively. Through the study of their strikes and community ties in small and medium-sized cities in the midwest, he traced "the worker's search for power in the gilded age" in several important early articles. Gutman was already moving away from the old institutional labor history which had dwelt upon the development of trade unions, and his concern with the community context of working-class existence was already evident. But the rebellion was as yet partial and muted.[5]

The decisive turning point for the reorientation of labor historiography away from an economic and institutional focus to one in which cultural issues were predominant came with the publication in 1966 of "Protestantism and the American Labor Movement: The Christian Spirit in the Gilded Age." In this article, Gutman traced the use made of "certain strands of pre-gilded age Protestantism" that sanctioned trade union radicalism and created a "working-class social Christianity" which enabled workers "to challenge the new industrialism." Gutman depicted workers as opponents of the economic-individualist view of man put forward by the upwardly mobile business elites; they sought instead to perpetuate an ethic (derived from preindustrial christianity) which emphasized man's communal, social, and humanitarian values and obligations.[6]

Gutman's article was notable first because it focused on the worker's mind: "the modes of thought and perception through which he confronted the industrialization process." The article was also important because of its use of the work of E. P. Thompson and, to a lesser extent, that of other British labor historians like Eric Hobsbawm. The two innovations were connected. The search for a focus that was not narrowly economic, but encompassed the cultural lives of the workers, led directly to the model of working-class life emanating from the writings of Thompson and other leftist British labor historians. American counterparts of Thompson, like Gutman, were concerned in the early 1960s to show that American history was not a story of bland consensus. They required, however, a new conceptual scheme with which to hammer home this point. If any radical analysis was to be credible, it would need to break decisively with the economic determinism which had tinged the progressive phase of liberal history. Gutman agreed with Hofstadter that scholars must shift away from "so narrow an emphasis" on "simple 'economic terms' " to encompass as well the symbolic and cultural forms in which material interests took shape.[7]

The search for nonconsensual models of worker behavior and thought that could avoid the mistakes of progressivism and incorporate the findings of the liberals on symbolic and cultural politics required borrowing from nonindigenous analytical concepts and labor traditions if it were to be successful. There was no inspiration to be found in a domestic labor movement which was increasingly part of the economic and political establishment. The fiery activism of the Congress of Industrial Organizations which mobilized leftist radicals in the 1930s was clearly on the wane in favor of business as usual. Nor could inspiration be gained from the state of labor historiography which, Robert Zieger observed, has since the days of Commons, Perlman, and Taft "largely justified and reinforced the conservative proclivities of the labor movement." The formation of a new journal, *Labor History*, at the end of the 1950s did not in itself spell a new beginning. The journal had among its prime movers end-of-ideology ideologues like Daniel Bell. Vaughn D. Bornet, another who influenced the founding of the journal, wrote that research in labor history would lead to support for organized labor's "leaders [and] organizations [as well as for] our balanced two-party system, and an economy based on the profit motive."[8]

In England, however, the work of the labor historians Thompson and Hobsbawm offered an attractive alternative to this conservative brand of labor history. Thompson in particular was an important influence because he had recently in a path-breaking work shifted away from a concern with narrow economic issues to focus on the cultural conflict manifest in the industrial revolution. The critical book was the justly famous *The Making of the English Working Class*, published in 1963. Within three years Gutman had published his first study drawing explicitly on Thompson's methodology. The method was elaborated in subsequent research, culminating in 1973 in "Work, Culture, and Society in Industrializing America." Acceptance of this article by the *American Historical Review* signified that the new labor history, focusing on the social and cultural rather than economic and union activities of the workers, had won legitimacy and a much wider audience in the profession.[9]

Gutman was not alone among left-leaning historians in this quest for a new way of conceptualizing working-class history in order to combat the hegemony of the liberal consensus approach. Jesse Lemisch likewise searched for English models to conceptualize popular resistance in the revolutionary period and found them in the work of George Rudé. Lemisch, too, was drawn to the study of noneconomic sources of class conflict. He even went so far as to note in a 1977 article that class was an "extremely complex affair" which must be understood "as a cultural phenomenon" rather than a structural or economic category. Yet it was Gutman who made the conceptual breakthrough. Lemisch himself acknowledged that "we have much to learn" from the approach of Gutman and others like him who have treated the cultural dimensions of class.[10] Gutman has written the most voluminous accounts illustrating the new cultural orientation, and achieved the most prestigious status in the profession. It is therefore upon his work that the analysis must concentrate, before the more general implications of radical social history for American historiography can be seriously considered.

When Gutman first began to emphasize the minds and values of the workers, he was quick to inform his readers that "in studying labor thought," historians should nevertheless remember Richard Hofstadter's admonition that "the material interests of politics" could not "be psychologized away or reduced to episodes in intellectual history." This admonition notwithstanding, the trend of Gutman's thinking as revealed in his later articles and books was precisely away from material interests to a study of working-class culture divorced from questions of power and economic structure. While Gutman's work was strong in the area of working-class culture, his "essays deal[t] with political power only tangentially." Yet, as David Montgomery notes, "politics and working-class culture impinged directly and decisively upon each other," through state legislation in favor of what can loosely be termed issues of public morality, through the state's exercise of power against popular disturbances, and by "the removal of the locus of economic decision-making . . . from the state" to private individuals.[11]

If power was neglected in Gutman's work, so too was the related phenomenon of class. David Brody has very perceptively noted that Gutman's work represented "a strategic retreat from Thompson's basic formulation. Class is, in fact, wholly jettisoned from Gutman's analysis."[12] Rather, Gutman's famous 1973 essay depicts a clash between a "modernizing" culture tied to the "factory and machine labor" and wave after wave of "preindustrial peoples" with their cultural baggage of "premodern" work habits.[13] Instead of the marxist class struggle over the control of the means of production, involving the expropriation of the surplus value of labor, there is a cultural struggle over customs and work habits.

The point is most certainly not that Gutman ought to have uncritically applied Thompson's specific evidence and conclusions to the analysis of the American class structure: that would have produced a much more distorted workers' history than appears in Gutman's pages. As Gutman never tired of pointing out, the American working-class experience was very different from the British because the former was continually reconstituted by European immigration from diverse cultural backgrounds. Herein lies the source of Gutman's major contribution to American historiography: the breaching of the artificial distinctions between ethnic and labor history that characterized progressive-era labor historiography inspired by John R. Commons. Gutman was certainly correct to move beyond these earlier economic and institutional analyses to emphasize the importance of ethnicity to the understanding of American working populations. Yet this subtle appreciation of the mutual overlaps and continuities between ethnicity and class should not lead, as it did in Gutman's case, to the dissolution of class into culture. Despite Gutman's repeated references to working-class behavior and belief, there is indeed little of a specifically class character in his work. Whereas Thompson treats class as a cultural and historical *process*, Gutman depicted the cultural continuities of the beliefs and behavior of workers' subcultures.

More important, the actual work experiences of American artisans, laborers, or factory workers were very narrowly treated. "Work, Culture, and Society" singled out the question of the industrial work ethic and its imposition, at the expense of analysis of a wide range of issues, such as the organization of labor, working conditions, the environment of industrial populations, cultural traditions formed in and growing out of workplace experiences, and political, union, and community questions. It is not good enough to claim that Gutman had already dealt with some of these in his earlier work, for the relations of these different elements remain crucial to a conceptualization of working-class history, as Gutman himself conceded. Gutman never published the synthesis of working-class experience that he had promised. Could he have successfully integrated the cultural perspective with these other matters? There is of course no answer to this question, but the record as demonstrated in his *The Black Family in Slavery and Freedom* gives little cause for optimism.[14] Like his histories of free workers, this book emphasized culture and socialization, even though slaves spent most of their conscious lives *working*. The slave narratives and their work songs testify to the importance of labor to the realization of slaves' material aspirations. Nonetheless, the specific cultural traits and values that emerged out of the work experience, both in factories and fields, is what is sadly absent.[15]

This point is worth reiteration. By neglecting the multifaceted dimensions of working experience, Gutman slighted something more than pure and simple economics. Rather he treated culture too narrowly in the range of phenomena studied in his essays. Work experience involves a structure of cultural relations. Culture is not something that is simply imported to economic or productive processes. The importance of prior cultural values as opposed to the cultural experiences of industrial labor forces intrinsic to the labor process (and the relations of these different aspects of culture) is a subject that requires analysis, not a priori exclusion.

Gutman's neglect of class, politics, other forms of power, and work in favor of culture had origins in two related aspects of his methodology. He accepted the fundamental distinction between culture and society made by such anthropologists as Clifford Geertz, Sidney Mintz, and Eric Wolff, and took a tactical decision to use that distinction to study working-class subcultures apart from and prior to their relationships with larger economic and power structures.[16] Gutman neglected the cultural experiences of work because he considered culture as a set of historically derived and collectively socialized patterns of behavior, and society as the circumstances or settings within which these forms may be used. According to Gutman, immigrants brought their cultural values to the workplace, which constituted the social arena in which the conflict between those forms and the cultural expectations of modernizing American factory owners took place. Given this analytical distinction, work experience cannot be an important part of the cultural lives of the workers studied. Gutman's method abandoned the crude distinction between class and ethnicity made by empiricist historians in the liberal tradition, but at the cost of substituting for it another analytical distinction between culture and society which obscures the subtle relations between those phenomena.

Gutman's emphasis on working-class culture at the expense of material interests essentially had the same defense as Hofstadter's brief for cultural analysis, and therefore it also has the same weaknesses. Gutman conceded that the influence of American capitalism on workers was indeed important, and "remains an essential subject for continuing study." What Gutman questioned was the emphasis given to that question to the exclusion of "the ways in which the behavior of working people affected the development of the larger culture and society in which they lived." Unfortunately, Gutman did not spell out in his work exactly what was the relationship between or the relative importance of the two types of studies: in this case, larger structures and workers' subcultures. Gutman implicitly conceded in his last book on working-class culture that the relationship between the power of American capitalism and the culture of workers must ultimately be treated, but he argued that such relationships can only be explored *after* "there is rich and detailed study of the many varieties of past American working-class experiences."[17]

Gutman's strategy of deferring the analysis of relationships between culture and the larger society was his crucial deficiency, and it reflects the profound empiricism of his historical method. His books and articles abound with the phrase "little is known about" a host of aspects of working-class (and ethnic and black) existence, and he argued that until such studies have been done, no theory of the relationship between subcultures and the larger culture can be ventured.[18] These antitheoretical leanings are further illustrated in his style of writing. The pages of his many articles and books are filled with case after case of detailed description of working-class behavior and belief. Yet the loving attention to detail and context often overwhelms the search for meaning. What is sometimes unclear is the relevance of the detail, let alone the contribution it makes to the development of an understanding of the place of working-class culture in relation to the larger society.

Despite his insistence that the rich evidence of workers' experiences must first be presented before a synthesis of labor history is possible, Gutman could not escape the choice of a synthetic conceptual scheme for the organization of his material. The choice compounds the difficulty. Gutman did not believe that the workers' lives ought to be divided into immigrant, ethnic, urban, business and other "special substudies," but his own explanatory device involved a truncation into the artificial polarity of modernization and tradition. Drawn from the efforts of American sociologists to assimilate third world experience to assumed patterns of development in American history, this dichotomy invents the static character of traditional society, homogenizes social conflict into the single typology of traditional versus modern, and obscures under the former guise the existence of aspects of working-class behavior that are products of the emerging class system, not the continuation of peasant mentalities. As several historians, David Montgomery and James Henretta among them, have argued, a modernization framework is incompatible with an analysis of class, since it draws attention away from economic exploitation to "an impersonal, value-free process" and "tempts the reader to assume that, when the process of industrialization had run its course and everyone had 'adapted' to the new ways, class conflict would come to an end.''[19] Gutman did not intend all of the implications which are part of the ideological freight of modernization theory, but the scheme's employment sits uncomfortably with his denial of deterministic formulas for comprehending the lives of workers, exposes the difficulties Gutman had in making sense of his rich material, and illustrates the tacit abdication of the class question.

The sources of Gutman's movement away from class are complex, but they undoubtedly involve a mutation in the theoretical and practical orientation of the book that inspired Gutman in the first place. *The Making of the English Working Class* has to be situated in its historiographical context if that mutation is to be understood. Thompson took issue with revisionist accounts of the early industrial revolution which emphasized economic growth and a rising standard of living. An orthodox marxist approach to this problem would have concentrated on the rate of expropriation of surplus value. That the standard of living did not fall and may even have risen was, according to analyses derived from Marx's *Capital*, irrelevant. Class struggle occurred over control of the means of production. Exploitation intrinsic to this struggle was taking place at the point of production as measured in the struggle over the surplus. Thompson bypassed such orthodox marxist responses. He did not deny the importance of economics and in a critical chapter on ''exploitation'' he evidenced his indebtedness to materialist conceptions of class. Nonetheless, he chose to emphasize the subjective, not the objective, experience of the workers. If English industrial workers had achieved a higher standard of living as a result of the industrial revolution, ''they had suffered and continued to suffer this slight improvement as a catastrophic experience.'' By this measure, there was irretrievable loss in the transformation of an agrarian way of life to that of the factory system. Thompson's discussion of how rural people were wrenched from their preexisting life and how they responded to the substitution of money values for the moral economy of the preindustrial order constituted a moving exercise. It made discussions of the price of corn relative to workers' wages pale into comparative insignificance.[20]

The reader of Thompson's pages, or even these lines, is bound to see immediately the indebtedness of Gutman to Thompson's formulations. Yet in Gutman's borrowing of this creative synthesis, something important was lost. Thompson had emphasized the subjective cultural experience of workers in an eight-hundred-page scholarly polemic against economic Gradgrinds like R. M. Hartwell. Gutman ignored the material basis of Thompson's interpretation, partly because Thompson did not emphasize that aspect. But Gutman also left out the political aspects of Thompson's approach in the ''Work, Culture, and Society'' essay, and Thompson certainly did not leave any doubts on that score. *The Making of the English Working Class* was such a good book in part because it did go beyond questions of working-class culture to consider the political struggle centered around the emergence of working-class radicalism that challenged the economic orthodoxy of Manchester liberalism. Thompson thus did not abandon the idea of class struggle, even if he did tend to concede to his opponents part of the economic argument over the emiseration of workers. Thompson was very much aware that any such class struggle had to emerge in political terms, and could not have much meaning as a class phenomenon without that political struggle. Thompson also managed through his brilliant attention to narrative, and his sensitivity to the processes of historical change, to convey a sense of the dynamic quality of the struggle over the impact of industrial capitalism. Gutman, in contrast, presented a strangely static picture of the persistence of cultural conflict divested of political significance.

Why did Gutman go much further than Thompson in emphasizing the non-political and cultural aspects of working-class behavior? It may be of note that this search took place at a time when the level of American unionization had already peaked, and when civil rights protests drew attention to new sources of activism and social conscience in an era of increasing middle-class prosperity. Perhaps the new approach also had something to do with the New Left's intellectual currents that devalued a mechanical marxism and exalted subjective experience. These currents also influenced Thompson, but they seem to have had a greater impact in the case of Gutman and other American radicals.

Gutman's reinterpretation of Thompson involved a perception of the difference between a clearly articulated class structure among people of common cultural origins in the English case, and the bewildering diversity of American ethnic experience. But recent British criticism of Thompson by Gareth Stedman Jones, Richard Price, Perry Anderson, and others emphasizes that the English working class was also extremely complicated in structure and culture. In no sense was there an English working class that had been made by the 1830s. These findings cry out for detailed comparative analysis of the English and American class structures and working-class experiences. Such comparisons may well find that cultural diversity was integral to the making of an English working class as it was to the American equivalent, and that diversity was linked to the changing composition of the labor market, the continual restructuring of the working class, and the unevenness of capitalist industrial development. American immigration may prove to be a superficial manifestation of these processes, but in the absence of comparative and international histories of the making of national working classes, it is not surprising that Gutman should focus on the most immediately apparent difference as a gold mine of evidence on which to erect an alternative, cultural history of American workers.[21]

Any account of the genesis of the new labor history under Gutman's influence has also to take notice of the specific political and academic contexts in which these perceptions of Thompson's work took shape. Here the power and pervasive influence of the liberal tradition was manifest. The most interesting historical work being done in the United States in the 1950s and 1960s emphasized the cultural, racial, ethnic, and social sources of conflict rather than economic ones. Not only was this work of the liberal historians increasingly influential in the profession as a whole. It was also especially important, as already noted, that Beardian and economistic interpretations of American history had been extensively criticized and subjected to a range of empirical refutations. Radical historians found it much simpler to accept the verdict of the liberal historians on this point, and employ the cultural analysis of the liberals while trying to turn that approach against consensus and anticlass viewpoints. Rather than question the way the liberals had framed the debate over the significance of Charles Beard's interpretation, and question the meaning of the empirical evidence and concepts which liberals had employed, radicals like Gutman chose to look for noneconomic sources of labor protest.

A historian looking for evidence of workers' struggle in the United States was bound to be impressed with the opportunities for analysis of immigrant and preindustrial artisan resistance to industrialization even if, on closer examination, the relationship between that struggle and class struggle was more apparent than real. If the class question remained obscure, the quantity of resistance to capitalist-induced change was being documented in ever greater detail. Gutman's effort thus fitted in with the concern of the New Left to produce a history from the bottom up, and to show that many people did not agree with the dominant economic trends. Industrial capitalism might have won out in the end, but the left-leaning labor and radical historians had at least discovered diverse patterns of cultural dissent with which they could identify.

Underlying this commitment to a cultural analysis in Gutman's work was the power and prestige of the discipline of anthropology, particularly cultural anthropology, within the American academy. The concept of culture derived from anthropology provided the conceptual tool for reframing the questions posed by British labor historiography to fit American circumstances. Here the work of Clifford Geertz was especially important. The liberal historians had been using the concept of culture as an alternative to an economic analysis of history since the 1940s. They had borrowed it initially from A. L. Kroeber of Berkeley and Clyde Kluckhohn of Harvard's School of Social Relations. But like many concepts drawn from social science, this one came under attack from the social scientists themselves, in this case for being too vague and imprecise. Geertz's contribution was to pare down the meaning of culture from its all-embracing formula under the Kroeber–Kluckhohn approach to something more manageable and empirically verifiable. It was from Geertz and others working in the same tradition that the analytical distinction between culture and society as variables came. Also connected with this more chastened concept of culture was Geertz's technique of thick description, in which he sought to give empirical illustration to anthropological theory through the observation of cultural rituals. In subtle fashion, he explored the relations between specific events and their cultural settings by situating them in a layer of anthropological meanings.[22]

Geertz's work was also important in its goal of seeking to adapt and hence to preserve Parsonian functionalist sociology so that it could "deal more adequately with processes of change." Geertz wanted to demonstrate how an analysis attuned to cultural symbols could explain much better than the static forms of functionalism in vogue in the early 1960s the conflict that occurred over change. Thus functionalist sociology could accommodate the revolt of the 1960s radicals against conservative conceptions of society without rooting the study of conflict in power relations or the material setting of culture.[23] This cultural analysis provided a theoretical framework for a historian like Gutman seeking to provide evidence of resistance to the dominant consensus, but prepared to concede the intellectual bankruptcy of the progressives' interpretation.

The sources of Gutman's emphasis on working-class culture are intriguing, but less important than the impact of his historical writing. Gutman's work has become a new historical orthodoxy exerting wide influence because it seemed, quite rightly, to represent a powerful advance over the old institutional labor history. Even marxist critics like Alan Dawley, who have noted that Thompson has received an essentially populist rather than marxist application in the United States, have praised the work of Gutman for presenting "the most probing radical analysis of the making of the American working class" to date, and for taking the ground of debate out of the sterile "economism" of the older labor history.[24]

Gutman's historiographical odyssey away from class toward cultural history is informative of certain trends in the study of inarticulate minorities and oppressed groups. Since the 1960s a common approach has coalesced in these fields. Historians of labor and ethnic groups, students of race and slavery, and the pioneers of women's history, have all emphasized how their own particular group, class, or sex has made its own history. There has been much concern with "human agency": the actions of men and women considered not merely as objects of historical change, but subjects in their own right. These studies have stressed the role of culture as the tool of human agency, and as the chief weapon against the oppression of whites, slave masters, men, or bosses.

Above all, these studies share a tendency to present their own groups as the creators or manipulators of an autonomous or separate culture. Typical of the genre in slavery studies is Thomas L. Webber's *Deep Like the Rivers: Education in the Slave Quarter Community, 1831–1865*. Webber breaks with the "historiographical models which stress the ability of whites to mold and control slave values and behavior to reveal the success of slaves in actively creating, controlling, and perpetuating their own education." The source of their autonomy was slave culture, which Webber, like Gutman, analyzed by drawing on the methodological and theoretical perspectives of American cultural anthropology. Webber uses "the methodology of Morris Opler's 'themes in culture,' " a "limited number of dynamic affirmations" which enable the character of that slave culture to be decoded.[25]

Gutman himself put foward a similar argument in his *The Black Family in Slavery and Freedom*. Gutman denied, of course, that he had presented a view of the slave family as culturally autonomous, and was indeed careful to leave open for further research the debate over the African origins of Afro-American culture. He also suggested the possible influence of whites from outside the planter class in the shaping of the black family, but *The Black Family* is still concerned with a view of culture that divorces it from the material conditions of everyday life in which culture takes shape. It is a culture formed out of the private, social lives of blacks and their Afro-American heritage. In that sense his work is inclined to stress cultural resources which are functionally independent of white power or material restraints, even if the specific language of autonomy is denied.[26] Gutman certainly succeeded very well indeed in establishing the existence of the black family as an important cultural resource for slaves and their descendants; he also made out a valid case for the eighteenth-century origins of Afro-American culture. But Gutman went further: he found family size, structure, or behavior to be independent of such influences as planter power, the economic character of plantations, and changing external political and legal structures.

For all his sensitivity to the dimension of time in the process of cultural change, Gutman did not show precisely how or why slave family structure altered in relation to the changing historical context of slavery. These deficiencies cannot be remedied and a case for the black family cannot be established until the relationship between slave family structure and wider social processes has been systematically assessed, and until the variations in slave family patterns that his own evidence revealed have been explained. Despite its eloquent testimony to the cultural resilience of a deeply oppressed people, *The Black Family* does not transcend the limitations of "Work, Culture, and Society." Both remain essentially static portraits of ethnic groups which have made their own history, largely through their culture and the historical transmission of that culture.[27]

Other examples come from the important field of women's history. There the concept of women's culture, "which grew out of the insistence that women in history have been actors rather than merely passive victims, is one of the most important [organizing principles] in the field."[28] Nancy Cott has emphasized the positive side of the women's sphere which allowed the development of close and sustained ties between young middle-class women in New England in the early part of the nineteenth century. Carroll Smith-Rosenberg had earlier offered a similar slant on women's culture in her analysis of "the female world of love and ritual."[29] These authors have been especially important because of their emphasis upon the private world of women, the separate support networks they developed, and because of the influence their innovative research has had on other scholars. A number of accounts have since emerged in the same genre, some explicitly drawing upon Cott and Rosenberg to depict the creation of a nineteenth-century women's sisterhood on the foundations of the concept of women's culture. Other studies, while not directly dependent on Cott and Rosenberg, also reflect the discovery of a separate culture.[30]

These diverse studies can only be adequately assessed as part of a larger system of historical interpretation that concerns the rescue of subordinate groups from the neglect, condescension, and misinterpretation of existing historiography. Assessed alone, they may be impressive enough, but it is their collective significance in the discourse of American historiography which is at issue here.

Rosenberg's article may serve as an exemplar of the new approach, not because it is a poor piece of work, but because its achievements are so impressive. Rosenberg had denied that she sought to establish an autonomous women's culture, and here and elsewhere she has been careful to suggest that the female world she studies ought to be related to the context of family history and that of male-female relations. She has herself acted on certain of these admonitions in earlier work. She has also argued that her article referred to woman's sexuality, not her culture.[31] This is technically correct, but the female world of love and ritual that involves cultural patterns and shared symbols is analogous to what other historians have described as sisterhood or the women's culture, and Rosenberg's work has with some justification been assimilated to such a broader interpretation and used as a foundation for other work in the same genre. Sarah Stage, for example, notes that Rosenberg's "homosocial networks" of women point to "a separate woman's culture, nurturing and supporting, in marked contrast to the industrial world of men." Leila Rupp argues that Rosenberg "described and analysed the domestic culture of friendship and intimacy women created."[32]

In this extremely influential piece, Rosenberg's focus is indeed on a separate and unchanging women's culture. She assumes on the basis of her literary evidence that the world of her women underwent no significant changes in its cultural and emotional dimensions over the course of one hundred years. This interpretation contrasts with Cott's picture of change in the dissemination of the women's culture from upper-middle-class younger women to middle-class women of all ages by the early nineteenth century. It also conflicts with the evidence of Catherine Clinton that the sorority of women did not extend to the southern plantation mistress, though many craved a sisterhood. Lower-class and immigrant women may also have fallen outside the sway of the kind of women's culture that Rosenberg depicts. Certainly the evidence that Rosenberg produces to show that the phenomenon may have crossed class or ethnic lines is thin indeed. Nor does the evidence from the variety of women's organizations in the nineteenth century which is now being more carefully studied suggest a homogeneous women's culture within the middle-class. Experiences and interests differed, and involvement in one cause did not lead automatically to involvement in others. Missing, too, is the need to reconcile the evidence of a woman's culture with other evidence presented, for example, by Anne Scott, that relations between men and women were more intimate and supportive than the now conventional view would suggest.[33]

Discovery of a women's sisterhood suggests the value of networks of support among American women, but also the choices historians have made in the subjects they have studied and the assumptions they have brought to their inquiries. Granted the importance of the evidence assembled, the relationship between this type of women's history and the broader field of social history still stands out. The concern with emotional connections rather than institutional settings, the emphasis on familial relations, on the personal and not the political, the examination of cultural resources which enabled oppression to be combated, all bear more than a casual resemblance to Gutman's depiction of the lives of slaves. The continuity of the subculture over time, independent of economic and political circumstances, is apparent in each case. Like Gutman, Rosenberg treats a subculture as developing within a circumscribed context but does not relate the subject to that context in a very convincing way. Rosenberg's female world focuses on the emotional and sexual ties between women, rather than the ways in which the culture was actually shaped by those restraints. The world of women thus seems to develop in a power vacuum in which material circumstances are the backdrop to the culture forged, not the conditions in which it was lived and experienced.

What is absent from the women's histories considered collectively is adequate treatment of the development of a gender-specific culture as a *product*—as a product of the actual experience of women. That absence contrasts with the work of Bonnie Gene Smith on French bourgeois women, a study which presents possible models for emulation. Smith did not focus on sisterhood, feminism, emotional, and sexual relations between women, women's networks, or any other formulation of the women's culture concept. Rather, *Ladies of the Leisure Class* shows how the domestic content of French, bourgeois women's culture was forged in the *material* context of their reproductive lives. Central to this interpretation are the material constraints upon women and the contest for power between the women's culture and the rational individualism of French bourgeois men. Ultimately, Smith shows, this culture took political and public forms.[34]

American feminist historians, too, are beginning to understand the limitations of studies that focus on women's culture or sexuality abstracted from the political and power context. Elizabeth Fox-Genovese has made out a general case for the importance of the political as opposed to the personal and noninstitutional values that recent women's historians have tended to emphasize. Ellen DuBois has through her work on the radical implications of nineteenth-century suffrage agitation given both theoretical and empirical backing to the strategy of relating women's studies to the contest for political power. Leila Rupp has argued that the concept of women's culture may be valid for the nineteenth century, but attacks women's historians for indiscriminately applying the same conceptual apparatus to the very different world of the twentieth century. Estelle B. Freedman testifies to the important cultural resources that the separate sphere developed for women, but also emphasizes that women's culture was not simply a private, noninstitutional affair.[35] Since women's culture had important public and political dimensions, its study must therefore surely be integrated with the analysis of problems of domination, subordination, and gender relations. This new emphasis on the importance of power is beginning to supersede the older preoccupation with women's culture which grew out of the radical impulses of the 1960s. But the effects of the search for cultural autonomy in this as in other fields still have to be transcended.

While minority history of the type written by Gutman on workers, Webber on slaves, and Rosenberg on women has immensely broadened the scope of

historical scholarship, it has merely forced the addition of specialist subdisciplines to the liberal tradition, and has not challenged the methods or the broad
outlines of the liberal synthesis. "History," Carl Degler candidly noted in 1980,
"as that word is defined by many citizens and most historians, still does not
include those activities women have engaged in; . . . *what is meant by history or
the past will have to be changed* before these two subdisciplines become an
integral part of it.''[36] Degler was talking about the history of women and the
family, but his conclusion could readily apply to labor, black, ethnic, slave, or
Indian history as well.

Instead of a serious reassessment of "what is meant by history," there has
developed an increasingly ramshackle structure within the discipline. Fragmentation of historical reality and specialization through the development of subdisciplines have taken place at the expense of serious reassessment of larger
theoretical perspectives and trends. Little attention has been devoted to the ways
in which these new fields hang together. As Peter Stearns has concluded, the
"steady development of topical subfields" that "marks social history in the
United States" still "lacks an overall conceptualization.''[37]

This process of eclectic assimilation to the existing historical tradition has also
made the new fields especially vulnerable to the changing political climate. Since
many of these specialized fields were established by beleaguered departments
and university administrations in the 1960s in response to radical demands for
relevance in the curricula, the dissipation of those political pressures and the
advent of severe budgetary restraints have posed a very serious threat to the
survival of these fields. This is especially clear in the case of black history,
where the civil rights and black power movements exerted pressures leading to
the establishment of black studies courses. Courses on Native Americans, ethnic
groups, women's studies, to name just a few of the proliferating special interest
groups, followed. By the early 1980s black rebellion no longer seems a pressing
political concern, and it is possible that an emphasis on black history in the
curricula will decline as a historiographical analogue to the current Republican
administration's neglectful policies toward black Americans. The *Mid-Atlantic
Radical Historians' Organization Newsletter* has noted that budgetary restraints
are becoming "a vehicle to eliminate black studies programs and cancel curricula
dealing with women's history, minority groups, or working people.''[38]

Whether or not these programs survive, the changing political climate in the
1970s and the obvious need to bring some order out of historiographical chaos
produced calls for reconsideration of what was common in the nation's past.
These calls have been reminiscent of the liberal, consensus history that minority
and radical history sought to supplant. *The Great Republic*, one of the most
sophisticated and academically oriented textbooks to appear in recent times, has
shifted the emphasis back from the history of minority groups to the development
of "free political institutions in the United States" and to "the tension between
majority rule and minority rights" as a way of incorporating the radical impulse
within a larger framework. More recently, James O. Robertson has attracted

attention through his attempts to analyze the myths that have shaped a common American experience in *American Myth, American Reality*. The bicentennial convention of the American Historical Association also saw an attempt by Robert Kelley to erect a new cultural synthesis which linked the ideologies of political elites in America to "mass cultural attitudes." This focuses attention back on national political history and assumes valid connections between that and mass culture. Although Kelley failed to establish those connections, the point remains that a decade of minority history had not shaken the central convictions of liberal historians such as Kelley. Indeed, they seemed even more convinced that the only way to synthesize America's diverse group, ethnic, class, and sex experience was in terms of national political elites and issues derived from the liberal-democratic experience.[39]

So-called "minority" history has successfully undermined the more simplistic varieties of consensus history of the 1950s. Liberal historians now vie with radicals for opportunites to criticize Louis Hartz's attempt to homogenize the political and ideological past of the United States. The work of Gutman and others discussed in this chapter has played an important part in this transformation of scholarship. The new work has been immensely important in resurrecting the experience of oppressed people and minorities that had been virtually ignored by mainstream historiography. To take the case of black history, the claims that blacks did not have a culture worthy of the name—that they lived in some kind of cultural no-man's land—have been systematically refuted and the ignorance of black history has been substantially reduced. The condescending views of Elkins, Stampp, and others have indeed been challenged, but what stands in their place? Here the ambiguous legacy of the new social history is very much in evidence. There is, for example, a strong populist strain running through a good deal of the radical social history. This work has been hailed by some as evidence of "progressive" or "democratic" forces emerging out of the "free space" which workers, women, and others have succeeded in creating. Yet it is not clear how these groups have created free space, whether they have created it, and how that development of "autonomous" traditions is connected to cultural resistance and to politically radical agitation.[40]

Given the concern of the radical social historians to transcend liberal history, it is ironic that the new social history may well be compatible with liberal and conservative viewpoints. Conservatives might well be able to say that slavery and industrial capitalism were less oppressive than commonly thought because they allowed the survival of independent cultural forms.[41] There is also the more immediate prospect that the radical historiography will be absorbed into a reconstructed liberal pluralism. The idea of a diversity of groups and individuals making their own history within the confines of liberal, capitalist civilization remains a possible misinterpretation of the significance of the new social history. The spectacle of women, post-Reconstruction blacks, ethnics, poor farmers, Indians, and workers all contributing in diverse ways to the story of American democratic progress is certainly the way textbooks have typically integrated the findings of the new social history.[42] (Talking about textbooks here is no minor point, since the new social history has been conceived and remains within the confines of traditional academic production and dissemination.) At the level of interpretive synthesis, too, there could be confirmation for those historians who emphasize the pluralistic character of the American past and the nation's capacity to provide for dissent and for orderly change. Already Robert Kelley has described life in the United States as "irreducibly pluralistic" in writing the interpretation which brought the ethnic history research of the 1960s and 1970s into a new synthesis of the meaning of the national political experience.[43]

The failure of historians of minority groups to confront the central methodological and epistemological assumptions of liberalism has entailed a lost opportunity presented by the energy and idealism of 1960s radicalism. It has given in effect a further lease on life to the sagging liberal tradition. This is not to deny the very real malaise within that tradition as the United States entered the 1980s and Americans sought to cope with diminished economic power and the erosion of confidence in the caliber of American political leadership. The challenge to the liberal synthesis has not, however, come from radical history alone. To the corrosive effects of the new social history there has been added a crisis in confidence rooted in the changing intellectual assumptions and material conditions of the profession.

NOTES

1. Peter N. Stearns, "Toward a Wider Vision: Trends in Social History," in Michael Kammen, ed., *The Past Before Us: Contemporary Historical Writing in the United States* (Ithaca, N.Y., 1980), pp. 212–13.

2. Herbert Gutman, *Work, Culture, and Society in Industrializing America: Essays in American Working-Class and Social History* (New York, 1976), is representative of the "new labor history." The larger field, and its theoretical and methodological weaknesses is illustrated in *Journal of Social History* (1967–   ).

3. David Brody, "Labor History in the 1970s: Toward a History of the American Worker," in Kammen, ed., *The Past Before Us*, p. 254.

4. See, for example, Harold D. Woodman, "Economic History and Economic Theory: The New Economic History in America," *Journal of Interdisciplinary History* 3 (1972): 323–25.

5. Herbert Gutman, "The Worker's Search for Power: Labor in the Gilded Age," in H. Wayne Morgan, ed., *The Gilded Age: A Reappraisal* (New York, 1963), pp. 38–68.

6. Herbert Gutman, "Protestantism and the American Labor Movement: The Christian Spirit in the Gilded Age," *American Historical Review* 72 (1966), reprinted in Alfred E. Young, ed., *Dissent: Explorations in the History of American Radicalism* (DeKalb, Ill., 1968), pp. 139, 146, 157, 160.

7. Ibid., p. 139.

8. Robert H. Zieger, "Workers and Scholars: Recent Trends in American Labor Historiography," *Labor History* 13 (1972): 247–48. Bornet (Ph.D., Stanford, 1951) was associated with the Rand Corporation between 1959 and 1963, when he became a professor

of history at the University of Oregon. See *Directory of American Scholars* (New York, 1969 ed.), 1:49.

9. E. P. Thompson, *The Making of the English Working Class* (New York, Vintage ed., 1966); Herbert Gutman, "Work, Culture, and Society in Industrializing America, 1815–1919," *American Historical Review* 78 (1973), reprinted in Gutman, *Work, Culture, and Society*, pp. 3–78.

10. Jesse Lemisch, "Bailyn Besieged in His Bunker," *Radical History Review* 4 (Winter 1977): 76.

11. Gutman, "Protestantism," p. 164; David Montgomery, "Gutman's Nineteenth-Century America," *Labor History* 19 (1978): 416–29, quotation at 426–27.

12. David Brody, "The Old Labor History and the New: In Search of an American Working Class," *Labor History* 20 (1979): 124.

13. Gutman, "Work, Culture, and Society," pp. 13–14.

14. Herbert Gutman, *The Black Family in Slavery and Freedom, 1750–1925* (New York, 1976).

15. The importance of work to the shop-floor culture is a theme pursued by Paul Willis, "Shop Floor Culture, Masculinity and the Wage Form," in John Clarke, Chas Chritcher, and Richard Johnson, eds., *Working-Class Culture: Studies in History and Theory* (London, 1979). See also F. M. L. Thompson, "Social Control in Victorian Britain," *Economic History Review*, 2d ser., 34 (1981): 204; on slaves and work, see Eugene Genovese, *Roll, Jordan, Roll: The World the Slaves Made* (New York, 1974); on work songs, see Lawrence Levine, *Black Culture and Black Consciousness: Afro-American Folk Thought from Slavery to Freedom* (New York, 1977).

16. Gutman, "Work, Culture, and Society," p. 16.

17. Gutman, "Work, Culture, and Society," p. xii.

18. Ibid.

19. Montgomery, "Gutman's Nineteenth-Century America," p. 425; James Henretta, " 'Modernization': Toward a False Synthesis," *Reviews in American History* 5 (1977): 445–52.

20. Thompson, *Making of the English Working Class*, pp. 203, 204, 205, 207, 212; Gareth Stedman Jones, "History and Theory," *History Workshop* 8 (1979): 199–200.

21. Gareth Stedman Jones, "Working-Class Culture and Working-Class Politics in London, 1870–1890: Notes on the Remaking of a Working Class," *Journal of Social History* 7 (1974): 460–508; Perry Anderson, *Arguments within English Marxism* (London, 1980), p. 45; Richard Price, "Edward Thompson and the Peculiarities of English History," paper presented at the American Historical Association convention, 29 Dec. 1983; Craig Calhoun, *The Question of Class Struggle: Social Foundations of Popular Radicalism during the Industrial Revolution* (Oxford, 1982).

22. Clifford Geertz, *The Interpretation of Cultures: Selected Essays* (New York, 1973), pp. 4–5, 250; Robert F. Berkhofer, Jr., "Clio and the Culture Concept: Some Impressions of a Changing Relationship in American Historiography," *Social Science Quarterly* 53 (1972): 299–301. Caroline Ware, ed., *The Cultural Approach to History* (New York, 1940), is illustrative of the older approach.

23. Geertz, *Interpretation of Cultures*, pp. 146, 165–69.

24. Alan Dawley, "E. P. Thompson and the Peculiarities of the Americans," *Radical History Review* 19 (1978–1979): 39.

25. Thomas L. Webber, *Deep Like the Rivers: Education in the Slave Quarter Community, 1831–1865* (New York, 1978), pp. xii, 263.

26. Herbert Gutman, "Slave Culture and Slave Family and Kin Network: The Importance of Time," *South Atlantic Urban Studies* 2 (1978): 80–81, 82, 83.

27. An astute assessment of Gutman's methodological problems in relation to the black family is Stanley Engerman, "Studying the Black Family," *Journal of Family History* 3 (1978): 78–101. The variations in Afro-American culture in different regions and periods, and their relations to the context of economy and society, are dealt with in a crucial modification of Gutman's work by Ira Berlin, "Time, Space and the Evolution of Afro-American Society on British Mainland North America," *American Historical Review* 85 (1980): 44–78.

28. Leila Rupp, "Reflections on Twentieth-Century American Women's History," *Reviews in American History* 9 (1981): 279.

29. Nancy Cott, *The Bonds of Womanhood: "Woman's Sphere" in New England, 1780–1835* (New Haven, 1977); Carroll Smith-Rosenberg, "The Female World of Love and Ritual: Relations between Women in Nineteenth-Century America," *Signs* 1 (1975): 1–29.

30. See, for example, Keith Melder, *The Beginnings of Sisterhood: The American Woman's Rights Movement, 1800–1850* (New York, 1977), p. 31; Mary Jo Buhle, "Politics and Culture in Women's History," *Feminist Studies* 6 (1980): 38; Karen Blair, *The Clubwoman as Feminist: True Womanhood Redefined* (New York, 1980); Barbara J. Berg, *The Remembered Gate: Origins of American Feminism: The Woman and the City, 1800–1860* (New York, 1978), pp. 173–75, 266–67, 334; Sara Evans, *Personal Politics: The Roots of Women's Liberation in the Civil Rights Movement and the New Left* (New York, 1979), esp. pp. 215–16, 218–19; Marilyn F. Motz, *True Sisterhood: Michigan Women and Their Kin, 1820–1920* (Albany, N.Y., 1983).

31. Rosenberg, "Female World," pp. 2–3; Carroll Smith-Rosenberg and Charles Rosenberg, "The Female Animal: Medical and Biological Views of Woman and Her Role in Nineteenth-Century America," *Journal of American History* 60 (1973): 332–56; Carroll Smith-Rosenberg, "The New Woman and the New History," *Feminist Studies* 3 (1975): 189, 193.

32. Sarah Stage, "Women's History and 'Woman's Sphere': Major Works of the 1970s," *Socialist Review* 10 (March-June 1980): 247; Rupp, "Reflections," p. 279.

33. Rosenberg, "Female World," pp. 3, 9–10; Catherine Clinton, *The Plantation Mistress: Woman's World in the Old South* (New York, 1983); Cott, *Bonds of Womanhood*; Anne M. Boylan, "Women in Groups: An Analysis of Women's Benevolent Organizations in New York and Boston, 1797–1840," *Journal of American History* 71 (1984): 497–523; Anne F. Scott, *The Southern Lady: From Pedestal to Politics, 1830–1930* (Chicago, 1970), esp. pp. 40–44.

34. Bonnie Gene Smith, *Ladies of the Leisure Class: The Bourgeoises of Northern France in the Nineteenth Century* (Princeton, N.J., 1981).

35. Elizabeth Fox-Genovese, "The Personal Is Not Political Enough," *Marxist Perspectives* 2 (Winter 1979–1980): 94–113; Ellen DuBois, *Feminism and Suffrage: The Emergence of an Independent Woman's Movement in America, 1848–1869* (Ithaca, N.Y., 1978); Rupp, "Reflections," pp. 275–84; Estelle B. Freedman, "Separatism as Strategy: Female Institution Building and American Feminism, 1870–1930," *Feminist Studies* 5 (1979): 512–29.

36. Carl Degler, "Women and the Family," in Kammen, ed., *The Past Before Us*, p. 326 (italics added).

37. Stearns, "Toward a Wider Vision," p. 222.

38. David B. Davis, "Slavery and the Post–World War II Historians," *Daedalus* 103 (1974): 8; *Mid-Atlantic Radical Historians' Organization Newsletter*, no. 36, Nov. 1981, pp. 1–2.

39. Bernard Bailyn et al., *The Great Republic: A History of the American People* (Lexington, Mass., 1st ed., 1977), from unpaginated introduction; James O. Robertson, *American Myth, American Reality* (New York, 1980); Robert Kelley, "Ideology and Political Culture from Jefferson to Nixon," *American Historical Review* 82 (1977): 567; Kelley, "The History the Masses Learn and Historians Ignore," *Reviews in American History* 8 (1980): 300–303.

40. Interpretations of slavery that Gutman superseded include Stanley Elkins, *Slavery: A Problem in American Institutional and Intellectual Life* (Chicago, 1959); Kenneth M. Stampp, *The Peculiar Institution: Slavery in the Antebellum South* (New York, 1956). The radical populist interpretation referred to is Harry Boyte, "Building the Democratic Movement: Prospects for a Socialist Renaissance," *Socialist Review* 8 (July/Oct. 1978): 17–63, esp. pp. 22–23; Boyte, *The Backyard Revolution: Understanding the New Citizen Movement* (Philadelphia, 1980).

41. Possible conservative uses of the new social history are illustrated in Aileen S. Kraditor, *The Radical Persuasion, 1890–1917: Aspects of the Intellectual History and the Historiography of Three American Radical Organizations* (Baton Rouge, 1981).

42. See, for example, the introduction by Winthrop Jordan and Leon Litwack to Richard Hofstadter et al., *The United States* (Englewood Cliffs, N.J., brief ed., 1979), pp. ix-x, 449–50; Richard N. Current, T. Harry Williams, and Frank Freidel, *American History: A Survey* (New York, 4th ed., 1975); Lloyd C. Gardner and William L. O'Neill, *Looking Backward: A Reintroduction to American History* (New York, 1974); Allen Weinstein and R. Jackson Wilson, *Freedom and Crisis: An American History* (New York, 1974); Bailyn et al., *The Great Republic*; Mary Beth Norton et al., *A People and a Nation* (Boston, 1982), is a partial exception in its greater attention to economic history and social process.

43. Kelley, "Ideology and Political Culture," p. 533. Kelley's analysis, however, failed to take into account the work of the new labor historians. Cf. Carl Degler, "Women and the Family," pp. 314–15.

7

Challenges to Empiricism

The new social history has eroded the intellectual coherence of the old liberal interpretations, but the current questioning of the liberal synthesis—either consensus or progressive—goes deeper still. There has occurred over the last fifteen years a cumulative loss of confidence in the theoretical and political efficacy of liberal history. Changes in the international and domestic political environment and a multipronged methodological challenge had by the late 1970s produced this malaise. Structuralism, antiempiricist philosophies, Freudian theory, structural-functionalism, and a modest marxian revival seriously undermined the empiricist and positivist assumptions of American historiography.[1]

Increased scholarly exchange since World War II and the growing international prestige of *Annales* historians led by Fernand Braudel made structuralist methods harder to ignore in the United States. Braudel's visit as a fellow of the Woodrow Wilson Center for International Studies at Princeton in 1968 helped spread the *Annales* methods, as much as it was a symbol of enhanced interest. Then the translation of his *La Méditerranée* into English in 1972 provoked a rash of enthusiastic appraisals, and the appetite for *Annales* history has continued to grow; it has resulted in frequent symposia, book-length assessments, and further translations of the important works of the senior *Annales* historians like Le Roy Ladurie, Febvre, Bloch, and Braudel. The *American Historical Review* recently carried an extensive appraisal of Bloch's work in comparative history, while as early as 1972, the *Journal of Modern History* devoted an entire issue to Braudel and his *histoire totale*. There has even appeared at the State University of New York, Binghamton, a Fernand Braudel Center for the Study of Economies, Historical Systems and Civilizations.[2]

The emphases found in historians associated with the *Annales* tradition have all received increasing attention in the American profession. These have included the commitment to total history, the importance attached to geography, the hostility to ideas of progress and to ethnocentricity, the assaults on concepts of voluntarism, the discovery of collective *mentalité*, the attack on the centrality of political elites for historical interpretation, and the relentless search for impersonal and deterministic structures.

Braudel's work has been especially important for the distinction he has drawn between the history of superficial events, and the structural history of the *longue durée*—the material constraints upon civilization that change only imperceptibly and over extremely long periods of time. Braudel clearly placed much greater value upon the latter in his work, and the ephemeral events of political and diplomatic history he relegated to the third and in some ways the least satisfactory part of his massive book. Braudel's distinction between the different temporal rhythms of superficial events and deeper structures is reminiscent in a concrete form of the epistemological stance of French structuralist method. From the point of view of this essay, that method, as much as Braudel's literary example, has posed a challenge for the empiricism of the liberal synthesis. According to structuralist epistemology, reality is not seen as something "out there" in surface events or facts but in deep structures which have to be penetrated by analysis. This approach has been profoundly influenced by structural linguistics and, particularly, by anthropology, where the work of Claude Levi-Strauss has been of immense importance in contesting the primacy of facts, and in positing the existence of a universalistic and rationalistic epistemology. Levi-Strauss has drawn a fundamental distinction between the empirical reality of social relations, and deeper patterns of social structure which go beyond any particular set of empirical phenomena, and have to be decoded by the anthropologist. After more than a decade of increasing influence in such subjects as literary criticism, communications, sociology, and anthropology, the work of Levi-Strauss is just beginning to permeate the conceptual frameworks of United States historians.[3]

Another challenge to empiricism came from the philosophers of science who argued that the practice of science itself conformed neither to empiricist notions of truth nor to conventional objectivist accounts of scientific method. From the American point of view, the chief influence has been that of Thomas Kuhn, through his *Structure of Scientific Revolutions*, published in 1962. Kuhn analyzed scientific practice and depicted the history of science not as the steady accumulation of empirical observations leading to incremental improvements in theory, but as a set of distinct intellectual paradigms, in which scientific truth was elaborated according to its conformity to a set of mutually agreed procedures. Facts contrary to existing scientific hypotheses did not necessarily lead to new theories or the demise of old ones. Scientific revolutions occurred dramatically at points of professional and societal crisis, at which times it was no longer possible for the paradigm to contain conflicting information.[4]

Kuhn's theories have probably been influential in the historical profession in part because they have taken a practical, historical form rather than a logical or philosophical one. But they have also appealed because, as David Hollinger, an important interpreter of Kuhn, has noted, they appear to provide a formula for reconciling relativism and objectivity, and for bringing the practice of historical scholarship back into line with a more modest scientific ideal. Kuhn's theory has not been interpreted by historians as a sanction for relativism, but it has made increasing numbers aware that scientific truth has a kind of objectivity which is limited by the questions and the language of the scholarly community. Its objectivity is thus not complete, but "socially grounded."[5]

A third challenge to empiricism came from the realm of psychoanalysis. Freudian theory claimed that reality could be explained not through observation of what actually happened in the Rankean sense, nor through an account of the thought of participants, as Collingwood and the idealist philosophers had contended, but through the application of a theory of childhood development to trivial and seemingly irrelevant experiences. Under Freudianism, like structuralism, the theoretical system had primacy over the facts; indeed, there was no such thing as "the facts," since the experience which Freudian theory mediated had to be dredged from the subconscious by the process of clinical therapy.

Yet Freudianism has not been as important as *Annales*, structural anthopology, Kuhn, or the philosophers of science in calling empiricism into question among American historians. Freudian techniques have met with considerable skepticism within the profession, and have only been very slowly and partially absorbed. The slow reception of Freud in the United States paralleled in its sources and meaning the animus toward marxism. Both sets of theories were typically seen as deterministic. Like marxism, too, Freudianism faced the standard objections that so much of psychohistory could not be verified by the evidence. The "patient" could not be called to testify or respond to the questions of the "therapist." Given the widespread distrust among historians of theoretical insights which were not clearly grounded in the phenomena historians could observe, it is small wonder that William L. Langer could still identify a Freudian-based psychology as the profession's "next assignment" in 1957. This was possible even though American historians had been exposed to Freudian theory for over forty years.[6]

Several developments over the past twenty years have served in significant ways to breach this climate of hostility, and to enlarge the area of impact of Freudian psychology in American scholarship, but at the cost of blunting the edge of the Freudian methodological impact. The gradual assimilation of Freudianism to American behaviorism, and the popularization of a modified Freudian theory by Erik Erikson in his studies of Luther and Gandhi, did much to soften the earlier antagonism, and by the early 1970s psychohistory had a foothold in United States history. In that decade, two major journals, the *Journal of Psychohistory* and the *Psychohistorical Review* had emerged, and the American Historical Association gave legitimacy to the movement in 1972 by accepting the Group for the Use of Psychology in History as an affiliate organization.[7]

A good deal of this work has involved the application of Freudian concepts alongside a range of social science techniques. Even when skillfully done, as in the case of David Donald's *Charles Sumner*, it is difficult to see how such work advances methodologically or theoretically beyond the 1950s conception of the role of social sciences in historical analysis. At the other end of the spectrum, however, the work of deeply committed psychohistorians seems on occasions to degenerate into an embarrassing form of crackpot positivism. As in the work of Lloyd DeMause, psychohistory has sometimes involved the reduction of complex historical processes to simplistic psychological motives. Such analyses hardly reconstitute historical theory; in fact they have tended to feed persistent objections to the legitimacy of psychohistory, while demonstrating the existence of yet another critique of empiricism from outside the conventional boundaries of the profession.[8]

Another intellectual movement which implicitly called into question the empiricism underlying American historiography was the structural-functionalism put forward in sociology by Talcott Parsons. Parsons conceived of society as a system in which the parts were interrelated and could not be understood as isolated facts. Parsons' work was, as Alvin Gouldner has shown, an attempt to import the theoretical perspectives of European sociology, particularly of Durkheim and Weber, and fashion these into a synthesis which would make values rather than material conditions, power relations, or the forces of production central to an understanding of society.

Parsons has been less directly influential than *Annales*, Kuhn, or structural anthropology (or even psychohistory). Despite Parsons' enormous influence in sociology in the 1950s, his opaque language and disdain for mere facts did not endear him to empirically minded historians. His failure to write historically made his work less attractive than Erikson's, Kuhn's, or Braudel's. Consequently, few American historians proclaimed themselves, as Paul Kleppner did, structural-functionalists, though Parsons might have had a more direct appeal had the disruptive effects of radical sociology in the late 1960s not interrupted the spread of his influence. Alvin Gouldner's critique of Parsons as a conservative theorist damaged his reputation in the 1960s when conflict seemed more pressing a concern than the supposed consensual values on which Parsons' structure rested. But his work has been influential in indirect ways, both through the work of historians such as Kleppner, and through sociologists and anthropologists like Robert Merton and Clifford Geertz, who have modified Parsons' synoptic vision, or expressed his ideas in more readable and historically concrete forms.[9]

These cumulative challenges to liberal assumptions are as much a product as a cause of declining confidence in existing historical syntheses. *Annales*, the search for alternatives to empiricism, indeed the vogue for marxism as well, all derive a certain currency from the increasing inadequacy of liberalism to explain the international and domestic situation, and from the changing sociology of the profession which is one small element of the current political, social, and economic conjuncture in western capitalism's history.

The political roots of the crisis in liberal historiography are vaguer and necessarily more intangible than its intellectual roots. Nevertheless, it is possible to give an outline of the main developments by tracing the changing intellectual orientation of the liberal historians. Since liberal intellectuals have defined themselves in relation to the power of the democratic state and have been distinguished by a deep attachment to the American political and economic system, changes in American power must provoke a profound reassessment of the liberal tradition which has grown up around American national myths of democracy, uniqueness, destiny, individualism, and freedom. Just as the dominance of liberal history in the 1950s rested heavily on the attachment of reform-minded liberal intellectuals to the pluralist, democratic, and antitotalitarian state associated with the New Deal experience, so too does the diminished authority of liberal history have deep roots in the declining efficacy of liberal ideology. Watergate, Vietnam, the energy crisis, and the economic stagnation of the 1970s have combined to unsettle the liberal intellectuals who had done much in their scholarly prime to perpetuate voluntaristic, individualistic, and other ideological conceptions of the American past. Participants in the bicentennial convention of the American Historical Association testified to the more pessimistic and even conservative mood that accompanied the nation's recent political embarrassments. C. Vann Woodward spoke of the gap between the ''reality'' of America's ''aging'' society and social structure, and the myths of perpetual innocence which continued to distinguish the official ideology of the American republic. While the general public and politicians seemed to respond well to the self-congratulatory rhetoric of bicentennial fervor, Arthur Schlesinger spoke at the same convention, deploring Jacksonian romanticism, innocence, and the missionizing impulse, while exalting the tradition of experience he found in the thought and practice of the founding fathers. David Donald went much further to proclaim the uselessness of American history in a much noticed article. ''The age of abundance'' which David Potter had analyzed ''has ended,'' Donald asserted. ''The 'lessons' taught by the American past are today not merely irrelevant but dangerous.''[10]

Underlying the erosion of confidence in liberal historiography is a new crisis in the sociology of the profession. Jobs in academia have only on rare occasions been plentiful for historians. In this sense the favorable market of the 1960s was the exception to the rule of persistent oversupply. Yet never before the 1970s had there been such a marked disparity between the realities of the academic employment market and the aspirations and qualifications of the pool of trained historians. The doctoral production in *American* history in the 1970s came close to exceeding *annually* the total number of living historians in all fields practicing in the 1920s. Whereas in the 1930s two-thirds of the output of 1935 had been employed in college jobs of some sort by 1939, projections had it that only one in ten of the much greater output of the 1980s will obtain academic employment. This abrupt shift back to a pattern of depressed demand came swiftly upon a buoyant period in which the hopes, and perhaps the reality of mobility within the profession, had been inflated. Given the excess of supply over demand, and given a background of declining confidence in historical thinking in American and indeed western culture, there has been a tendency for graduate programs to place increasing emphasis on methodological and/or theoretical sophistication.

In this way the young Ph.D. degree holders can (hopefully) distinguish themselves from their competitors and so obtain that elusive university or college appointment.[11]

A related development concerns the inception of so-called applied history programs which seek to train historians in such a way as to make their skills marketable in government, research, or business employment. These programs involve necessarily an interdisciplinary focus; an example would be historical and archival management training, or history and law. The programs, such as that set up at the University of Pittsburgh, also incorporate internships where practical on-the-job experience is earned, usually as part of the degree program. Because the programs break across the traditional specializations of academic study and because they involve practical training, they do hold out the possibility of methodological innovation which may feed back to the historical profession a new vitality. More certain is the judgment that the existence of such programs testifies to the current state of methodological innovation within the profession which has stemmed in part from the gloomy academic employment market.[12]

Another trend involves the movement of trained historians into the academic fringe occupations—such as community college teaching—where the limits of the ideology of social mobility for both staff and students are clearer, and where the class-based character of American higher education is readily apparent. The kind of history which has emphasized the opportunities for individuals to advance within the American class structure can be (though not necessarily is) called into question by this experience. For some young radical historians drawn into teaching in the late 1960s and early 1970s, this experience has left them increasingly disillusioned with the possibilities of advancement within the academic world, as well as more concerned with probing the social functions and implicit political content of much academic scholarship in history.[13]

Spurred by these intellectual and political changes, a major upheaval of method and conception is underway. The profession is more open to criticism and reassessment than at any time since the relativist controversy of the 1930s, and historiographers now widely recognize that the liberal synthesis lacks coherence and persuasive power. The change can be seen in the spate of books and articles focusing explicitly on theoretical and conceptual issues, beginning with the publication of David Hackett Fischer's *Historians' Fallacies* in 1970, and Gene Wise's *American Historical Explanations* in 1973. New journals addressed partially or primarily to these methodological and theoretical questions have proliferated, among them the *Historical Methods Newsletter* (1967–   ), the *Journal of Interdisciplinary History* (1970–   ), *Reviews in American History* (1973–   ), and *Social Science History* (1976–   ).[14]

Historians are now seeking to encompass the methodological innovations of the *Annales* historians and at the same time are beginning to review the ideological assumptions and social functions of liberal historical scholarship. From the point of view of this study, the most important development has been the willingness of a few intrepid souls to criticize the empiricist assumptions underlying liberal methodology. Amid an outpouring of reevaluations at the bicentennial American Historical Association Convention, Leo Marx attacked "the influence of the reigning ideology of the American academy: a form of empiricism" which assumed "a reality immediately visible and observable in the historical data." Michael Frisch has noted the conceptual poverty characteristic of American urban history because of its empiricist and antitheoretical biases. Alan Dawley has denounced "crackpot empiricism" in which data accumulation drowns out theory. Commenting on the persistence of positivist and empiricist notions in American historical practice, Jackson Lears claimed that "historical facts are not simply 'out there' but rather embedded in the questions historians frame." Most of the assimilation of the anti-empiricist critique and realization of its implications for the liberal tradition has occurred either among European historians like Richard Andrews or among radical and marxist historians like Dawley and James Green.[15] But in the work of James Henretta, one of the most eloquent younger Americanists of first rank, the antiempiricist influence has resulted in a serious and sustained critique of liberal methodology that deserves detailed discussion.

Henretta's "Social History as Lived and Written" offers a shrewd overview of marxist and structuralist currents, as well as a devastating attack on the empiricist epistemology dominant for so long among historians. Nevertheless, his proposed solution to the challenge of European intellectual currents continues to illustrate the limitations of the liberal perspective in theory and method. He stops short of accepting the implications of his criticisms of liberal epistemology. Instead, he tries to synthesize the new approaches with the American tradition of pragmatism in what he calls an action model. This seeks to incorporate analysis of the objective characteristics of society through the application of the techniques of marxist, structural-functionalist, and *Annales* historians, but then insists that these new intellectual currents be "subordinated to the subjective experiences of the historical actors" through a phenomenological perspective. The result may be a practical compromise, but it does little to dispel the very real methodological problems facing the discipline.[16]

Henretta does not offer a logical justification for his decision to reject a reconstruction of historical practice in favor of assimilating the *Annales* methods and marxism to the existing intellectual structures. Indeed, Henretta admits that pragmatism's attention to technique at the expense of theory has "narrowed the critical scope and interpretive range of American historical analysis." His justifications are instead derived essentially from the political and ideological aspirations of pragmatism. The value of methodology is assessed not in terms of its objective validity or even its heuristic possibilities, but rather in terms of its ability to depict and to popularize a democratic history. Much emphasis is put, therefore, on the reading of history and its reception in the larger society, and on a recognition of the obligations that this purpose imposes on historical method. "If American social historians are to reach a wide audience," Henretta argues, "then they must fashion a rhetorical mode of presentation that reconciles narration and analysis." Reaching a wide audience is imperative, Henretta believes, because "in a society formally committed to the democratic ideals of liberty and equality, the ultimate test of a historical method must be its capacity to depict the experiences of all members of the culture and to comprehend the ability of all individuals in the culture to make their own history."

To achieve these goals Henretta places great reliance on an historical narrative which enables the historian to employ a phenomenological perspective. "By placing as much (or more) emphasis upon the subjective perceptions of the actors as upon the objective circumstances of existence, narratives underscore the importance of human agency." Narratives are also compatible with the aim of appealing to the lay reader, since "most readers view the past in the same manner that they comprehend their own existence— . . . in terms of a series of overlapping and interwoven narrative life-stories."[17]

Henretta's narrative mode of presentation does not circumvent the need for judgment, selection, organization, and attention to causal connection on the part of the historian. The subjective experiences of the historical actors can only be presented through the analytical and theoretical mediation of the historian. Henretta in part admits this when he says that there will always be "some degree of artifice" entering "the construction of the narrative," because the author knows the outcome of the story, and develops it accordingly. It would seem that the capacity to present the subjective experiences of the historical actors has been crucially undermined here, but unperturbed, Henretta shifts his case to one of presentation, arguing that the *reader* perceives the story in the same open-ended way as the original historical participant. It is doubtful, however, whether the "reader's imperfect knowledge" does approximate "that of the historical actor" since the participant may not know so much about the experiences of the other actors as the reader can through the narrator's sophisticated presentation of the subjective experiences of *all* the participants. Moreover, Henretta had begun by extolling narrative as a means of *knowing* the open-endedness of history, only to move later from historical explanation to the comprehension of historical explanation by the reading public. Once again, as in the more general matter of method, he has allowed his democratic and pragmatic historical purpose to override questions of historical interpretation and theory.[18]

The theoretical weakness in Henretta's attempt to synthesize objective historical structures with a narrative mode of presentation was observed by Robert Berkhofer. After noting that Henretta's action model began with the definition of a historical problem—a "paradigmatic episode" which would illuminate historical structures and mentalities—Berkhofer simply pointed out that by conceding the importance of an analytical focus on the part of the historian, Henretta undermined the emphasis on the narrative mode or the subjective presentation of the points of view of historical actors. In an equally telling criticism, he noted that Henretta's narrative itself still seemed to embody the concept of the omniscient narrator, and was thus incompatible with his phenomenological perspective.[19]

Henretta's reply to these observations was a startling revelation of the weaknesses inherent in his attempted synthesis. He conceded that to follow his method through, it might indeed be necessary to abandon the perspective of an omniscient narrator in favor of a fragmented and pluralistic perspective in the "form of a montage composed of individual life-histories." How this adoption of modern literary consciousness might be compatible with the analysis of objective structures was not made clear, as could be gathered from his reply to Berkhofer's criticisms. Here Henretta was forced to concede the theoretical difficulties, and fall back upon the weak working justification that "this method succeeds in many instances." Again, this reply showed he has shifted ground away from theory to the justification of a practical compromise between liberal history and competing traditions.[20]

Undermining Henretta's synthesis is the suspicion that despite his strictures on the epistemological weakness of liberal empiricism, he has not transcended that way of knowing the world. Henretta does not really accept the antiempiricist perspectives in marxism and structuralism. He does ask for "discussion and debate" between these traditions and American pragmatism, but then merely absorbs particular insights from structuralism and marxism within the framework of pragmatism. His brief for a narrative presentation is fundamentally empiricist in its implications. Narrative, Henretta believes, entails a "mode of cognition" which "approximates the reality of everyday life." In that admission, commonsense observations of what is real—to use his earlier phrase, "the surface of events"—are raised to the level of historical theory and the highest form of historical activity. Finally, his belief that the historian can and ought to aim primarily at the presentation of the subjective experiences of the historical participants still embodies the assumption of a reality "out there" subject to direct historical observation and unmediated presentation. Despite Henretta's concession elsewhere in the argument that history inevitably involves the mediation of the historian, for him the most convincing and satisfying historical account is one "designed to discover and depict history as it was lived by men and women in the past" through a kaleidoscope of individual and group perspectives. Henretta's synthesis fails to resolve the epistemological dilemmas facing liberal historiography: instead, it is illustrative of the problem it seeks to surmount. The foundations of the old liberal history have been undermined both from within and from without, but a coherent and theoretically adequate alternative has yet to be found.[21]

Judging by the space devoted to it in the scholarly journals, the *Annales* School must be considered as the leading candidate for a new conceptual framework to replace a moribund liberal synthesis. The current structuralist vogue among American historians has several sources, and some of them have nothing to do with the undoubted quality and international prestige of the *Annales* scholarship. To speak of *Annales* is merely a convenient shorthand way of describing, like liberal history, a historical tradition in which there has been much complexity, historical development, internal transformation, and permutation. To go further and claim that there is today any such thing as a coherent, unified, historiographical paradigm called *Annales* is itself a curious product of the recent intellectual history of American historians. The anticipated demise of the liberal approaches has produced an intimidating volume of ponderous and often adulatory theorizing upon *Annales*, much to the mystification of the French scholars themselves.[22] The enthusiastic reception given Braudel's work in the United States in the 1970s, in comparison with the 1950s, points to political and ideological changes, and not just to the impact of a great work spreading through translation and the effusion of time. The structuralist vogue reflects above all the attraction of its promise to replace the liberal synthesis while not conceding the territory of history to marxist historiography, for it must never be forgotten that *Annales* is in the last analysis incompatible with marxist history. *Annales* is, however, compatible with the new conservative mood of the world-weary liberal historians who, like Schlesinger, now take pessimistic views of the future of the republic and invoke those cautious principles of the founding fathers rather than the romantic radicalism of Jacksonian America.[23]

Despite the growing appeal and prestige of *Annales*, there is reason to doubt that it offers to American historians a convincing new framework for the study of their own nation's past. Certainly, *Annales* methods and assumptions have not yet had much direct influence on the writing of United States history. When the Fernand Braudel Center at SUNY-Binghamton held a conference in 1977 to discuss the impact of *Annales*, the application of its principles to American history was left to a Europeanist, albeit an American-born one. Few Americanists, it seems, were either able or willing to do the job.[24]

Even where *Annales* scholarship has been a source of inspiration, its deployment has been extremely selective and limited. American historians have employed particular demographic techniques derived from the *Annales* tradition but its larger historical concepts, such as the notion of collective *mentalité* have been much less utilized. *Mentalité* had in the 1970s begun to be noticed in American historical interpretation, but either as general cultural attitudes or as the equivalent of material culture rather than collective representations.[25]

It is not just, as Henretta has pointed out, that *Annales* conflicts with the nation's liberal-voluntarist self-conception, because it is precisely that conception which has been called into question. Because the *Annales* historians have been most concerned with enduring economic and demographic patterns over many centuries, their conclusions do not seem to many American historians to apply to an American past the basic contours of which they still take as a given. Perhaps for this reason, and also because of direct emulation of particular techniques, utilization of *Annales* scholarship has tended to concentrate on the colonial period, especially the seventeenth century, where conditions were most similar to those depicted by the French historians of early modern Europe. The most obvious work in this genre has been done by the colonial demographer and social historian, Kenneth Lockridge, in his pioneering study of Dedham, Massachusetts.

Another related area conducive to application of *Annales* techniques is the history of slavery, particularly in the colonial period. Studies of the transatlantic slave economy which have appeared over the last ten or fifteen years bear important similarities to *Annales* methodology. Here it was Philip Curtin who pioneered the depiction of the complex demographic, economic, ecological, and biological processes that shaped the patterns of the international slave trade. Peter Wood and others have carried these matters further to show how attention to the international demographic and epidemiological settings of the trade can illuminate large areas of the history of what later became the United States.[26]

Despite the heuristic possibilities of *Annales* methods for certain topics, areas, and periods of American history, there are serious problems in using *Annales* to replace the liberal synthesis, without abandoning the notion of a United States history as a central concept. French historians have been successful, through the employment of demographic analysis, in showing quantitative variations within particular social structures over long periods of time. They have not, however, advanced a conceptual framework for analyzing the transformation of social systems by revolutionary or quasi-revolutionary change. When, for example, Le Roy Ladurie turns from the question of the great agrarian structure which forms the substance of his *Les Paysans de Languedoc* to explain the nature of the changes which ruptured its Malthusian cycle, his account becomes strangely sketchy. This unsatisfactory final section of his book is largely a result of his choice of focus. Continuity, not revolutionary change, was his subject, but as in other academic endeavors, such choices are important. What is excluded sets into relief what is satisfactorily treated.[27]

The preference of recent *Annales* historians for the study of the enduring structures of premodern societies poses a grave problem for the study of American history. That problem is how to comprehend the political and ideological changes which surrounded the Revolution, and the social and economic transformations which have created American industrial capitalism. These changes loom large in any attempt to come to grips with the meaning of the American experience, or of modern history generally. The liberal tradition, for all its defects, treats these issues much more effectively than any *Annales* method could ever do. Liberal history also provided superior though incomplete analytical tools for studying the ideology and politics of the modern United States. The liberal tradition did not succumb to the critical failure that has since become characteristic of much post–World War II writing associated with *Annales*, and neglect the dimension of human action and its relation to historical circumstances. It is possible, for example, to read hundreds of pages of *Annales* scholarship on the history of labor in nineteenth-century France without encountering an outline of the process of strike action as it was actually experienced in particular cases. The ways in which men and women attempted to shape their lives in dialectical relations with larger historical circumstances are simply not discussed in this work.[28] To rephrase this important matter in another and more general way, *Annales* historians have often tended to write as if the economic and demographic systems they describe were biological facts with an organic unity. In contrast, the American liberal tradition at its best, in the work of the progressives, attempted with some success to escape from this organicist delusion. The progressives' emphasis upon the interplay of interest groups and individuals at least avoided the pitfalls of an *Annales* historiography in which consciousness and ideology were too often discounted, even if the progressives' pluralism failed to attend adequately to the power relations which structured group interaction.[29]

In yet another way the vogue for *Annales* is a tempting though inadequate framework for comprehending American history. Aspects of *Annales* scholarship have appealed to some American historians because of the attention given to the study of locality. The United States as a society encompassing vast regional diversities seems therefore a natural target for *Annales* methods, as Richard Andrews has recently pointed out.[30] However, the *Annales* tradition is not able to handle with the same ease the understanding of the relationship between the microcosm of local society, and the macrostructure of politics, power, and ideology. The United States is not merely a set of discrete regions; while geo-historical regions ought to be studied, it is also necessary to analyze the realities of American state power and its ideological and political apparatus. The Civil War, for example, illustrates the reality of sectional diversity, but the meaning and impact of the war can scarcely be understood without reference to the changing role and character of the state, and to the influence of political ideologies which transcended regional boundaries in their impact.

Perhaps the passage of time and the imperial decline of the republic may make the *Annales* synthesis a more attractive one. What now seems to American patriots as the glory and greatness of the American nation may one day be viewed as a passing phase in a historical cycle of a civilization's expansion and contraction. For the time being, however, *Annales* does not seem to offer a convincing way of treating a nation's history, the defining characteristics of which have been massive change and the brutal mastery of man over the environment through the application of material force.

An alternative synthesis which does offer an explanation of those forces which have transformed the world since the eighteenth century is, of course, marxism. It has become commonplace to note the increasing prestige, volume, and sophistication of marxist scholarship in the United States. The *American Historical Review*, the *Journal of Social History*, and the *Journal of Interdisciplinary History* have all published explicitly marxist articles by Jonathan Wiener, Christopher Clark, and Daniel D. Luria respectively. The marxist Eugene Genovese, and the quasi-marxist William Appleman Williams, have both served recent terms as president of the Organization of American Historians. Genovese and Alan Dawley won successive Bancroft prizes for their books, *Roll, Jordan, Roll*, and *Class and Community: The Industrial Revolution in Lynn*. Critical marxist work of a high academic and intellectual standard has been done through *Marxist Perspectives* (1978–1981) and the earlier inception of *Radical History Review* in 1975. Though in absolute numbers marxist historians still constitute only a small group within the profession, their influence has been growing and their prestige has been considerable over the last fifteen years. For the first time, nonmarxists have been prepared to admit the existence of a highly sophisticated alternative to the liberal tradition in American marxist historiography.[31]

The emergence of marxism as a significant force in history and the social sciences has been closely connected with the transformation of the New Left. Those who took part in the Conference on the Political Economy of Higher Education, held at New York University in the fall of 1978, "as a whole shared a new left background: they had been students or teachers in the late 1960s and early 1970s and now identified themselves as Marxists, socialists, or radicals."[32] Similarly, Ellen Schrecker's 1979 survey of the marxist revival found a strong connection between the up-and-coming marxist historians and participation in the New Left in the 1960s. Schrecker, however, tried to explain the movement from New Left activism to 1980s marxism as "a natural one." "Discouraged by their failure to build a viable left wing movement, the student activists of the late 1960s went back to their books" and they "began to read Marx."[33] This assessment ignores the fact that a good deal of the New Left had been anarchistic in its thinking and practice. Nor can such a view account for the move to a conservative politics among certain erstwhile radicals like Aileen Kraditor and David Horowitz. How the New Left spawned the new marxism cannot therefore be deduced from the logic of radical thought and practice. It is also worth noting that several of the most prominent marxist historians, such as Eugene Genovese and David Montgomery, were never truly members of the New Left movement. Their political education took place much more firmly within orthodox marxist and communist experience in the 1950s, before the emergence of the New Left.[34]

The new marxist history is the hybrid product of the mature work of these older scholars (now given a legitimacy within the profession it would have been denied twenty years ago), and the emergence of younger marxist historians, often from the ranks of the New Left, but also from a post–New Left generation of graduate students impressed by the sophistication of British marxist history. These diverse sources must not, however, obscure a common theme behind the intellectual attraction and the growing prestige of marxist work. This involves the attempt of intellectuals to grapple with the failure of both radical and liberal ideologies to account satisfactorily for the changing economic and political conditions of the American nation in the 1970s. The intellectual reorientation of the younger historians is especially important, because it is from them that much of the new marxist analysis is coming. Recognizing that the student revolt had not developed "theoretical and strategic viewpoints that went beyond the ad hoc and empiricist perceptions" pervading both the movement of the 1960s and the liberal political culture from which it sprang, a number of radicals began in the late 1960s to make "their first serious study of Marxism." Radicals wanted to explain why the revolution had not begun at the first romantic flourishes of student unrest, and to understand "the complex interrelationships between institutional and cultural change which the dominant liberal and radical paradigms could not explain." They were particularly concerned with those strains of twentieth-century marxism which dealt with popular culture, mass communication, and capitalist domination in advanced capitalist societies. Above all, this new interest took in the work of the young Georg Lukács on consciousness, and that of Herbert Marcuse, whose attempted synthesis of Freudianism and marxism was already popular in the 1960s.[35]

The concern with analyzing why the revolution did not occur in 1968 was not the only outcome of changing historical circumstances. As Robert DuPlessis has pointed out, young radicals quickly found the liberal (and radical) intellectual frameworks incapable of providing more than trivial or irrelevant comprehension of the deteriorating economic prospects of the capitalist world in the early 1970s. Even though "economic history has always been regarded as central to the elaboration of a Marxist historiography," the radicals had neglected economic history and economic theory. They had been nurtured in a period in which the liberal-capitalist framework seemed strong, and the main issues were for them political or cultural because these questions, not economics, dominated the events of the day. All this changed in the 1970s, as the maturation of marxist scholarship occurred alongside "the festering depression" which has made the economic aspects of Marx's analysis of capitalism seem much more relevant than they did in the 1960s.[36]

That process of maturation has, because it is a product of reflection upon the 1970s, only just begun to emerge. It is not my purpose, therefore, to engage here in a systematic exposition, let alone critique, of the views of these diverse inheritors of the mantle of Marx. Instead, the remainder of this chapter will sketch the major contributions to the marxist revival since the 1960s from the perspective of the discipline of history, and thus lay the groundwork for an assessment of the present achievements and future prospects of American marxist history.

By way of caveat, it must first be noted that much marxist history, both American and non-American, continued to appear in the pages of *Science and Society*, an academically oriented marxist journal which has been published continuously since 1937. It survived (narrowly) the ideological and political pressures of the cold war, probably because it maintained a rather detached stance on the immediate political implications of marxist thought. *Science and Society* originally reflected the orthodox positivistic marxist tradition of the 1930s American Communist Party milieu in which it took shape. Since that time it has weathered considerable ideological and political controversy while maintaining its orthodoxy. Nonetheless, it has often published or publicized the work of marxists with rather diverse approaches; work by or about Paul Sweezy, Louis Althusser, and Antonio Gramsci has figured in its pages. From the point of view of history, perhaps *Science and Society* remains most notable as the forum for debate in the 1950s on the transition from feudalism to capitalism. While this debate was not of direct relevance to American history, its theoretical and methodological impact has been far-reaching, and influenced in different ways Eugene Genovese and Immanuel Wallerstein.[37]

Also emanating from the orthodox American marxist tradition was the work of the American Institute for Marxist Studies (AIMS) and its director Herbert Aptheker. AIMS was established in 1964 upon the realistic assessment that political repression had virtually ruled out the possibility for marxist political action as an organized movement in America. AIMS' function in this context was to disseminate knowledge about marxism and promote "a dialogue among Marxists and non-Marxists" that would bridge the climate of suspicion and intolerance fostered during the cold war. To this end, the institute claimed that it "shunned sectarianism" and publicized the works of socialists, radicals, feminists, and labor activists. In the decade after 1964, AIMS established offices in New York City, collected a library of some eight thousand volumes on marxist criticism, and published a steady stream of monographs, reprints, bibliographies, and newsletters, all under the indefatigable leadership of Aptheker. The director of AIMS was himself a historian of some note writing extensively on the history of blacks and slavery, and much of the material AIMS published was historical.[38]

If the revival of American marxist history depended, however, on the contributions of those like Aptheker who are identified with the defense of marxist-leninist "science," then that revival would not have proceeded very far. In fact, a number of younger and more flexible scholars stand out. One tendency appears in the many works of the maverick Gabriel Kolko, and another among those influenced by the comparative historical approach adopted by Barrington Moore, Jr. Better known, though not confined to or even principally concerned with American history, has been the work of Immanuel Wallerstein and his colleagues at the Fernand Braudel Center. They have produced an especially important journal, *Review*, which began publication in 1977. Finally, there has been the contribution of Eugene Genovese at the University of Rochester, and as a principal driving force behind the short-lived *Marxist Perspectives*. It is perhaps indicative of the still marginal status of marxism in the American academy relative to bourgeois social science that two of these four—Moore and Kolko—eschew the marxist label while drawing on marxist insights to a considerable extent.

Even though Kolko has specifically announced his heterodoxy by critical comments on marxism his interpretation of American history was derived in part from the American neomarxist tradition of Paul Baran and Paul Sweezy, as expounded in their book *Monopoly Capital*. Baran and Sweezy departed from orthodox marxism by adopting an analysis of the systemic crises of modern capitalism that drew upon Keynesian theories of underconsumption. Linked to their theory of the tendency of the economic surplus to rise under conditions of monopoly capitalism, they used the concept of underconsumption to predict economic stagnation rather than apocalyptic collapse as the likely fate of the modern American economy. Without directly acknowledging his intellectual debts, Kolko essentially built upon this analysis in a series of important synthetic works. In *Main Currents in Modern American History* and in his earlier book, *The Triumph of Conservatism*, Kolko analyzed in economic structural terms the characteristics of modern American corporate capitalism, and attacked traditional marxist analyses for failing to comprehend the processes whereby capitalism adapted to changing circumstances and thus stabilized itself. His gloomy prognosis for a revolutionary potential in the United States is especially at odds with orthodoxy. Kolko's thesis on the links between business and government in the early twentieth century received some support from James Weinstein, who was, however, quite happy to make explicit his connections with the marxist tradition. Weinstein argued that the corporate liberal ideology was the product of the most advanced sectors of business in alliance with government, to achieve the integration of farmers, unions, and businessmen in the corporate state. Despite this corroborating analysis, it would be correct to see Kolko's work as sui generis. Though widely known for his substantial output, he has not generated a school of followers, and his relation to the developing marxist history of the 1980s is problematic.[39]

Barrington Moore, another who has drawn on the marxist tradition while forging his own synthesis of social change, is a different case. The breadth and audacity of Moore's *Social Origins of Dictatorship and Democracy* has exerted an influence over a number of young scholars. They have been busy over the past few years applying Moore's comparative perspective and class analysis to southern history. Moore stressed that societies took diverging paths toward modernization which reflected the different content and balance of class forces. His book included a chapter on the American south and the Civil War, which emphasized the south's aristocratic political ethos and stressed its antagonism toward the democratic aspirations of northern capitalist society. Though criticized by such marxists as Genovese for failing to incorporate an understanding of the economic aspects of the antagonism between north and south, Moore's work inspired Dwight Billings and Jonathan Wiener to develop class analyses of the process of economic development in the postbellum south. These historians offer different interpretations of the dynamics of modernization in their respective case studies, but both take as their point of departure the model of a "Prussian road" to industrialization and modernization first developed in Moore's comparative history. Billings, Moore, and Wiener have all found the German comparison relevant because of the peculiar processes of industrialization in the south. The growth of an industrial sector amid a largely agrarian society characterized by extremely repressive labor relations prompted the use of Moore's model.[40] These attempts to apply in creative ways the class analysis advanced by Moore have provoked critical reactions from other marxists like Harold D. Woodman. But Woodman concedes that these works have attempted "to break away from the narrow perspective of cost accounting and income analysis" that characterizes work in the neoclassical tradition of economic history. Wiener and Billings have thereby issued a challenge to the dominance of that tradition, and opened a dialogue on the relevance of marxist analyses for yet another period of American history.[41]

Immanuel Wallerstein has had little impact on United States history, but the challenging nature of his methodological innovation and the breadth of his interpretation could undermine that judgment very quickly. Wallerstein has developed the concept of a world-system to explain the rise of capitalism, which he relates to the exploitation of periphery areas based upon the use of unfree labor by the capitalist core based on wage labor. He has thus reopened the debate over the origins and character of early capitalism and the transition from feudalism which figured so prominently on the pages of marxist journals in the early 1950s. To sustain his arguments, he has drawn not only upon the literature of early capitalist development, but has blended the work of *Annales* history, particularly Braudel's, with theories of underdevelopment derived from the work of the Chilean marxist economist Andre Gunder Frank.[42]

Thus far there have been few attempts to apply Wallerstein's theories to American history, probably because his range is global, total history, while most American historians remain interested in the United States separate from the international context. However, in 1977, Sidney Mintz made a thoughtful and mostly favorable scrutiny of the approach with reference to the Caribbean, and Wallerstein himself has written an important critique of Genovese's work, suggesting that the world-system approach can help comprehend the capitalist character of early slave production on the mainland of the American continent.[43]

Another sign that the Wallerstein approach may be gaining favor, and may help to reconceptualize United States history, is in ethnic and immigrant history. It has long been emphasized by a variety of radical and marxist scholars that American immigration was part of a larger international capitalist labor market. But little had been done on either a theoretical or empirical level by marxists to make the intersection of ethnicity, labor, capitalism, and international migration the subject of systematic analysis. Now an entire issue of *Review* has been devoted to these questions, and has quite rightly focused attention on the much neglected case of Chicano labor in the southwestern United States. The members of the Chicano Political Economy Collective have taken mostly world-systems ground, and demonstrated how Wallerstein's work can be used to illuminate first as well as third world history.[44]

Neither Wallerstein, nor Moore, nor Kolko has had the widespread recognition and success in American history that Eugene Genovese has achieved since the publication of *The Political Economy of Slavery* in 1965. So important has his influence been for the revival of marxism in the historical profession that his work deserves more than the passing mention possible in this introductory sketch. Genovese's contribution is also so closely tied to his specific interpretations of slavery and paternalism that its critical assessment will be deferred until the concepts and empirical work of contemporary American marxist historians are considered in Chapter 9.[45]

These scholars, and the approaches associated with them, by no means exhaust the range and complexity of contemporary marxist history, but it is difficult to talk about other schools or subgroups because so much is still in the process of research and publication. A good deal of the best new work has come from the *Radical History Review*. The *Review* is the outgrowth of the establishment in

1973 of a *Newsletter* by the Mid-Atlantic Radical Historians' Organization (MARHO). The group has operated through its collectives of interested academics, graduate students, and others in Boston, New Haven, and New York. MARHO has held its own conferences, continued to publish a separate newsletter, and encouraged the development of other radical history collectives throughout the country. In the pages of *Radical History Review*, we find a range of marxist viewpoints, sometimes agreeing with Genovese, sometimes with Wallerstein, sometimes launching out on their own path-breaking perspectives. *Radical History Review* cannot therefore be said to have a consistent party line or theoretical position. Like its British counterpart, *History Workshop*, it concentrates on detailed empirical work *and* theoretical and methodological discussion. It has also been distinguished, like the *Workshop* group, by attempts to take history beyond the narrow confines of traditional academia, "to present works by left historians and others in non-print formats to a wide audience." Lest this descriptive summary be considered an attempt to slight the theoretical contributions of *Radical History Review* to American historiography, it is worth noting that innovative thematic issues have appeared on a host of conceptual questions. These have included British marxist historiography, western European communism, history and sexuality, and the spatial dimensions of historical analysis.[46]

Differences aside, these approaches all share a common commitment to transcend the limited worldview of liberal empiricism. Attacks on narrow empiricism have come from historians associated with the radical history group, such as Alan Dawley and Michael Merrill. Merrill, for example, in an article on modes of production, made the sensible point that such marxist categories "do not stalk around on the surfaces of society, immediately visible to the untutored eye. Rather they exist as discoverable patterns in the events of everyday life" through the application of "intellectual work and empirical research."[47] Other marxist historians have drawn on intellectual traditions that diverge from the empiricism that has informed so much of American scholarship. Eugene Genovese, for example, has invoked the organic theories of the Hegelian dialectic and the concept of cultural hegemony advanced by Gramsci, whose intellectual debts ran back not to positivism or empiricism but to the confrontation of Italian idealist philosophers with marxist thought. Still others—like Wiener and Billings—have given more attention than has been common among liberals to the development of a holistic approach to social change that has involved the study of the interrelations of politics and economics as a central and critical concept.

Their departure from the orthodox fragmentation of historical reality and the heuristic potential of their theories are what makes these authors so exciting and so full of promise for the revitalization of American history. It is clear that revitalization has already begun, as seen in the very favorable reception given to Genovese's recent work. But can the marxist offensive continue? To answer this very difficult question we must necessarily probe the limitations, both theoretical and empirical, of current marxist historical scholarship. We will then be in a position to assess the prospects for marxist history in the United States.

NOTES

1. For a valuable study of these "subtle pressures" from "various theoretical systems," see James Henretta, "Social History as Lived and Written," *American Historical Review* 84 (1979): 308 and passim.

2. Fernand Braudel, *The Mediterranean and the Mediterranean World in the Age of Phillip II*, trans. Sian Reynolds, 2 vols. (New York, 1972–1973); J. H. Hexter, "Fernand Braudel and the 'Monde Braudellien,' " *Journal of Modern History* 44 (1972): 480–539; Robert Forster, "Achievements of the Annales School," *Journal of Economic History* 38 (1978): 58–76; Boyd H. Hill, Jr., and Alette Olin Hill, "Marc Bloch and Comparative History," *American Historical Review* 85 (1980): 828–57.

3. Samuel Kinser, "*Annaliste* Paradigm? The Geohistorical Structuralism of Fernand Braudel," *American Historical Review* 86 (1981): 63–105; Claude Levi-Strauss, *Structural Anthropology* (New York, 1963); Levi-Strauss, *Triste Tropiques*, trans. John and Doreen Weightman (New York, 1975).

4. Thomas Kuhn, *The Structure of Scientific Revolutions* (Chicago, 1962). A more general survey of developments in the philosophy of science is Harold Morick, ed., *Challenges to Empiricism* (Belmont, Calif., 1972); for criticisms of Kuhn, see Imre Lakatos and Alan Musgrave, eds., *Criticism and the Growth of Knowledge* (Cambridge, Eng., 1970).

5. David Hollinger, "T. S. Kuhn's Theory of Science and Its Implications for History," *American Historical Review* 78 (1973): 381.

6. William L. Langer, "The Next Assignment," ibid., 63 (1958): 283–304. Typical criticisms can be found in David Stannard, *Shrinking History: On Freud and the Failure of Psychohistory* (New York, 1980); and Oscar Handlin, *Truth in History* (Cambridge, Mass., 1979), pp. 274–75.

7. Edward N. Saveth, "A Decade of American Historiography: The 1960s," in William L. Cartwright and Richard L. Watson, eds., *The Reinterpretation of American History and Culture* (Washington, D.C., 1973), p. 28; Erik Erikson, *Young Man Luther: A Study in Psychoanalysis and History* (New York, 1958); Erikson, *Gandhi's Truth: On the Origins of Militant Nonviolence* (New York, 1969).

8. David Donald, *Charles Sumner and the Coming of the Civil War* (New York, 1960); Lloyd DeMause, "What Is Psychohistory?" *Journal of Psychohistory* 9 (1981): 179–84. For criticisms of the abuse of psychohistory, see Elizabeth Fox-Genovese, "Psychohistory versus Psychodeterminism: The Case of Rogin's Jackson," *Reviews in American History* 3 (1975): 407–17; *Newsweek*, 18 April 1977, p. 96; Peter Loewenberg, "Psychohistory," in Michael Kammen, ed., *The Past Before Us: Contemporary Historical Writing in the United States* (Ithaca, N.Y., 1980), pp. 408–32, has a useful survey of the field.

9. Parsons appears not to have done any historical research himself, and when he did late in his career pursue his structural-functionalism into a systematic study of past societies, his efforts were still cast at too general a level of abstraction to be of use to historians. See Talcott Parsons, *The Evolution of Societies*, revised by Jackson Toby (Englewood Cliffs, N.J., 1977); Paul J. Kleppner, *The Cross of Culture: A Social Analysis of Midwestern Politics, 1850–1900* (New York, 1970), pp. 1–2; Clifford Geertz, *The Interpretation of Cultures: Selected Essays* (New York, 1973); Alvin Gouldner, *The Coming Crisis of Western Sociology* (New York, 1970), pp. 242, 331–33; James Green,

"Behavioralism and Class Analysis: A Review Essay on Methodology and Ideology," *Labor History* 13 (1972): 92, 94. A widely cited but nevertheless rather obscure case of Parsonian influence is Janet Zollinger Giele, "Social Change in the Feminine Role: A Comparison of Woman's Suffrage and Woman's Temperance, 1870–1920," Ph.D. diss., Radcliffe College, 1961.

10. David Donald, "Our Irrelevant History," *New York Times*, 8 Sept. 1977, p. A27; Arthur M. Schlesinger, Jr., "America: Experiment or Destiny?" *American Historical Review* 82 (1977): 505–22; C. Vann Woodward, "The Aging of America," *American Historical Review* 82 (1977): 583–94.

11. Michael Kammen, "Introduction: The Historian's Vocation and the State of the Discipline in the United States," in Kammen, ed., *The Past Before Us*, pp. 44–45; James Henretta, "The Study of Social Mobility: Ideological Assumptions and Conceptual Bias," *Labor History* 18 (1977): 165; Ellen Schrecker, "The House Marxists," *The Nation* 228 (27 Jan. 1979): 82; Frank Freidel, "American Historians: A Bicentennial Appraisal," *Journal of American History* 63 (1976): 10.

12. For a good discussion of the limitations of these programs, see Howard Green, "A Critique of the Professional Public History Movement," *Radical History Review* 25 (1981): 164–71.

13. Berenice Fisher and Floyd M. Hammack, "Contradictions of Work: The New Left Professors," *Socialist Review* 8 (Nov.-Dec. 1978): 94; *Mid-Atlantic Radical Historians' Organization Newsletter* 1 (no. 6, 1973–1974): 6, and 2 (no. 1, 1974–1975): 3–5.

14. Gene Wise, *American Historical Explanations: A Strategy for Grounded Inquiry* (Minneapolis, 2d ed., 1980); David Hackett Fischer, *Historians' Fallacies: Toward a Logic of Historical Thought* (New York, 1970).

15. Leo Marx, "Comments," AHR Forum, *American Historical Review* 82 (1977): 597; Green, "Behavioralism and Class Analysis," pp. 89–106; Alan Dawley, "E. P. Thompson and the Peculiarities of the Americans," *Radical History Review* 19 (1978–1979): 40, 58 n. 11; Michael Merrill, "Raymond Williams and the Theory of English Marxism," *Radical History Review* 19 (1978–1979): 15, 30 n. 18; Richard Andrews, "Some Implications of the *Annales* School and Its Methods for a Revision of Historical Writing about the United States," *Review* 1 (1978): 165–80; Michael Frisch, "American Urban History as an Example of Recent Historiography," *History and Theory* 18 (1979): 370–71; Jackson Lears, letter to editor, *New York Review of Books*, 16 Dec. 1982.

16. Henretta, "Social History," pp. 1309, 1314, 1318–19.

17. Ibid., pp. 1309, 1314, 1318–19.

18. Ibid., p. 1319.

19. Robert F. Berkhofer, Jr., "Comments," ibid., p. 1330.

20. Henretta, "Reply," ibid., pp. 1332–33.

21. Henretta, "Social History," pp. 1308, 1319, 1321.

22. Fernand Braudel, "Foreword," to Traian Stoianovich, *French Historical Method: The "Annales" Paradigm* (Ithaca, N.Y., 1976), p. 11.

23. Schlesinger, "America: Experiment or Destiny?" pp. 505–22.

24. *Review* 1 (1978); Andrews, "Some Implications," ibid., pp. 165–80. The best-equipped liberal historian was probably Bernard Bailyn. See his "Braudel's Geohistory— A Reconsideration," *Journal of Economic History* 11 (1951): 277–82.

25. James Henretta, "Families and Farms: *Mentalité* in Pre-Industrial America," *William and Mary Quarterly*, 3d ser., 35 (1978): 3–32; Kenneth A. Lockridge, "Historical

Demography," in Charles F. Dalzell, ed., *The Future of History: Essays in the Vanderbilt University Centennial Symposium* (Nashville, Tenn., 1977), pp. 53–64.

26. Kenneth A. Lockridge, *A New England Town: The First Hundred Years: Dedham, Massachusetts, 1636–1737* (New York, 1970), p. viii; Lockridge, "Historical Demography," pp. 53–55; Philip D. Curtin, *The Atlantic Slave Trade: A Census* (Madison, Wis., 1969); Peter Wood, *Black Majority: Negroes in Colonial South Carolina from 1670 through the Stono Rebellion* (New York, 1974). For a recent disappointing application of a structural framework to the sweep of American history, see Walter Nugent, *Structures of American Social History* (Bloomington, Ind., 1981).

27. Emmanuel Le Roy Ladurie, *The Peasants of Languedoc*, trans. with an introduction by J. Day (Urbana, Ill., 1974), p. 302.

28. Michelle Perrot, *Les Ouvriers en grève (France, 1871–1890)* (Paris, 1974).

29. Eugene Weber, "About Marc Bloch," *American Scholar* 51 (1981): 82.

30. Andrews, "Some Implications," pp. 165–80.

31. Kammen, "Introduction," p. 25; Schrecker, "House Marxists," pp. 81–84; Carl Degler, "Remaking American History," *Journal of American History* 67 (1980): 17; Daniel D. Luria, "Wealth, Capital, and Power: The Social Meaning of Home Ownership," *Journal of Interdisciplinary History* 7 (1976): 261–82; Jonathan M. Wiener, "Class Structure and Economic Development in the American South, 1865–1955," *American Historical Review* 84 (1979): 970–92; Christopher Clark, "Household Economy, Market Exchange and the Rise of Capitalism in the Connecticut Valley, 1800–1860," *Journal of Social History* 13 (1979): 169–89; Alan Dawley, *Class and Community: The Industrial Revolution in Lynn* (Cambridge, Mass., 1976); Eugene Genovese, *Roll, Jordan, Roll: The World the Slaves Made* (New York, 1974); "An Interview with William Appleman Williams," *Radical History Review* 22 (1979–1980): 65–92; "The Rise of a Marxist Historian: An Interview with Eugene Genovese," *Change* 10 (Nov. 1978): 31–35.

32. Fisher and Hammack, "Contradictions of Work," p. 94.

33. Schrecker, "House Marxists," p. 81; Howard Zinn, "Marxism and the New Left," in Alfred F. Young, ed., *Dissent: Explorations in the History of American Radicalism* (DeKalb, Ill., 1968), pp. 355–72; Staughton Lynd, "Historical Past and Existential Present," in Theodore Roszak, ed., *The Dissenting Academy* (New York, 1968), pp. 96–97, 105, 109.

34. "Once Upon a Shop Floor: An Interview with David Montgomery," *Radical History Review* 23 (1980): 37–51; "Rise of a Marxist Historian," pp. 31–34; Robert Westbrook, "Good-bye to All That: Aileen Kraditor and Radical History," *Radical History Review* 28–30 (1984): 69–89.

35. "Introductory Notes," *Radical History Review* 3 (Fall 1976): 2; Mary Jo Buhle, "Recent Contributions to Women's History," ibid., 2 (Summer 1975): 5.

36. Robert DuPlessis, "From Demesne to World-System: A Critical Review of the Literature on the Transition from Feudalism to Capitalism," ibid., 4 (Winter 1977): 3.

37. Henry F. Mims, "*Science and Society*: The Early Years," *Science and Society* 45 (1981): 85–88; Rodney Hilton, ed., *The Transition from Feudalism to Capitalism* (London, 1976 ed.). An example of *Science and Society*'s orthodox historical materialism in the early period is Lewis Feuer, "The Economic Factor in History," *Science and Society* 4 (1940): 168–92.

38. Herbert Aptheker, "Introduction," to *American Institute for Marxist Studies Newsletter* (New York, Kraus repr., 1978). Of Aptheker's own voluminous works, see *Amer-*

ican Negro Slave Revolts (New York, 1943); and Aptheker, ed., *The Correspondence of W. E. B. DuBois*, 3 vols. (Amherst, Mass., 1973–1978).

39. Paul Baran and Paul Sweezy, *Monopoly Capital* (New York, 1966); Gabriel Kolko, *Main Currents in Modern American History* (New York, 1976), pp. 2, 66–67, 68, 398–99; Kolko, *The Triumph of Conservatism: A Reinterpretation of American History, 1900–1916* (Glencoe, Ill., 1963); Victor Perlo, rev. of Kolko, *Wealth and Power in America: An Analysis of Social Class and Income Distribution* (New York, 1962), in *Science and Society* 27 (1963): 502–4; James Weinstein, *The Corporate Ideal in the Liberal State: 1900–1918* (Boston, 1968).

40. Barrington Moore, Jr., *Social Origins of Dictatorship and Democracy: Lord and Peasant in the Making of the Modern World* (Boston, 1966); Dwight B. Billings, Jr., *Planters and the Making of a "New South": Class, Politics, and Development in North Carolina, 1865–1900* (Chapel Hill, 1979); Jonathan M. Wiener, *Social Origins of the New South: Alabama, 1860–1885* (Baton Rouge, 1978); Wiener, "Class Structure and Economic Development," pp. 970–92; Wiener, "Review of Reviews: *Social Origins of Dictatorship and Democracy,*" *History and Theory* 15 (1976): 146–75.

41. Harold D. Woodman, "Comments," AHR Forum, *American Historical Review* 84 (1979): 997–1001; Woodman, "Sequel to Slavery: The New History Views the Post-bellum South," *Journal of Southern History* 43 (1977): 552–53.

42. Immanuel Wallerstein, *The Modern World-System: Capitalist Agriculture and the Origins of the European World-Economy in the Sixteenth Century* (New York, 1974).

43. Sidney Mintz, "The So-Called World System: Local Initiative and Local Response," *Dialectical Anthropology* 2 (1977): 253–70; Immanuel Wallerstein, "American Slavery and the Capitalist World-Economy," *American Journal of Sociology* 81 (1976): 1199–213; Eugene Genovese, "Class, Culture, and Historical Process," *Dialectical Anthropology* 1 (1975): 71–79.

44. *Review* 4 (no. 3, 1981); for example, Tomás Almaguer, "Interpreting Chicano History: The World-System Approach to Nineteenth-Century California," ibid., pp. 459–507. It should be noted that the participants in this special issue do not work in history departments in the United States, and their research testifies to the revival of a historical sociology in the United States stimulated in part by Wallerstein's own efforts.

45. Eugene Genovese, *The Political Economy of Slavery: Studies in the Economy and Society of the Slave South* (New York, 1965); Genovese, *The World the Slaveholders Made: Two Essays in Interpretation* (New York, 1969); Genovese, *In Red and Black: Marxian Explorations in Southern and Afro-American History* (New York, Vintage ed., 1972); Genovese, *Roll, Jordan, Roll.*

46. *Radical History Review*, nos. 19, 20, and 21; ibid., 19 (1978–1979): 59.

47. Michael Merrill, "Cash Is Good to Eat: Self-Sufficiency and Exchange in the Rural Economy of the United States," ibid., 4 (Winter 1977): 64.

8

Empiricism and the Marxist Tradition

Though marxism constitutes one important element in the current critique of empiricism in the liberal tradition, the marxist historian is not necessarily immune to the same criticisms. Considerable confusion and disagreement persist among marxists over the relation of theory and evidence, and marxist thought covers the range of philosophical positions on the issue, from empiricism to rationalism to realism.[1] Of these, an empiricism indistinguishable from the assumptions of the larger profession has sometimes characterized marxist work, despite the implications of the marxist dialectic to the contrary.[2] A residual hostility to theory seen in some English and American marxist or quasi-marxist writers has undoubtedly had its advantages, since ideological disputation could be minimized through a concentration on the facts. But there have been costs as well. To tell the story of the past as fully and as accurately as possible has constituted a kind of Hippocratic oath among historians, but when marxists fail to write a theoretically informed empirical history, they capitulate to their opponents on the validity of important areas of historical discourse which are not readily observable facts. The whole question of class is one of these. To be sure, marxists are committed to the principle of reasoning and analyzing in ways discussed later in this section, but the historical practice of marxists does not always conform to these principles. A recent example was Eugene Genovese's response to theoretical critiques of his work on slavery by other marxists. The suggestion that Eric Perkins should write his own books rather than write critiques of Genovese's work sounded very much like the criticism that David Donald made of Robert Skotheim's work when the latter demonstrated the methodological weaknesses of Donald's study of antebellum abolitionists. The underlying suggestion that historians need to steep themselves in the sources before they venture theories or critiques remains very pervasive, and evidently not limited to nonmarxists.[3]

Empiricism also presents problems at the level of specific interpretations and theories, where some American marxists have absorbed the work of nonmarxist social scientists without sufficient critical scrutiny. Thus Gabriel Kolko focuses on elites of businessmen, the most obvious level of capitalist social relations, and tends to give a rather simplified picture of a process of capitalist control that is monolithic. He gives extended and valuable discussion of the distribution of wealth and income, but such analysis does not constitute an adequate coverage of class processes, and neither does his emphasis upon elites and the power of businessmen in politics. Had Kolko made class processes and capitalist relations of production more central, he might have produced a more complex account of American society and its processes of domination, subordination, and resistance.[4]

THE PROBLEM OF "THEORY" AND THE CHALLENGE OF STRUCTURALIST MARXISM

The structuralist marxism of Louis Althusser, if taken to a logical extreme, avoids the pitfalls of empiricism, even if nothing else positive can be said about it. By insisting that the evidence is entirely a product of the conceptual and theoretical apparatus, historical research becomes an automatic confirmation of general theories which are rationalistically derived from marxist texts. Indeed, in the work of the English structuralist marxists Barry Hindess and Paul Q. Hirst, this logical conclusion (and absurdity) is reached, with drastic results for the discipline of history. Instead of history, Hindess and Hirst extoll theoretical practice applied to the materials of history and put to work in the service of present political and ideological objectives. Their position is logical, but arid. "Empiricism" (which they unfortunately tend to confuse with "empirical") is the method of bourgeois ideology under this formulation. Against this discredited ideological method, marxist science is posited with its own concepts, methods, proofs, and refutations, which involve essentially the validation of empirical phenomena against a priori theory. Thus, for example, their work on *Pre-Capitalist Modes of Production* expresses nothing but scorn for Genovese's attempts to define the system of slavery not in terms of some abstract concept of a slave mode of production, but in terms of the system's empirical divergence from a capitalist mode of production. In the more recent *Mode of Production and Social Formation*, Hindess and Hirst carry this argument to its logical conclusion when they divorce theoretical discourse from the realm of the existent or the real. Against the marxist notion that theory appropriates reality in thought, they now advocate the "construction of problems for analysis and solutions to them by means of concepts." This circular enterprise does more than complete the logical progression of their thought; it leaves no room for both marxism and history. Indeed, in their earlier work, Hindess and Hirst had already proclaimed the study of history "not only scientifically but also politically valueless." Now classical marxism joins the list of tabooed practices. Yet it is not clear that they have reached the nirvana of pure discourse untainted by epistemological weakness, since what is left unspecified in their polemic is where the concepts come from and how they relate to the nondiscursive realities that Hindess and Hirst continue to admit do exist.[5]

Not all those influenced by Althusser take so extreme a stand, and indeed Hindess and Hirst have turned on their source of inspiration and denounced Althusser as infected with empiricism! Among those stimulated by Althusser, empirical research has not been eliminated, and some like Perry Anderson argue that Althusser's concern with the specification of the logical character of class and class relations under different modes of production has produced a good deal of valuable empirical research. But this work has been concentrated in the disciplines of political science and sociology.[6] Very little *historical* research of an Althusserian kind has transpired. Anderson himself is a political scientist who synthesizes the research of historians, and Stedman Jones, possibly the most able historian influenced by Althusser, is hardly a full-blown Althusserian either by his own admission or his actual historical practice.[7]

The failure of Althusserian marxism to appeal to historians is linked no doubt to some extent with the antitheoretical cast of historical practice, but it is not theory as such which makes the Althusserian enterprise insufficient for historical analyses. The theoretical universe of the Althusserian revolves around a set of dominant instances that combine in specific social formations. I shall argue in a later chapter that this formulation does not explain historical process, as any adequate analysis of social structure must move that structure through time. Insofar as Althusser tends to treat historical epochs in terms of a set of illustrations of logical combinations of theoretical constructs, he cannot explain historical change. But that admission neither rules out the selective use of Althusserian concepts, nor the relevance of the theoretical interrogation of concepts in historical analysis. What is eliminated as valueless is the theoretical equation found in structuralist analysis in which the formal characteristics of structure take precedence over content, and in which the actual people and products that constitute structures are reduced to their abstract structural relations.[8]

Thus far, structuralist marxism has had little impact on American marxist historians, influenced as they have been overwhelmingly by the anti-Althusserian E. P. Thompson, or by Hegelian marxist currents derived from the New Left experience. Historians of the latter persuasion denounce Althusserianism as a resurrected bourgeois positivism; the Thompsonians treat it as an abstract system imposing theory upon the richness and diversity of historical experience. It is unlikely that an Althusserian marxist history will have much more influence in the future either, since it has passed its peak in France, and has been discredited in England by E. P. Thompson's stupendous attacks in *The Poverty of Theory*. When Americanists have noticed this debate at all, they have tended to be critical of Althusser and sympathetic to Thompson's political position.[9] Given Thompson's enormous prestige in the United States, as well as a natural distaste for theories which play down the role of human agency in history which many

American marxist historians share with a number of English colleagues, structuralist marxism of the Althusserian variety may well become a pariah before it has even been cursorily examined by American marxists.

Historians must not, however, be tempted to throw out the baby of theory with the bathwater of Althusserian criticism. Thompson's brilliant polemic against the Althusserian fad has encouraged a Neanderthal approach to theory which in the English context has reinforced the deeply ingrained empiricism of sections of the historical profession. The understandable revolt against the aridity of Althusserian theory should not be allowed to obscure the important role the structuralist marxists have had in reopening debates about the pertinence of theory to the construction of marxist history. If these debates in England have so far generated more heat than light, it is all the more vital that the channels between theoretical work and historical practice be kept open if further progress in the writing of the history of society is to be maintained. For American historians, the new marxist work in the Althusserian tradition is particularly important because it raises theoretical issues touched upon during the relativist controversy of the 1930s, but which were effectively shelved in favor of a renewed concern with data accumulation and the refinement of historical technique.

Is there a way of mediating between the logical extremities of structuralist theory and the existing historiographical practices? While ultimately history cannot be validated independently of evidence, the Althusserians have been important in reminding us that history cannot proceed very far without the construction, criticism, and application of theory to prize meaning from the residues of the human past. Partly this approach involves the old relativist question of bias and selectivity, but it goes beyond this point to construct systematic, theoretically informed research strategies as a way out of subjectivity. This is what makes theoretical discussion of such critical importance to the advancement of history as a discipline. If history is to move beyond its ad hoc and descriptive practice, more attention must be given to the formulation and logical content of the concepts and methods that are used to identify and solve historical problems. Further attention must also be given to the necessary though often implicit relations of these concepts and methods to systematic theories of power and historical change.

The connection between this intellectual activity and the realities of the human past are extremely complex. We are not examining anything so simple as the past or the evidence—some kind of entity "out there" with a mind of its own. We are examining a reality which is conceptually mediated. That takes us back to the need for the construction of concepts, which involves necessarily the intervention of theoretical perspectives of various kinds.

THEORY AND EVIDENCE

The relationship between theory and evidence is perhaps best understood through some practical examples. Historians are well aware of the extent to which concepts and theories can produce some types of evidence, in the sense of drawing attention to previously neglected blocks of material. Intrinsic to the birth of national, secular history in the nineteenth century was the assertion of the importance of evidence and its critical assessment according to the canons of Rankean method. But the evidence deemed relevant to this new history was very specific and limited. Before the triumph of scientific history, historians had frequently made use of oral sources and folklore. As Paul Thompson shows, these traditions were gradually replaced by an emphasis upon public documents and the letters of great statesmen, both because documents and manuscripts could be subjected to the methods of textual criticism, and because such records were appropriate to an elite theory of politics as the subject matter of history.[10] There was no point in examining, for example, the songs, artefacts, and oral traditions of the lower orders, because these groups were deemed to be inconsequential to the making of history. The revival of interest in such sources had to await a shift in historical consciousness. The growing concern in recent decades with the history of peoples and societies has prompted searches for evidence that would be appropriate to the new social history. The emphasis since the 1960s on the cultural autonomy of slaves has been heavily influenced by the evidence of the slave narrative collections which had been available, if in restricted form, since the 1930s.[11] But these sources were neglected as late as the 1950s, because slavery was still regarded essentially in political, legal, and institutional terms.

Prior to the 1960s, these sources had to contend not only with the assumption that they were irrelevant to the most important historical subjects, but also with the related theoretical premise that nonwritten sources were inherently more suspect. When Kenneth Stampp wrote the most important study of slave life to appear in the 1950s, he slighted the slave narratives, apparently because they were not "of much value to historians." While they might be useful for students of folklore, they apparently lacked the self-evident facticity of documents in Stampp's mind since, he later admitted, he could "seldom be sure that what they contain are true expressions of the slaves." Stampp agreed that other sources also did not directly express the "firsthand testimony" of "the slaves themselves," but he nevertheless used these sources routinely in preference to oral history.[12]

Historians would still maintain that even though the questions asked had elicited new evidence, the evidence remained completely distinct from its production. Attention had been drawn to the evidence by historical concepts, but the evidence could then modify or discredit as well as validate the concept. Yet certain categories of evidence will not fit into so simple a framework. Demographic and economic structural changes revealed, for example, by historians of early modern Europe are not facts or even "events."[13] These and some other kinds of statistical evidence are intellectual reconstructions quite literally produced by historians. The procedures involved in such work include estimation, extrapolation, aggregation, and correlations which are inconceivable without carefully articulated methodologies and implicit or explicit theoretical assumptions. A good deal of evidence appropriate to the study of popular culture is similar. "The evidence" is so fragmentary and so obscure that it literally lacks meaning until interpreted. It is not simply that the historian regards the evidence in question as unimportant: he or she cannot understand it. Evidence must therefore be interpreted in much the same way as anthropologists interpret alien cultures. Theory, it would appear, cannot be invalidated by appeal to a body of evidence in these cases because it is precisely the theory which supplies the meaning.[14]

In yet another way, evidence is conditioned by the theories used to interpret it. This is the critical *reading* of the evidence as text. Many historians would recoil from the Althusserian notion of a "symptomatic reading" in which hidden or displaced meanings are elicited and the deeper structures of a text presumably revealed. That seems to be playing fast and loose with the facts. But every good historian knows that no piece of historical evidence can be taken at face value. As a recent manual on method reminds us, historians quickly move beyond the "surface content" of a document to examine such questions as "what the document might have said but did not."[15] Often the latter can be more illuminating than what the document did say, especially when both are incorporated into a comprehensive interpretive framework. But to read the historical evidence for the reconstruction of hidden patterns involves theorizing upon the data. Many a historian has followed this method but usually without realizing the extent to which it calls into question the very foundations of time-honored assumptions about facts, their perception, and their explanation.

Though some philosophers of history would go further in the attack on empiricism and treat history simply as a creative, literary synthesis, marxists cannot accept this idealist alternative. True, some of the greatest marxist work has had a narrative form, such as C. L. R. James' *The Black Jacobins* (1938), and all historians routinely use narrative, but that is not the only dimension to historical writing. History is produced in a variety of genres, such as the historiographical survey, the monograph focused narrowly in place or time, the analytical essay, the interpretive synthesis, the documentary account, and so forth. Narrative may enter these works but they are not only or even mainly narratives. This point is often misunderstood because historical works rightly convey the importance of the dimension of time and give central consideration to historical process. They are not, however, narratives in the same sense as the great literary syntheses of the nineteenth century. Nor is their significance assessed by the profession in terms of a narrative intelligibility. Rather, they are criticized and assimilated in complex ways through attention to their *analysis* of evidence and their contribution to a particular problem or thesis. They may be partly accepted and partly rejected, or taken apart and used in many different contexts. For these reasons, the cognitive questions which the "new rhetorical relativism" claims to have circumvented persist in importance for academic historians.[16]

A marxist contribution to this quest for explanations that can better comprehend the real world involves the ways in which material life has been produced and reproduced, including the forms in which humans became conscious of conflicts which arise from "conditions and changes of condition in economic production." The range of concepts derived from this theory is the cumulative result of work done by thinkers who identify with the theoretical stance first taken by Karl Marx. That tradition claims, if it has any validity at all, to represent the appropriation of reality in thought, not the reflection, observation, or representation of reality. The patterns that marxists claim to discover will not be readily observable to purely empiricist analysis of discrete facts wrenched out of context, because marxists are concerned with the relationships between the phenomena under study, and because marxist method involves the analysis of phenomena in terms of their internal oppositions and transformations over time. This is a historical approach that contrasts with the static and positivist analysis of the social science models that have been most influential in the American academy. The positivist tradition involves the testing of theories against the data, and the principle of causal attribution in which cause and effect are separable and subject to some kind of measurement or estimation. Marxist analysis of the type discussed above does not avoid this formulation merely because the variables in history are too numerous to permit complete specification, but also because "human beings change their social practice in the light of knowledge and self-consciousness. Agency and thought are thus constitutive of the object of study. As a consequence," argues Richard Johnson, "social theory is necessarily historical, because the relations of social structure to knowledge are, necessarily, relations over time."[17]

This does not mean that a single epistemological stance is commonly accepted by marxists. Althusser, for example, would be denounced by many other marxists as a rationalist, structuralist thinker whose idealist cast has lost touch with the real world Marx sought to understand. This diversity of philosophical positions in marxism is in part a reproduction of Marx's own epistemological elusiveness. As Pierre Vilar states, Marx "discovered his method by practising it." Therefore, we "can only recover it in his practice."[18] That practice involved several different levels beginning with "the detailed appropriation" of the material under study, its digestion and reformulation in a process of theorization and abstraction, the tracking down of the inner structural connections of the material, and its presentation in concrete forms as if the construction had been a priori rather than the product of a complex mental process.[19] Historical investigation for Marx consisted not in the testing of theories against the evidence but a much more complex and synthetic notion of mental production.

Such a position does not make evidence unimportant. It makes argument with evidence critical in historical accounts. In turn, arguments with evidence imply that evidence is not subsumed into theory. Even if, as some structuralists claim, theory and evidence are both in some sense conceptual *representations* of reality, accessible to us only through language, those representations occur in more or less concrete forms, and we cannot ignore those more concrete forms. Stedman Jones sensibly concludes that the materials from which history is constructed do not "lose their autonomous character in history any more than other branches of knowledge. . . . In their original phenomenal form, they remain objects of alternative possible theorization. Theory in history as in natural sciences always has a provisional status, and its power is no greater than what it can successfully explain."[20]

To take again the example of popular culture and the difficulties of interpretation it necessarily involves, the fact that the evidence has no meaning without theory does not mean that it is subservient to any one conceptual framework. Otherwise there would be no way of evaluating different theoretical assessments of the same evidence. Nor, to put the matter another way, does the role of theory mean that the diverse evidence of popular culture ought to be homogenized into one gigantic anthropological system in which the complexities of time and place are ignored. We must look for the context of the data in order to interpret it. Here E. P. Thompson gives some help in an article entitled "Anthropology and the Discipline of Historical Context."[21] Thompson points out that one cannot probe popular culture without sensitivity to regional variations and to the cultural contexts that go with these variations. Perusals of pamphlet collections analyzed according to anthropological theory will not do. They must be treated in a manner akin to literary criticism, with a sensitivity to dialect and to the poetic meaning of words. These variations do not sanction an abandonment of theory, however. Thompson's position is in itself a theoretical one, since it does not free him from the dilemma of an epistemological and theoretical choice. But Thompson's position does remind historians of a valuable convention: that historians must be sensitive to the context in which theoretically derived research strategies are operating, if the meaning of obscure and often fragmentary data is to be maximized. (The social science–influenced history of the 1950s and 1960s often ignored this problem of contextualism, and marxists are not impervious to the same arrogance.) The meanings historians assign to such data and the connections they establish still remain, moreover, provisional and subject to alternative theorization.

To leave the debate at this point with pious admonitions on the importance of theory would be sterile indeed. The interrelations of all phenomena, the search for systematic connections between facts that are partly hidden to observation, the dynamic conception of dialectical change, all suggest a subtle approach to historical knowledge, but marxist theory and marxist historical writing has of course not always justified the faith that inheres in these high-sounding phrases. If marxism has produced much work that makes modern historiography incomprehensible without its theoretical contribution, there are countless instances, even within the oeuvre of Marx himself, of mechanical use of these same marxist categories. The whole notion of the dialectic can be, as C. Wright Mills recognized, a sophisticated way of conveying a sense of the "fluidity and many-sided nature of history-making," of rendering the interconnections of forces, and of revealing the "genuine conflict" in "every historical situation."[22] But as Mills also noted, too often the dialectic becomes, in the hands of "self-appointed 'insiders,' " a metaphysical concept employed in ideological battles to justify disregard for historical experience, so much so that some marxists are coy in invoking the dialectic, even where they remain indebted to dialectical forms of analysis. Consequently, the fruits of marxist theory can never be manifest purely at the level of theory or epistemological critique; the ultimate test resides in the way those concepts and theories are used in practice to illuminate history, to construct new histories and to marshal new evidence in creative syntheses of theory and evidence. The question of theory and evidence cannot therefore be divorced from analysis of the actual body of work which historians of marxist persuasion have produced, and from the future prospects for a marxist historiography.

NOTES

1. For a discussion of these three themes, see Gregor McLennan, "Philosophy and History: Some Issues in Recent Marxist Theory," in Richard Johnson et al., *Making Histories: Studies in History-writing and Politics* (London, 1982), pp. 133–52.

2. Empiricism among English marxists is discussed in Keith Nield, "A Symptomatic Dispute? Notes on the Relation between Marxian Theory and Historical Practice in Britain," *Social Research* 47 (1980): 479–506; Nield and John Seed, "Waiting for Gramsci," *Social History* 6 (1981): 210–11.

3. Eugene Genovese, "A Reply to Criticism," *Radical History Review* 4 (Winter 1977): 98; Robert A. Skotheim, "A Note on Historical Method," *Journal of Southern History* 25 (1959): 356–65; David Donald, letter to editor, *Journal of Southern History* 26 (1960): 156–57.

4. Gabriel Kolko, *Main Currents in Modern American History* (New York, 1976).

5. Louis Althusser, *For Marx*, trans. Ben Brewster (New York, Vintage ed., 1970); Althusser and Etienne Balibar, *Reading "Capital"* (London, 1970); Barry Hindess and Paul Q. Hirst, *Pre-Capitalist Modes of Production* (London, 1975), pp. 150–56, 312; Hindess and Hirst, *Mode of Production and Social Formation: An Auto-Critique of Pre-Capitalist Modes of Production* (London, 1977), p. 7.

6. Perry Anderson, *Arguments within English Marxism* (London, 1980), pp. 7, 125–26; Erik Olin Wright, *Class, Crisis and the State* (London, 1978), pp. 9–14; Wright, *Class Structure and Income Determination* (New York, 1979); Nicos Poulantzas, *Fascisme et Dictature* (Paris, 1970).

7. Perry Anderson, *Passages from Antiquity to Feudalism* (London, 1974); Anderson, *Lineages of the Absolutist State* (London, 1974); Gareth Stedman Jones, "History and Theory," *History Workshop* 8 (1979): 198–202.

8. Jones, "History and Theory," pp. 198–202; see pp. 226–27.

9. E. P. Thompson, *The Poverty of Theory* (London, 1978); Paul Buhle, "E. P. Thompson and His Critics," *Telos* 49 (1981): 133, who noted that structuralism recapitulated nominalist academic thought and compared it to American social science of the 1950s. Jonathan Wiener, "Marxist Theory and History," *Socialist Review* 10 (July-Aug. 1980): 141, leans in an anti-Althusserian direction, claiming that Jean-Paul Sartre's existential marxism supplies the dimension of human activity lacking in Althusser's work. See also Michael Merrill, "Raymond Williams and the Theory of English Marxism,"

Radical History Review 19 (1978–1979): 13–15; Bryan Palmer, *The Making of E. P. Thompson: Marxism, Humanism, and History* (Toronto, 1981).

10. Paul Thompson, *The Voice of the Past* (Oxford, 1978), chap. 2.

11. George P. Rawick, ed., *The American Slave: A Composite Autobiography*, 19 vols. (Westport, Conn., 1972).

12. Kenneth M. Stampp, "Rebels and Sambos: The Search for the Negro's Personality in Slavery," *Journal of Southern History* 37 (1971): 367–69.

13. Bernard Bailyn, "The Challenge of Modern Historiography," *American Historical Review* 87 (1982): 10–11, treats "latent" and "manifest" events.

14. Clifford Geertz, *The Interpretation of Cultures: Selected Essays* (New York, 1973), is an anthropological model which many American historians have been happy to follow.

15. John W. Davidson and Mark Lytle, *After the Fact: The Art of Historical Detection* (New York, 1982), pp. 66, 70; Althusser, *For Marx*, pp. 39, 69, 253–54.

16. "The new rhetorical relativism" is summarized by Louis O. Mink, "Philosophy and Theory of History," in Georg G. Iggers and Harold T. Parker, eds., *International Handbook of Historical Studies: Contemporary Research and Theory* (Westport, Conn., 1979), pp. 17–28; see esp., Hayden V. White, *Metahistory: The Historical Imagination in Nineteenth-Century Europe* (Baltimore, 1973).

17. Raymond Williams, *Keywords: A Vocabulary of Culture and Society* (London, rev. ed., 1983), p. 156 (first quote); Richard Johnson, "Reading for the Best Marx: History-Writing and Historical Abstraction," in Johnson et al., *Making Histories*, pp. 156–57 (second quote).

18. Pierre Vilar, "Marxist History, A History in the Making: Towards a Dialogue with Althusser," *New Left Review* 80 (1973): 67.

19. Johnson, "Reading for the Best Marx," pp. 156–57.

20. Jones, "History and Theory," p. 199; Richard Johnson, "Edward Thompson, Eugene Genovese, and Socialist-Humanist History," *History Workshop* 6 (1978): 87–88.

21. E. P. Thompson, "Anthropology and the Discipline of Historical Context," *Midland History* 3 (1972): 41–55.

22. C. Wright Mills, *The Marxists* (New York, 1962), p. 128.

9

New Directions in Marxist Historiography: The 1970s and Beyond

The theoretical vacuum left by the fragmentation of the liberal tradition cannot be automatically occupied by a marxist alternative. The claims of marxism as a coherent historical synthesis must first be scrutinized. If liberal history is suffering from a lack of confidence, marxist history too has become fragmented and its more rigid formulations severely tested. Radical but nonmarxist history has been of particular relevance in this process by raising questions neglected in class analysis. This chapter examines the impact of the radical subversion, charts the efforts of a new generation of marxist scholars to incorporate the insights of the new social history, and analyzes the implications of the new departures in empirical research for the coherence of the marxist tradition. The new work documents the vitality and complexity of contemporary marxist historiography, but also raises difficult questions concerning the reconciliation of diverse work with the emphasis upon mode of production as the distinctive organizing category of a marxist approach. While American marxist historians have produced excellent work on cultural hegemony, politics, ideology, and the labor process, other important areas of a marxist interpretation remain almost totally missing. The succeeding chapter will then explore these absences: class structure, capital and its trajectory, and the role and forms of state power. Until marxists have matched the exciting new work on class and culture with more detailed and extensive analysis of economic and political power structures, the full significance of the new approaches, and the adequacy of a marxist synthesis of the American past will remain in doubt.

THE DECOMPOSITION OF A MONOLITHIC MARXISM

There can be no denying that the marxist tradition has itself been in a state of theoretical ferment. The fragmentation of marxist political movements on the national and international level since the 1950s has been reproduced on the level of marxist theory and marxist history. The decomposition of a monolithic marxism has occurred, and the label of "marxist" has become ever more problematic. Observation of this process has led some commentators, such as Laurence Veysey, Bernard Bailyn, and Carl Degler, to claim either that the impact of marxism on scholarship has been absorbed or that the cutting edge of marxist theory has been blunted by the modification of orthodoxy. "There are signs," Veysey argued in 1979, "that the marxist shock wave has been increasingly assimilated. It has lost some of its force by internal splintering. In the last few years varying conceptions of it among its practitioners have made the label seem almost meaningless." Bernard Bailyn has recently reinforced this "damned if you do, damned if you don't" assessment of marxist history in his presidential address before the American Historical Association. The explosion of historical data since the 1950s has outstripped the marxist capacity to interpret it, he argues. "The more technically strict the Marxist interpretation, the less comprehensive the coverage of the data is likely to be; the more comprehensive the coverage, the less strictly Marxist—the more diffuse—the interpretation will be."[1]

These and similar views rest on two connected liberal shibboleths. One is that there exists a fixed body of data waiting for historical interpretation: historical work must therefore be assessed according to its "fit" with the data. The other involves the unwarranted assumption that liberal social theory is pluralistic and diverse by nature, while marxism must necessarily involve a monolithic interpretive framework. In this line of thinking, diversity appears as a sign of debilitation in the marxist scheme. These views may seem reasonable enough if only the usual caricatures of marxism are considered, but they rest on a long inheritance of misconception about the nature of both liberal and marxist historiography. If stereotypes of marxism can be put aside, it may be possible to consider diversity in that tradition as a sign of a renewed vitality, complexity, and growth.

Further conceptual advance may well come from tension between competing formulations of marxism. Even if significant differences are not adequately resolved, there is still the prospect of much useful historical work to enrich American historiography. Rather than a static and monolithic doctrine, marxism might be more fruitfully conceived as a theoretical field which generates a number of related research strategies that together comprise a broad research program. The validity of theory must then be measured in terms of its overall performance across a broad period of time, not in terms of the invalidation of any particular concept or line of investigation. Since so little *serious* marxist historical work has been done, particularly in the United States, it is clearly too early to pronounce the program as discredited.[2]

THE CHALLENGE OF RADICAL HISTORY

The main problem comes not from the growing diversity of marxist scholarship per se, but from the challenge presented by radical historiography and the new social history. For all its limitations, the work done since the 1960s has revealed the limitations of many traditional marxist concepts and interpretations. Radical scholarship has produced volumes of research to demonstrate the importance of race, gender, ethnicity, and other issues in American life, and to many American historians, these seemed more important than class issues. Certainly it had become clear that there were many other conflicts over the distribution of power in society than those between capital and labor. A great deal of the research done since the 1960s on sex, women, and family history can be taken to document this conclusion. On a theoretical and paradigmatic level, the work done by Michel Foucault from the time of *Madness and Civilization* onwards also points toward a radical critique of power arrangements in modern societies without involving a recognition of the primacy of economic class relationships. A new international genre is emerging which treats such subjects as scientific practice, deviancy and its control, sexual relations, bureaucratization, and professionalization, and argues that these phenomena cannot be reduced to class relations. Within the next few years, American historical studies using Foucauldian concepts of discourse are likely to appear, but the implications of the attack on marxist theories of power posed by Foucault are already evident in general commentaries on the French thinker.[3]

Quite apart from its emphasis on nonclass phenomena, radical historiography has had a direct impact on the study of class relations and class formation. For the historiography of working-class and radical movements, the new research has been of critical importance in demonstrating that resistance to the spread of industrial capitalism did not take the form of a simple economistic struggle organized along institutional and political lines. The preservation of traditional cultures could contribute as much to the shaping of working-class behavior and beliefs as the struggle for wage justice. Gutman's immigrants were structurally members of the working class, but much would be lost if only their economic and trade union connections were regarded as vital. In the area of slavery, the importance of cultural struggle has also come to be regarded as critical to the making of a laboring class.[4]

Marxists must take the essential empirical findings of these works, develop critiques of their blind spots, and seek to enrich this tradition of social history by linking it to the analysis of class and capitalism. How this daunting program may be organized is suggested in the following chapters, but nothing of value will be achieved if marxist history reduces these other categories to purely class explanations. True, a marxist approach would remain rooted in investigations of the organization of capitalist society over time for purposes of production and reproduction, and of the ways in which the conflicts over this organization were articulated. Yet this inquiry would have to situate the issues of class analysis realistically in the context of the society in which class operates. It would be necessary to show the ways in which class and nonclass phenomena relate to one another.[5] This would be the open-ended empirical inquiry which constitutes the only hope for a sustained and serious marxist historiography. Thus conceived, marxist approaches could contribute to the revitalization of American historiography by showing that the analysis of the *interaction* of such phenomena as class and gender is more fruitful than their treatment as factors to be weighed against each other, and stripped from their historical context.

A good deal of evidence can be produced to demonstrate that marxist history in the United States is entering a new period of maturity, in which marxist categories are indeed being employed in a heuristic project to construct a new history of American society. This work has abandoned the intellectual barricades of the New Left and is seeking to incorporate the valuable insights of the new social history of race, ethnicity, gender, and popular culture.

Of these issues, race is probably the one with the longest pedigree in American marxist circles, going back to the efforts of the American communists to recruit blacks to their ranks in the 1930s. Academically, this political interest produced the early work of Aptheker, at a time when few white, liberal historians paid any attention to the role of the Negro in American history and life. Though the communist effort of the 1930s has been often denounced as simplistic and self-serving, the legacy remains, for two of the most important American marxist contributions of the 1960s and early 1970s, Genovese's several volumes and Robert Starobin's *Industrial Slavery*, reflect this continuing marxist interest in the slavery question that began with Aptheker's study of slave revolts. These works aside, there is still much untouched territory. No adequate study covers, from a marxist point of view, the black nationalism manifest in movements like Garveyism. The study of black trade unions and their leaders, too, is in its infancy. In the field of race relations, nothing matches the achievements of the British-centered Institute of Race Relations and its journal *Race and Class*. In contrast to promising work being done there, in the United States most of the innovative work on race has been done by American liberals working in the context of the great upheavals over civil rights. If American marxism is to produce an adequate historiography, it must surely take up the challenge first essayed by W.E.B. DuBois in *Black Reconstruction* in 1935, and tackle the complex intersection of race and class relations.

Marxists do have much to add to this question. Instead of focusing on the development of individual political rights as in the liberal tradition, the marxist historian could put the question of racial discrimination and the development of black culture in the context of the economic roles of blacks. Even for slavery, little of this has been done. The analysis of the slaves as workers has lagged behind the study of their culture. Yet the full measure of the culture of a people forced to work for so long for others, and since repeatedly coerced and subjected to discrimination in the labor market, remains unclear while their place in the system of social relations is narrowly conceived.[6]

Marxists have responded more positively to the challenges posed by the development of women's studies. That field illustrates the contribution marxists can make to the analysis of gender, and to its integration with the larger field of American history. Historically, the relations between marxism and feminism have generated considerable friction. The sexism of Old Left politics and the consequent rejection of orthodox marxism by some feminist writers in the 1960s testifies to a divergence in practical and theoretical interests.[7] The best early feminist writing among historians was done, as in the case of race relations, by nonmarxists whose attention to questions of gender in United States history has been very fruitful. Gender has been established as a separate force that cannot be simply explained in class terms. Marxists must therefore pay attention to the new feminist history if their own work is to increase in subtlety and complexity. On the other hand, gender and class are often closely connected, and marxists who are concerned with principles of interrelatedness can, if they take gender seriously, illuminate both women's history and class.

An instructive example of the marxist potential is Thomas Dublin's investigation of the mill women of antebellum Lowell, Massachusetts. Dublin utilizes the concepts of the historians of women's culture and sisterhood, but links his analysis of these phenomena to the changing composition of the working population. In the mills a women's culture did indeed exist, according to Dublin. Its operation underpinned a transient solidarity and militancy among the women workers of the 1830s and 1840s, but the vitality and indeed the actual content of the women's culture depended very heavily on the conditions under which the women lived and worked, and on the demographic composition of the labor force. Once the homogeneous work force of young, single, Yankee farm girls had been replaced with an older, married work force in which Irish immigrants figured strongly, the labor militancy among the women workers declined along with expressions of their sisterly solidarity. Dublin shows how the study of the role of women in American history can be further illuminated by relating gender to its class coordinates. Conversely, the class analysis of labor relations in the Lowell mills is strengthened by the incorporation of insights derived from the new social history. Dublin provides a case in point for the general rule that class relations do not occur in a vacuum. The values and the consciousness of workers could not be divorced from the cultural context within which they experienced class relations.[8]

This book is but one example of a larger historiographical trend. In Britain and the United States, socialist-feminist historians are beginning to challenge both the isolation of gender relations from class categories, and the subordination of women's issues to a traditional, economistic marxism.[9] Sociological and anthropological studies have showed clearly that in many third world countries experiencing industrialization, women's work-force participation has been shaped by the interaction of gender and economic questions.[10] In particular, socialist-feminists have drawn attention to the relations of reproduction. They have shown how women's tasks of reproducing and nurturing the family "have determined the opportunities open to them in new economic structures." Old inequalities between men and women "have been intensified as a result of the different ways they are absorbed into those structures."[11] The question of women's role in the

family and its relation to the development of industrial capitalism is, consequently, now on the historical agenda. Alice Kessler-Harris' *Out to Work*, which
deals with the sweep of women's experience in wage labor over the last two
centuries in the United States, is sensitive to these theoretical debates, though
Harris' position is not explicitly marxist. Her book goes further than other
available studies in American historiography towards integrating questions of
women's wage work with their domestic situation by showing the tensions and
contradictions between wage work and the domestic ideology.[12]

But Harris' book, like much of the literature on women's work that she
synthesizes, concentrates on the opening of opportunities for women in the paid
work force. This emphasis reflects a present political concern of feminists for
social and economic equality, not a considered theoretical orientation. The latter
would require much more attention to the political economy of housework. Given
the explosion of theoretical and sociological literature on the relations of reproduction, both biological and social, it seems that the study of the political
economy of the home and of domestic work is one important direction in which
American marxist historians could move. Some, like Susan Strasser, have followed the lead and made the issue of housework central, but in most cases work
is treated too narrowly to be fully comprehended. In Harris' account, the domestic
situation is merely a backdrop to the process of integrating women into the
market society. Because Harris does not make the reproduction of gender inequality in the home a central consideration in the analysis of "work," her
conclusion that inequality is being steadily undermined by incremental change
in the post–World War II period remains overly optimistic and unconvincing.
She does not show how and why the patterns of gender inequality which, by
her own account, profoundly structured earlier phases of women's wage work,
have ceased to be equally potent today.[13]

Apart from the obvious area of women's work in all its forms, marxist influence
has begun to be felt in a reaction against the purely behaviorist approach of the
new social history. Thus the birth control question, which social historians have
analyzed extensively, is linked by Linda Gordon in *Woman's Body, Woman's
Right* to sexual and class struggles. Gordon shows in a lively and often iconoclastic account how the birth control issue cannot be discussed simply as a matter
of individual behavior. Rather, birth control was unavoidably political in the
sense that control of women's reproductive functions was a matter of state policy
with class and feminist implications. Gordon thereby offers a cogent critique of
liberal feminist accounts which treat birth control unproblematically as a reform
and of conventional marxist theory which has neglected the politics of social
and biological reproduction.[14]

Equally important are the signs that marxist feminists will not isolate the study
of women as a separate category as has been typical of some recent liberal and
radical scholarship. They seek instead to study the relations between men and
women, and thus to develop a systematic and empirically informed theory of
the social relations of gender to complement theories of class relations. The

potential of the feminist movement is at last being harnessed to this socialist-feminist task. After a decade or more of scholarship emphasizing such themes as the progress of women's rights, the oppression of women, or women's positive achievements in the domestic realm, the appearance of Barbara Epstein's study of women's temperance in her *Politics of Domesticity* signals an important conceptual advance. Epstein agrees that women's temperance involved a separate culture. That culture, however, she finds circumscribed in profound ways. Especially important was the relationship between men and women, the study of which reveals deep sexual antagonism expressed through temperance. The Woman's Christian Temperance Union (WCTU) she depicts as an expression of the aspirations of women that arose from this struggle to embody at times a critique of the (male) industrial order that economically and politically subordinated women. By realizing the dialectical tensions involved in women's temperance, Epstein goes closer than other authors toward resolving the sterile debate over the progressive or regressive nature of women's temperance.[15]

These efforts in women's history have been more than matched by important work in the study of working-class culture and politics. A series of essays edited by Michael Frisch and Daniel Walkowitz exemplifies the achievement. Extending the insights of the new labor history and the English marxists, several contributors explore the community, cultural, and work experience of diverse groups of American workers. They show that despite the absence of class-conscious politics in the marxist mold, nineteenth-century American history in the period of industrialization could in no sense be described as one of a Lockean consensus. Class antagonism abounded, and working-class political and union activity was endemic. The essays are especially successful where they give attention, as Sean Wilentz does for Jacksonian artisans, to the rituals and symbols which expressed the aspirations of workers experiencing the industrializing process. And that process is not shown to have been a homogeneous or unilinear development along the lines suggested by orthodox marxist interpretations and the modernization formula of American social scientists. Both Wilentz and Christine Stansell follow the English marxists Stedman Jones and Raphael Samuel who argue that industrialization proceeded in an uneven pattern which complicated class relations.[16]

These essays are part of a much larger range of scholarship which includes important contributions on the southern yeomanry by Steven Hahn, the politics and culture of class in the revolutionary era by Gary Nash and Edward Countryman, the shaping of popular culture and leisure among Worcester, Massachusetts, workers by Roy Rosenzweig, and the grass-roots struggles of the Knights of Labor by Leon Fink. None of these authors ignores the significance of the new social history of quantification, or the study of mobility, family life, and ethnocultural affiliation. Rather, genuine efforts are made to link these social processes with the organization of production and with the contest for political and social power. Thus ethnicity is not treated by Leon Fink in *Workingmen's Democracy* as a factor to be weighed against class. Fink shows, for example, how ethnicity can sometimes work against class identification, but on other occasions can reinforce class solidarity. Unlike Gutman's seminal essay of 1973, Fink's account also contains a renewed emphasis on politics. Working-class culture is depicted as continuous with labor organization, not diametrically opposed as so often claimed in American historiography. By bringing questions of political power and ideology into relation with class forces, scholars such as Fink and Wilentz draw upon the marxist intellectual legacy, and integrate it with the new social history.[17]

Despite the appeal of marxist doctrines in the contemporary world, much of the current marxist historical scholarship deals with the last century. The modern era has been much less attractive. Some would say the neglect of twentieth-century topics signifies the passing of the kind of capitalism Marx analyzed. To many commentators, marxists have appeared unable or unwilling to confront the experience of societies in which the class conflict between proletariat and bourgeoisie seems to be receding in importance. Yet far from demonstrating a blind commitment to classical marxist propositions, modern marxist theory has repeatedly attempted to come to grips with the development of a more complex capitalism, and with the failure of revolutionary optimism. On the economic front, the work of Baran and Sweezy explored the development of monopoly capitalism and the alliance of the corporations with the bureaucratic state; the work of the Frankfurt School critical theorists also analyzed the issues of culture and class consciousness in a period of capitalist reorganization, and pointed to the deployment of ever more sophisticated techniques of persuasion, surveillance, and control. The mark of these theorists is evident in the stimulating critiques of aspects of modern American society contained in the historical works of David Noble, Stuart Ewen, and Christopher Lasch. Noble has written on technology, industrial capitalism, and higher education in his *America by Design*. Taking as his starting point Marcuse's observation that technology in modern capitalist society had become a vehicle for class hegemony but not for human liberation, Noble demonstrates how technology did not develop in an impersonal and deterministic manner. Its transformation was linked intimately with the rise of corporate capitalism and the changing social relations of production. In *Captains of Consciousness*, Ewen takes on another aspect of the reorganization of modern capitalism, the role of advertising in the production of a capitalist mass culture in the twentieth century. Just as Noble relates technology and social relations, so too does Ewen emphasize that advertising was more than a business enterprise. Ewen argues that the 1920s was for capitalism an era of restructuring, and he connects anxieties over the instability in the social relations of capitalism to attempts by advertising ideologues to foster an ethic of mass consumption among workers.

The marriage of psychoanalysis and political economy attempted by the Frankfurt School is also an influence on the more iconoclastic work of Christopher Lasch. In *Haven in a Heartless World*, Lasch scrutinized the intrusion of professionalized experts and the state into the previously private realm of family life, as the functions of reproduction became steadily more socialized. A more recent book, *The Culture of Narcissism*, builds on this argument but puts the entire range of American cultural institutions and norms under the spotlight. Sport, education, culture, psychology, and family life all reveal for Lasch the self-obsession of a dying culture which is the *reductio ad absurdum* of classical capitalism's competitive individualism. A bureaucratic and corporate order has stripped work and achievement of its intrinsic values, and replaced them with a culture of commodities which intrudes into the most private spheres. Lasch appears today more in the guise of an eclectic contemporary cultural critic than as either a conventional historian or a marxist whose ideological position can be easily pidgeon-holed, but his analysis is distinguished by often insightful historical perspectives on modern culture, and by the marxist concern with capitalism's historical trajectory and its interconnections with other aspects of social life.[18]

Marxists are also making an important contribution to the understanding of the social history of ideas by relating systems of thought and belief to the class relations of society through the concept of ideology. Until recently, ideology was rather crudely treated, particularly in the texts of the vulgar marxists of the 1930s and 1940s. Engels and Marx had set the tone for this pejorative treatment of ideas as "mere illusion" or "false consciousness." Intellectual historians had no difficulty undermining this cruder usage, but as Raymond Williams points out, marxism has always been ambiguous on the subject. An alternative tendency in marxist work treated ideology not as a smoke screen for real economic interests but rather as "the forms in which men become *conscious* of the conflict arising from conditions and changes of condition in economic production."[19] It is this sense of ideology as social consciousness which many modern, marxist historians increasingly utilize. This approach has by no means dispensed with the study of the internal structures and contents of ideas as they changed over time, but for the study of the connections between ideas and their social context, the marxist insight holds out hope for conceptual advance. In the work of a number of American historians, the promise is being realized.

Just at a time when many social historians were beginning to embrace the deterministic explanations characteristic of behaviorism, and to treat ideas as reflexes of social forces, the American historian Eric Foner was adopting a more dialectical approach. In *Free Soil, Free Labor, Free Men: The Ideology of the Republican Party before the Civil War* (1970), and in a series of influential essays, Foner dealt with the interaction of politics and ideology on the one hand with social and economic change on the other. He was able thereby to throw new light on that hardy perennial, the "causes of the Civil War," especially by circumventing unprofitable arguments over the relative importance of moral and economic factors in the coming of the war. Later, in *Tom Paine and Revolutionary America*, Foner related the radical ideas of the American Revolution to the social world of the artisan classes. Foner's work was symptomatic of a willingness among American marxists by the 1970s to take ideas seriously and to treat them more sympathetically than earlier generations had done. *Marxist Perspectives*, for example, paid particular attention to the study of religion as a form of social consciousness in a class society through contributory essays by Michael Greenberg and Jack P. Maddex. This concern may have been connected to Eugene Genovese's own interest in both paternalism and slave religion in his study of slave–master relations.[20]

Marxists have not been the only contributors to the study of the history of ideas conceived as ideological systems of thought. The major syntheses of Wood, Pocock, and Bailyn remind us that republicanism and republican ideology are concepts derived from nonmarxist work.[21] But the marxist may be able to add something of value because liberal versions have tended to treat ideas in isolation from the social relations in which they were produced and given meaning. A gulf remains, despite the effort of Foner and others, between the study of ideological systems and the social history constructed by the radical and marxist historians. If this gulf is to be bridged, marxists must not treat the ideology of a republican equalitarianism as a formal system of belief to be dredged up to organize otherwise inexplicable data. The new working-class histories illustrate the danger. Republicanism in too many of these studies is loosely employed as the American equivalent of the cultural traditions of English preindustrial workers analyzed so effectively by E. P. Thompson. No matter how ingenious, such transpositions of the explanatory schemes of English marxism will hardly account for the complexities of American class relations. In *Class and Community*, for example, Alan Dawley explains labor solidarity in the ante-bellum period in terms of the Equal Rights doctrine drawn from the republican tradition. Yet the connection of that ideology to the intellectual and social context of workers' lives is not adequately treated. Equal rights is not set within the context of what Sean Wilentz calls "the entire moral order" of republicanism with its concepts of virtue, citizenship, and independence. Nor is it clear that Equal Rights conceived as a class ideology articulates the consciousness of the workers themselves. Absent from the analysis are the day-to-day linkages between republicanism and the structural conditions which shape the meanings assigned to the ideology through the experiences of workers in the changing organization of social relations. Instead, we are presented with a rather abstract account of the economic changes, and then the ideology is deduced from these conditions through a selective analysis of the rhetoric of labor radicals.[22]

A more complex investigation of the relationship between the structure of social relations and the larger context of political ideology is necessary. Wilentz has indicated what is possible in his work on the ideology and culture of artisan radicalism in early republican and Jacksonian New York. That study charts the complex patterns of negotiation and redefinition of the meanings of ideas as part of the actual process of class relations in the society. Unlike much of the new labor history, Wilentz recognizes that the ideology of employers as well as workers must be more fully understood, and the emergence of both treated dialectically as forged in a relationship of contestation and compromise between labor and capital. Friedrich Lenger has made similar comments in relation to the class consciousness of New England shoemakers in the nineteenth century. He emphasizes correctly that a materialist perspective must treat ideology not as "separate from and largely independent of the everyday experience of its bearer" but as "lived" and experienced in "a real historical process."[23] To execute this strategy, Lenger calls for a more careful social history of the ideas and culture of workers. If this injunction is to be more than a form of words, however, great demands will be placed on the delineation of much more precise connections between the changing nature of the economic productive system, the class structure, and the beliefs and actions of workers. Whether marxists can construct adequate accounts of these processes depends not simply upon a more sophisticated rendering of intellectual systems but upon the as yet fragmentary construction of a marxist history of class and economic process.

That is another way of saying that perhaps the new preoccupation with ideology, culture, and consciousness has led marxist historians to lean over backwards to compensate for the sterile economism of much traditional marxist thinking. The stress on consciousness and ideology can certainly have its limitations if it occurs at the expense of an investigation of material relations. The scholarship on working-class culture which neglects to map the material settings of class risks failing to explain why class consciousness did not develop further, and why working-class movements seemed to end so often in defeat. Another related danger involves the failure to show that the cultures and ideologies studied were actually experienced by large numbers of people. That is, the behavior of workers, women, and other groups is too often neglected in favor of a purely ideological analysis. Despite its insights, the relationship between ideology and behavior remains problematic in the otherwise exemplary study of women and temperance undertaken by Epstein. If that work falls short of its potential, it is because Epstein follows too closely the findings of other women's historians on the influence of the concept of women's culture. One would have expected in a socialist-feminist analysis a more differentiated portrait linking the material situation of groups of women to the ways in which their social circumstances were articulated. Instead, the WCTU is taken as a phenomenal expression of an essence: a generalized women's culture that underlies the nineteenth-century history of American women. How the particular experiences of women within the institution of the WCTU shaped their consciousness and culture, and how that specific cluster of beliefs conditioned their behavior, is not treated, except at the most general level. This is a deficiency in an important work, since any study that seeks to synthesize the experience of class and gender should surely move beyond ideological representations to map the actual social history of the women studied. One historian has already criticized Epstein on this ground, for portraying temperance women as asexual despite behavioral evidence to the contrary. Another has complained that her work fails to take into account the specific experiences of temperance women with alcohol and its related social problems.[24] All this is not to deny the value of Epstein's work, but it is not sufficiently grounded in the material circumstances of women's lives, like so much radical and liberal women's history from which her historical problematic of feminist consciousness is partly drawn.

Ewen's study of advertising is another case in point. Despite its strengths, *Captains of Consciousness* does not fully convince as a social history of modern advertising's cultural significance. Too often its analysis concerns the ideology of consumer capitalism, without relating advertising strategies and intentions to their mode of operation or their behavioral impact. As a consequence, Ewen's book takes on a somewhat abstract air that fails to do justice to the drift of its theoretical promise. That is not to suggest that a marxist analysis of culture is impossible, but rather that some existing accounts have not been sufficiently materialist to qualify either as marxist or as adequate social history.[25] But the answer to this dilemma, marxist historians would argue, is not to produce an apolitical history of social behavior, but to link ideology and behavior together in analyses that make class, power, and politics central. Some of the works so far discussed can be distinguished from much of the new social history precisely because they do take these matters as critical to a historical synthesis.

It is undeniably true, as Eric Foner has argued, that there is a pressing need to give renewed attention to politics as a way of reintegrating the diverse insights of a fragmenting American historiography. Because of its traditional concern with the analysis of political action, marxism may have much to offer such an enterprise. This does not entail agreement with those who announce a return to a conception of history as the narrative of events. Foner has something else in mind, since he conceives of politics more broadly than most practitioners of political history usually do to include all varieties of domination, subordination, and resistance. "The way in which power was wielded and conceptualized" ought, in Foner's estimation, to stand "at the forefront of analysis" of politics.[26]

Too often marxists have in the past depicted power as purely economic, and have identified its exercise with the exertion of a ruling-class domination of workers. Power has typically been seen as a matter of coercion, and the analysis of the production of more positive types of power has been neglected. But this crudity in power analysis is really only one tendency within the broad boundaries of the marxist tradition over the last century. It is always possible to find other more sophisticated views, and certainly there would be few marxists today prepared to accept a simple top-down conception of the exertion of power in everyday social relations. A good deal of contemporary marxist theory recognizes the dispersal of many of the mechanisms of power, of social cohesion, authority, legitimacy, and control in complex modern societies. The most famous contribution in this genre has been that of Gramsci, whose writings tackled the important question of the exercise of cultural hegemony within the framework of class analysis. The exercise of power by a ruling class with the consent of other classes does not mean the absence of class conflict, but rather that conflict is contained within a terrain which recognizes the legitimacy of ruling-class rule.[27]

HEGEMONY AND SUBVERSION

This more sophisticated study of power relations is perhaps most useful in the case of the modern United States, but curiously the most important application of Gramsci's ideas of hegemony has come in the study of slave society. Because Genovese's work is so often cited as the most influential marxist study by an American historian, and because of the concepts of power he employs, it is fitting to give his treatment in *Roll, Jordan, Roll* extensive appraisal here. In that book, Genovese located the development of slave society within the context of the cultural hegemony of the planters' paternalistic ideology. Like serfs and lords in seigneurial Europe, slaves and masters were bound together in a web of reciprocal obligations and customary rights. The complex elements of a slave culture, such as religion, family structure, and community life, are treated with this overarching conception in mind.[28]

This approach represented an advance over the class determinism of much earlier marxist history in the United States. Genovese's focus also avoided the search for radical activist heroes and seething slave rebellion that has sometimes characterized both marxist and radical historiography.[29] By discussing the slaves and the masters together as a social relation, he also began the process of putting the fruits of the new social history to work in a new synthesis with the issues of power and authority. Yet his use of Gramsci's hegemony concept requires more careful scrutiny and further research before its value as an explanation for the behavior and beliefs of subordinate classes can be accepted. In part the controversy over Genovese's notion of planter paternalism can be settled through an empirical inquiry. The accumulation of evidence could establish the operation and importance of hegemonic values under slavery. Empirical objections of this sort constitute the burden of criticism developing among American historians in consideration of Genovese's work. In particular, it has been argued that Genovese failed to establish the cultural hegemony of paternalistic values in the slave quarters. Gutman, for example, depicted a vital slave community resisting planter domination and transmitting its values through distinctive family patterns. Drew Faust's case study of the Hammond plantation in Georgia describes a complex power struggle between a paternalistic planter and slaves who resisted his authority. Other critics have argued that the planters themselves did not follow the norms of paternalism in their behavior toward slaves, particularly in the matter of slave sales. One author, James Oakes, has even gone so far as to write a book-length critique which purports to show the capitalistic and antipaternalistic character of the typical planter.[30]

Marxists have also been critical of Genovese, and their objections have combined the two central elements of empirical refutation apparent in the larger profession. It is in this context that the work of the historical sociologist Immanuel Walerstein is of importance in underpinning the marxist critique. Though not responsible as yet for much direct research into aspects of American history, the world-systems theory has been employed in disputes within the fraternity of marxist historians in the United States. To understand this point, the theoretical divergence of Wallerstein and Genovese must be probed. Genovese treats slavery as a reciprocal social system in which slaves cannot be considered as pure property. He argues along classic marxist lines that only with the advent of wage labor can the purely economic rationality of the capitalist marketplace be completely followed by employers. Under slavery, like but not the same as under feudalism, relations at the point of production are not determined by profits, but rather by the questions of paternalism, dependence, domination, and subordination, which are cultural, psychological, and social in character. In contrast, Wallerstein argues that there has been since the sixteenth century a capitalist world economy necessarily international in scope, and that the social organization of production in its various areas is part of this system and subordinate to its needs. Unfree labor is, according to Wallerstein, entirely compatible with the system of capitalist market relations. Free labor characterizes the core capitalist economies, while the peripheral parts of the system have a variety of coercive labor systems. Since the latter produce for the market, for profit, their businesses respond to market forces.[31]

The implications for Genovese's marxism are now clear. Wallerstein provides the theoretical underpinning for a challenge to paternalism and the entire theory of hegemony. If planter attitudes and behavior are formed in an economy that is part of the capitalist world-system, and not some prebourgeois order, then planter behavior can only be explained in terms of the rational demands of the capitalist marketplace. Taking up this argument, Eric Perkins seizes on the contradiction between loving paternal masters and the huge numbers of slave sales. Over a million slave sales took place during the first fifty years of the nineteenth century. He goes on: "Planters violated their duty as paternalists when they sold slaves, and contributed a great vacuum in the slaves' acceptance of such authority. . . . The paternal ideology becomes unglued when the reality of slave sale is put back into the historical picture."[32]

Genovese has not replied directly to his critics over his neglect of the interregional slave trade and its effects on the slave's acceptance of paternalism (or one might add, the master's attempts to adhere to it). Genovese concentrated instead on a more general defense in which he agreed that "with the rise of a worldwide capitalist mode of production, every attempt to resurrect an archaic social system or to defend a dying one had to bend its economy to the political and economic power of the world market and its competitive demands." But "the difference between the buying and selling of labor-power and the extra-economic compulsion of direct human labor constituted the essence not only of a divergence of material interests but of the deepest moral sensibilities."[33]

If Genovese's paternalist thesis could be shown to be incompatible with the dynamics of the slave economy, then the question of the slaves' independent cultural formations could again be opened. Instead of subordination within the hegemony of the planters' paternalism, Perkins portrays an implicitly political struggle between an Afro-American culture and planters dominated increasingly by the coercive, profit-oriented forces of the capitalist marketplace. With Perkins, the cultural question is ironically reversed. The slaves have their own independent culture, but the masters do not.[34]

Genovese's opponents have not, however, yet succeeded in establishing "the existence of an autonomous slave cultural tradition outside of Genovese's parameters," as Eric Foner points out. While some of Genovese's critics, including Perkins, have suggested that Herbert Gutman's book on the slave family would provide that evidence, Gutman too has asserted rather than convincingly established the cultural independence and self-generating character of slave family life. Ultimately, Gutman's portrait cannot be sustained, for all its anthropological and empirical nuances. Already it has been subjected to searching analytical criticism from Stanley Engerman and, partly as a result, Gutman himself began to shift his ground perceptibly, and to emphasize less the study of the slave family and more the study of the community as a kind of surrogate kinship system.[35]

Alan Dawley notes that in any case "most of the apparent counter-evidence" showing that the paternalistic ideology did not conquer the quarters "could be conceded without surrendering the field."[36] This is precisely the strategy that Genovese has already followed in his treatment of slave religion. Critics of his thesis have difficulty in combating the subtle way that he has incorporated the question of cultural autonomy into his hegemonic analysis. In effect, Genovese agrees that slaves fought for and were granted a measure of cultural autonomy that made their lives bearable. But Genovese, adopting a dialectical approach, insists quite correctly that any autonomy was granted at a price, and that the price of the struggle was exacted upon both slaves and masters. If Genovese's claims were to be replaced by a view emphasizing cultural autonomy, it would be necessary to show that planters did not determine the *terrain* on which the cultural struggle took place. This Genovese's critics have not demonstrated so far.[37]

To make this point convincingly, opponents must do more than marshal evidence of economic motives among planters and a culture among slaves that diverges from planter norms. They must construct an alternative model of slave society that accounts for the phenomena they have discovered. So far, an alternative perspective has not emerged, despite the use of Wallerstein's world-systems theory. Wallerstein's main contribution so far has been his concentration on market forces at the broadest levels of historical generalization. Yet Wallerstein is being used to provide theoretical underpinning for an argument concerned with a subject of very different scope and content: the slaves' own cultural forms and their significance. There is an anomaly here, because the critics have not reconciled the culture of the slaves and the logic of the capitalist marketplace. Eric Perkins raises the question of the importance of the slave's labor to a realization of slave autonomy without pursuing the implications of this fruitful idea. He relies mainly, notwithstanding his emphasis on the mediation of slave-master relations through the productive process, on the creation and maintenance of slave culture through slave family life. The relationship between slave labor and slave culture thus remains as unclear as that between the economics of a rapacious capitalist agriculture and the autonomy of slave family life. As it now stands, one could just as easily employ Wallerstein's account of the logic of capitalist exploitation (particularly as it relates to slave sales) in order to cast doubt on the viability of the slave family or other cultural patterns. The whole matter therefore cries out for further interpretation.[38]

When the insights of Wallerstein *are* confronted by Americanists, it will be necessary at that stage to take note of the criticisms that have been leveled at world-systems theory by Robert Brenner and others. American historians cannot add much that is novel to these already copious arguments, but they can confront abstraction with the actual social processes in which class and capitalism operated over time in particular historical situations. Historians can also contribute to the development of a more complex, multilevel analysis than one couched purely or largely in terms of an economic rationale. Wallerstein's approach provides descriptions of early capitalist development in its global setting, but it cannot explain the specific historical development of particular social formations. Why, for example, does the penetration of capitalist social relations in some societies dominated by slavery end in armed rebellion? Why the accentuation of precapitalist types of behavior among planters in some social settings but not in others? Just because there are market relations of exchange does not mean that the social relations of production or the cultural forms of those societies are capitalistic. The study of class forces in the regional setting of the slave south must be joined to an analysis of the capitalist tendencies in market relations if this problem is to be resolved. Genovese more than his critics has addressed the issue, even if his answers are far from definitive.[39]

Though Genovese's use of hegemony renders his account superior as historical analysis to more economistic versions of marxism, this does not mean that his work is beyond possible theoretical criticism. Doubts remain whether Genovese's notion of paternalism provides the best way to conceptualize relations between slaves and masters in the context of the larger southern society. Some of these doubts arise from the theoretical appropriation of hegemony from the context of Gramsci's thought. In the first place, it is very difficult to get a clear definition of what hegemony is, partly because Gramsci's writings on the subject are so cryptic and episodic. These characteristics arose from the conditions of prison censorship and deprivation under which Gramsci tragically wrote. Thus much of the Italian marxist's meaning has depended on critical *readings* of his texts, and there has been no shortage of commentators providing their own glosses on Gramsci. Interpreters have typically truncated the complexities of his thought in the process of translation, exposition, and interpretation. As Keith Nield and John Seed point out, "even the best" of the commentators "has tended to abstract the concept of hegemony from its locus within a much broader analysis of power." The "characteristic thrust of Gramsci's project—the state, forms of political organization, the concrete institutional structures of culture (civil society)—remains strategically absent'' in the thinking of marxists who have appropriated Gramsci's legacy.[40] Since in Gramsci the hegemony of the dominant classes was broadly based on all of the institutions of civil society, it is difficult to see how the concept can illuminate the study of slave-master relations. For the essence of hegemony resides in the consent of the ruled, yet slavery as an institution and the slave-master relationship would appear to rest by definition on explicit coercion.[41]

The question is not so simply settled, however. All societies, including the "civil society" of western, liberal democracies, depend on some combination of consent and coercion. The real question concerns the relation between coercion and consent, and the gradations of intimidation and influence that lie between. Genovese actually develops a sophisticated analysis in which power is an omnipresent backdrop to the process of cultural persuasion and contestation. But several problems remain, and these are rooted in his Hegelian analysis of the slave–master dialectic as the essence of slavery. Virtually all empirical detail flows from this theoretical stance which abstracts the analysis of slavery from the context of the larger social formation of the antebellum south. It follows that the historical and temporal specificity of American slavery is neglected in a study of the essence of the system. Further, the role of diverse forms of compliance (not simply physical and legal coercion) is undervalued because these are mediated through the psychological and cultural dimensions of the slave–master dialectic. These "mechanisms of compliance" emanated from the larger structure of class power and the economic relation of slave production. Physical punishment, psychological coercion, and military force were only superficial manifestations of the structures of power that impinged upon the lives and behavior of slaves. There is a pressing need for extended analysis of the diverse responses of slaves to the economic structures that through the market distributed and redistributed slave labor; the productive processes that organized work and shaped the structures of community life, black and white; the constellation of class forces in the south; the distribution of wealth and political and legal power; and the ideological fields of southern nationalism, popular democracy, and white racism. Elsewhere, Genovese has made important contributions to our understanding of some of these forces, but they nevertheless demand greater attention here. They are crucial to an analysis of the specific processes of domination and subordination centered around the cultural struggle between slaves and masters. These material and class determinations help to explain far better than hegemonic notions of paternalism the limits to any slave oppositional culture, but they also remain vital to any understanding of the degree of autonomy that slaves fought for and won.[42]

The importance of such an analysis is brought into sharp relief if we consider the seventeenth- and eighteenth-century origins of North American slavery. There the "external mechanisms of compliance" were more obvious, and the system apparently more brutal in its impact on slaves. Genovese's study suffers because he does not deal with slavery before the emergence of benevolent paternalism

after the American revolution. This absence reflects in turn the neglect by most
historians of the changing temporal context of slavery. Gutman has been among
the leaders in directing our attention to the eighteenth-century origins of Afro-
American *culture*, but we still know very little about how the structure of class
power intersected with the emerging patterns of slave behavior and belief. One
study in progress on eighteenth-century North Carolina is directed toward these
very issues, and rightly focuses on the regional context of early American slavery.
That study emphasizes the mobilization through the state of an apparatus of terror
and intimidation, and treats the behavior of slaves, including their forms of
resistance, in relation to these patterns of power. But there is much more to be
done in building upon the pioneering work of Peter Wood on the emergence of
slave economy and society in colonial South Carolina.[43]

For the years between the Civil War and the Great Depression, the prospects
for an analysis employing the terms of hegemony seem better. Particularly in
the area of cultural studies does the legacy of Gramsci appear important, and
the use of hegemony becomes steadily more sophisticated. Nowhere is that point
made clearer than in the recent work of Jackson Lears on "anti-modernism"
and the revitalization of elite culture at the turn of the century in his *No Place
of Grace*.[44] Yet the major thrust in marxist studies for the period since Reconstruction has not been the discovery of the dissemination of a shared view of
reality in society, but the revelation of both massive industrial conflict and a
contest of values as well as of class interests. That much has been clear ever
since David Montgomery published *Beyond Equality*, his path-breaking study
of class and politics in the Reconstruction era. Since that book appeared in 1967,
the most fruitful research has aimed at providing American historiography with
something it has sadly lacked: a reliable set of accounts covering the processes
of class contestation centered on the reorganization of work. The earlier emphasis
upon the clash of modern and premodern work habits has given way to a more
precise analysis of the conflict over changes in the organization of production
in the workplace, particularly the contest over scientific management. The principal impetus has come from Montgomery's more recent essays in *Workers'
Control in America*, and from a number of students influenced by him at the
University of Pittsburgh who have investigated labor militancy, mainly in the
late nineteenth and twentieth centuries. Their careful studies of the workplace
in different historical, industrial, and regional contexts have been complemented
by a more general theoretical interest in the reorganization of work coming from
the sociologists and economists.[45]

This emphasis upon workplace studies is valuable provided it does not lead
to an exaggeration of working-class activism and economic conflict. Montgomery, for one, is well aware of the dangers of romanticizing worker protests.
He admits the limitations of movements for control of work processes in the
contest against scientific management. These have been typically centered in
skilled crafts, and isolated from questions of the political transformation of
society which alone could make the dream of worker cooperatives of which

Montgomery writes come true. To argue otherwise and to exaggerate radical tendencies by setting them apart from structures of class power would be to focus unduly upon the surface of economics and political life.[46]

Several complementary topics must be developed if the new studies of class contestation in the workplace are not to be wrenched from the community, cultural, and political context. To avoid the faulty equation of American marxist history with the history of workers' struggles at the point of production, historians must embark upon a more comprehensive study of class structures and relationships; they must also analyze the role of the state in the development of industrial capitalism and liberal democracy; and they must broach the issue of the economic dynamic of capitalism as a system of production, distribution, and exchange. In short, they must integrate the new social history with the legacy of economic history and political economy.

NOTES

1. Laurence Veysey, "The 'New' Social History in the Context of American Historical Writing," *Reviews in American History* 7 (1979): 1; Bernard Bailyn, "The Challenge of Modern Historiography," *American Historical Review* 87 (1982): 6; Carl Degler, "Remaking American History," *Journal of American History*, 67 (1980): 17. The extent of the turmoil in marxist circles can be measured by a perusal of Stanley Aronowitz, *The Crisis in Historical Materialism: Class, Politics and Culture in Marxist Theory* (New York, 1981).

2. I am influenced in suggesting this comparison by the work of Imre Lakatos, "Falsification and the Methodology of Scientific Research Programmes," in Lakatos and Alan Musgrave, eds., *Criticism and the Growth of Knowledge* (Cambridge, Eng., 1974), pp. 91–96. I do not, however, accept all of the implications of the view of philosophy and history of science which Lakatos has developed. In particular, I have reservations about his theory of a scientific method divorced from the conditions of real scientific practice. For criticism from a marxist viewpoint, see Alan F. Chalmers, *What Is This Thing Called Science? An Assessment of the Nature and Status of Science and Its Methods* (Brisbane, Qld., 1976), pp. 137–42.

3. The theories and influence of Foucault can be traced through Hayden V. White, "Foucault Decoded: Notes from the Underground," *History and Theory* 12 (1973): 23–54; Larry Shiner, "Reading Foucault: Anti-Method and the Genealogy of Power/Knowledge," ibid., 21 (1982): 389–90, 396; Jan Goldstein, "Foucault among the Sociologists: The 'Disciplines' and the History of the Professions," ibid., 23 (1984): 170–92; Alan Sheridan, *Michel Foucault: The Will to Truth* (London, 1980), p. 225; Hubert L. Dreyfus and Paul Rabinow, *Michel Foucault: Beyond Structuralism and Hermeneutics* (Chicago, 1982). Foucault's most intellectually accessible works are *Madness and Civilization*, trans. Richard Howard (New York, 1965); and *The History of Sexuality*, vol. 1, *An Introduction*, trans. Robert Hurley (New York, 1978).

4. Herbert Gutman, *Work, Culture, and Society in Industrializing America* (New York, 1976), is a good place to begin. For a summary of much of the work, see James Green, "Culture, Politics and Workers' Response to Industrialization in the US," *Radical America* 16 (Jan.–April 1982): 101–27.

5. On the need to take account of nonclass elements, see Stephen Resnick and Richard Wolff, "A Reformulation of Marxian Theory and Historical Analysis," *Journal of Economic History* 42 (1982): 53–59.

6. See esp., Robert S. Starobin, *Industrial Slavery in the Old South* (New York, 1970); Eugene Genovese, *Roll, Jordan, Roll: The World the Slaves Made* (New York, 1974); Genovese, *In Red and Black: Marxian Explorations in Southern and Afro-American History* (New York, Vintage ed., 1972); Herbert Aptheker, *American Negro Slave Revolts* (New York, 1943); Jeff Henderson, "A. Philip Randolph and the Dilemmas of Socialism and Black Nationalism in the United States, 1917–1941," *Race and Class* 20 (1978): 143; Mark Naison, *Communists in Harlem during the Depression* (Urbana, Ill., 1983); W.E.B. DuBois, *Black Reconstruction in America* (Cleveland, Ohio, 1969 ed.). Nonmarxist scholarship on race since the 1950s has been abundant. See esp., Lawrence W. Levine, *Black Culture and Black Consciousness: Afro-American Folk Thought from Slavery to Freedom* (New York, 1977); George M. Fredrickson, *The Black Image in the White Mind: The Debate on Afro-American Character and Destiny, 1817–1914* (New York, 1971); Carl Degler, *Neither Black nor White: Slavery and Race Relations in Brazil and the United States* (New York, 1971).

7. Robert Shaffer, "Women and the Communist Party, 1930–1940," *Socialist Review* 9 (May–June 1979): 73–118; Shulasmith Firestone, *The Dialectic of Sex: The Case for Feminist Revolution* (New York, 1970), pp. 6, 28.

8. Thomas Dublin, *Women at Work: The Transformation of Work and Community in Lowell, Massachusetts, 1826–1860* (New York, 1979).

9. Kate Young, Carol Wolkowitz, and Roslyn McCullagh, eds., *Of Marriage and the Market: Women's Subordination in International Perspective* (London, 1981); Rayna R. Reiter, ed., *Toward an Anthropology of Women* (New York, 1975), esp. Gayle Rubin's essay, "The Traffic in Women: Notes on the 'Political Economy' of Sex," pp. 157–210; and Michelle Rosaldo and Louise Lamphere, eds., *Woman, Culture, and Society* (Stanford, Calif., 1974), are representative of theoretical developments and empirical work in feminist anthropology, influenced by marxist perspectives. Among historians, see "Politics and Culture in Women's History: A Symposium," *Feminist Studies* 6 (1980): 26–64, esp. Ellen DuBois' contribution, pp. 28–36.

10. See, for example, "Development and the Sexual Division of Labor," *Signs* 7 (1981, special issue).

11. Gay Seidman, "Women in the Third World," *Socialist Review* 12 (Sept.–Oct. 1982): 133–34.

12. Alice Kessler–Harris, *Out to Work: A History of Wage-Earning Women in the United States* (New York, 1982), pp. 44–72, 321.

13. Ellen Malos, "Housework and the Politics of Women's Liberation," *Socialist Review* 8 (Jan. Feb. 1978): 41–71; Ann Oakley, *Woman's Work: The Housewife, Past and Present* (London, 1974); Heidi Hartmann, "The Family as the Locus of Gender, Class, and Political Struggle: The Example of Housework," *Signs* 6 (1981): 366–94. Valuable historical works that are beginning to address the issue of housework, and its ideology and political economy, include Susan Strasser, *Never Done: A History of American Housework* (New York, 1982); Kathryn Sklar, *Catharine Beecher: A Study in American Domesticity* (New Haven, 1973); Dolores Hayden, *The Grand Domestic Revolution: A History of Feminist Designs for American Homes, Neighborhoods, and Cities* (Cambridge, Mass., 1981).

14. Linda Gordon, *Woman's Body, Woman's Right: Birth Control in America* (New York, 1977).

15. Barbara Epstein, *The Politics of Domesticity: Women, Evangelism, and Temperance in Nineteenth Century America* (Middletown, Conn.: 1980).

16. Michael H. Frisch and Daniel Walkowitz, eds., *Working-Class America: Essays on Labor, Community, and American Society* (Urbana, Ill., 1983); Sean Wilentz, "Artisan Republican Festivals and the Rise of Class Conflict in New York City, 1788–1837," ibid., pp. 37–77; Christine Stansell, "The Origins of the Sweatshop: Women and Early Industrialization in New York City," ibid., pp. 78–103; Leon Fink, "The Uses of Political Power: Toward a Theory of the Labor Movement in the Era of the Knights of Labor," ibid., pp. 104–22.

17. Leon Fink, *Workingmen's Democracy: The Knights of Labor and American Politics* (Urbana, Ill., 1983), pp. 72–75, 221; Steven Hahn, *The Roots of Southern Populism: Yeoman Farmers and the Transformation of the Georgia Upcountry, 1850–1890* (New York, 1983); Roy Rosenzweig, *Eight Hours for What We Will: Workers and Leisure in an Industrial City, 1870–1920* (Cambridge, Eng., 1983); Edward Countryman, *A People in Revolution: The American Revolution and Political Society in New York, 1760–1790* (Baltimore, 1981); Gary B. Nash, *The Urban Crucible: Social Change, Political Consciousness, and the Origins of the American Revolution* (Cambridge, Mass., 1979); Herbert Gutman, "Work, Culture, and Society in Industrializing America, 1815–1919," *American Historical Review* 78 (1973): 531–87.

18. Paul Breines, "Toward an Uncertain Marxism," *Radical History Review* 22 (1979–1980): 102; David Noble, *America by Design: Science, Technology, and the Rise of Corporate Capitalism* (New York, 1977); Stuart Ewen, *Captains of Consciousness: Advertising and the Social Roots of Consumer Culture* (New York, 1976); Christopher Lasch, *Haven in a Heartless World: The Family Besieged* (New York, 1977); Lasch, *The Culture of Narcissism: American Life in an Age of Diminishing Expectations* (New York, 1978). See also Elizabeth and Stuart Ewen, *Channels of Desire: Mass Images and the Shaping of American Consciousness* (New York, 1982).

19. Raymond Williams, *Keywords: A Vocabulary of Culture and Society* (London, rev. ed., 1983), p. 156.

20. Eric Foner, *Politics and Ideology in the Age of the Civil War* (New York, 1980), p. 9; Foner, *Free Soil, Free Labor, Free Men: The Ideology of the Republican Party before the Civil War* (New York, 1970); Foner, *Tom Paine and Revolutionary America* (New York, 1976); Michael Greenberg, "Revival, Reform, Revolution: Samuel Davies and the Great Awakening in Virginia," *Marxist Perspectives* 2 (Summer 1980): 102–19; Jack P. Maddex, Jr., " 'The Southern Apostasy' Revisited: The Significance of Proslavery Christianity," *Marxist Perspectives* 2 (Fall 1979): 132–41; "Editorial Note," *Marxist Perspectives* 2 (Fall 1979): 7.

21. J.G.A. Pocock, *The Machiavellian Moment: Florentine Political Thought and the Atlantic Republican Tradition* (Princeton, N.J., 1975); Gordon Wood, *The Creation of the American Republic, 1776–1787* (Chapel Hill, 1969); Bernard Bailyn, *Ideological Origins of the American Revolution* (Cambridge, Mass., 1967).

22. Wilentz, "Artisan Republican Festivals," p. 63; Alan Dawley, *Class and Community: The Industrial Revolution in Lynn* (Cambridge, Mass., 1976), esp. p. 229; Dawley and Paul Faler, "Working-Class Culture and Politics in the Industrial Revolution: Sources of Loyalism and Rebellion," *Journal of Social History* 9 (1976): 466–80; Faler, "Cultural Aspects of the Industrial Revolution: Lynn, Massachusetts Shoemakers and Industrial

Morality, 1826–1860," *Labor History* 15 (1974): 376–94; Daniel J. Walkowitz, *Worker City, Company Town: Iron and Cotton-Worker Protest in Troy and Cohoes, New York, 1855–84* (Urbana, Ill., 1978), pp. 135–38.

23. Wilentz, "Artisan Republican Festivals," pp. 37–77; Friedrich Lenger, "Class, Culture and Class Consciousness in Ante-bellum Lynn: A Critique of Alan Dawley and Paul Faler," *Social History* 6 (1981): 323, 325; see also Wilentz, *Chants Democratic: New York City & the Rise of the American Working Class, 1788–1850* (New York, 1984).

24. Epstein, *Politics of Domesticity*; Estelle B. Freedman, "Sexuality in Nineteenth-Century America: Behavior, Ideology, and Politics," *Reviews in American History* 10 (1982): 209; Jack S. Blocker, Jr., "Separate Paths: Suffragists and the Women's Temperance Crusade," *Signs* 10 (1985): 460–76.

25. Ewen, *Captains of Consciousness*, esp. pp. 185–220. A "concern with the hegemonic role of elites in the formation of a consumer culture" continues to distinguish better and more recent work on this subject. See Richard Wightman Fox and T. J. Jackson Lears, "Introduction" to Fox and Lears, eds., *The Culture of Consumption: Critical Essays in American History, 1880–1980* (New York, 1983). None of the authors examines "patterns of consumption themselves," nor "the lives of ordinary consumers" (p. x).

26. Foner, *Politics and Ideology in the Age of the Civil War*, p. 9; cf. Lawrence Stone, "The Revival of Narrative: Reflections on an Old New History," *Past and Present* 85 (1979): 3–24; Richard T. Vann, "The Rhetoric of Social History," *Journal of Social History* 10 (1976): 223; Bailyn, "Challenge of Modern Historiography."

27. Eugene Genovese, "On Antonio Gramsci," *Studies on the Left* 7 (March–April 1967): 83–108. On the "productive aspects of power" and criticism of "repressive" formulations, see Michel Foucault, *Power/Knowledge: Selected Interviews and Other Writings, 1972–1977*, ed. Colin Gordon (New York, 1980), p. 119.

28. Eugene Genovese, *Roll, Jordan, Roll*, esp. pp. 25–49, 161–284.

29. Eugene Genovese, "Marxian Interpretations of the Slave South," in Barton Bernstein, ed., *Towards a New Past: Dissenting Essays in American History* (New York, 1968), pp. 90–105.

30. Herbert Gutman, *The Black Family in Slavery and Freedom, 1750–1925* (New York, 1976), pp. 309–19; Drew Gilpin Faust, "Culture, Conflict, and Community: The Meaning of Power on an Ante-bellum Plantation," *Journal of Social History* 14 (1980): 83–97; James B. Oakes, *The Ruling Race: A History of American Slaveholders* (New York, 1982); James D. Anderson, "Aunt Jemima in Dialectics: Genovese on Slave Culture," *Journal of Negro History* 41 (1976): 99–114; Fred Siegel, "The Paternalist Thesis: Virginia as a Test Case," *Civil War History* 25 (1979): 247–61; Siegel, "Parameters for Paternalism," *Radical History Review* 3 (Fall 1976): 62–63.

31. Immanuel Wallerstein, *The Modern World-System: Capitalist Agriculture and the Origins of the European World-Economy in the Sixteenth Century* (New York, 1974); Wallerstein, *The Modern World-System II: Mercantilism and the Consolidation of the European World-Economy, 1600–1750* (New York, 1980); Wallerstein, *The Capitalist World-Economy* (New York, 1979).

32. Eric Perkins, "Roll, Jordan, Roll: A 'Marx' for the Master Class," *Radical History Review* 3 (Fall 1976): 56–57; see also Siegel, "Parameters for Paternalism," pp. 62–63.

33. Eugene Genovese, "A Reply to Criticism," *Radical History Review* 4 (Winter 1977): 104.

34. Perkins, "A 'Marx' for the Master Class," pp. 45, 47. Genovese's "model of slave and planter behavior hardly comes to grips with the issue of how slaves developed

a culture and belief system, independent of the planter, and such development is itself testimony to some kind of autonomy'' (p. 47).

35. Eric Foner, "Introductory Notes" to "Symposium on Roll, Jordan, Roll," *Radical History Review* 3 (Fall 1976): 27; Perkins, "A 'Marx' for the Master Class," pp. 48– 49; Gutman, *Black Family*, pp. 309–19 and passim; Stanley Engerman, "Studying the Black Family," *Journal of Family History* 3 (1978): 78–101; Herbert Gutman, paper on the slave family delivered at Australian and New Zealand American Studies Association conference, University of New South Wales, August 1980.

36. Alan Dawley, "E. P. Thompson and the Peculiarities of the Americans," *Radical History Review* 19 (1978–1979): 47–48.

37. In addition to the items cited in n. 30 above, see Perkins, "A 'Marx' for the Master Class," pp. 41–59.

38. Perkins, "A 'Marx' for the Master Class," p. 45; cf. pp. 48–49.

39. C. H. George, "The Origins of Capitalism: A Marxist Epitome & A Critique of Immanuel Wallerstein's Modern World-System," *Marxist Perspectives* 2 (Summer 1980): 70–99; Robert Brenner, "The Origins of Capitalist Development: A Critique of Neo-Smithian Marxism," *New Left Review* 104 (1977): 25–93; Vincente Navarro, "The Limits of the World Systems Theory in Defining Capitalist and Socialist Formations," *Science and Society* 46 (1982): 77–90; Robert DuPlessis, "From Demesne to World-System: A Critical Review of the Literature on the Transition from Feudalism to Capitalism," *Radical History Review* 4 (Winter 1977): 3–41.

40. Keith Nield and John Seed, "Waiting for Gramsci," *Social History* 6 (1981): 209–10.

41. Fred Siegel appears to be making this point when he writes that hegemony implies consent, "something slaves were notoriously unable to give." "The Paternalist Thesis," p. 249; Genovese, *Roll, Jordan, Roll*, pp. 25–26 and passim.

42. For suggestive comments on the relations between hegemony and compliance, see Gareth Stedman Jones, "From Historical Sociology to Theoretical History," *British Journal of Sociology* 27 (1976): 303–4. On the concept of hegemony, see Perry Anderson, "The Antinomies of Antonio Gramsci," *New Left Review* 100 (1976–77), pp. 5–78. The origins of Genovese's approach in the controversies of the 1960s over the issue of slave "accommodation" can be found in Eugene Genovese, "The Legacy of Slavery and the Roots of Black Nationalism," *Studies on the Left* 6 (Nov./Dec. 1966): 3–27.

43. For an installment, see Lee Cary and Marvin Kay, " 'The Planters Suffer Little or Nothing': North Carolina Compensations for Executed Slaves, 1748–1772," *Science and Society* 40 (1976): 288–306; see also Peter Wood, *Black Majority: Negroes in Colonial South Carolina from 1670 through the Stono Rebellion* (New York, 1974); Herbert Gutman, *Black Family*; Michael Mullin, "Introduction," to Mullin, ed., *American Negro Slavery: A Documentary History* (New York, 1976), pp. 1–29.

44. T. J. Jackson Lears, *No Place of Grace: Antimodernism and the Transformation of American Culture, 1880–1920* (New York, 1981), pp. xv, 10.

45. David Montgomery, *Beyond Equality: Labor and the Radical Republicans 1862– 1872* (New York, 1967); Montgomery, *Workers' Control in America: Studies in the History of Work, Technology, and Labor Struggles* (Cambridge, Eng., 1979); Bryan Palmer, "Class, Conception and Conflict: The Thrust for Efficiency, Managerial Views of Labor and the Working Class Rebellion, 1903–22," *Review of Radical Political Economics* 7 (Summer 1975): 31–49; Ronald Schatz, *The Electrical Workers: A History of Labor at General Electric and Westinghouse, 1923–60* (Urbana, Ill., 1983); Harry

Braverman, *Labor and Monopoly Capital: The Degradation of Work in the Twentieth Century* (New York, 1974); Richard Edwards, *Contested Terrain: The Transformation of Work in the Twentieth Century* (New York, 1979); Dan Clawson, *Bureaucracy and the Labor Process* (New York, 1980). For an excellent survey, see Richard Price, "Theories of Labor Process Formation," *Journal of Social History* 18 (1984): 91–110.

46. "Once Upon a Shop Floor: An Interview with David Montgomery," *Radical History Review* 23 (1980): 48–50.

10

Prospects for Marxist History: An Agenda

In all the words that have been expended on the subject of class in American history, a most significant absence is the careful study of class structure. That curious lacuna constantly threatens to vitiate the developing marxist project, and is part of a larger failure to confront the classical themes of historical materialism. This chapter delineates these gaps, and charts the key directions in which marxist history would have to move if its coherence were to be maintained, and its explanatory power effectively exploited. At times it will be necessary to dwell upon marxist work by non-Americans, particularly in the realm of theory, to illustrate the potential for future research using American materials.

Though class activism and class culture have attracted considerable attention, American marxist historians have not investigated with anything like the same vigor the so-called objective dimensions of the phenomenon of class. Labor historians have studied the question of trade union membership and its relation to the size of the working class, however defined, but on the larger issues of class structure little at all has been done by marxists or anybody else, and what has been accomplished fits, like Edward Pessen's ubiquitous work on wealth, into a stratificationist mold.[1] Despite the rise of a new marxist historiography, neither has the relationship between capital formation and working-class composition been extensively studied by American historians. These are peculiar deficiencies in a society characterized by rapid economic, technological, and demographic change that has reflected the changing composition and deployment of capital. Answers to these questions hardly tell us everything we need to know. To deal with "objective" structures in isolation from analysis of the processes of class formation and class action would be to return to a mechanical conception at odds with the notion of classes as historical creations. Attention to structures must be complemented with analysis of the intellectual and political content of class action. Ultimately, historians must take up David Montgomery's exhortation that "the dialogue between social being and social consciousness, which produces the action of the workers themselves," should "move to the center of our attention."[2] Nevertheless, until the structural coordinates of class cohesion and conflict have also received attention from historians, the meaning and limits of class conflict and cultural resistance to capitalism will remain in doubt.

Radical historians have concentrated on an analysis of class which gives special and sometimes exclusive importance to class culture and class activism in an attempt to overturn the stratificationist views so long ascendant in American sociological thinking. But radical history has too often confused stratification and structure. What is noticeable about American class relations is the potential of a structural approach to class suggested by the vast disparities of wealth, income, and employment opportunities which historians and social scientists have repeatedly documented. Even though this data is often cast in a misleading and ahistoric framework, and does not itself establish the existence of classes, the distribution of resources in society can be used to identify and analyze class processes. In a recent study of nineteenth-century Buffalo and of Hamilton, Ontario, Michael Katz observes that while class is indeed a relationship—and hence not amenable to stratificationist analysis—class relations "affect the way in which people behave and the distribution of resources." Katz discovered an association between the analysis of his populations in terms of employer–employee relations, and the "structure of inequality." Class relations have thus been used by Katz to help explain patterns of behavior such as wealth distribution for which statistical evidence is more readily available than for questions of class relations themselves.[3]

POLITICAL ECONOMY: THE ANALYSIS OF CAPITAL

Just as clearly, class must be complemented with study of the economic processes of the capitalist system which are connected with class but cannot be reduced to class struggles at the level of the workplace, trade unions, or electoral politics. Marxism requires this emphasis, though it is often forgotten that marxism is a theory of *capital* as well as class. Marx's major achievement was in the area of economics, and since Marx's time, there have been many other marxists who have contributed to the development of a marxian economic theory which is historically grounded. The path-breaking contributions of Marx in this regard have been continuously modified and specific predictions discarded, but the tradition of political economy remains as a theory in which "markets distribute income according to relative power," not "efficiency."[4] Profound differences exist within this tradition, of course. Orthodox marxist economists continue to emphasize the falling rate of profit and the expropriation of surplus value, while among the revisionists are the members of the political economy group associated with the *Cambridge Journal of Economics* in England. These economists concentrate on questions of distribution, argue that surplus value is a metaphysical concept, and question the logic of the argument that rates of profit tend to fall under capitalist conditions of production.[5] The work of Joan Robinson, Piero Sraffa, and others connected with the Cambridge group has resulted in controversial revisions of marxist shibboleths, but more important has been the impact of this work upon the now shaky edifice of neoclassical economics. As Edward Nell points out in his summary of these developments, "it is now widely agreed," in the light of the studies of political economy of capital by the Cambridge group, that "neo-Classical capital theory is defective."[6] Yet it is precisely the same neoclassical assumption that "markets allocate scarce resources according to relative efficiency" which underlies the contribution of econometric historians Fogel and Engerman in *Time on the Cross*, and which has become so fashionable in departments of economics in the United States. Econometric critics of Fogel and Engerman have usually proceeded from the same technical and conceptual assumptions, and have reinforced the increasingly prestigious and analytical method of econometrics while censoring slipshod use of the conceptual apparatus. Historians have, on the other hand, concentrated on the handling of evidence and context in *Time on the Cross*, and have raised echoes of old and unprofitable debates about the possibility of an objective and scientific history. The underlying assumptions of motivation and causality have gone largely untouched. Even some marxists have been inclined to reduce slave–master relations to the cash nexus of marketplace behavior, though it is also true that some of the most penetrating critiques of faulty econometric assumptions have come from marxist historians.[7]

If the controversy over the economics of slavery illustrates the value of remaining in touch with the traditions of economic analysis contained in political economy, it is nevertheless easy to see why marxist historians so often do not pursue the issues which that tradition raises. Much of the new work in political economy is highly technical because it is locked into specific debates generated by the discourse of modern economic theory, and its methodology is often heavily quantitative. This technical gulf characterizes marxian economics almost as much as its conventional equivalent, and reflects deep disciplinary divisions, particularly the institutional division of the historical profession into history and economic history, and the assimilation of the latter to economic theory. It is important that economic history be reclaimed and integrated into an analysis of social change in which power relations, not the abstract concept of free markets inhabited by *homo economicus*, is the central organizing principle. The prospects for such a reintegration have improved a little as a result of the work done on the economics of the advanced capitalist societies and on underdevelopment by marxists associated with the Union for Radical Political Economics (URPE) in the United States.[8] That work demonstrates a commitment to the study of large issues of economic policy, the critique of neoclassical economic theory, and the development of dynamic theories of capitalist development. Unfortunately, most of the research generated by radical political economy has been more useful in developing critiques of mainstream social science than in stimulating empirical studies of marxist history. The historical material produced by the Union's *Review of Radical Political Economics* usually consists of review articles and syntheses in which detailed historical works are employed to illuminate the theoretical concerns of political economy. Where original analysis has been attempted by those associated with URPE, as in the case of economist Daniel D. Luria's study of social mobility and home ownership in turn of the century Boston, or Bowles and Gintis' survey of the relationship between political economy and education, the result has often seemed to historians to be flawed by an economistic bias.[9]

It would be a shame, however, if the failure of political economists to explore the cultural dimensions of their analyses of class actions led historians to repudiate the entire project of political economy. The theoretical insights of radical economics can be used to complement and perhaps integrate the studies of worker activism. In *Segmented Work, Divided Workers*, Michael Reich, Richard Edwards, and David Gordon attempt to do just that, to provide an account of how capitalism operates to structure the labor process. They seek to link the successive transformations in the labor market and in the organization of work with recurrent crises in the process of capital accumulation that have accompanied the long swings of expansion and stagnation in the capitalist world economy. Within the framework of the exploration, consolidation, and decay of different structures of accumulation, their historical analysis seeks to reformulate United States labor history around three periods: an initial proletarianization from the 1820s to the late nineteenth century, the homogenization of the labor force through the wresting of control of labor processes from skilled workers from the 1890s to World War II, and the increasing segmentation of the work force that involves more complex structures of labor–management cooperation, and bureaucratic and corporate deployment of job hierarchies and skills.[10]

This is not the place to assess the value of their model for analyzing the labor process, but their approach is stimulating enough because it does offer a manageable way of exploring empirically the limits of class activism. Too often we are told by radical or marxist historians that workers in various situations have been expressing class cohesion, only to find that these same manifestations of worker solidarity repeatedly failed to survive over long periods. Emphasis upon the relationship between working-class activity and the strategies of capital in the organization of work allows us to appreciate the structural conditions of class cohesion. Daniel Walkowitz's study of the working-class community in Troy, New York, illustrates the point. The demise of Troy's iron industry undermined the solidarity of the working-class community, and the economic shift reflected the tendency of Troy iron manufacturers to relocate their plants to escape from the pressures exerted by Troy trade unionists. As Walter Licht remarks, "class conflict, in effect, broke class cohesion."[11] On a larger scale, we are all familiar with the relocation in the late nineteenth century of a large part of the New England cotton textile industry to the south, and in contemporary America with the general decline of the industrial northeast and the emergence of new tertiary industries in the southwestern United States. These developments have not just happened through the workings of the invisible hand. They have been the product of political decisions, state support, and management strategies as well as technological change which in turn has been closely related to the changing organization of work and production. A convincing account of American class relations will not be possible until the new working-class history has been more effectively linked with these structural conditions.

Much unexploited evidence is available in business archives to provide the empirical foundation for a historical study of these processes. Paysheets, directors' reports, rule books, company letterbooks, and the like would allow historians to investigate the structure of the work force in various industries and to link those structures with worker activity. Occasionally these records are effectively employed, as in Dublin's study of the Lowell mill girls or Walter Licht's monograph on nineteenth-century railroad workers. More often, these sources have been neglected in favor of newspaper accounts and the decennial population schedules of the United States census. The neglect stems in part from the fragmentary character of the records which document the relations of management and labor in the workplace, but also reflects the disciplinary gulf separating labor history from business history. Gordon, Reich, and Edwards believe that marxist political economy can help bridge the gap. Through the development of middle-range theories of the labor process, they hope to link the grand and synoptic theories of traditional marxist accounts of capitalism with the empirical studies of the labor historians.[12]

BASE AND SUPERSTRUCTURE

This emphasis upon structures, particularly economic structures, is sure to elicit once more the old images of a mechanical marxism. The nineteenth-century charge that Marx and Engels subordinated the superstructure of philosophy, culture, politics, religion, and government to the economic base produced some important qualifications from Engels, but the difficulty remained unresolved in the minds of many critics. Raymond Williams has attempted to surmount this difficulty by recasting the notion of "base" to include all of the productive aspects of society. The productive base ought not, he believes, be limited to the study of basic industry or productive labor, and he thinks it legitimate to talk about cultural as well as economic production. It would be possible under this formula to think of all human activity as some kind of production or reproduction, and as part of the base of a society's social organization.[13] This is a useful formulation, because it is thoroughly grounded in the study of *practice*—the real social conditions under which a society's forms are produced and reproduced. And it is equally clear that Williams' rendition of this materialist formula is extremely subtle, depicting the base not in static but in dynamic terms involving the possibility of real contradictions, and in understanding the notion of determination as setting broad limits to human actions.

But the question remains: what aspects of the productive processes are dominant or determinant? Or to put the matter in a broader way, what is the relationship between the different subsystems of production and reproduction? Williams himself is unhappy with the strategy of abandoning the notion that some things are truly derivative and superstructural. Certain kinds of ideologies and political activity on the surface of a society's history would, he feels, still be better regarded as determined and superstructural. If this principle were abandoned, he believes marxism would lose entirely its distinctiveness as a social theory.[14] It is undoubtedly true that marxist theory has traditionally held that the ways in which societies have organized for the purposes of production and reproduction have determined in some form or other the structure of their ideological, cultural, and political systems. It is equally true that this principle must be adhered to if marxism is to retain its intellectual coherence. Yet it is not at all clear how or why Williams is able to draw the line between the different sorts of activity he calls superstructural and those he does not.

Louis Althusser provides another answer to this recurrent difficulty. When pressed, marxists have usually adopted the formula of Engels, and insisted that the material base of society was determinant "in the last instance." The French philosopher agrees with Engels' terminology, but he has reformulated the notion in an important way, though one which still leaves considerable problems for marxist historians. Althusser has pointed out that there is never a pure contradiction between labor and capital, or between the forces and relations of production. The process of class struggle is always "overdetermined" because it is embodied in particular "social formations" that have existed historically. He has emphasized the "relative autonomy" of the different levels in society, and has argued for a distinction between the determination of the economic structure and the dominance of other levels which are selected by the economic in particular historical epochs.[15]

Althusser's solution, as developed by such sympathetic English interpreters as Robin Blackburn and Gareth Stedman Jones, is probably the most interesting and innovative attempt to solve this old and difficult problem. Their notion of the marxist totality as "a complex structure of objective and specific levels that are not equivalent and are relatively autonomous within a historically determined social formation" is an impressive attempt to think through the structure of societies in a way that is neither purely functional nor based on the kinds of simplistic analogies that have been common in bourgeois social science.[16] But the formula is less useful for explaining historical change at the level on which most historians, including most marxists, operate. As Williams points out, marxism has typically been "very much better at distinguishing the large features of different epochs of society . . . than at distinguishing between different phases" of historical epochs, and "different moments within the phases: that true historical process which demands a much greater precision and delicacy of analysis than the always striking epochal analysis which is concerned with main lineaments and features."[17] For marxist historians it is important to be able to specify historical *process*, and to be able to say not merely that culture, ideology, or politics is relatively autonomous, but to demonstrate in historical situations what were the real structures of social relations in a particular society over time. Nothing, it seems, can substitute for empirical investigation informed by marxist categories to elicit those changing relationships.

THE PROBLEM OF MATERIALISM AND MARXISM

When they investigate these relations, marxists will need to focus, more than in the past, upon ''material life.'' It has not been fashionable until very recently to reassert the materialist character of marxism, because such an assertion is bound to be taken for a ''vulgar'' or ''economistic'' reading of marxist principles. Yet there can be, as the work of Raymond Williams demonstrates, a materialistic history of culture or ideology without reducing that history to a technological determinism or to a simplified and mechanical evocation of class forces. Nor does materialism involve the search for ''economic causes'' in the manner of positivism, but rather the analysis of the processes of material production and reproduction, and their contradictions, as they have been experienced historically in the social relations of everyday life.

One does not deny the existence or importance of ideas by arguing, as marxists have traditionally done, that ideas are the products of thinking heads, and that human history therefore remains fundamentally concerned with material context, its determinations, and its transformations. Yet marxists have, to their loss, usually concentrated on the processes of transformation and have left to others the pursuit of the determinations of material life. (There is, for example, little marxist work on the environmental dimensions of the growth of industrial capitalism in the nineteenth century and beyond.) That is why all historians, including marxists, have much to learn from the attention of *Annales* scholars to such questions as geography, climate, disease, and death. But that is merely to say that marxists may not have been sufficiently materialist in the past. In addition to the *Annales* emphasis upon structures, marxists need to discuss the ways in which material restraints have been experienced in class settings according to the forms of social organization and differentiation. (Work on the spatial dimensions of class struggle is one but by no means the only aspect of this question.) A marxist approach to impinging material conditions ought not to take the form of a simple geographic or climatic determinism, but rather treat the relation between material constraints and material transformation.[18]

Marxists are already beginning to give the question of materialism increasing attention. The English philosopher G. A. Cohen's defense of a materialist reading of Marx's work and of the central place of productive forces in marxist theory is one recent example. Some historians, too, have been prepared to defend a materialist interpretation as Steve Hochstadt has done in an important article criticizing the neglect of demography and statistical methods by some marxists. Wal Seccombe has shown how analysis of the processes of reproduction—

fertility, family structure, and the like—can complement analysis of the mode of production, and has argued for a reconceptualization of marxist historical analysis around the interaction of economic and demographic systems and processes. Such an approach transcends the traditional marxist analysis of reproduction as derivative of the economy, and is best understood as a materialist approach in the larger sense rather than a strictly class approach.[19]

But before we assume uncritically the validity of this new tendency, it is worth observing that "materialism" can easily become—like Gramscian notions of hegemony, structuralism, or any other conceptual apparatus—a mere mechanical invocation rather than a truly creative approach to historical theory. A historian cannot help but observe the close correlation between the materialist tendency and the larger economic and cultural situation of western capitalism. In the 1960s the emphasis in marxism was very much upon an elaboration of the subjective traditions of western marxism: that is, the marxism that evolved in the western European context in the aftermath of the failure of the Bolshevik revolution to spread to the so-called advanced capitalist countries. These variants of marxism have, as we have seen, been imported into the United States, particularly since the New Left period, and produced a flowering of marxist studies in the 1970s. But the character of marxism is constantly changing. The economic crisis of western capitalism and the failure of the cultural radicalism of the 1960s brought increasing emphasis upon larger structures and the economic determinants of history. The vogue for Althusser reflected this tendency, though ironically structuralism is itself now being denounced as an idealist or theoretical movement, and contrasted unfavorably with materialism. No one can guarantee, however, that a materialist approach will provide the key to a reinvigoration of marxism any more than the other approaches already discussed. No tendency can be considered above the flow of history and entirely independent of historical conditions.

Already Cohen's materialist insistence on the primacy of productive forces has prompted a rejoinder from other marxists emphasizing the social relations of production, and hence class struggle. If productive forces are indeed to be given primacy, then why is it that societies with similar technological organization of the labor process often display considerable variation in their social, political, and ideological structures? Nor does an excessive emphasis on productive forces explain the transitions from feudalism to capitalism and from capitalism to socialism which have taken particular routes in different societies. Only an analysis of class capacities to generate the changes which will serve rational class interests, argue American critics Andrew Levine and Erik Olin Wright, can explain those changes and provide the underpinning of marxist political action. But they correctly concede their indebtedness to Cohen for his lucid and vigorous statement of the materialist position, and agree it is essential that such a creative dialogue between marxism's competing tendencies be kept open if further conceptual advance is to be achieved.[20]

THE STATE

One further topic has been a part of the marxist intellectual inheritance, but has not as yet produced any significant body of research in American history. The role of the state has always been an important part of marxist theory, but until fairly recently, the quality and quantity of marxist theoretical work on the subject left much to be desired. Both Marx and Lenin had a good deal to say about state power in the context of the classical marxist theory of revolution, but Marx did not systematically work through his thoughts on the subject, and Lenin's work was so closely bound up with the specifics of the Russian revolutionary conjuncture that its relevance to historians of vastly different historical experiences is questionable. Orthodox marxist theory and propaganda shared the crude tendency to depict the state as either a naked expression of class rule, or a mere epiphenomenon of economic productive processes.[21] In the last twenty years, however, a good deal of more sophisticated thinking and research has emerged in the marxist tradition to treat the nature of the state and its relation to class processes. Some recent theorists have seen the state as a separate force managing the economy and assisting profit maximization; others have depicted the state as expressing complex balances of class forces that cannot be reduced to a blunt exertion of class power but rather suggest the role of the state as a mediating or legitimating process for the system as a whole.[22] We do not need to pick our way through the contentious alternative positions which have arisen from this debate, but marxist historians might well be able to contribute to the discussion by providing the historical dynamic to analyses which are often culturally or temporally limited. Within the discipline of history, the work of E. P. Thompson and his collaborators on the subject of crime and society in Georgian England is an important example of what can be done. In Thompson's *Whigs and Hunters*, and in Douglas Hay's article in *Albion's Fatal Tree*, "Property, Authority, and the Criminal Law," the subtle interplay of coercion and consent organized as the legitimate force of the state constitutes a theme employed to great effect. Against vulgar marxist and structural-functionalist views of the law as superstructure or value system, Thompson and Hay investigate its actual historical operation. They show how the rhetoric of law bound rulers and ruled, though in unequal relationships, and how the law and its traditions could be the subject of contestation between these different social strata.[23]

In American history, calls for critical analysis of the role of the state have come from Alan Dawley, a historian who very much admires Thompson's contribution. Dawley has pointed out that an excessive concentration on working-class activism might produce a romanticized history of workers in the United States. The new studies of workplace conflict and the "world of the worker" need to be related, Dawley believes, to the "structure of power in the modern capitalist state." He specifies for treatment "the vast fortresses positioned atop the workplace—finance, insurance, investment—and the way these are linked by a labyrinth of more or less hidden tunnels" to the various arms of the state bureaucracy and, especially, the "maze of state and local authorities—tax assessors, housing authorities, school boards, local police, and small claims court—those very arms of the state with which workers are in most immediate contact."[24]

This is an imposing program, and its dimensions illustrate the difficulties in conceptualizing state power in the United States and in linking that power to economic and class processes. There is a danger involved in an application of theories of the state derived from contemporary circumstances or from other national historical experiences. One key problem is the use of theories of the state developed for economies and societies where the role of state intervention and the scope and structure of state power have been vastly different. It is not that the state has been unimportant in American history, but as Marx recognized in the *Grundrisse*, its position in the national formation was distinctive in the nineteenth century.[25] Much of American economic and political history from the 1820s to the 1920s has involved either the demolition of particular institutions of state regulation or the persistent invasion of those spheres by private interests. Many functions of government, from concrete economic to symbolic legitimating roles, have been relegated in American historical experience to local government or voluntary action. Even today, in a transformed economy, the dispersal of certain kinds of power over, for example, education, taxes, social welfare, and matters of morality, seems noticeably greater than in many comparable modern societies. Dawley has recognized the importance of the dispersal of power, since a study he has done of antiradical mobilization in the World War I period emphasizes that ideas of a centralized application of state repression cannot comprehend the very localistic sources of popular mobilization in the defense of capitalist "order." Dawley's research program also acknowledges that power has been parceled out among a variety of private community and business groups. He includes, at the end of his catalogue of topics, the role of "schools, churches, mass media, and commercial entertainment in shaping critical assumptions and attitudes towards authority."[26]

Dawley's ordering of this program still suggests, however, a top-down conception of power, and it is clearly influenced by the perception of bureaucratic and corporate power in modern-day America. Moreover, to talk of schools, the churches, and mass media still suggests an institutional manipulation as the prime force. There is still some way to go before American marxism can match Gramsci's notion of the complexities of state power, which went well beyond "a tangible set of institutions" to include "the whole tissue of everyday social relations."[27] In their analysis of the state, American historians of marxist persuasion must come to terms with the concrete level of ordinary experience that has about it an amorphous quality of flux and diversity, which for liberal historians has suggested an absence of any coherence at all.[28] If this perception of pluralism has prompted certain American liberal historians to ask whether any alternative theory can square with evidence and experience, marxist historians could take the same observations to imply the need for ever more complex models to specify the relations between political economy, the cultural context of capitalist social relations, and the particular structures of authority and tradition that constitute the historical inheritance of American civilization. At this quite legitimate level of analysis, marxists must confront the reality of a historical experience not characterized simply by coercive power relations on a crude marxist model, but by the self-regulating power relations of communities and groups as well. Michel Foucault's recent pronouncements that power relations have no center but that power is dispersed almost invisibly in complex societies is a useful insight that marxists may be able to appropriate to complement their own analyses of state power as mentioned in this essay. How the particular structures of civil society in the United States have complicated class relations and how those structures relate to the developing power apparatus of the capitalist state remain important problems facing future marxist analysis and historical research.[29]

INTERNATIONAL COMPARISON AND THE "PECULIARITIES" OF AMERICAN HISTORY

This does not mean that marxism must reinforce traditional liberal concepts of American uniqueness. It simply means that there has been in the United States—as in all countries—a peculiar combination of various elements which has determined the precise shape of American history. Marxist theory can provide ways of investigating the American past that will focus on key issues of social process and structure, but the elements of that theory cannot specify the content of the analysis, nor the ways in which the different elements of a social process have interacted over time. If this point is kept in mind, it is possible to speak of the distinctiveness of American history without succumbing to the delusion that it is therefore incomprehensible in marxist terms.

The peculiarities of the American past can, paradoxically, only make sense through rigorous international comparison. Here too marxism can be very helpful because of its traditional concern for such analysis, and because of the interests of certain modern marxist thinkers. While some notable contributions to comparative analysis have come from nonmarxists, marxists have generally been more alive to the comparative dimensions of human experience than other historians, because their marxism has made comparison necessary. The nature of marxist theory implies consideration of the sweep of human history in a cross-cultural analysis. The long-standing marxist interest in the transition from feudalism to capitalism and the good work that has been done on slavery exemplify the real benefit of this cross-cultural perspective.[30] The recent work of Immanuel Wallerstein could provide further incentives to broaden the scope of analysis beyond the nation-state. The world-systems approach reminds us that the modern nation-state may not be the best framework for comprehending the long-term dynamics of capitalism, nor its regional diversities. Gabriel Kolko's work, too, has in a more specific way been notable for its attention to the connections of international and domestic labor markets, and to the international ramifications of the contradictions and crises that plague modern American "political capitalism." While these transnational approaches are most notably useful in analyzing foreign relations, labor, and the crises in the economy, there is also some indication that national boundaries are ceasing to define the historical problematic in women's history, where cross-cultural analysis of women's subordination has proceeded apace. It is possible, using these and other insights derived from marxism, to analyze the American past without taking the national historical unit as an unexamined assumption.[31] Marxists can thereby contribute to the emerging body of work on international history that includes the United States in its frame of reference. An international analysis as conceived here would hardly eclipse either national or comparative frameworks, but there is nothing to prevent these modes of analysis from being employed in a complementary fashion. Nor would marxists be the only contributors to this field, since a number of distinguished nonmarxist examples could easily be provided, but the marxists' intellectual inheritance and their particular theoretical interests make international history an obvious and valuable extension of the marxist project.[32]

None of this amounts to a coherent and comprehensive marxist interpretation, nor to a marxist system in which the particulars of history are routinely slotted. The kind of unified synthesis which liberal history once provided and which some American marxist writers of the 1930s appeared to advocate is no longer a realistic possibility, nor is it intellectually defensible. To offer such a completed alternative to the fragmentation of current American historiography would be to deny the whole movement of modern historiography and methodology which has been toward the concept of a historical tradition that is being constantly recreated. To erect an a priori system of marxist interpretation to be applied to American history would also be at odds with the active, developing, unfinished, and persistently contentious character of a marxist tradition which currently engages so many writers precisely because it does represent the possibility of an open-ended and variable empirical inquiry. Yet the heuristic potential of this theoretical invigoration is now threatened by a resurgence of circumstances that lie outside the domain of routine academic controversies. Marxist history is not seriously threatened because it has been tried and found wanting, since relatively little serious marxist work has yet been done of a kind which has distinguished French, British, and other European historiographies in the last twenty years. Rather, it is external political and institutional circumstances which command attention now.

NOTES

1. Edward Pessen, "Social Structure and Politics in American History," *American Historical Review* 87 (1982): 1290–1325, illustrates the point and constitutes an impressive bibliography. Useful for the trade unions and the working class are Melvyn Dubofsky, "Workers' Movements in North America, 1873–1970: A Preliminary Analysis," in Immanuel Wallerstein, ed., *Labor in the World's Social Structure* (Beverly Hills, Calif.,

1983), pp. 22–43; and Albert Syzmanski, "Trends in the American Class Structure," *Socialist Revolution* 10 (July/Aug. 1972): 101–22.

2. David Montgomery, "Introduction," to Wallerstein, ed., *Labor in the World's Social Structure*, p. 16.

3. Michael Katz, "Social Class in North American Urban History," *Journal of Interdisciplinary History* 11 (1981): 579–605.

4. Edward Nell, "Economics: The Revival of Political Economy," in Robin Blackburn, ed., *Ideology in Social Science: Readings in Critical Social Theory* (Glasgow, 1972), pp. 76–95, esp. p. 95.

5. Ibid. A compendium of these views, but sympathetic to the Cambridge School, is Karl Kuhne, *Economics and Marxism*, 3 vols. (London, 1979 ed.).

6. Nell, "Economics," pp. 84, 95.

7. This position was well represented at the Mathematical Social Sciences Board—University of Rochester Conference, "*Time on the Cross*: A First Appraisal," 24–26 Oct. 1974. Some of the papers were printed in Paul David et al., *Reckoning with Slavery: A Critical Study in the Quantitative History of American Negro Slavery* (New York, 1976). The econometric contributions to this volume follow the analysis referred to in the text. For marxist responses, see Elizabeth Fox-Genovese, "Poor Richard at Work in the Cotton Fields: A Critique of the Psychological and Ideological Presuppositions of *Time on the Cross*," *Review of Radical Political Economics* 7 (Fall 1975): 67–83; Eugene Genovese, "A Reply to Criticism," *Radical History Review* 4 (Winter 1977): 105, 110 n. 8; Sarah Elbert, "Good Times on the Cross: A Marxian Review," *Review of Radical Political Economics* 7 (Fall 1975): 55–66.

8. See Union for Radical Political Economics, *Review of Radical Political Economics* (1969–   ).

9. Daniel D. Luria, "Trends in the Determinants Underlying the Process of Social Stratification: Boston, 1880–1920," *Review of Radical Political Economics* 6 (Summer 1974): 174–93; Luria, "Wealth, Capital, and Power: The Social Meaning of Home Ownership," *Journal of Interdisciplinary History* 7 (1978): 261–82; Samuel Bowles and Herbert Gintis, *Schooling in Capitalist America: Educational Reform and the Contradictions of Economic Life* (New York, 1976). For criticisms, see David Hogan, "Education and the Making of the Chicago Working Class, 1880–1930," *History of Education Quarterly* 18 (1978): 227–70; Michael Katz, Michael J. Doucet, and Mark J. Stern, *The Social Organization of Early Industrial Capitalism* (Cambridge, Mass., 1982), pp. 413–14.

10. David Gordon, Richard Edwards, and Michael Reich, *Segmented Work, Divided Workers: The Historical Transformation of Labor in the United States* (Cambridge, Eng., 1982).

11. Walter Licht, "Labor and Capital and the American Community," *Journal of Urban History* 7 (1981): 231; Daniel J. Walkowitz, *Worker City, Company Town: Iron and Cotton-Worker Protest in Troy and Cohoes, New York, 1855–85* (Urbana, Ill., 1979).

12. Walter Licht, *Working for the Railroad: The Organization of Work in the Nineteenth Century* (Princeton, N.J., 1983), pp. 273–310; Thomas Dublin, *Women at Work: The Transformation of Work and Community in Lowell, Massachusetts, 1826–1860* (New York, 1979), pp. 209–49, for the methodology and sources; Gordon, Edwards, and Reich, *Segmented Work*, p. 22.

13. Raymond Williams, "Base and Superstructure in Marxist Cultural Theory," *New Left Review* 82 (1973): 3–16.

14. Ibid., p. 7.

15. Friedrich Engels to J. Bloch, 21 Sept. 1890, in Karl Marx and Friedrich Engels, *Selected Works*, 3 vols. (Moscow, 1966), 3: 487–89; Louis Althusser, *For Marx*, trans. Ben Brewster (New York, Vintage ed., 1970), pp. 111–13. "From the first moment to the last, the lonely hour of the 'last instance' never comes" (p. 113). See also Jerzy Topokski, "Methodological Problems of the Application of Marxist Theory to Historical Research," *Social Research* 47 (1980): 463–64.

16. The complex notion of structural causality, on which the Althusserian analysis is grounded, receives detailed exposition in Robin Blackburn and Gareth Stedman Jones, "Louis Althusser and the Struggle for Marxism," in Dick Howard and Karl Klare, eds., *The Unknown Dimension: European Marxism since Lenin* (New York, 1972), pp. 370–72. Structural causality represents an attempt to conceive the effects of the whole on the parts of the social structure, where the structure represents its effects, "the structure being merely a specific combination of its peculiar elements and nothing beyond its effects" (p. 372). The concept thus differs from both the positivist concept of a transitive, mechanistic sum of its parts, and the Hegelian concept of an "essence" in which "the elements of the whole are . . . no more than its phenomenal expressions" (p. 371). Using the concept of structural causality, Stephen Resnick and Richard Wolff define "overdetermination" for their purpose as "each class position exists only as the locus of effects exerted by all other class and nonclass processes constituting [the social] formation." Resnick and Wolff, "A Reformulation of Marxian Theory and Historical Analysis," *Journal of Economic History* 42 (1982): 53–59, quote at p. 57.

17. Williams, "Base and Superstructure," p. 8.

18. Besides the contributions of *Annales* historians discussed in Chapters 1 and 7, see Sebastiano Timpanaro, *On Materialism* (London, 1975); Raymond Williams, "Problems of Materialism" *New Left Review* 109 (1978): 3–17; and "Editors' Introduction," *Radical History Review* 21 (1979): 3–10.

19. G. A. Cohen, *Karl Marx's Theory of History: A Defence* (London, 1978); Steve Hochstadt, "Social History: A Materialist View," *Social History* 7 (1982): 75–83; Wal Seccombe, "Marxism and Demography," *New Left Review* 137 (1983): 22–47.

20. Andrew Levine and Erik Olin Wright, "Rationality and Class Struggle," *New Left Review* 123 (1980): 47–68.

21. V. I. Lenin, "The State and Revolution," in V. I. Lenin, *Selected Works*, 2 vols. (Moscow, 1952 ed.), 2: 199–325.

22. Bob Jessop, "Recent Theories of the Capitalist State," *Cambridge Journal of Economics* 1 (1977): 353–73; Nicos Poulantzas, *Political Power and Social Classes* (London, 1973); Erik Olin Wright, *Class, Crisis and the State* (London, 1978); James O'Connor, *The Fiscal Crisis of the State* (New York, 1973); Alan Wolfe, *The Limits of Legitimacy* (New York, 1977).

23. Douglas Hay et al., *Albion's Fatal Tree: Crime and Society in Eighteenth-Century England* (New York, 1975 ed.), pp. 17–63; E. P. Thompson, *Whigs and Hunters: The Origins of the Black Act* (London, 1975). For a fatally flawed attempt at refuting the thrust of these studies, see John H. Langbein, "Albion's Fatal Flaws," *Past and Present* 98 (1983): 96–120. In *Roll, Jordan, Roll: The World the Slaves Made* (New York, 1974), Eugene Genovese developed an analysis similar to Thompson's, but as has already been implied, the content of power in slave society was very different from that in Georgian England, and slaves did not have the rights of free-born Englishmen.

24. Alan Dawley, "American Workers/Workers America: A Review of Recent Works

by David Brody and James Green,'' *International Labor and Working Class History* 23 (Spring 1983): 42; Dawley, ''E. P. Thompson and the Peculiarities of the Americans,'' *Radical History Review* 19 (1978–1979): 57.

25. Karl Marx, *Grundrisse*, ed. Martin Nicolaus (New York, 1973), p. 884.

26. Alan Dawley, ''The State Made Visible,'' paper presented at the Third Annual North American Labor History Conference, Wayne State University, 8 Oct. 1981; Dawley, ''Workers America,'' p. 42. Dawley's ''E. P. Thompson,'' pp. 52–57, is more suggestive in its attention to the pecularities of state power and cultural context in the larger sweep of American history.

27. Keith Nield and John Seed, ''Waiting for Gramsci,'' *Social History* 6 (1981): 226. The closest approximation to the tissue of relations that constitutes the state in actual practice can be found in Thompson, *Whigs and Hunters*. See pp. 258–69 for his conclusions.

28. Ronald Walters, ''Signs of the Times: Clifford Geertz and Historians,'' *Social Research* 47 (1980): 551.

29. Michel Foucault, *Power/Knowledge: Selected Interviews and Other Writings, 1972–1977*, ed. Colin Gordon (New York, 1980). For a sympathetic analysis of points of convergence between Foucault's recent preoccupation with power analysis and various strands within modern marxist theory, see Carla Pasquinelli, ''Sex, Power, and Knowledge,'' *Radical History Review* 22 (1979–1980): 174–79. The divergence of marxism and the work of Foucault is of course not to be denied. That divergence centers around the concern of marxists to distinguish qualitative and quantitative differences in power relations, and to provide explanations of changes in the domains of political and economic power.

30. Rodney Hilton, ed., *The Transition from Feudalism to Capitalism* (London, 1976 ed.); Eugene Genovese, *The World the Slaves Made: Two Essays in Interpretation* (New York, 1969), part 1, is a good example of the comparative insights that have sometimes been stimulated by marxist debates. Carl Degler, *Neither Black Nor White: Slavery and Race Relations in Brazil and the United States* (New York, 1971); and George Fredrickson, *The Arrogance of Race: Patterns of Inequality in American and South African History* (New York, 1981), are representative of liberal scholarship.

31. Immanuel Wallerstein, *The Modern World-System: Capitalist Agriculture and the Origins of the European World-Economy in the Sixteenth Century* (New York, 1974); *Review: A Journal of the Fernand Braudel Center for the Study of Economies, Historical Systems, and Civilizations* (Binghamton, N.Y., 1977–   ); Gabriel Kolko, *Main Currents in Modern American History* (New York, 1976), pp. 29, 68, 201–2; Kate Young, Carol Wolkowitz, and Roslyn McCullagh, eds., *Of Marriage and the Market: Women's Subordination in International Perspective* (London, 1981).

32. In this genre of international history, see, for example, David Brion Davis, *The Problem of Slavery in Western Culture* (Ithaca, N.Y., 1966); Davis, *The Problem of Slavery in the Age of Revolution* (Ithaca, N.Y., 1975); Robert Kelley, *The Transatlantic Persuasion: The Liberal Democratic Mind in the Age of Gladstone* (New York, 1969). George Fredrickson's critical remarks on the latter volume in ''Comparative History,'' in Michael Kammen, ed., *The Past Before Us: Contemporary Historical Writing in the United States* (Ithaca, N.Y., 1980), p. 471, are, however, accurate.

11

Politics and Practice in Contemporary Marxist History

American marxism has always been a product of a recognizeably American set of conditions and experiences, despite the attempts of certain commentators to assert its exclusively foreign content. Since recent American marxist history has taken shape within a distinctive milieu, it is reasonable to suppose that its future is also bound up with certain practical questions of a political and institutional kind that are defined in large measure by American circumstances. Some of these conditions are shared by marxists elsewhere, but their specific combination in the American case demands attention here. These influences include the still very small and marginal position of marxist scholarship in the professional environment of American historiography, the tendency toward excessive factionalism and internal disputation, the cultural and political hostility toward marxist concepts and practice in the larger society, and the absence of a strong working-class political movement or labor agitation.

The challenges posed by the external political and cultural environment are enormous. From one point of view the marxist history which did begin to appear in the 1970s could be seen as an elitist phenomenon, evidenced only in intellectual circles. The general public seemed as hostile to marxism as it had since the beginnings of the cold war. The brief détente under Nixon and Ford was quickly replaced during the late 1970s by a major deterioration in United States–Soviet relations of which the Reagan administration's foreign policies represent only an accentuation. Publicly, it is as difficult as ever to say anything mildly favorable about the Soviet Union without being branded by radicals and conservatives alike as Stalinist. Even within intellectual communities the swing to the right has been manifest. The erosion of the liberal tradition may have seemed, for a time, to work in favor of more radical analysis, but on a popular and intellectual level conservative and antimarxist views have taken on a new virulence. The intellectual polarization that parallels the political conjuncture was seen clearly between 1978 and 1981 in the pages of *Marxist Perspectives*, which devoted a section to views of marxism from "the other shore." Recently, too, a conservative historians' newsletter has been announced, and a new journal edited by a number of self-proclaimed conservatives has appeared under the title *Continuity*. One key focus of the conservative historians' work so far has been, as in Aileen Kraditor's most recent book, an attack on the alleged biases in recent marxist and radical historiography.[1]

While many American historians were not prepared any longer to dismiss marxism by definition, the influential liberal center of the profession still displayed at times, in prominent individuals and publications, a skepticism toward marxist concepts and the marxist contribution to the revival of American scholarship. A liberal historian like Carl Degler still tended to see marxism in rigid terms, and identified the tradition with its economic determinist caricatures. Only to the extent that marxists departed from a purely economic and class analysis and recognized the importance of other factors did they tend to receive accolades from mainstream American historians. Scholarly discussion still revealed grave ignorance or neglect of such modern marxist innovators as Gramsci, despite the publicity given to Gramsci's work by Genovese. American historians still tended, moreover, to dismiss marxism as incompatible either with the facts or with the anti-ideological pragmatism of "the American mind."[2]

The impressive achievements of a handful of highly successful marxist historians and the undoubted quality of much other marxist scholarship does not alter the strategic assessment: American marxist history remains numerically insignificant in comparison with the volume of history produced in the social science or empiricist genres, and in the liberal progressive tradition generally. The record expressed in terms of what came before looks good, but compared with other disciplines, the advances made by American marxist historians cannot be stated without major reservations. Eugene Genovese has ventured the opinion that "we have gone much further in history" in the direction of a marxist influence in historiography "than in other disciplines," but a comparative appraisal of the place of marxism in the larger perspective of higher education does not support this sanguine estimation. There is no radical political caucus within the professional historical associations, whereas sociology has two marxist or quasi-marxist sections. In economics, a powerful radical group withdrew from the American Economic Association to form the Union for Radical Political Economics "which has its own journal and holds its own annual conferences." The University of Massachusetts–Amherst has established through the hiring of leading marxist economists "what is probably the most comprehensive Marxist-oriented graduate program in the country." History does have its Radical Historians group, but its members are mostly people on the fringe of academia, either graduate students, unemployed historians, or untenured faculty. *Marxist Perspectives*, the leading marxist journal for history and related disciplines, collapsed in 1981 due to internal dissension. *The Review of Radical Political Economics* had been running for seven years before the radical historians succeeded in establishing their journal, the *Radical History Review*, in 1975, while

Insurgent Sociologist had over two thousand subscriptions and this had grown to around three thousand by 1977. The economists were also extremely well organized and articulate, and they seemed to command a measure of popular support which was lacking among historians. The Union for Radical Political Economics grew rapidly in membership from 821 at its inception in 1969 to 2178 by 1975. Nor did anything in the historical profession compare with *The Capitalist System*, edited by Richard Edwards and others in 1972. As a marxist work, this book's analysis was pervasively historical even though it was written by economists. By 1979, it had entirely sold out its first edition of eighty thousand copies. In history, texts with a New Left flavor appeared, like Howard Zinn's *A People's History of the United States*, but nothing specifically marxist. The most prestigious new text of the period, *The Great Republic*, was very much within the liberal tradition.[3]

The explanation for the slower pace of radical and marxist scholarship in history, relative to social science disciplines, is probably tied up with the reproduction of forms of positivism and empiricism in American historical practice. Though American social scientists of all types were strongly influenced by empiricist notions of reality, the disciplines of sociology, anthropology, and economics were nevertheless fundamentally conceptual and theoretical in character. They simply could not proceed very far without theorizing. An anthropologist, for example, faced with thousands of villages to choose from, simply had to put a premium on methodological construction and theoretical significance, even if these justifications for fieldwork were made within the context of empiricist assumptions about the nature of reality and human perception of that reality. Similarly, the impulse to prediction and control which had long informed economics involved of necessity a level of abstraction absent from most traditional historical scholarship. As a radical sociologist, Martin Shaw, has noted, what defines sociology (and economics) is the "carving out of a structure of ideas, a context of argument. . . . Within this framework, empirical study is validated. Only by endowing his work with 'theoretical' significance can the empirical researcher aspire to a place in the upper echelons of the profession."[4] In contrast, the discipline of history from its inception as a professional subject has been dominated for a variety of reasons by empiricist and positivistic conceptions, and has allowed only a limited role for theorizing. Theory was employed by the liberal historians, but essentially to provide new interpretive power to the traditional intellectual synthesis, not to replace it. For these reasons, a theory like marxism with a legacy of claims to systematic knowledge could make little headway in history, in comparison with its influence in related disciplines.

The problem of numbers is compounded in some ways by the tendency toward factionalism among American marxist historians. Since the revival of American marxist history began in the 1960s, there have been some legendary examples of fragmentation on the left, most notably the acrimonious exchanges between Herbert Aptheker and Eugene Genovese.[5] Nor is it uncommon for marxist works to receive much more critical treatment in the radical and marxist press than in the regular academic publications. Reviews in the former are frequently more uncharitable, and sometimes embody an unwillingness to recognize that divergent marxist interests may be "complementary rather than inherently oppositional," as one marxist victim of such views lamented.[6] The issue is a complex one, since critique has been a time-honored avenue for the development of marxist theory, and the polemics of today's marxist historians sometimes echo the language and the sentiments of Marx's own polemical attacks on his nineteenth-century opponents. Such disputation can be productive, but frequently the tenor of ideological disputes within academic marxism has been bitter and pointless. A recent example occurred through the debates in England over the alleged culturalism of E. P. Thompson's interpretations and methods. The positions taken in this debate became so polarized that, according to one observer, they "cast a pall" over the question of the role of theory in English marxism. Other scholars found the "antinomies" of the debate totally unacceptable insofar as they forced combatants—and that is what they were—to make spurious and Manichean choices that were inconsistent with any claim to consider marxism as an open and developing tradition.[7]

The sources of ideological disputes within marxism are several and complex. It is difficult to judge whether or not the small scope of the marxist fraternity in the United States has actually accentuated the divisions. While there are some indications that the amount of acrimony rises as the size of the disputing force dwindles, there is also evidence that marxist factionalism has deep roots in both the political character of marxism and the recent assimilation to academia of the marxist left. Because theoretical coherence has always been important within marxism, both in the United States and elsewhere, ideological disputation over that coherence has always been present. Yet the tone and content of that bitterness has recently been exacerbated by the academicization of marxism. "Traditional sectarian tendencies" have been compounded, Dan Clawson believes, by "an uncritical acceptance of the usual ways in which academic careers are built, combined with the geniune insecurity of the positions in which most [radical scholars] find ourselves" in the institutions of academia in the 1980s. Compelled to compete with one another for scarce jobs, marxists are too often reproducing, Clawson suggests, the individualism of academic scholarship at the expense of the development of a cooperative and complementary oeuvre.[8]

Theoretical disputes within American marxism reflect in part the institutional structures of academic life. A prominent example is the controversy between Wallerstein and Genovese discussed in the last chapter. Though this divergence of interpretation has theoretical roots, it also has practical sources in disciplinary divisions. Wallerstein is committed to the interdisciplinary study of civilizations and economies, and has drawn historians, sociologists, and economists together in cooperation. But it is nevertheless true that the main strongholds of world-systems theory have been sociology departments; historians committed to the study of individual countries and particularities have tended to distrust the production of cosmic formulas for interpretation and synthesis of historical realities.

Perhaps this is why Wallerstein's theories have made relatively little progress in the historical discipline, while Genovese's work is so well-known. He does conform much more than Wallerstein to history as historians have known and produced it since the 1880s.

One last set of practical and institutional obstacles to the development of marxist history in the United States must be confronted. This concerns the difficulties of establishing a viable marxist tradition in the absence of a strong working-class movement. Here the British marxist tradition has invariably been invoked to emphasize the weaknesses of American academic marxism. The special issue of the *Radical History Review* devoted to "Marxism and History: The British Contribution" noted that "Marxist history in Britian today is too complex, too vigorous ever to be simply captured and imported into the United States without major distortion and damage."[9] According to the editors, two key differences stemmed from the enduring working-class experience. One was the workers' education movement which had served for more than fifty years as an alternative to elitist universities as a channel for education and research. The other was the mass political movement of the Labour Party, trade unions, and intellectual leftists which had established links between popular and academic history, and posed important theoretical and methodological questions which were not raised until nearly twenty-five years later in the United States.

British marxism is without doubt much more varied and much more entrenched academically than American marxism, which remains still marginal to the historical discipline. Where whole areas of English historiography have been influenced by marxists, most importantly Eric Hobsbawm, Rodney Hilton, Christopher Hill, Thompson, and Raymond Williams, only Eugene Genovese's study of slavery remotely approximates the English case. (And it has always been possible for Americans to think of the south as somehow different and hence the methods and conclusions reached by students of southern history can be still quarantined from general circulation.) British marxism has indeed exhibited in recent decades significant and sophisticated marxist theory. It does have supportive political and social institutions to back it up, including some trade unions and the worker education tradition. There are, too, several vital and long-standing journals that have been influenced by marxism or remain forums for marxist work. *Past and Present* and the *New Left Review* are examples which today are being reinforced by such innovative journals as *Social History* and *History Workshop*. Criticism does in some areas accept marxist or quasi-marxist assumptions, and debate in these cases occurs over which version of marxism to use. In contrast, the American issue is still, marxist historian Mary Nolan notes, whether to use Marx at all.[10]

Yet a direct relationship between marxist history in Britain and the strength of working-class organization and culture has never been demonstrated. Until the 1950s, English marxism was both rudimentary and marginal to British historiography, as the accounts of Raphael Samuel and Gareth Stedman Jones suggest.[11] People's history and labor history there was but not much in the way of *marxist* interpretation. English marxism in historical analysis is *mainly* a product of the period since the early 1950s. What has happened in Britain is the growth of a historical tradition of marxism which has become increasingly detached from practical politics and is the result of wider intellectual and social trends rather than any fixed or derivative relationship with the vitality of working-class culture and politics. Samuel correctly summed up the current historiographical conjuncture when he concluded: "Paradoxically in a period of retreat by the Left, the constituency of socialist historians seems to be growing."[12]

In finding a better explanation, it may be helpful to note that English marxist scholarship began to emerge as a serious force in the late 1950s, and that this coincided with the decline of Britain as an imperial power. The subject of history as we know it took shape in the nineteenth century as an adjunct of nationalism. In Britain and America, the dissemination of historical consciousness was closely tied up with ideas of progress and the extension of liberal freedoms realized in the context of the nation-state. In Britain, history also had an important role in educating colonial administrators, and through the Whig approach, in providing explanations for the progressive spread of British rule. Though Britain has long since ceased to be the dominant world power, and though facile concepts of progress had been challenged by the traumas of World War I, it was not until the shock of decolonization occurred in the post–World War II period that Britain lost its imperial functions, and the whole rationale behind the liberal interpretation was finally torn away. A similar development occurred in France, where military defeat and then decolonization after World War II provided institutional, political, and intellectual conditions spurring the increased legitimacy and then domination of *Annales* within the French historical profession.[13]

Whatever the reason, British historiography has only truly lost its Whiggish cast since the 1950s, and labor and socialist historians are among those who have stood out in their criticism of crude notions of unilinear progress. E. P. Thompson, for example, has found in his account of class conflict in the industrial revolution irreparable cultural loss, centered in the conversion of man from a noneconomic being to a market-oriented one. The pessimism is even more strongly shown in the work of the newer marxist historians influenced by structuralist thinking. They, like Gareth Stedman Jones and Perry Anderson, have openly repudiated ideas of progress and displayed considerable detachment from the liberal institutions of the modern British state.[14]

Besides Britain's imperial decline, an equally important condition of the surge of creative marxist scholarship was the dissension within the British Communist Party which saw many young and able communists like Hill, Thompson, and Hilton repudiate Stalinism after the events of 1956 in Hungary. Spurred by this break, they were able to crystallize their discontent with existing orthodoxy. Thompson in particular set out in new directions to study the cultural dimensions of class. More generally, there was a release of critical energy which produced an enormous increase in the output of socialist scholars, both those who, like Christopher Hill, broke with the party, and those who, like Eric Hobsbawm, did not. By all accounts the Historians' Group of the British Communist Party was not subject to very tight ideological control before 1956, but whatever inhibitions did exist were removed thereafter. As far as the academic prominence of this new marxist history is concerned, it is also of some significance that the university system slowly expanded beyond its older Oxbridge constituency with the building of "redbrick universities." By the 1960s were many universities like Warwick, where E. P. Thompson achieved a more conventional academic influence and eminence through the founding of the Centre for the Study of Social History and the publication, with students and colleagues, of important studies of authority, crime, and popular resistance in eighteenth-century England.[15]

The circumstances which explain the emergence of marxist historical criticism in Britain are equally relevant to understanding the failure of the United States to produce a similarly sophisticated marxism among its historians. To explain the difference, it is necessary to restate the arguments developed in chapter 3. The United States inherited a marxist tradition that was, as in Britain, orthodox and marginal to academic history. But in the United States, the postwar academic and political context was different in three ways. Beardian history had created a unique American formulation in historiography that neutralized the impact of marxism as an intellectual force. This was the process of inoculation. After World War II, accounts would be settled with Beard, not Marx, and a new historiographical compromise would be forged around the selective impact of social science concepts to constitute, in effect, a mutation of the progressive tradition. That was the process of transformation. Then there was the element of exclusion, exerted in a complicated way through the ideological battles of the cold war era. In Britain, McCarthyism existed too, but there it was not a quasi-populist movement of disclosure at the public and political level. Historians were not hauled out, interrogated, intimidated, suspended, and fired, although those marxists who did not already have jobs found it difficult for a time to get them. With the exception of "one or two cases," Eric Hobsbawm recalls, "it was a bad period but it was nowhere near as bad in England as it was in the United States."[16] In the latter case, a smaller and less secure party faced a more overt form of opposition, and the reaction was, almost inevitably, one of purely political self-defense. For American historians committed to the Communist Party as the supposed inheritor of Marx's mantle, like Philip Foner, Herbert Aptheker, and Herbert Morais, there was no course but orthodoxy and self-justification. Those who went through the ordeal of McCarthyism and the rest of the anti-communist hysteria exhibited, as one participant historian has claimed, a "siege mentality." Another witness to the process has testified to a spirit of self-righteousness among party leaders, and still another to a failure of intellectual leadership and creativity. Forced to remain political operatives rather than intellectuals, tacticians rather than theorists, American communists were less favorably placed than their British counterparts to rethink and to build a complex and considered marxist historiography.[17]

The comparative position of the liberal community was also different. If the imperial decline forced a reassessment of British attitudes, the American liberal self-image still held conviction. Not until the Vietnam period of the 1960s did the ascendance of liberal values in historiography begin to shatter, though not necessarily in directions favorable to marxism. At first New Leftists tried, as Staughton Lynd's example testifies, to implement American democratic traditions rather than to transcend their limitations. Yet the decline of the international power of the United States, the enervating experience of Watergate, the shock of the oil and energy crisis, and the festering economic recession together produced among liberals and conservatives as well as radicals gloomy prognostications that American exceptionalism was at an end. Even a cold war intellectual like Daniel Bell has made precisely that claim.[18] Whereas the period from 1945 to the mid–1960s had seen the United States both economically and politically dominant on the world stage, American power has become much more attenuated into the subsequent period.

The movement of New Left activists into academic work, together with the current questioning of America's imperial role and its myths of uniqueness and invincibility, could easily produce a flowering of historical studies in the United States, centered as in the British case around a revival of marxist history. The absence of a growing working-class political movement is not in either case of crucial importance. To argue otherwise would be to reduce historical scholarship to a crude reflection of socioeconomic structures, unmediated by intellectual and theoretical activity. The current state of marxist history is, I would submit, impressive evidence that such an intellectual shift may be taking place.

Yet it is impossible to end on quite so positive a note. There are further ways in which the absence of a working-class political movement needs to be confronted. The first involves the political threat of a swing to the right. I do not mean 1950s style political repression, though signs of resurgent McCarthyism are by no means entirely absent, as observers of the case of Professor Bertell Ollman at the University of Maryland will know.[19] More important is the general contraction of university finances along with the conservative tax revolt and the attempts to reinstate the political and economic panaceas of the era of Calvin Coolidge. In this hostile environment of supply-side economics, there is no need for political repression. Without available jobs, few marxists are likely to penetrate the halls of academe. Moreover, embarrassing radical or socialist history programs in universities can be cut for financial reasons. Another aspect of this problem is the attack of the Reagan administration on the funding of projects in popular and radical history by the National Endowment for the Humanities over the past few years. This attack clearly illustrates, if nothing else does, the practical impossibility of completely divorcing scholarship of a radical kind from the pressures of politics.[20]

Though radical historiography needs the political networks of support that a strong trade union movement and democratic socialist politics could provide, there is little evidence that a revival of strength in the labor movement in the United States is in sight. The decline in the blue-collar component of the working class since the 1950s, the falling level of unionization, and the current dein-dustrialization of certain areas where labor had been strong does not make for confidence. The prospects for a socialist politics probably depend on the extent to which it is possible to convince white-collar workers that their interests lie in the direction of greater collective control over economic processes. Socialist historians have something to contribute to this work in studying and demon-strating the multilevel transformation of modern capitalism. Already available are impressive studies of the spread of consumer capitalism and other aspects of the hegemony of liberal, capitalist values in the twentieth century. Much more, however, could be done to study the historical character of this transfor-mation, and to disseminate the results of such broad-ranging studies to a larger audience.[21]

There is also in the American case the problem presented by a weaker popular tradition of radical and working-class history.[22] British marxist history has drawn upon the rich labor tradition. What is known as people's history (labor history, the history of popular culture, workers, peasants, women, and minorities) has not been dominated by left-liberals as in the United States. Rather, radical and socialist perspectives of various kinds have since the turn of the century been of much greater importance. It is here that labor politics and its ancillary insti-tutions assume crucial importance. In Britain, an oppositional history has been sustained and advanced by the workers' education movement, by such institutions as Ruskin College in Oxford, by a number of trade unions, and by the work of socialist and radical publicists and intellectuals. Marxist theory has played an indispensable role in providing radical impetus and coherence to the very diverse legacy of people's history, but in turn marxist history and theory would be much poorer if its inspirational sources lay only in the academy and the aspirations of individual historians for advancement within it. The sense of belonging and contributing to an oppositional movement that is much larger than the academic community has been very important. It would be impossible to understand, for example, the greatness of E. P. Thompson's *Making of the English Working Class* without taking into account the moral energy which informs its outlook, and the experience in adult education in the Yorkshire region, on which the work so profoundly draws for its inspiration. Raymond Williams is similarly unintel-ligible without an understanding of his roots in regional working-class culture and the perspectives on the world induced by that experience. The moral inspi-ration, the empirical data, and the fresh perspectives of people who have not been in positions of power and who have not espoused the dominant ideology have been repeatedly drawn upon by British marxist historians.

Neither the intellectual tradition of people's history nor the institutions sup-porting it have been entirely absent in the United States. Particularly in the 1930s, American Communist Party historians had begun, under the impetus of the Popular Front, to create a similar tradition of people's history. Also active at that time were the various worker education groups and labor schools affiliated with factions of the Communist Party and the socialists.[23] But these groups and individuals did not have sufficient grounding in the diverse American working class to make more than a superficial impression upon the dominance of the liberals. Then, as we have seen, the nascent oppositional tradition was cut short by the political repression of the McCarthyite period.

Today in the United States, radical historians are doing much valuable work by sponsoring history workshops in industrial towns and through wider use of films, television, photographs, music, and other popular media. The most promising initiative in this field, eagerly awaited by all who are interested in the construction of a working-class historiography, is the "American Working-Class History Project" initiated under the supervision of Herbert Gutman. Local, regional, and national trade union officials have been used in an advisory capacity, and the project itself arose from a series of social history seminars attended by trade union men and women. The materials in preparation are specifically designed "for working adults enrolled in community colleges and labor-studies and trade-union programs." Since the "changing status and behavior of America's working people" is to be set "within the larger context of American economic, social, political, and cultural development," this forthcoming study may well overcome the limitations of radical historiography discussed in an earlier chapter. Especially important are the audiovisual components of the study, and the plans to produce versions of the curricula in languages other than English. Yet still more remains to be done. Nothing comparable exists, for example, to match the efforts of radical economists, sociologists, and political scientists in spreading marxist ideas through such publications as *Dollars and Sense*, published by the Union of Radical Political Economics.[24]

For all these valuable initiatives, the verdict at present must remain a pessimistic one. American leftist historians tend to talk and think in terms of a people's history, without sufficient attention to the other (and equal) part of the British History Workshop movement's enterprise, the development of socialist theory, and its interaction with people's history. This interaction has not been without its persistent tensions in the British case, but it is only out of such tension that creative and cumulative socialist work can arise. Moreover, special circumstances in the American case must be considered by the advocates of people's history. A viable United States equivalent to the British tradition cannot be easily or quickly created. Precisely because liberal history has influenced radical assumptions as well as shaped popular consciousness of history in the United States, the task of marxist historians cannot be equated with strategies associated with British marxism. American marxist historians must concentrate much more than their British counterparts on developing alternative theoretical perspectives and empirical work to contest the continuing prominence of liberal points of view within the historical profession.

This is not to deny the importance of the dimensions of politics, power, and practical activity. For many marxists, including E. P. Thompson, nuclear insanity constitutes the critical case which can and must take precedence over academic or theoretical activity. In the shadow of a nuclear "exterminism," nice historical points assume a ridiculous posture. One can agree with the importance of this issue, while also agreeing with Raymond Williams that such a struggle, divorced from questions of political economy, power, and the analysis of capitalism and imperialism would be theoretically and practically inadequate.[25]

The prospects for a radical oppositional movement to contest the process of capitalist restructuring currently taking place lie beyond the scope of this essay. Marxist historians will presumably want to advance any such movement, if its aims and methods are directed toward the eradication of the manifest injustices inherent in the present world economic order. However politically valuable these sympathies may be, they should not be allowed to preempt the important tasks of historical analysis in the present political conjuncture. Standing back from the ephemera of current trends requires courage in a world in which detachment is considered a luxury. Yet detachment is a necessary prerequisite to a realistic appraisal of the underlying trajectory of capitalist civilization. Marx's famous aphorism in the *Theses on Feuerbach*—"the philosophers have only interpreted the world . . . the point, however, is to change it"—haunts marxist scholarship even today. If Marx's much quoted message has conjured up for some a simple subordination of scientific inquiry to revolutionary goals, the actual process of Marx's own intellectual activity demonstrates a more complex and ambiguous relationship between theory and practice. As Jerrold Seigel's study of Marx's life points out, Marx did not himself produce a single, coherent position on the relation between theory and political action. He wrote both highly concrete and theoretical studies, both revolutionary pamphlets and thoroughly reflective works. These oscillations in his intellectual production reflected the changing political prospects for revolution and capitalism in his own experience.[26]

It is of course as easy to theorize this experience in terms of the relative autonomy of academic practice as it is to denounce a purely academic marxism that pursues its specialty with indifference to the very real processes of class exploitation and struggle in the larger world. But the point remains that marxist historians must either abandon their role in the development of historical understanding to which they have made important contributions, or continue to live with the moral and intellectual dilemmas that Marx's aphorism posed, and with the tensions that Marx's life embodied.

NOTES

1. *Continuity*, ed. by Paul Gottfried of Rockford College, noted in *Marxist Perspectives* 2 (Winter 1979–1980): 6; *Mid-Atlantic Radical Historians' Organization Newsletter*, no. 30, Nov. 1979, p. 3, announcing the *Conservative Historians' Forum*, ed. by Joseph T. Fuhrmann of Murray State University; Aileen S. Kraditor, *The Radical Persuasion: 1890–1917: Aspects of the Intellectual History and the Historiography of Three American Radical Organizations* (Baton Rouge, 1981).

2. Edward Pessen, "Reply," AHR Forum, *American Historical Review* 87 (1982): 1337, for a dismissal of Gramsci; Darrett Rutman, "Comment," AHR Forum, *American Historical Review* 84 (1979): 1324–25, for an invocation of empiricism and pragmatism;

Carl Degler, "Remaking American History," *Journal of American History* 67 (1980): 17.

3. "The Rise of a Marxist Historian: An Interview with Eugene Genovese," *Change* 10 (Nov. 1978): 34; Ellen Schrecker, "The House Marxists," *The Nation* 228 (27 Jan. 1979): 82; Moishe Gonzales, "*Marxist Perspectives* (1978–81) and Beyond," *Telos* 47 (1981): 184; *New York Times*, 1 Feb. 1981, p. 16; *Insurgent Sociologist* 3 (Spring 1973), and 7 (Summer 1977), no pagination, for circulation figures; Richard Edwards, Michael Reich, and Thomas Weisskopf, eds., *The Capitalist System: A Radical Analysis of American Society* (Englewood Cliffs, N.J., 1972); Howard Zinn, *A People's History of the United States* (New York, 1980).

4. Martin Shaw, "The Coming Crisis of Radical Sociology," in Robin Blackburn, ed., *Ideology in Social Science: Readings in Critical Social Theory* (Glasgow, 1972), p. 33.

5. Eugene Genovese, "The Legacy of Slavery and the Roots of Black Nationalism," and Herbert Aptheker, "Comment," *Studies on the Left* 6 (Nov./Dec. 1966): 3–35.

6. Dan Clawson, "Reply to Benenson," *Insurgent Sociologist* 11 (Fall 1982): 77.

7. Raphael Samuel, "Editorial Note," in Samuel, ed., *People's History, Socialist Theory* (London, 1980), p. 378; Gareth Stedman Jones, "History and Theory," *History Workshop* 8 (1979): 198–202; Keith Nield, "A Symptomatic Dispute? Notes on the Relation between Marxian Theory and Historical Practice in Britain," *Social Research* 47 (1980): 479–506.

8. Clawson, "Reply to Benenson," p. 77.

9. "Editors' Introduction," *Radical History Review* 19 (1978–1979): 5.

10. Mary Nolan, "New Perspectives on Social History," *Socialist Review* 8 (May/June 1978): 34 n. 3.

11. Raphael Samuel, "On the Methods of History Workshop: A Reply," *History Workshop* 9 (1980): 169; Samuel, "British Marxist Historians, 1880–1980, Part One," *New Left Review* 120 (1980): 21–96; Gareth Stedman Jones, "History: The Poverty of Empiricism," in Blackburn, ed., *Ideology in Social Science*, pp. 107, 109–110.

12. Samuel, "Methods of History Workshop," p. 169.

13. Traian Stoianovich, *French Historical Method: The "Annales" Paradigm* (Ithaca, N.Y., 1976), pp. 13–14, 41–43; Terry N. Clark, *Prophets and Patrons: The French Universities and the Emergence of the Social Sciences* (Cambridge, Mass., 1973), pp. 234–35; Gareth Stedman Jones, "From Historical Sociology to Theoretical History," *British Journal of Sociology* 27 (1976): 299.

14. E. P. Thompson, *The Making of the English Working Class* (New York, Vintage ed., 1966); Jones, "Poverty of Empiricism"; Perry Anderson, "Components of the National Culture," in Alexander Cockburn and Robin Blackburn, eds., *Student Power: Problems, Diagnosis, Action* (Harmondsworth, Middx., 1969), pp. 214–86.

15. "An Interview with Eric Hobsbawm," *Radical History Review* 19 (1978–1979): 116–17, 120; Eric Hobsbawm, "The Historians' Group of the Communist Party," in Maurice Cornforth, ed., *Rebels and Their Causes: Essays in Honour of A. L. Morton* (London, 1978), pp. 21–47; "An Interview with E. P. Thompson," *Radical History Review* 3 (Fall 1976): 14. For work of the Centre for the Study of Social History, see Douglas Hay et al., *Albion's Fatal Tree: Crime and Society in Eighteenth-Century England* (New York, 1975).

16. "An Interview with Eric Hobsbawm," p. 120; Edward A. Shils, *The Torment of Secrecy: The Background and Consequences of American Security Policies* (London,

1956); Bill Schwarz, " 'The People' in History: The Communist Party Historians' Group, 1946–56," in Richard Johnson et al., *Making Histories: Studies in History-Writing and Politics* (London, 1982), pp. 44–95.

17. Joseph R. Starobin, *American Communism in Crisis, 1943–1957* (Cambridge, Mass., 1972), p. 197; "Once Upon a Shop Floor: An Interview with David Montgomery," *Radical History Review* 23 (1980): 42–43; confidential interview with a former member of the American Communist party, June 1981.

18. Daniel Bell, "The End of American Exceptionalism," *Public Interest* 41 (1975): 193–224; Laurence Veysey, "The Autonomy of American History Reconsidered," *American Quarterly* 31 (1979): 459.

19. The Board of Regents of the University of Maryland blocked Ollman's appointment as chairman of the department of politics after considerable media and political criticism of his marxism. See Greg Mitchell, "Ollman Plays 'Class Struggle' for Real," *The Nation* 227 (18 Nov. 1978): 541–43; James J. Kilpatrick, "Maryland Should Reject Marxist Prof," *Newark, N.J., Star Ledger*, 29 May 1978, is typical of conservative responses.

20. *Mid-Atlantic Radical Historians' Organization Newsletter*, no. 36, Nov. 1981, pp. 1–2.

21. Stanley Aronowitz, "The Labor Movement and the Left in the United States," *Socialist Review* 9 (March/April 1979): 19; Stuart Ewen, *Captains of Consciousness: Advertising and the Roots of Consumer Culture* (New York, 1976); David Noble, *America by Design: Science, Technology, and the Rise of Corporate Capitalism* (New York, 1977).

22. Raphael Samuel, "People's History," in Samuel, ed., *People's History*, p. xxxi; Michael Merrill, "Raymond Williams and the Theory of English Marxism," *Radical History Review* 19 (1978–1979): 9–31.

23. Rand School of Social Science, *The American Labor Year Book 1932* (New York, 1932), pp. 173–79.

24. "American Working Class History Project," brochure in possession of the author; Susan Levine, "History for Non-Historians," *Radical History Review* 18 (1978): 95–96; report on the Lynn History Workshop, *History Workshop* 10 (1980): 209–10; *Program on Workers' Culture in the Institute of Labor and Industrial Relations, University of Michigan–Wayne State University*, vol. 1, no. 1 [1981]; Schrecker, "House Marxists," p. 84.

25. Cf. E. P. Thompson, "Notes on Exterminism: The Last Stage of Civilization," *New Left Review* 121 (1980): 3–25; Raymond Williams, "The Politics of Nuclear Disarmament," ibid., 124 (1981): 25–42.

26. Karl Marx and Friedrich Engels, *Selected Works*, 3 vols. (Moscow, 1966), 1: 15; Jerrold Seigel, "Consciousness and Practice in the History of Marxism: A Review Article," *Comparative Studies in Society and History* 24 (1982): 176–77.

Bibliographical Essay

This project would have been unthinkable without the rich historiographical literature available for many aspects of American historical writing. My considerable indebtedness to other scholars for particular points is indicated in the notes to each chapter. Those who wish to pursue the subject further will find the best introduction in John Higham, with Leonard Krieger and Felix Gilbert, *History: The Development of Historical Studies in the United States* (Englewood Cliffs, N.J.: Prentice-Hall, 1965), which may be supplemented by Higham's *Writing American History: Essays on Modern Scholarship* (Bloomington: Indiana University Press, 1970). Richard Hofstadter, *The Progressive Historians: Turner, Beard, Parrington* (New York: Alfred A. Knopf, 1968), has excellent essays on its three central figures and the historiographical literature they have provoked. Gene Wise, *American Historical Explanations: A Strategy for Grounded Inquiry*, rev. ed. (Minneapolis: University of Minnesota Press, 1980), is unfortunately marred by the search for conflicting paradigms. There are excellent essays and bibliographies on major figures in modern American historiography in Marcus Cunliffe and Robin Winks, eds., *Pastmasters: Some Essays on American Historians* (New York: Harper and Row, 1969).

Other works of a general kind which should be consulted: Michael Kraus, *The Writing of American History* (Norman: University of Oklahoma Press, 1953); Harvey Wish, *The American Historian: A Social–Intellectual History of the Writing of the American Past* (New York: Oxford University Press, 1960); Robert A. Skotheim, *American Intellectual Histories and Historians* (Princeton, N.J.: Princeton University Press, 1966); Oscar Handlin, *Truth in History* (Cambridge, Mass.: Harvard University Press, 1979), which has an excellent overview and shrewd comments on marxism; David Hackett Fischer, *Historians' Fallacies: Toward a Logic of Historical Thought* (New York: Harper and Row, 1970); W. Stull Holt, *Historical Scholarship in the United States and Other Essays* (Seattle and London: University of Washington Press, 1967).

A number of compendiums are useful for documenting the patterns of historiographical change in the 1950s and 1960s. See two works by William Cartwright and Richard L. Watson, Jr., eds., *The Reinterpretation of American History and Culture* (Washington, D.C.: National Council for the Social Studies, 1973); and *Interpreting and Teaching American History* (Washington, D.C.: NCSS, 1961); Herbert J. Bass, ed., *The State of*

American History (Chicago: Quadrangle, 1970); A. S. Eisenstadt, ed., *The Craft of American History: Selected Essays*, 2 vols. (New York: Harper and Row, 1966); C. Vann Woodward, ed., *The Comparative Approach to American History* (New York: Basic Books, 1968); John A. Garraty, *Interpreting American History: Conversations with Historians*, 2 vols. (New York: Macmillan, 1970); and John Higham, ed., *The Reconstruction of American History* (New York: Harper and Row, 1962).

Of particular interest to the accommodation between history and the social sciences are Seymour Martin Lipset and Richard Hofstadter, eds., *Sociology and History: Methods* (New York: Basic Books, 1968); Edward N. Saveth, ed., *American History and the Social Sciences* (Glencoe, Ill.: The Free Press, 1964); *The Social Sciences in Historical Study: A Report of the Committee on Historiography* (New York: Social Science Research Council, 1954); Lee Benson, *Toward a Scientific Study of History: Selected Essays of Lee Benson* (Philadelphia: J. B. Lippincott, 1972).

The historiography of the 1950s has received fewer serious appraisals than for earlier periods, but see John Higham, "The Cult of the 'American Consensus': Homogenizing Our History," *Commentary* 27 (1959): 93–100; Richard Reinitz, *Irony and Consciousness: American Historiography and Reinhold Niebuhr's Vision* (Lewisburg, Pa.: Bucknell University Press, 1980); Jesse Lemisch, *On Active Service in War and Peace: Politics and Ideology in the American Historical Profession* (Toronto: New Hogstown Press, 1975), is essential reading but only partially valid as a critique. Most attention has been given to individual figures, especially Hofstadter. See the bibliography and essays in Stanley Elkins and Eric McKitrick, eds., *The Hofstadter Aegis: A Memorial* (New York: Alfred A. Knopf, 1973); a useful review of that book, Paul Bourke, "Politics and Ideas: The Work of Richard Hofstadter," *Historical Studies* 67 (1976): 210–18; Christopher Lasch, "Foreword," to Hofstadter, *The American Political Tradition and the Men Who Made It*, 2d ed. (New York: Alfred A. Knopf, 1973); Daniel J. Singal, "Beyond Consensus: Richard Hofstadter and American Historiography," *American Historical Review* 89 (1984): 976–1004; Richard Gillam, "Richard Hofstadter, C. Wright Mills, and the 'Critical Ideal,' " *American Scholar* 47 (1978): 69–85. On Boorstin, see especially John P. Diggins, "Consciousness and Ideology in American History: The Burden of Daniel J. Boorstin," *American Historical Review* 76 (1971): 99–118.

The impact of the anticommunist hysteria on historians is nowhere satisfactorily treated, but see Michael Rogin, *The Intellectuals and McCarthy* (Cambridge: Massachusetts Institute of Technology Press, 1967).

Reading on the beginnings of professional and scientific historical writing can best start with J. Franklin Jameson, *The History of Historical Writing* (New York: Antiquarian Press, 1961, orig. pub., 1891); A. S. Eisenstadt, *Charles McLean Andrews: A Study in American Historical Writing* (New York: Columbia University Press, 1956); Edward N. Saveth, *American Historians and European Immigrants, 1875–1925* (New York: Columbia University Press, 1956), which is disappointing; and an excellent essay by David D. Van Tassel, "From Learned Society to Professional Organization: The American Historical Association, 1884–1900," *American Historical Review* 89 (1984): 929–56.

In addition to the manifesto of *The New History* discussed in the text, see especially, on the reform movement in historical practice, Arthur M. Schlesinger, Sr., "History," in Wilson Gee, ed., *Research in the Social Sciences: Its Fundamental Methods and Objectives* (New York: Macmillan, 1929); and Harry Elmer Barnes, *A History of Historical Writing* (Norman: University of Oklahoma Press, 1938). A critique of both the scientific and the New History approaches from an idealist viewpoint is Lloyd Sorensen,

"Historical Currents in America," *American Quarterly* 7 (1955): 234–46. The transformation of the New History beginning just before World War II is documented in Caroline Ware, ed., *The Cultural Approach to History* (New York: Columbia University Press, 1940); and Richard H. Shryock, "American Historiography: A Critical Analysis and a Program," American Philosophical Society, *Proceedings* 87 (July 1943): 35–46, an unjustly obscure piece.

The literature on the central figures in the progressive tradition is too vast to list here. For Beard, Ellen Nore, *Charles A. Beard: An Intellectual Biography* (Carbondale and Edwardsville: Southern Illinois University Press, 1983), is excellent, notwithstanding the critics who feel she has judged Beard by ahistoric standards. In fact, Nore's portrayal is a justly sympathetic one, and reveals a deep knowledge of the social and political context in which Beard's thought developed. See Howard K. Beale, ed., *Charles A. Beard: An Appraisal . . .* (Lexington: University of Kentucky Press, 1954), for bibliographies of Beard's work and critical essays. Obscure but valuable essays by John Braeman and Eugene Genovese appear in Marvin C. Swanson, ed., *Charles A. Beard: An Observance of the Centennial of His Birth* (Greencastle, Ind.: DePauw University, 1976). A recent defense of Beard against his critics is John Patrick Diggins, "Power and Authority in American History: The Case of Charles A. Beard and His Critics," *American Historical Review* 86 (1981): 701–30. The critics have of course included Forrest McDonald, *We the People: The Economic Origins of the Constitution* (Chicago: University of Chicago Press, 1958); and Robert E. Brown, *Charles Beard and the Constitution: A Critical Analysis of "An Economic Interpretation of the Constitution"* (Princeton, N.J.: Princeton University Press, 1956). For Turner, there is a bibliography of his writings in F. J. Turner, *Early Writings of Frederick Jackson Turner* (Madison: University of Wisconsin Press, 1938); and of historians' views of Turner in Ray Allen Billington, *The American Frontier* (Washington, D.C.: Service Center for Teachers, 1971). Billington's own *Frederick Jackson Turner: Historian, Scholar, Teacher* (New York: Oxford University Press, 1973) is unsurpassed and invaluable. It is faithful to the rich Huntington Library collection. Richard M. Andrews, "Some Implications of the *Annales* School and Its Methods for a Revision of Historical Writing about the United States," *Review* 1 (1978): 165–80, includes an important reassessment of Turner's place in American historiography. Lee Benson, *Turner and Beard: American Historical Writing Reconsidered* (Glencoe, Ill.: The Free Press, 1960), was influential in its critique of economic determinism. The frontier influence has been wider than the work of Turner alone. See Wilbur Jacobs, John W. Caughey, and Joe B. Frantz, *Turner, Bolton, and Webb: Three Historians of the American Frontier* (Seattle and London: University of Washington Press, 1965); Gregory M. Tobin, *The Making of a History: Walter Prescott Webb and "The Great Plains"* (Austin: University of Texas Press, 1976), an excellent critical study; John F. Bannon, *Herbert Eugene Bolton: The Historian and the Man* (Tucson: University of Arizona Press, 1978), is filiopietistic.

Other studies of progressive era writing include Cushing Strout, *The Pragmatic Revolt in American History: Carl Becker and Charles Beard* (New Haven: Yale University Press, 1958); Burleigh T. Wilkins, *Carl Becker: A Biographical Study in American Intellectual History* (Cambridge: Massachusetts Institute of Technology Press, 1961); and David Shi, *Matthew Josephson: Bourgeois Bohemian* (New Haven: Yale University Press, 1981), which confuses progressive and marxist.

Marxism: Clinton Rossiter, *Marxism: The View from America* (New York: Harcourt, Brace, 1960), is an apparently sincere attempt to come to grips with its subject, but fails to escape from the usual stereotypes. C. Wright Mills, *The Marxists* (New York: Dell Publishing, 1962), captures the complexity of marxism while maintaining an independent critical stance. Very impressive. So too on a different level is Jon Cohen, "The Achievements of Economic History: The Marxist School," *Journal of Economic History* 38 (1978): 29–57. David McLennan, *Marxism after Marx: An Introduction* (Boston: Houghton Mifflin, 1981, c. 1979), is faithful to its title. Jean L. Cohen, *Class and Civil Society: The Limits of Marxian Critical Theory* (Amherst: University of Massachusetts Press, 1982), is dialectically formidable but treats certain works of Marx as the essence of marxism. More convincing is Melvin Rader, *Marx's Interpretation of History* (New York: Oxford University Press, 1979). See also, for the relevance of Marx to history, William Appleman Williams, *The Great Evasion: An Essay on the Contemporary Relevance of Karl Marx . . .* (Chicago: Quadrangle, 1964); Leonard Krieger, "The Uses of Marx for History," *Political Science Quarterly* 74 (1960): 355–78; and "Studies in Marxist Historical Theory," Beiheft 20, *History and Theory*, 1981. For the British marxists, see Harvey J. Kaye, *The British Marxist Historians: An Introductory Analysis* (Cambridge, Eng.: Polity Press, 1984).

Comparisons with other historiographies: Georg G. Iggers, *New Directions in European Historiography* (Middletown, Conn.: Wesleyan University Press, 1975); Georg G. Iggers and Harold T. Parker, eds., *International Handbook of Historical Studies: Contemporary Research and Theory* (Westport, Conn.: Greenwood Press, 1979); Boyd C. Shafer et al., *Historical Study in the West* (New York: Appleton-Century-Crofts, 1968); William R. Keylor, *Academy and Community: The Foundation of the French Historical Profession* (Cambridge, Mass.: Harvard University Press, 1975); Terry N. Clark, *Prophets and Patrons: The French University and the Emergence of the Social Sciences* (Cambridge, Mass.: Harvard University Press, 1973); H. Stuart Hughes, *Consciousness and Society: The Reorientation of European Social Thought, 1890–1930* (London: Harvester Press, 1979, orig. pub., 1958); John P. Kenyon, *History Men* (London: Weidenfeld and Nicholson, 1982); "Theory and Social History," special issue of *Social Research* 47 (Autumn 1980); "Marxism and History: The British Contribution," special issue of *Radical History Review* 19 (Winter 1978–1979).

On *Annales* specifically, see "The Impact of the *Annales* School on the Social Sciences," special issue of *Review* 1 (Winter/Spring 1978); Marc Bloch, *French Rural History: An Essay on Its Basic Characteristics*, ed. Bryce Lyon (Berkeley and Los Angeles: University of California Press, 1966). Though I have focused on Bloch in the text, Lucien Febvre is equally pertinent to the argument. See *Phillipe II et la Franche-Comté: étude d'historique, religieuse et sociale* (Paris, 1912, repr., 1970); Peter Burke, ed., *A New Kind of History: From the Writings of Febvre* (London: Routledge and Kegan Paul, 1973). Among more recent *Annales* historians, see especially Georges Duby, *The Three Orders: Feudal Society Imagined*, trans. Arthur Goldhammer (Chicago: University of Chicago Press, 1980), for the possibilities of a history of *mentalité*.

A good history of economic history is badly needed. In the absence of anything satisfactory, see Joseph Dorfman, *The Economic Mind in American Civilization*, vol. 3, 1865–1918 (New York: The Viking Press, 1949), for the early period. Donald McCloskey, "The Achievements of the Cliometric School," *Journal of Economic History* 38 (1978): 13–28, defends the new trends in economic history; Harold D. Woodman, "Economic History and Economic Theory: The New Economic History in America," *Journal of Interdisciplinary History* 3 (1972): 323–50, is a fine critique. Business and entrepreneurial history are, however, well covered. See Steven A. Sass, "Entrepreneurial Historians and

History: An Essay in Organized Intellect,'' Ph.D. diss., Johns Hopkins University, 1977; Louis Galambos, *American Business History* (Washington, D.C.: Service Center for Teachers, 1967).

Historical practice: Dexter Perkins, John Snell, and the Committee on Graduate Education of the American Historical Association, *The Education of Historians in the United States* (New York: McGraw-Hill Book Company, 1962); and William B. Hesseltine and Louis Kaplan, ''Doctors of Philosophy in History: A Statistical Study,'' *American Historical Review* 47 (1942): 765–800, are indispensable. Frances Fitzgerald, *America Revised: History Textbooks in the Twentieth Century* (Boston: Little, Brown, 1979), is a pioneering study of an important subject. So too is Carol S. Gruber's *Mars and Minerva: World War One and the Uses of the Higher Learning in America* (Baton Rouge: Louisiana State University Press, 1975).

Further study of the New Left must begin with Barton Bernstein, ed., *Towards a New Past: Dissenting Essays in American History* (New York: Random House, 1968). Useful for its bibiographies and essays, especially on foreign relations, is Bernstein and Allen J. Matusow, eds., *Twentieth Century America: Recent Interpretations* (New York: Harcourt, Brace, and World, 1969). A trenchant critique of radical historiography can be found in Aileen Kraditor, ''American Radical Historians on Their Heritage,'' *Past and Present* 56 (1972): 136–53.

More recent trends in areas like social history, quantification, women's history, labor history, and so on are best approached through the many collections which are part of the current intellectual stocktaking. See Michael Kammen, ed., *The Past Before Us: Contemporary Historical Writing in the United States* (Ithaca, N.Y.: Cornell University Press, 1980), which has excellent essays and bibliographical footnotes, but avoids economic history and marxism, thus reflecting the conventional disciplinary divisions and theoretical assumptions. See also Charles F. Dalzell, ed., *The Future of History: Essays in the Vanderbilt University Centennial Symposium* (Nashville, Tenn.: Vanderbilt University Press, 1977); John Higham and Paul K. Conkin, eds., *New Directions in American Intellectual History* (Baltimore: Johns Hopkins University Press, 1979); Theodore K. Rabb and Robert I. Rotberg, eds., *The New History: The 1980s and Beyond* (Princeton, N.J.: Princeton University Press, 1982); ''The Promise of American History: Progress and Prospects,'' special issue of *Reviews in American History* 10 (Dec. 1982).

The debt to Gareth Stedman Jones' work is evident throughout the text, but equally influential for my thinking has been Perry Anderson, *Arguments within English Marxism* (London: New Left Books, 1980); and Anderson, *Considerations on Western Marxism* (London: New Left Books, 1976). The English journals *Social History* and *History Workshop* have been an inspiration. My critique of social science in social history is largely acknowledged in the text, but see also Tony Judt, ''A Clown in Regal Purple: Social History and the Historians,'' *History Workshop* 7 (1979): 66–94; which ought, however, to be read again against the demur of Steve Hochstadt, ''Social History: A Materialist View,'' *Social History* 7 (1982): 75–83. Another stimulating but sharp marxist contrast appears in Elizabeth Fox-Genovese and Eugene Genovese, ''The Political Crisis of Social History,'' *Journal of Social History* 10 (1977): 205–20. T. L. Jackson Lears, ''The Concept of Cultural Hegemony: Problems and Possibilities,'' *American Historical Review* 90 (1985): 567–93, appeared after this study was completed.

It goes without saying that the major journals remain vital to any historiographical study. In addition, there are several periodicals outside of ''professional history'' which contain historical material of increasingly important value. See *Radical America*; *Socialist*

Revolution (since 1978 *Socialist Review*); *Dialectical Anthropology*; *Insurgent Sociologist*; *Review of Radical Political Economics*; *New Left Review*; *Review: A Journal of the Fernand Braudel Center for the Study of Economies, Historical Systems, and Civilizations*. These journals are often of more relevance to historical scholarship than the conventional journals of the social sciences. Such material, for all its deficiencies, brings into question glib assertions that the historical approach is in irrevocable decline.

Index

About the Author

IAN TYRRELL is a senior lecturer at the University of New South Wales, Sydney, Australia. A specialist in antebellum social history and comparative women's history, he is the author of *Sobering Up: From Temperance to Prohibition in Antebellum America, 1800–1860*, articles on social history published in the United States and Australia, and a forthcoming study of the Woman's Christian Temperance Union in international perspective.

DATE DUE
